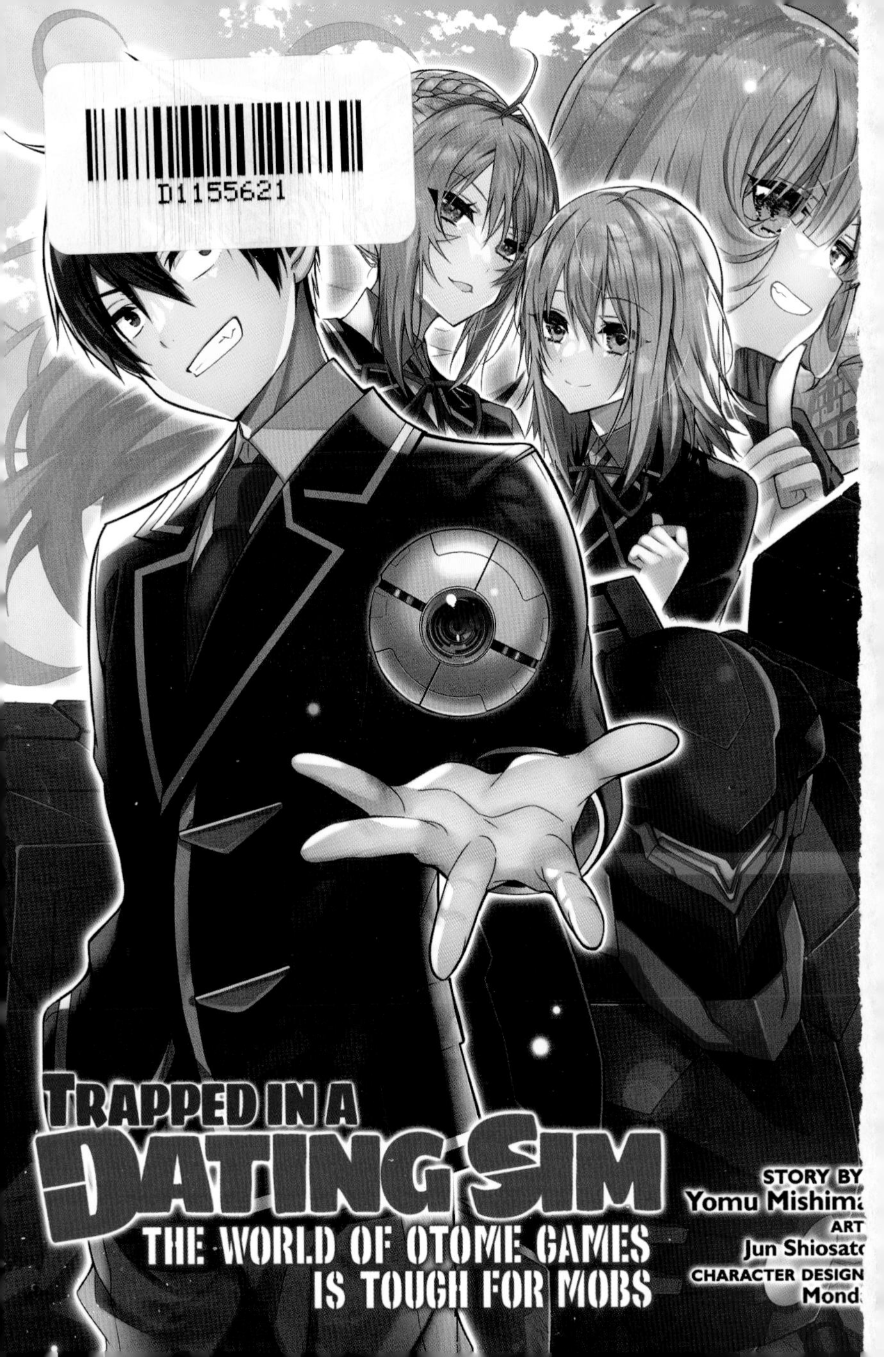
TRAPPED IN A
DATING SIM
THE WORLD OF OTOME GAMES
IS TOUGH FOR MOBS
STORY BY
Yomu Mishima
ART
Jun Shiosato
CHARACTER DESIGN
Monda

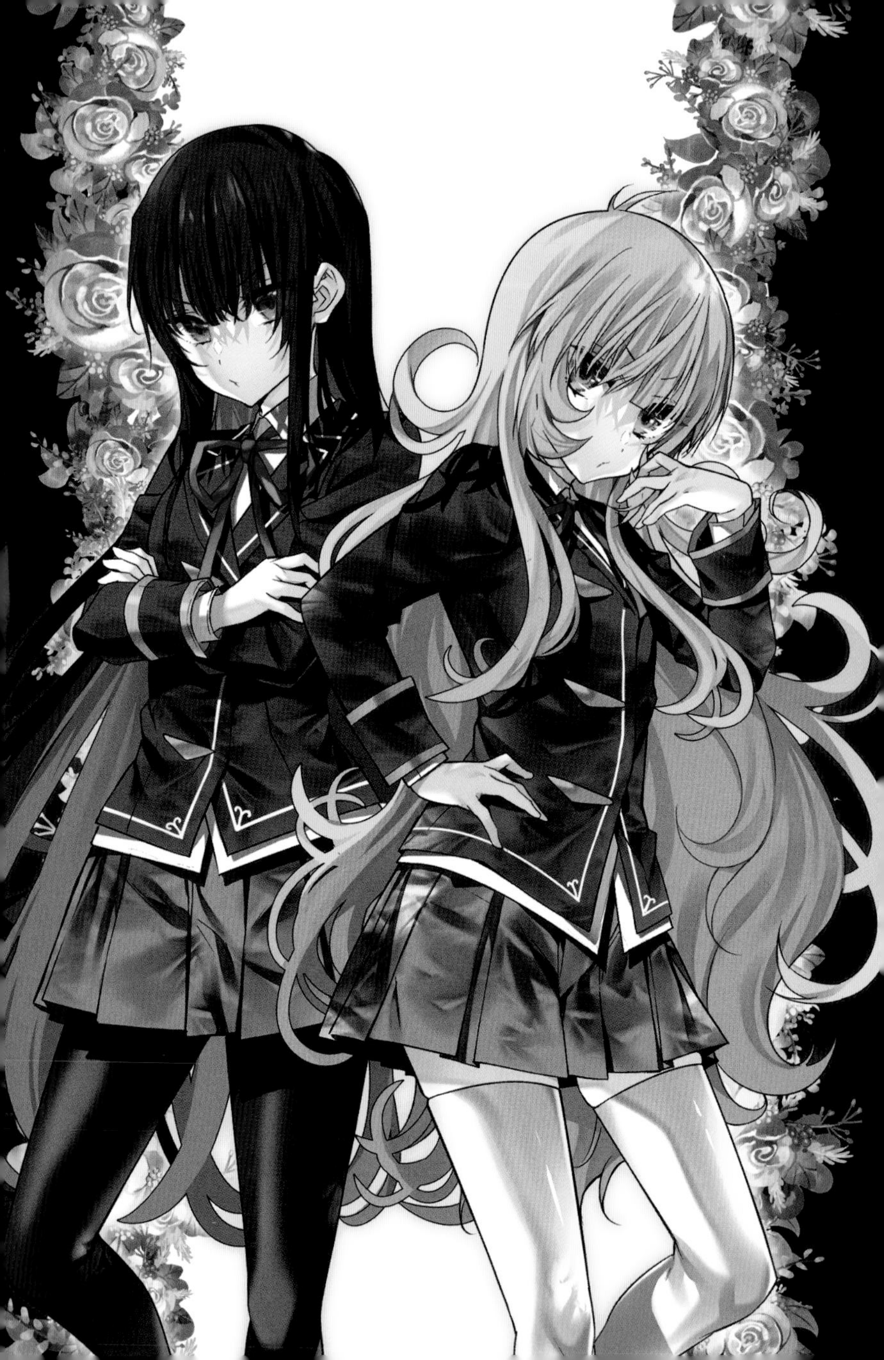

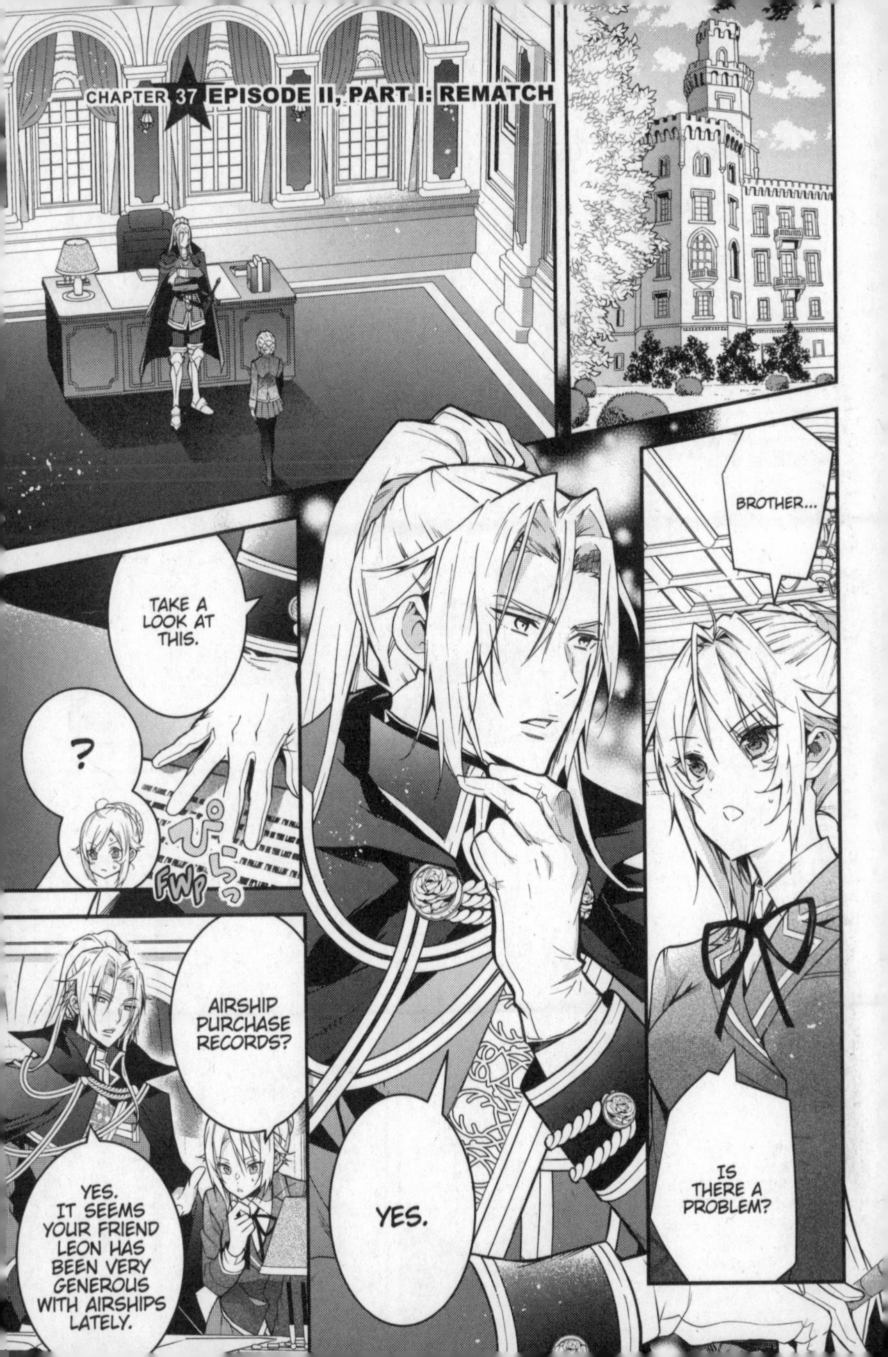
CHAPTER 37 EPISODE II, PART I: REMATCH
BROTHER...
IS THERE A PROBLEM?
YES.
TAKE A LOOK AT THIS.
?
FWP
AIRSHIP PURCHASE RECORDS?
YES. IT SEEMS YOUR FRIEND LEON HAS BEEN VERY GENEROUS WITH AIRSHIPS LATELY.

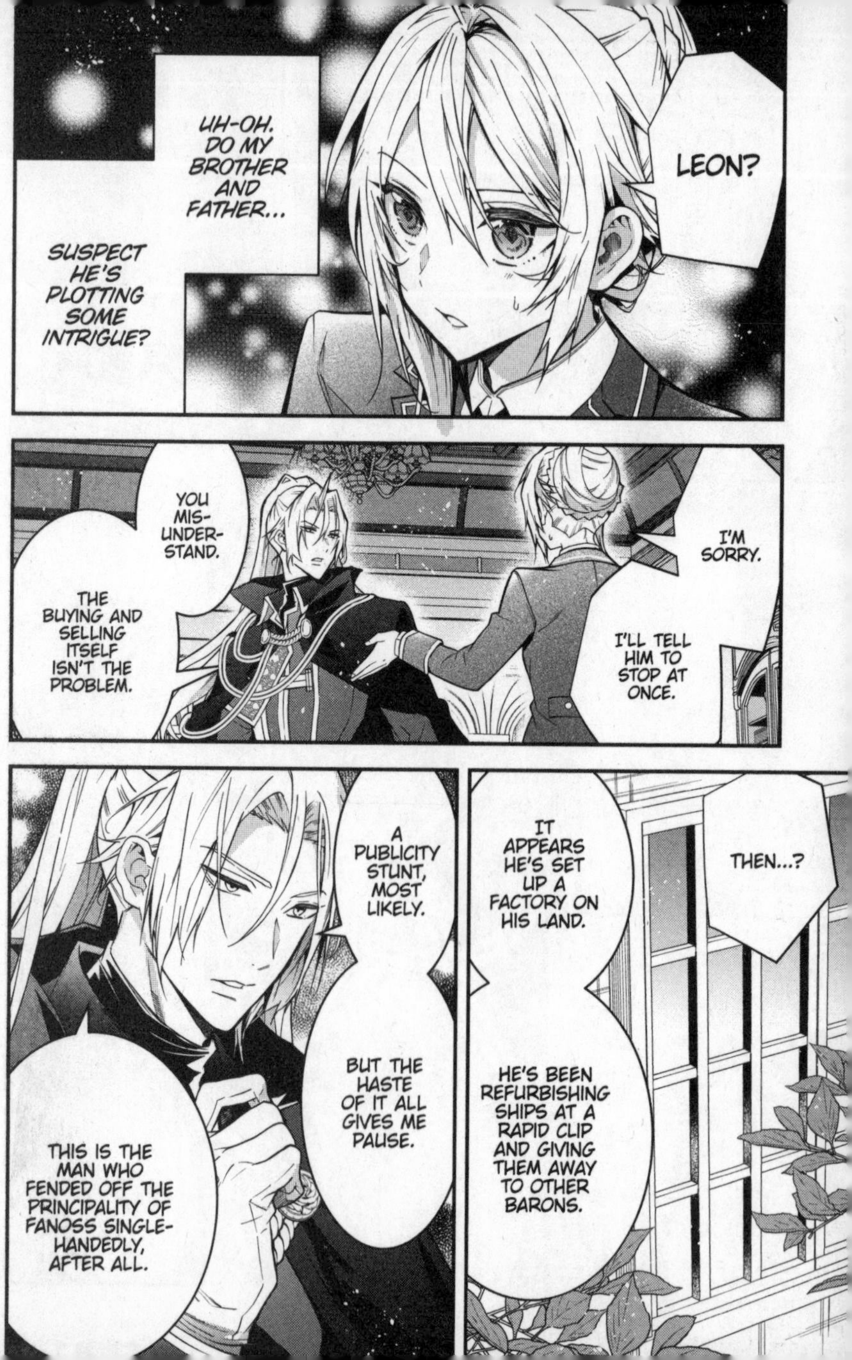
LEON?
UH-OH. DO MY BROTHER AND FATHER...
SUSPECT HE'S PLOTTING SOME INTRIGUE?
I'M SORRY.
I'LL TELL HIM TO STOP AT ONCE.
YOU MISUNDERSTAND.
THE BUYING AND SELLING ITSELF ISN'T THE PROBLEM.
THEN...?
IT APPEARS HE'S SET UP A FACTORY ON HIS LAND.
HE'S BEEN REFURBISHING SHIPS AT A RAPID CLIP AND GIVING THEM AWAY TO OTHER BARONS.
A PUBLICITY STUNT, MOST LIKELY.
BUT THE HASTE OF IT ALL GIVES ME PAUSE.
THIS IS THE MAN WHO FENDED OFF THE PRINCIPALITY OF FANOSS SINGLE-HANDEDLY, AFTER ALL.

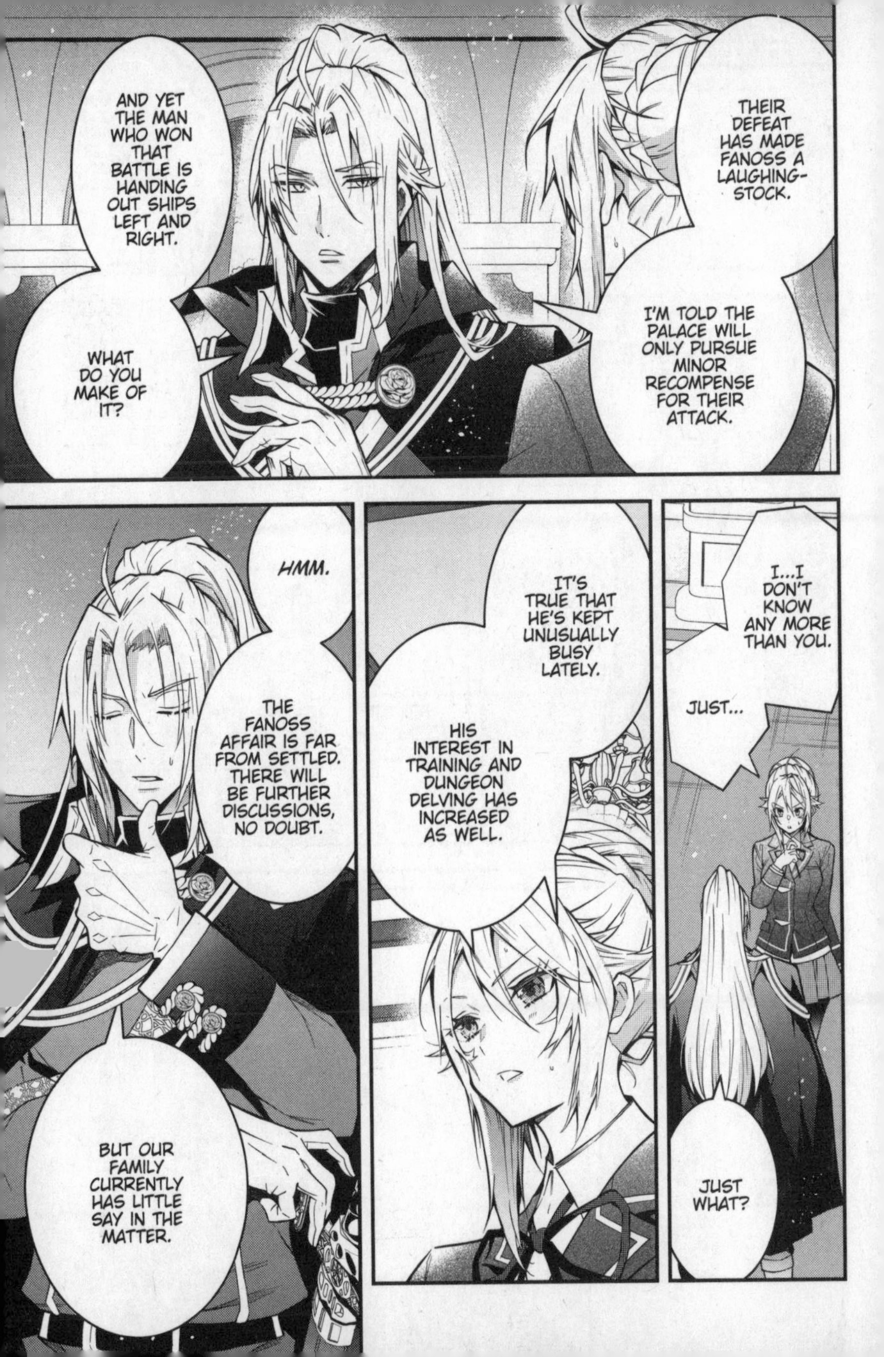
THEIR DEFEAT HAS MADE FANOSS A LAUGHING-STOCK.
I'M TOLD THE PALACE WILL ONLY PURSUE MINOR RECOMPENSE FOR THEIR ATTACK.
AND YET THE MAN WHO WON THAT BATTLE IS HANDING OUT SHIPS LEFT AND RIGHT.
WHAT DO YOU MAKE OF IT?
I...I DON'T KNOW ANY MORE THAN YOU.
JUST...
JUST WHAT?
IT'S TRUE THAT HE'S KEPT UNUSUALLY BUSY LATELY.
HIS INTEREST IN TRAINING AND DUNGEON DELVING HAS INCREASED AS WELL.
HMM.
THE FANOSS AFFAIR IS FAR FROM SETTLED. THERE WILL BE FURTHER DISCUSSIONS, NO DOUBT.
BUT OUR FAMILY CURRENTLY HAS LITTLE SAY IN THE MATTER.

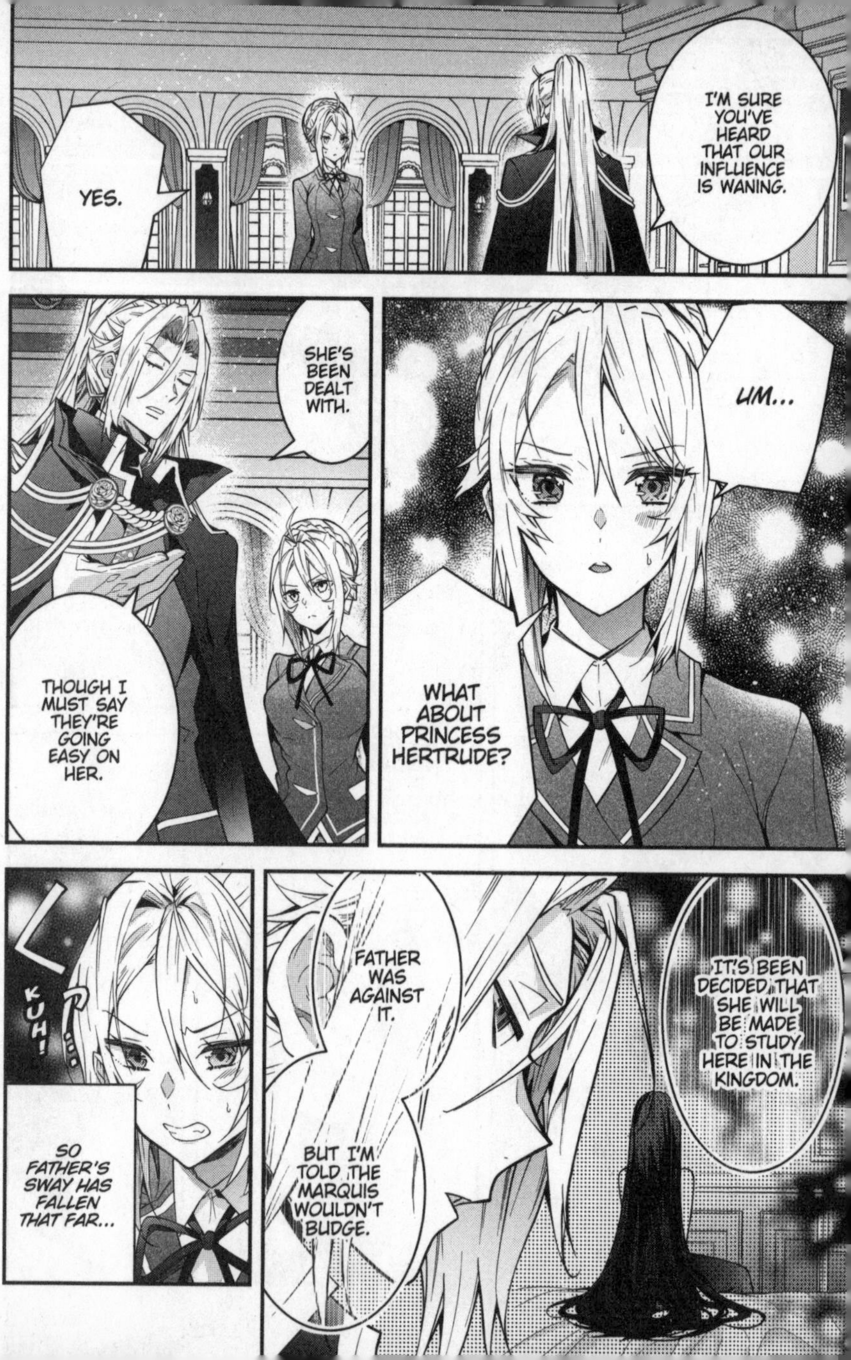
I'M SURE YOU'VE HEARD THAT OUR INFLUENCE IS WANING.
YES.
UM...
WHAT ABOUT PRINCESS HERTRUDE?
SHE'S BEEN DEALT WITH.
THOUGH I MUST SAY THEY'RE GOING EASY ON HER.
IT'S BEEN DECIDED THAT SHE WILL BE MADE TO STUDY HERE IN THE KINGDOM.
FATHER WAS AGAINST IT.
BUT I'M TOLD THE MARQUIS WOULDN'T BUDGE.
KUH!
SO FATHER'S SWAY HAS FALLEN THAT FAR...

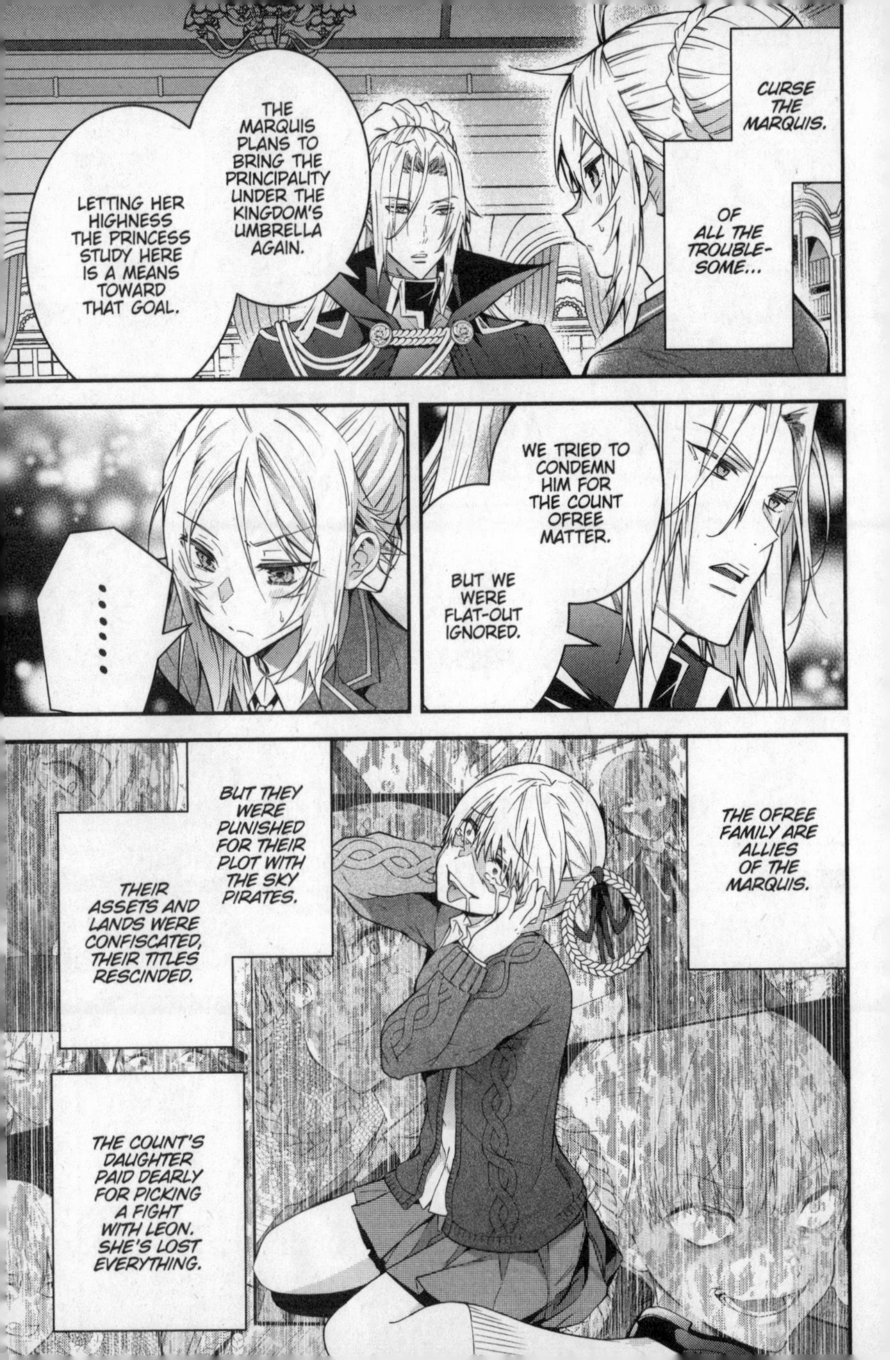
CURSE THE MARQUIS.
OF ALL THE TROUBLE-SOME...
THE MARQUIS PLANS TO BRING THE PRINCIPALITY UNDER THE KINGDOM'S UMBRELLA AGAIN.
LETTING HER HIGHNESS THE PRINCESS STUDY HERE IS A MEANS TOWARD THAT GOAL.
WE TRIED TO CONDEMN HIM FOR THE COUNT OFREE MATTER.
BUT WE WERE FLAT-OUT IGNORED.
......
THE OFREE FAMILY ARE ALLIES OF THE MARQUIS.
BUT THEY WERE PUNISHED FOR THEIR PLOT WITH THE SKY PIRATES.
THEIR ASSETS AND LANDS WERE CONFISCATED, THEIR TITLES RESCINDED.
THE COUNT'S DAUGHTER PAID DEARLY FOR PICKING A FIGHT WITH LEON. SHE'S LOST EVERYTHING.

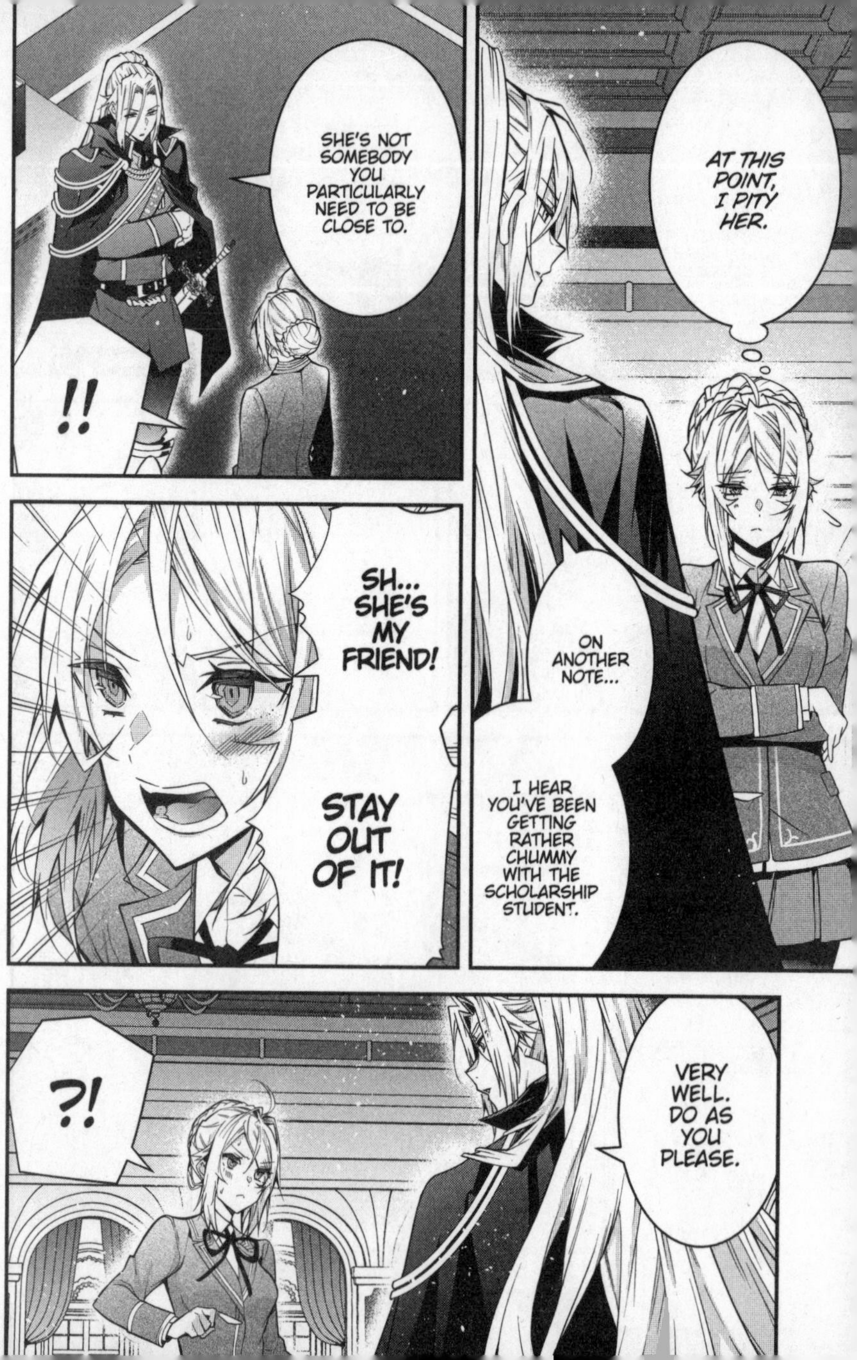
AT THIS POINT, I PITY HER.
ON ANOTHER NOTE...
I HEAR YOU'VE BEEN GETTING RATHER CHUMMY WITH THE SCHOLARSHIP STUDENT.
SHE'S NOT SOMEBODY YOU PARTICULARLY NEED TO BE CLOSE TO.
!!
SH... SHE'S MY FRIEND!
STAY OUT OF IT!
VERY WELL. DO AS YOU PLEASE.
?!

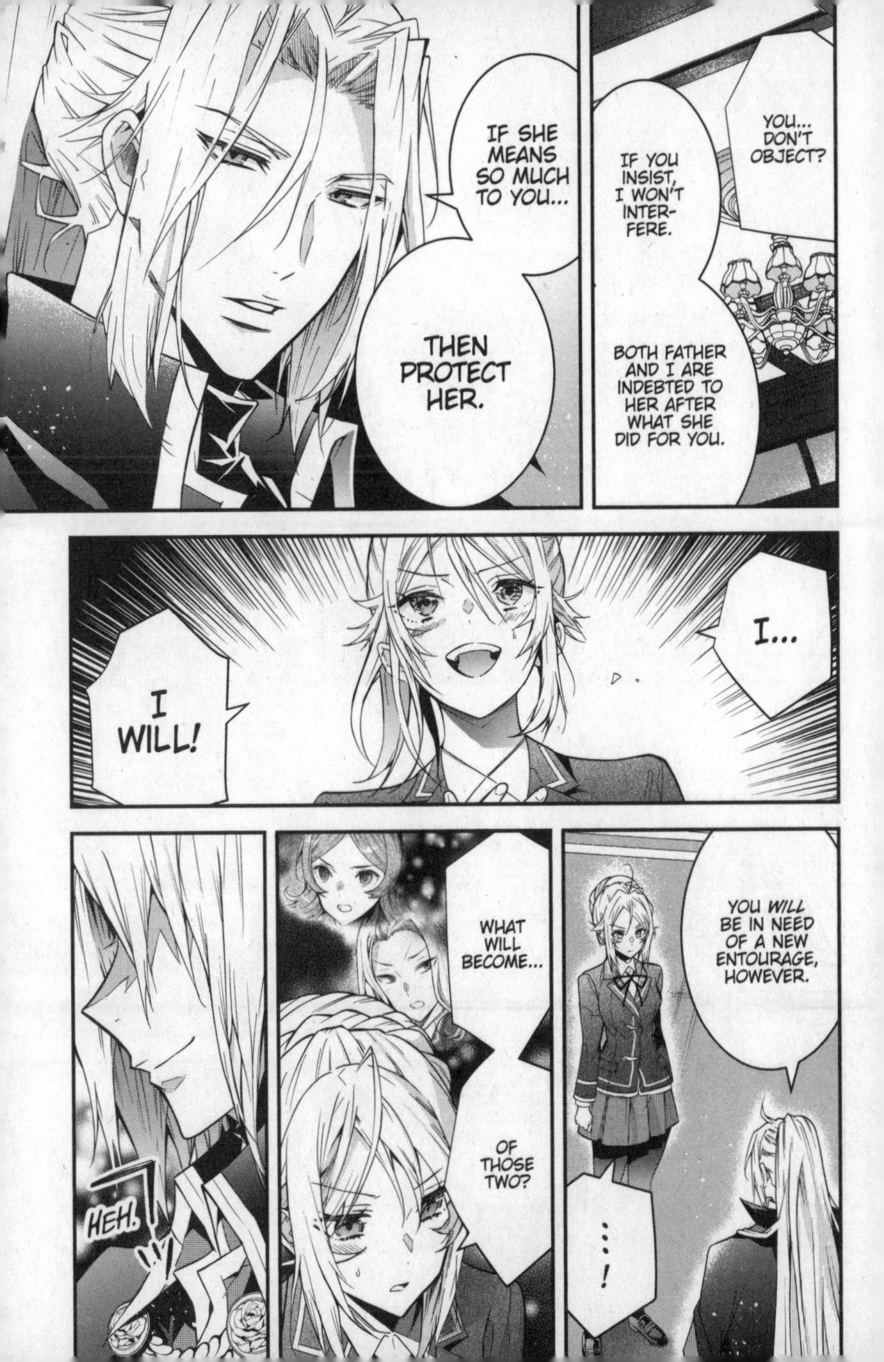
YOU... DON'T OBJECT?
IF YOU INSIST, I WON'T INTER-FERE.
BOTH FATHER AND I ARE INDEBTED TO HER AFTER WHAT SHE DID FOR YOU.
IF SHE MEANS SO MUCH TO YOU...
THEN PROTECT HER.
I...
I WILL!
YOU *WILL* BE IN NEED OF A NEW ENTOURAGE, HOWEVER.
...!
WHAT WILL BECOME...
OF THOSE TWO?
HEH.

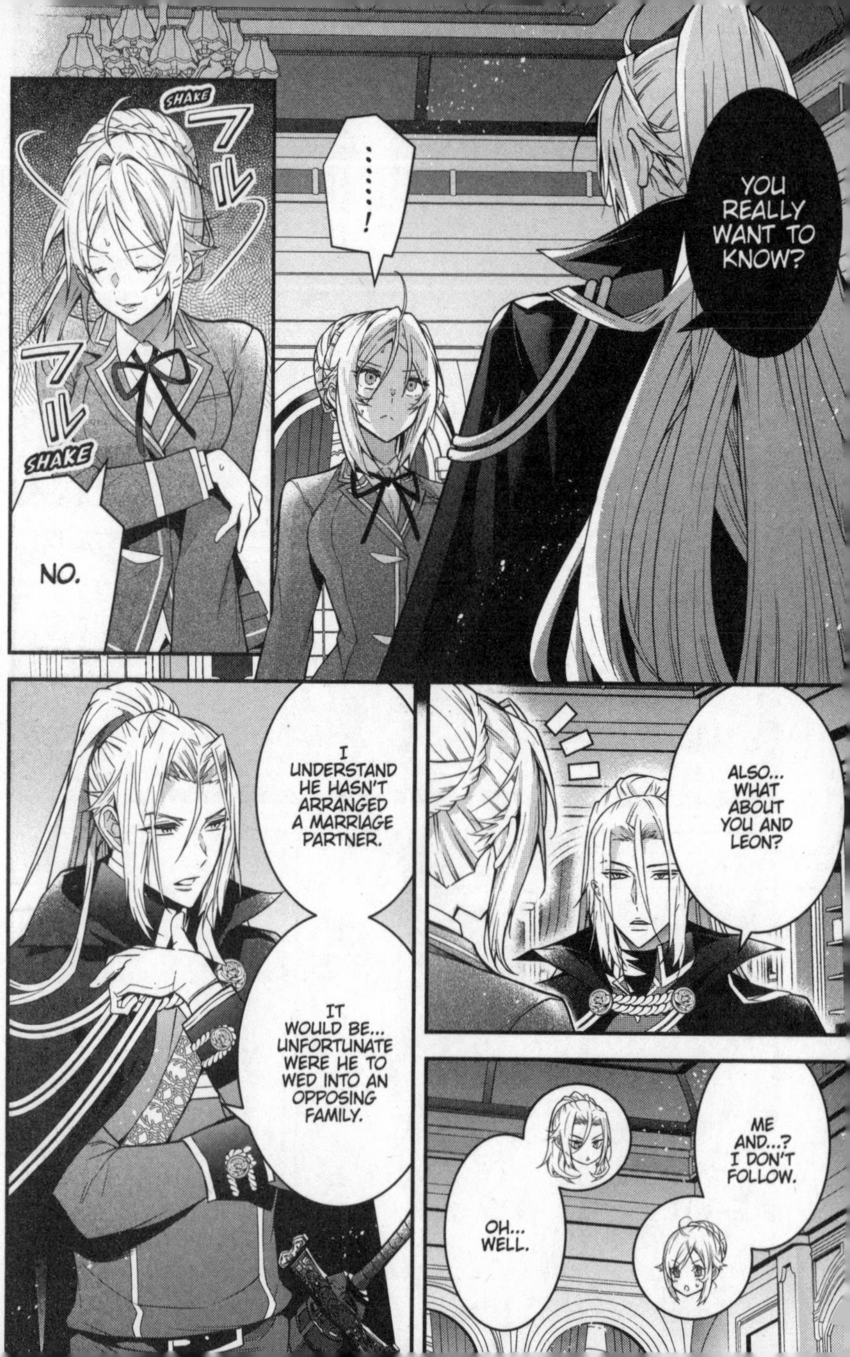
YOU REALLY WANT TO KNOW?
......!
SHAKE
フル
フル
SHAKE
NO.
ALSO... WHAT ABOUT YOU AND LEON?
ME AND...? I DON'T FOLLOW.
OH... WELL.
I UNDERSTAND HE HASN'T ARRANGED A MARRIAGE PARTNER.
IT WOULD BE... UNFORTUNATE WERE HE TO WED INTO AN OPPOSING FAMILY.

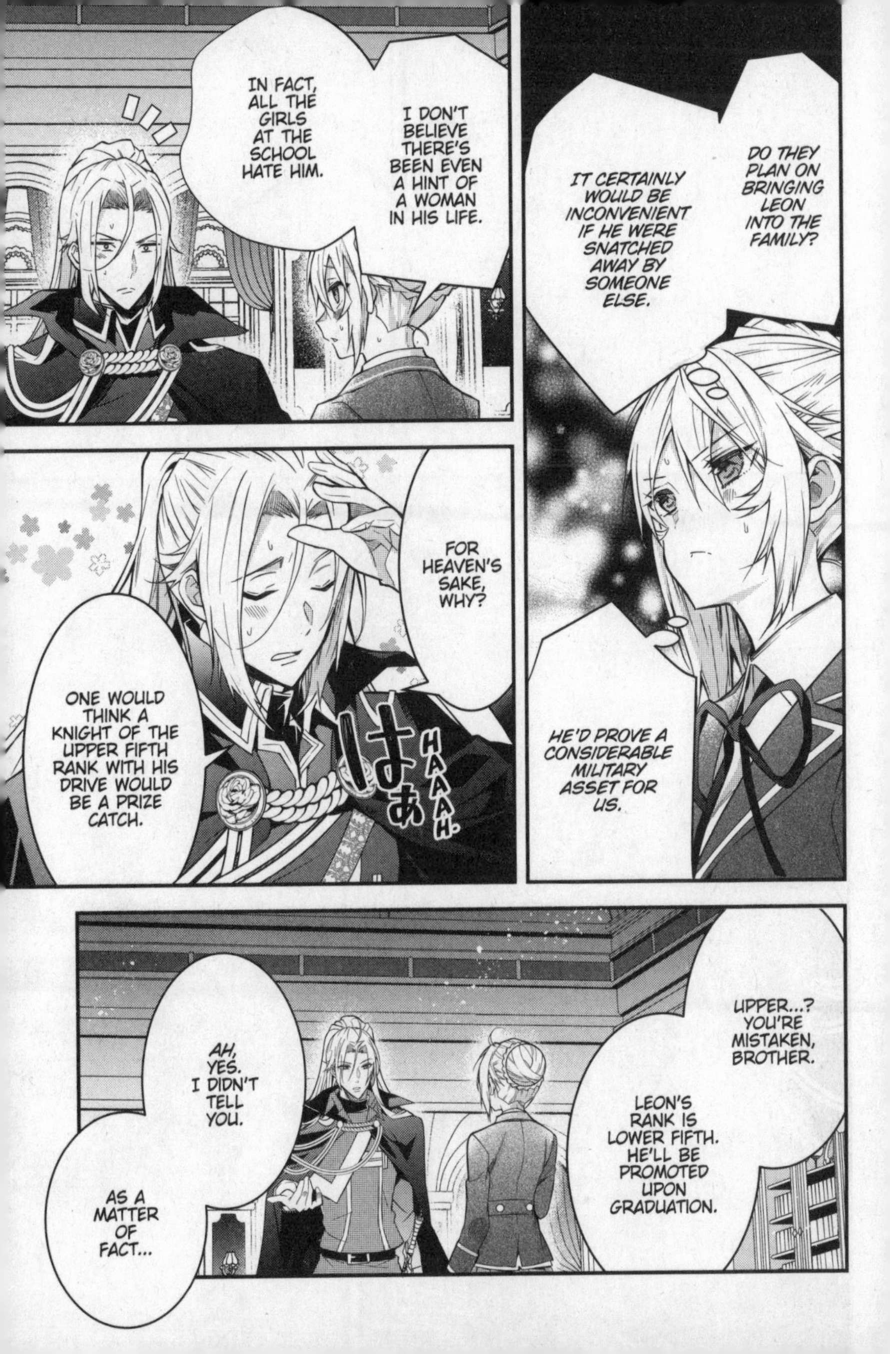
DO THEY PLAN ON BRINGING LEON INTO THE FAMILY?
IT CERTAINLY WOULD BE INCONVENIENT IF HE WERE SNATCHED AWAY BY SOMEONE ELSE.
HE'D PROVE A CONSIDERABLE MILITARY ASSET FOR US.
I DON'T BELIEVE THERE'S BEEN EVEN A HINT OF A WOMAN IN HIS LIFE.
IN FACT, ALL THE GIRLS AT THE SCHOOL HATE HIM.
FOR HEAVEN'S SAKE, WHY?
はあ HAAAH.
ONE WOULD THINK A KNIGHT OF THE UPPER FIFTH RANK WITH HIS DRIVE WOULD BE A PRIZE CATCH.
UPPER...? YOU'RE MISTAKEN, BROTHER.
LEON'S RANK IS LOWER FIFTH. HE'LL BE PROMOTED UPON GRADUATION.
AH, YES. I DIDN'T TELL YOU.
AS A MATTER OF FACT...

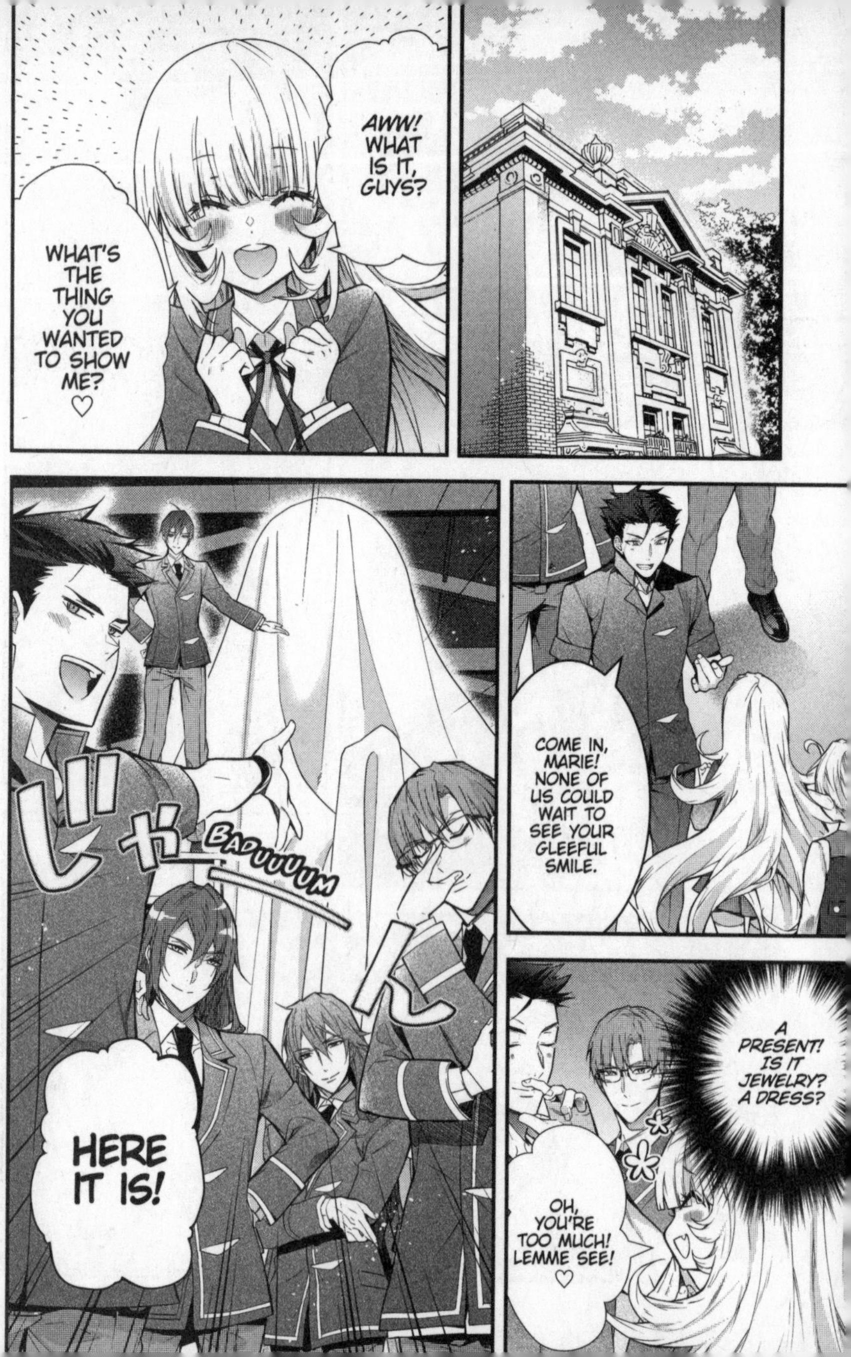
AWW! WHAT IS IT, GUYS?
WHAT'S THE THING YOU WANTED TO SHOW ME? ♡
COME IN, MARIE! NONE OF US COULD WAIT TO SEE YOUR GLEEFUL SMILE.
A PRESENT! IS IT JEWELRY? A DRESS?
OH, YOU'RE TOO MUCH! LEMME SEE! ♡
じゃーん
BADUUUUM
HERE IT IS!

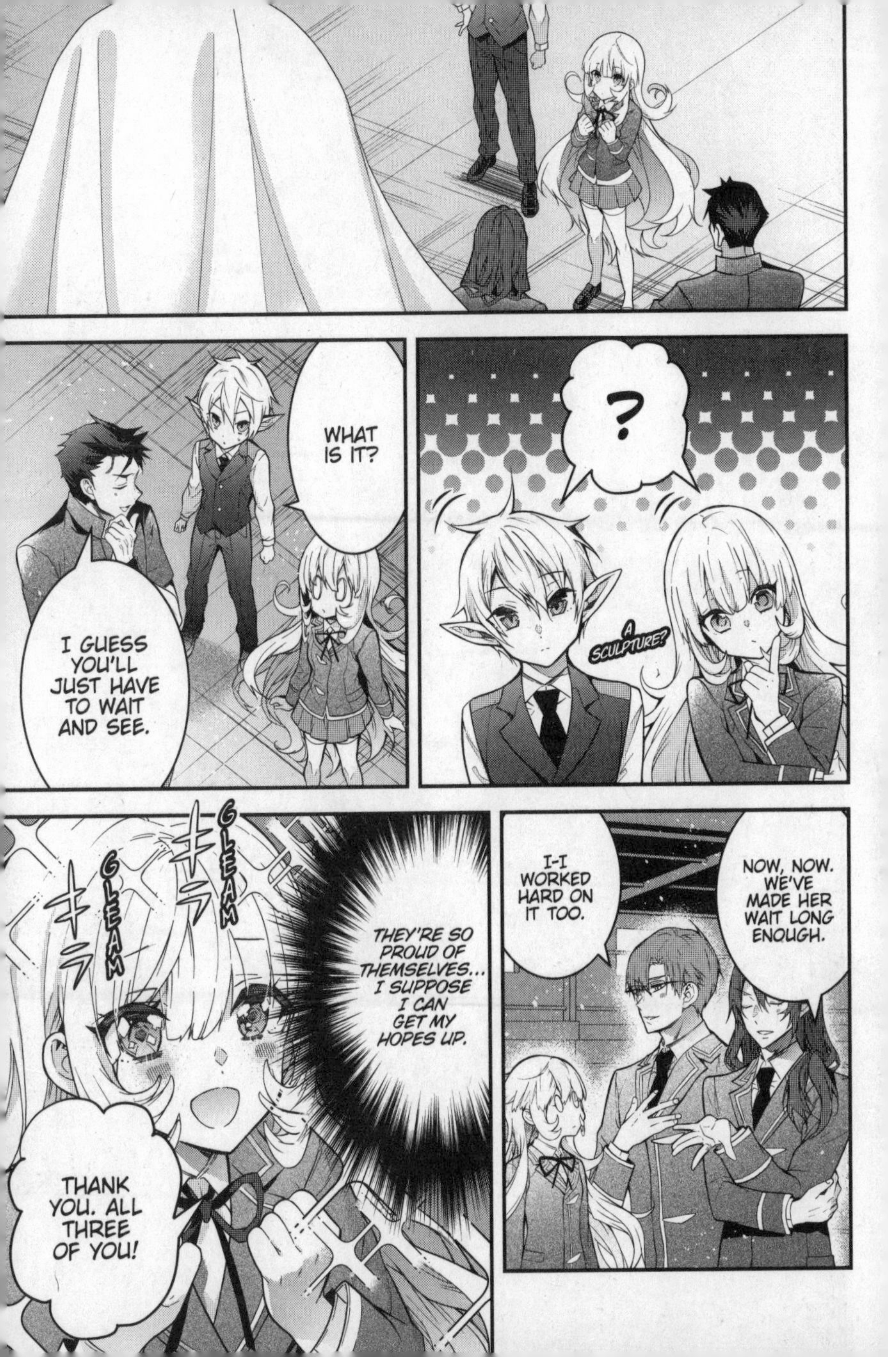
?
A SCULPTURE?
WHAT IS IT?
I GUESS YOU'LL JUST HAVE TO WAIT AND SEE.
NOW, NOW. WE'VE MADE HER WAIT LONG ENOUGH.
I-I WORKED HARD ON IT TOO.
GLEAM
GLEAM
THEY'RE SO PROUD OF THEMSELVES... I SUPPOSE I CAN GET MY HOPES UP.
THANK YOU. ALL THREE OF YOU!

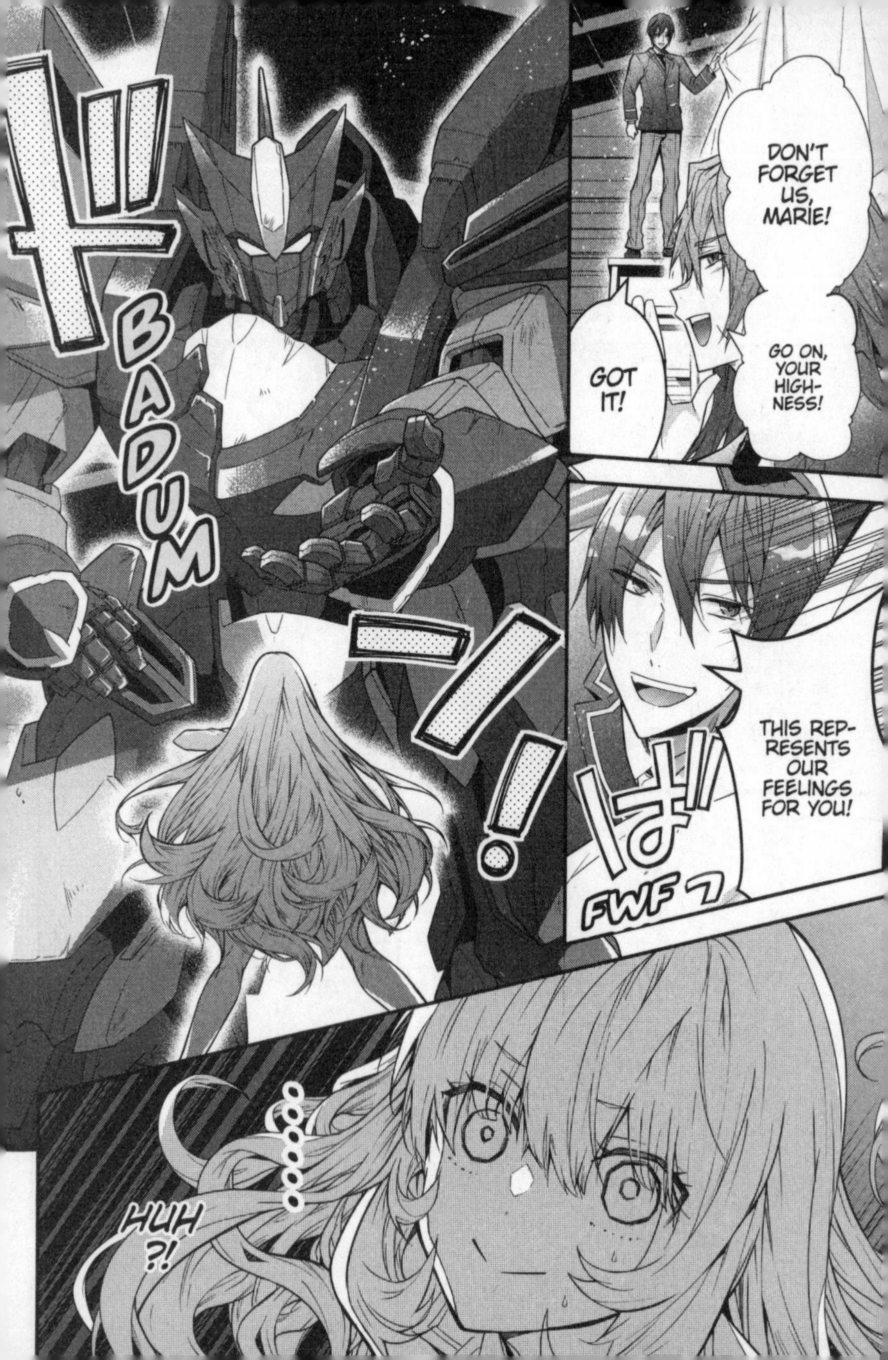
DON'T FORGET US, MARIE!
GO ON, YOUR HIGHNESS!
GOT IT!
THIS REPRESENTS OUR FEELINGS FOR YOU!
ぱ
FWF
BADUM
HUH?!

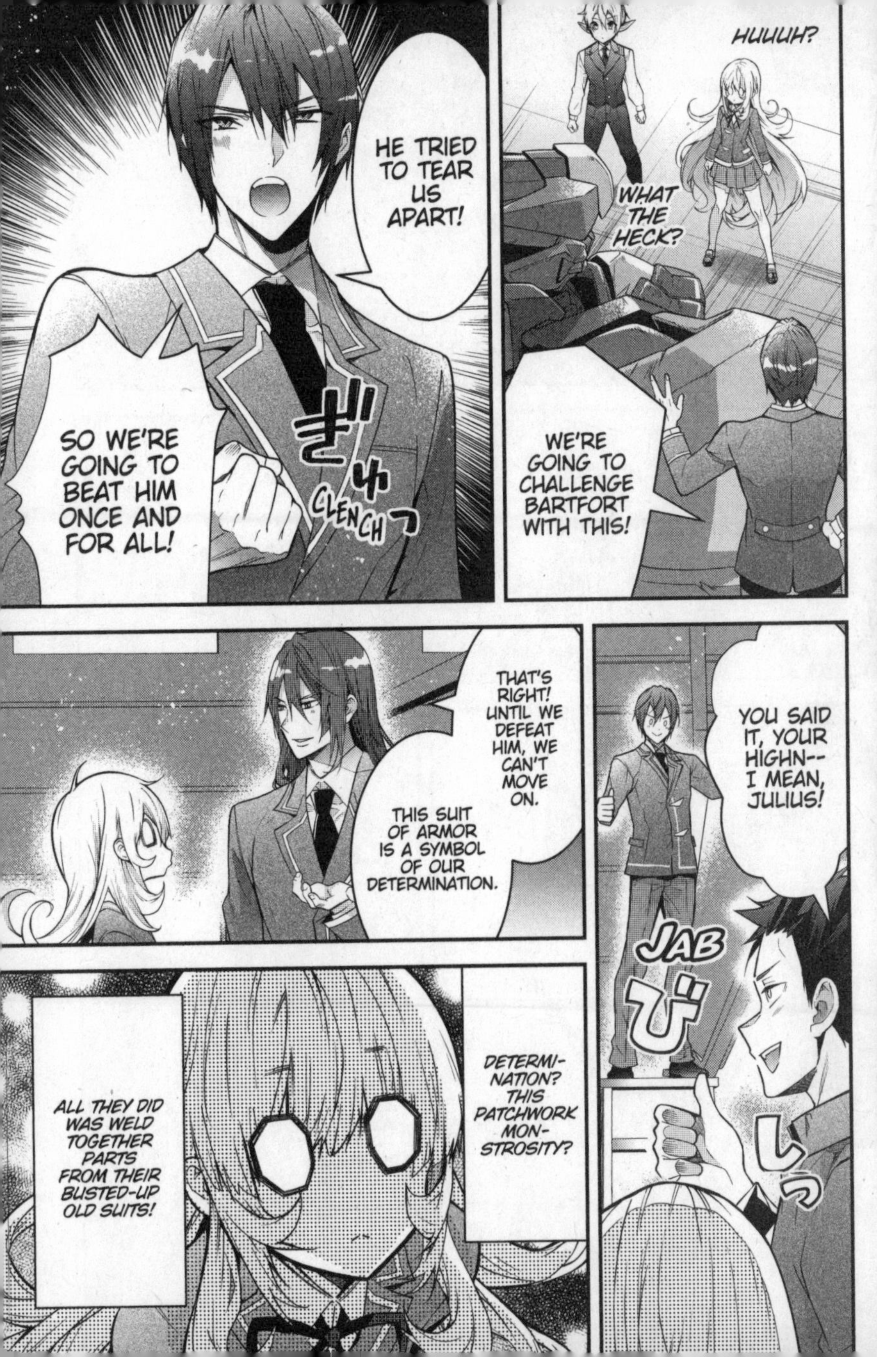
HUUUH?
WHAT THE HECK?
WE'RE GOING TO CHALLENGE BARTFORT WITH THIS!
HE TRIED TO TEAR US APART!
SO WE'RE GOING TO BEAT HIM ONCE AND FOR ALL!
ぎゅっ
CLENCH
YOU SAID IT, YOUR HIGHN-- I MEAN, JULIUS!
JAB
びしっ
THAT'S RIGHT! UNTIL WE DEFEAT HIM, WE CAN'T MOVE ON.
THIS SUIT OF ARMOR IS A SYMBOL OF OUR DETERMINATION.
DETERMI-NATION? THIS PATCHWORK MON-STROSITY?
ALL THEY DID WAS WELD TOGETHER PARTS FROM THEIR BUSTED-UP OLD SUITS!

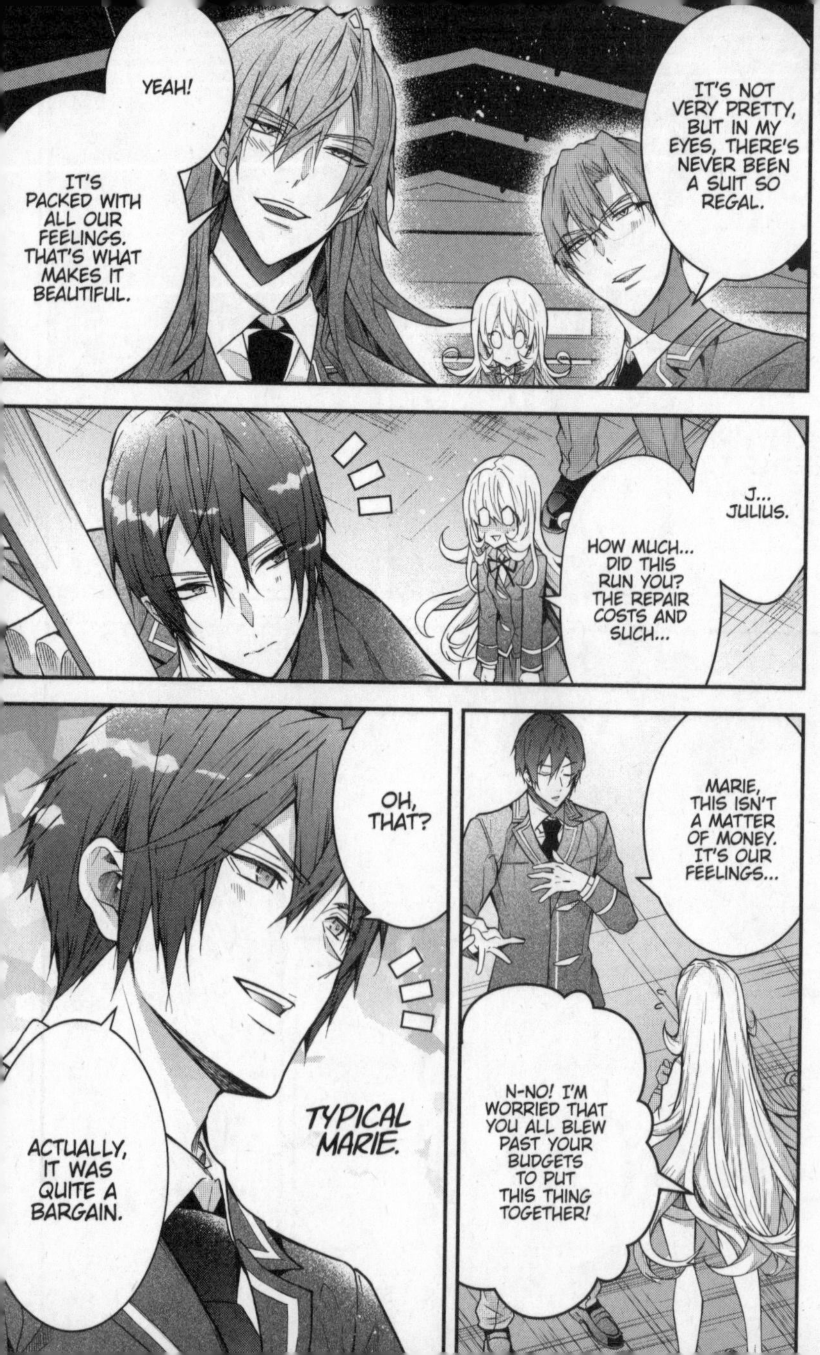
IT'S NOT VERY PRETTY, BUT IN MY EYES, THERE'S NEVER BEEN A SUIT SO REGAL.
YEAH!
IT'S PACKED WITH ALL OUR FEELINGS. THAT'S WHAT MAKES IT BEAUTIFUL.
J... JULIUS.
HOW MUCH... DID THIS RUN YOU? THE REPAIR COSTS AND SUCH...
MARIE, THIS ISN'T A MATTER OF MONEY. IT'S OUR FEELINGS...
N-NO! I'M WORRIED THAT YOU ALL BLEW PAST YOUR BUDGETS TO PUT THIS THING TOGETHER!
OH, THAT?
TYPICAL MARIE.
ACTUALLY, IT WAS QUITE A BARGAIN.

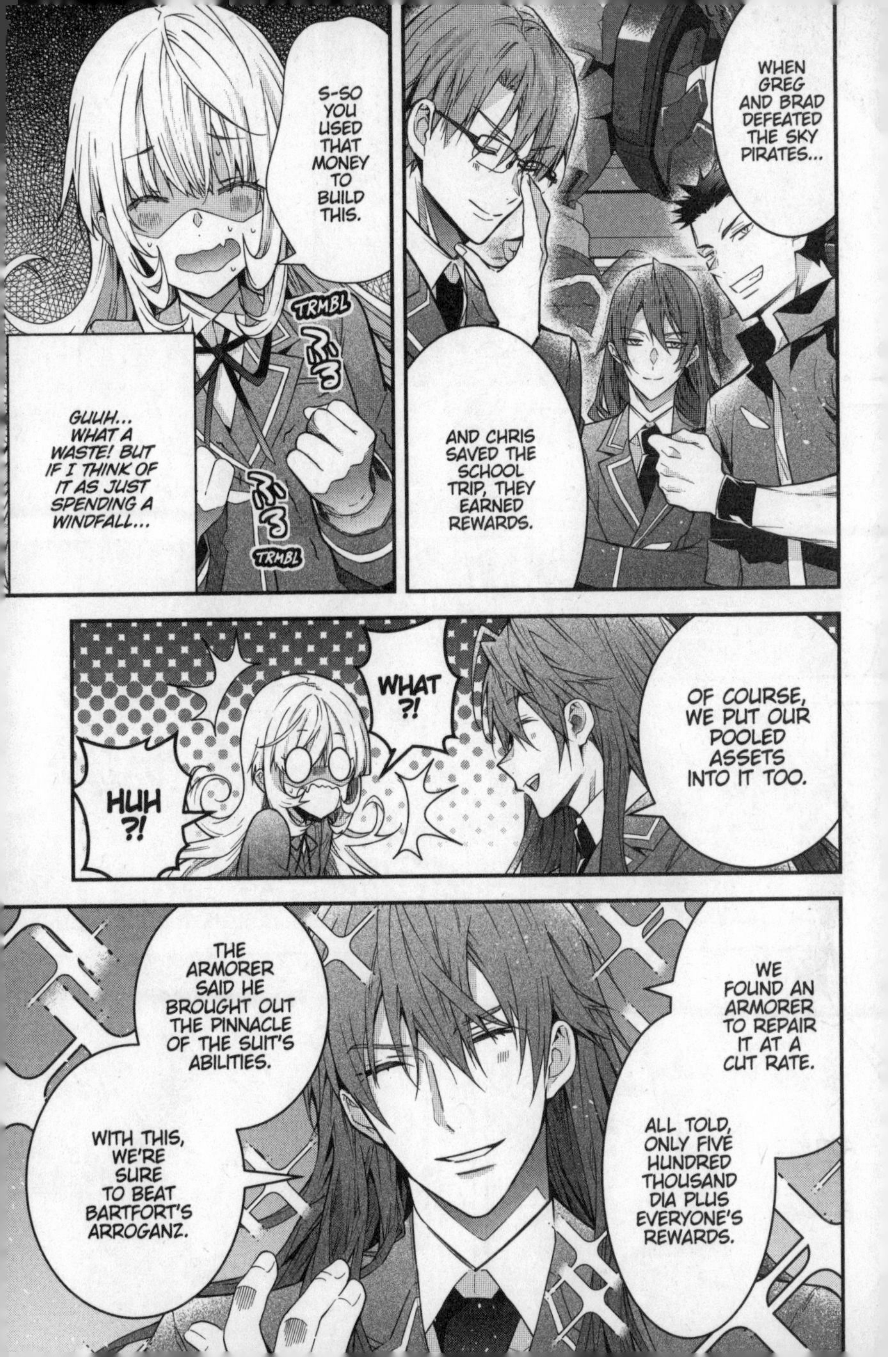
WHEN GREG AND BRAD DEFEATED THE SKY PIRATES...
AND CHRIS SAVED THE SCHOOL TRIP, THEY EARNED REWARDS.
S-SO YOU USED THAT MONEY TO BUILD THIS.
TRMBL
ぷる
ぷる
TRMBL
GUUH... WHAT A WASTE! BUT IF I THINK OF IT AS JUST SPENDING A WINDFALL...
OF COURSE, WE PUT OUR POOLED ASSETS INTO IT TOO.
WHAT ?!
HUH ?!
WE FOUND AN ARMORER TO REPAIR IT AT A CUT RATE.
ALL TOLD, ONLY FIVE HUNDRED THOUSAND DIA PLUS EVERYONE'S REWARDS.
THE ARMORER SAID HE BROUGHT OUT THE PINNACLE OF THE SUIT'S ABILITIES.
WITH THIS, WE'RE SURE TO BEAT BARTFORT'S ARROGANZ.

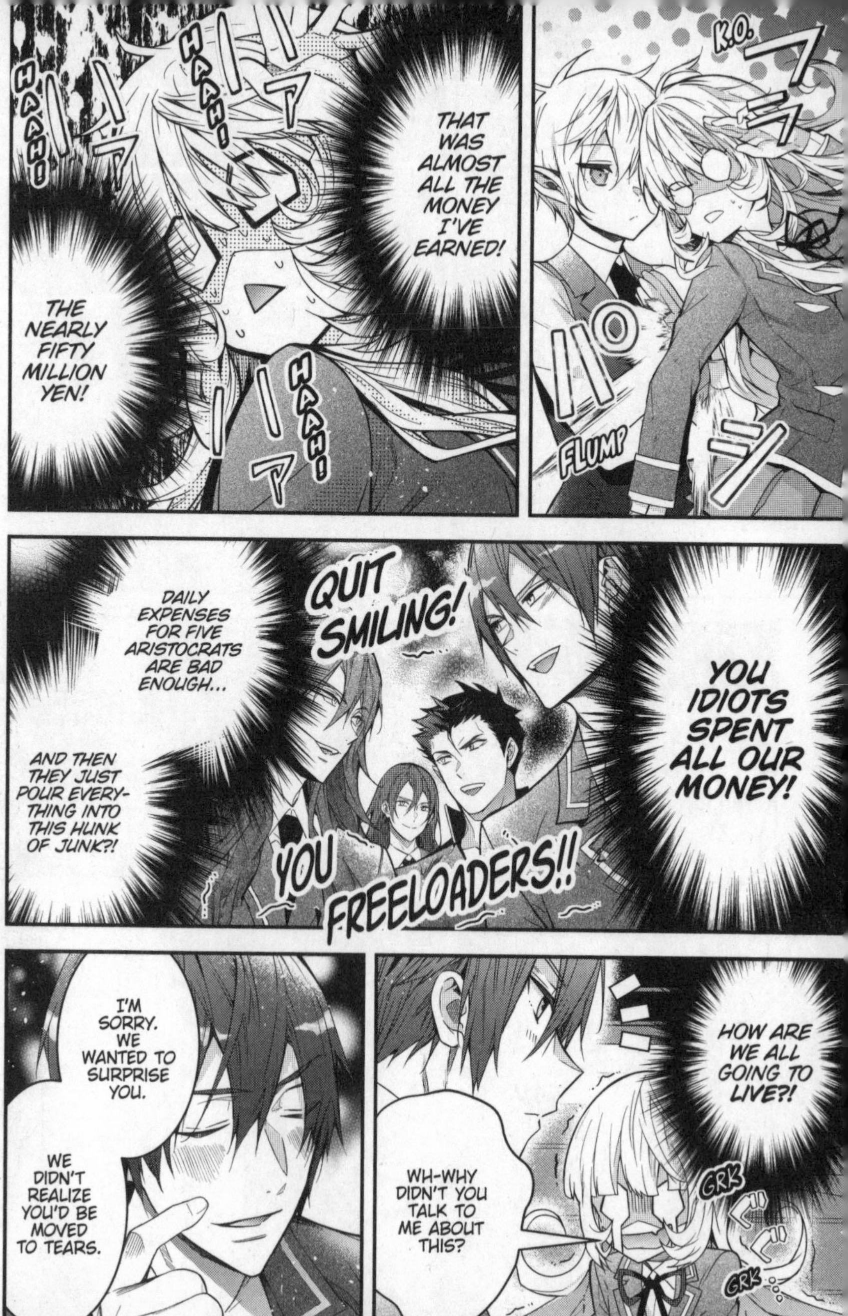
K.O.
FLUMP
HAAAH!
HAAAH!
THAT WAS ALMOST ALL THE MONEY I'VE EARNED!
THE NEARLY FIFTY MILLION YEN!
HAAAH!
YOU IDIOTS SPENT ALL OUR MONEY!
QUIT SMILING!
DAILY EXPENSES FOR FIVE ARISTOCRATS ARE BAD ENOUGH...
AND THEN THEY JUST POUR EVERY-THING INTO THIS HUNK OF JUNK?!
YOU FREELOADERS!!
HOW ARE WE ALL GOING TO LIVE?!
GRK
GRK
WH-WHY DIDN'T YOU TALK TO ME ABOUT THIS?
I'M SORRY. WE WANTED TO SURPRISE YOU.
WE DIDN'T REALIZE YOU'D BE MOVED TO TEARS.

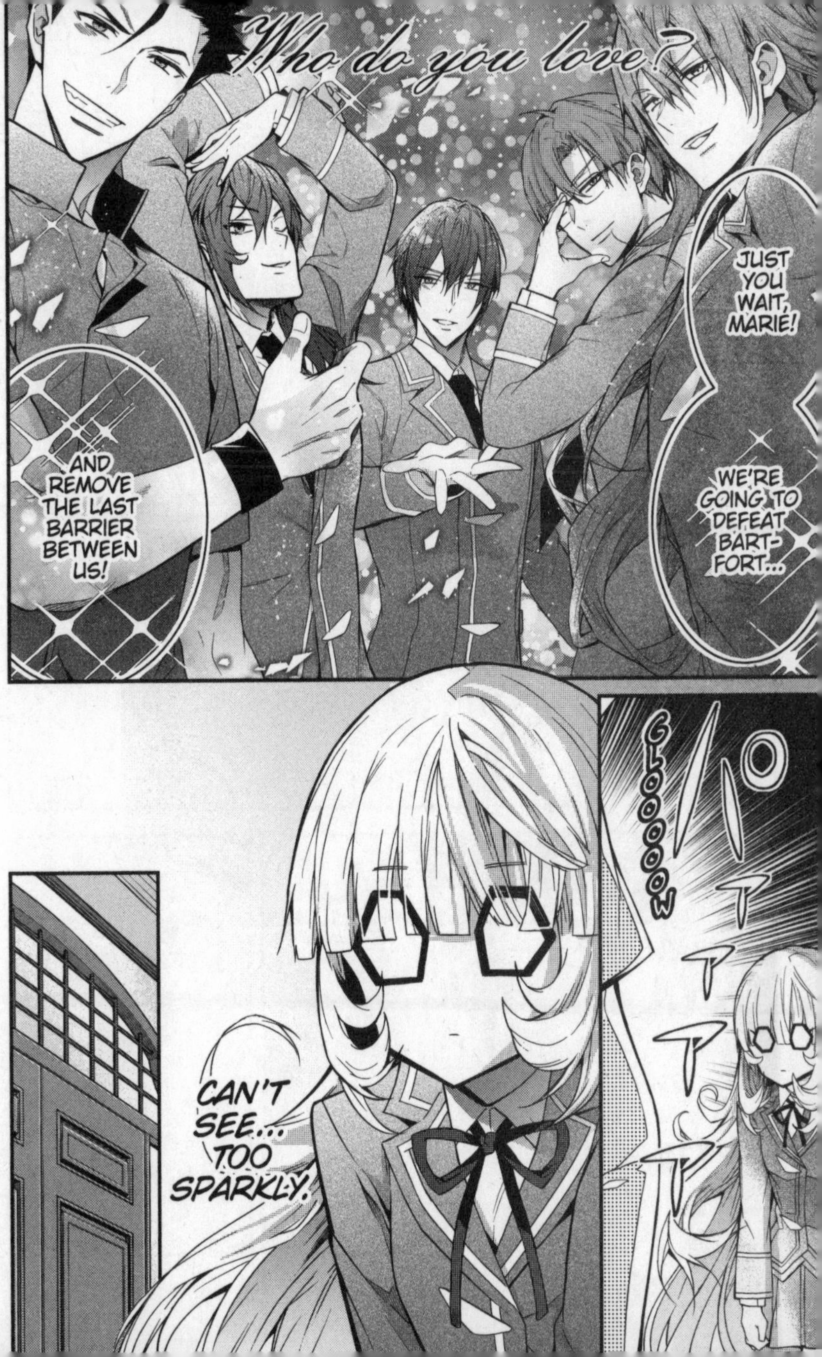
Who do you love?
JUST YOU WAIT, MARIE!
WE'RE GOING TO DEFEAT BART-FORT...
AND REMOVE THE LAST BARRIER BETWEEN US!
GLOOOOOOW
CAN'T SEE... TOO SPARKLY.

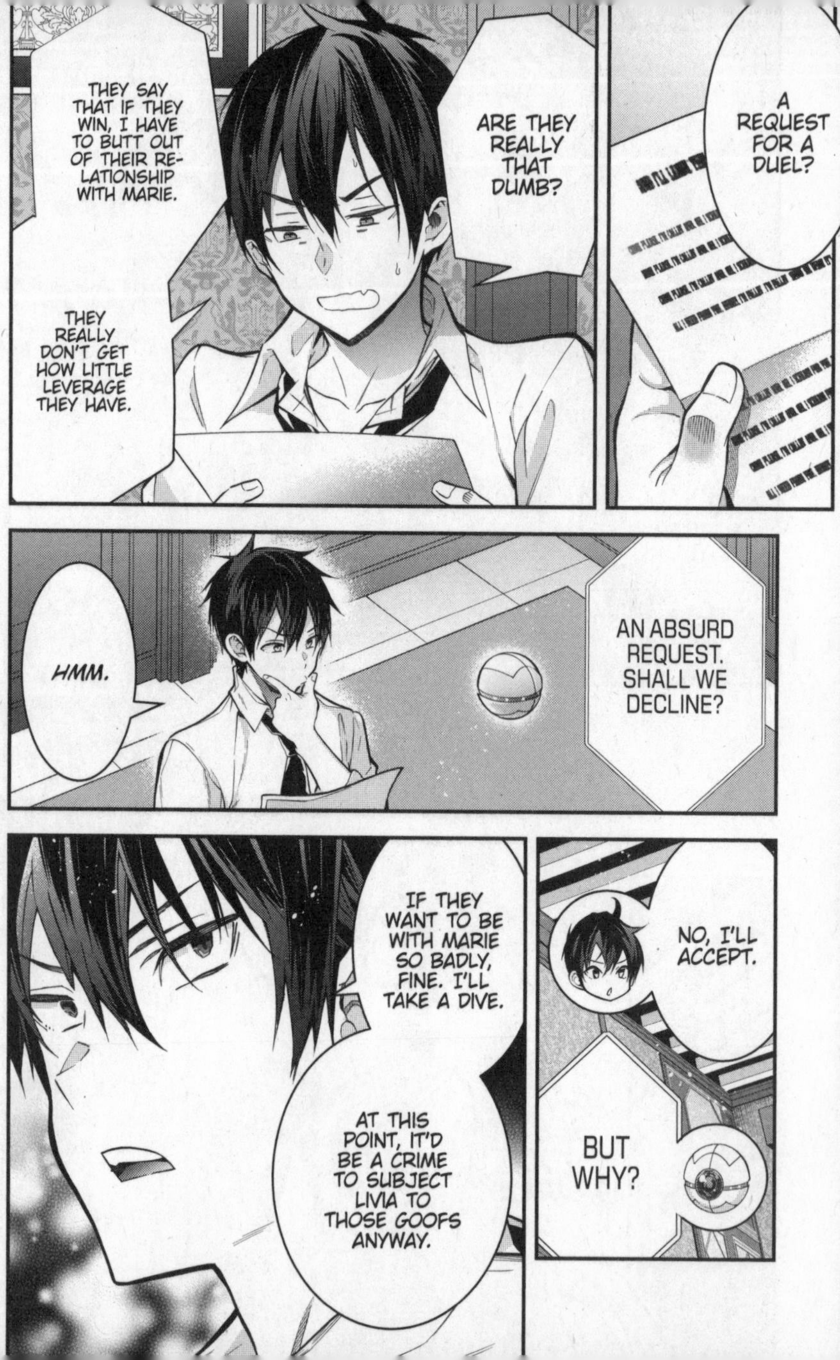
A REQUEST FOR A DUEL?
ARE THEY REALLY THAT DUMB?
THEY SAY THAT IF THEY WIN, I HAVE TO BUTT OUT OF THEIR RE-LATIONSHIP WITH MARIE.
THEY REALLY DON'T GET HOW LITTLE LEVERAGE THEY HAVE.
AN ABSURD REQUEST. SHALL WE DECLINE?
HMM.
NO, I'LL ACCEPT.
BUT WHY?
IF THEY WANT TO BE WITH MARIE SO BADLY, FINE. I'LL TAKE A DIVE.
AT THIS POINT, IT'D BE A CRIME TO SUBJECT LIVIA TO THOSE GOOFS ANYWAY.

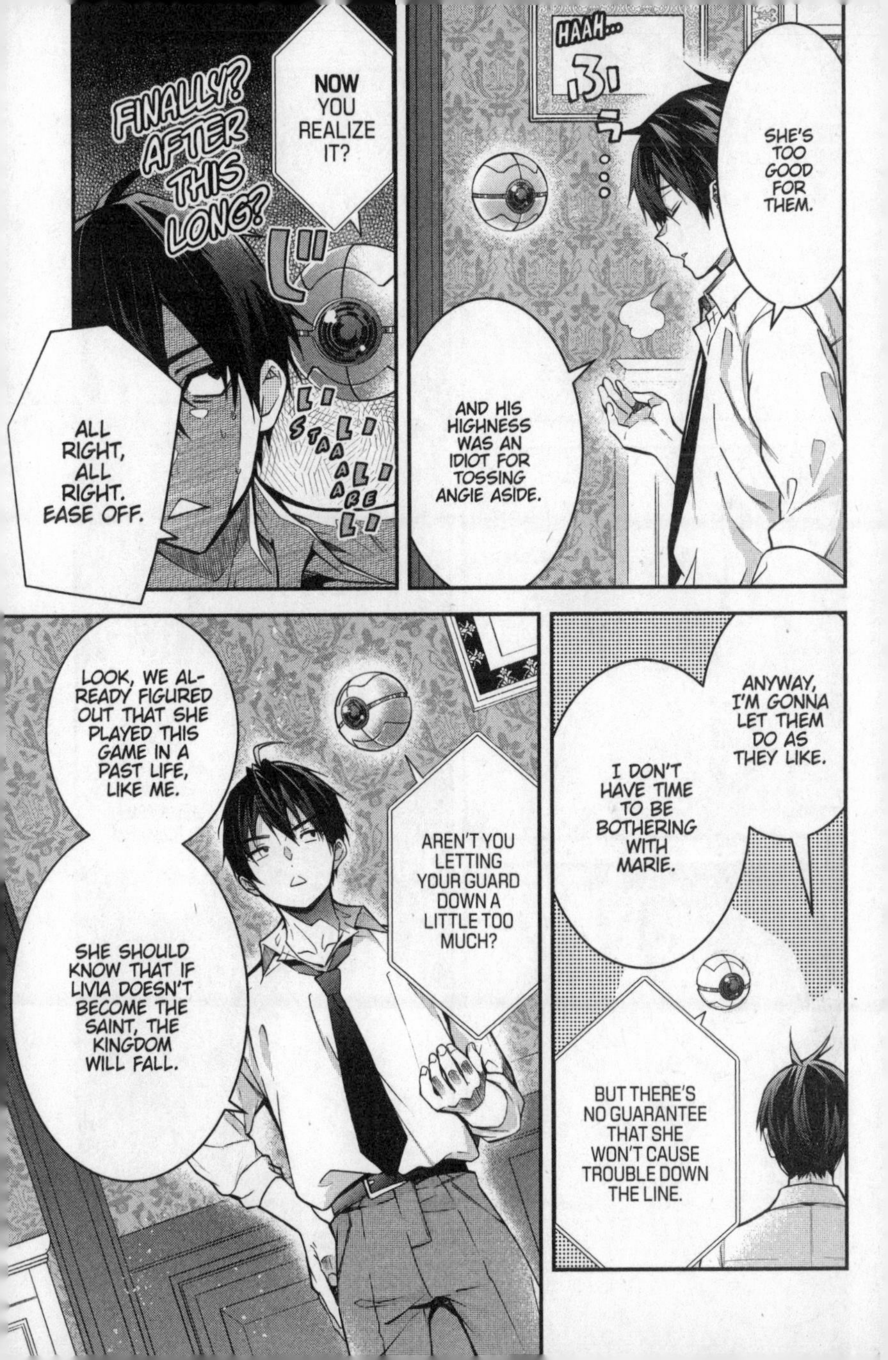
HAAH...
SHE'S TOO GOOD FOR THEM.
AND HIS HIGHNESS WAS AN IDIOT FOR TOSSING ANGIE ASIDE.
NOW YOU REALIZE IT?
FINALLY? AFTER THIS LONG?
STAAARE
ALL RIGHT, ALL RIGHT. EASE OFF.
ANYWAY, I'M GONNA LET THEM DO AS THEY LIKE.
I DON'T HAVE TIME TO BE BOTHERING WITH MARIE.
BUT THERE'S NO GUARANTEE THAT SHE WON'T CAUSE TROUBLE DOWN THE LINE.
AREN'T YOU LETTING YOUR GUARD DOWN A LITTLE TOO MUCH?
LOOK, WE AL-READY FIGURED OUT THAT SHE PLAYED THIS GAME IN A PAST LIFE, LIKE ME.
SHE SHOULD KNOW THAT IF LIVIA DOESN'T BECOME THE SAINT, THE KINGDOM WILL FALL.

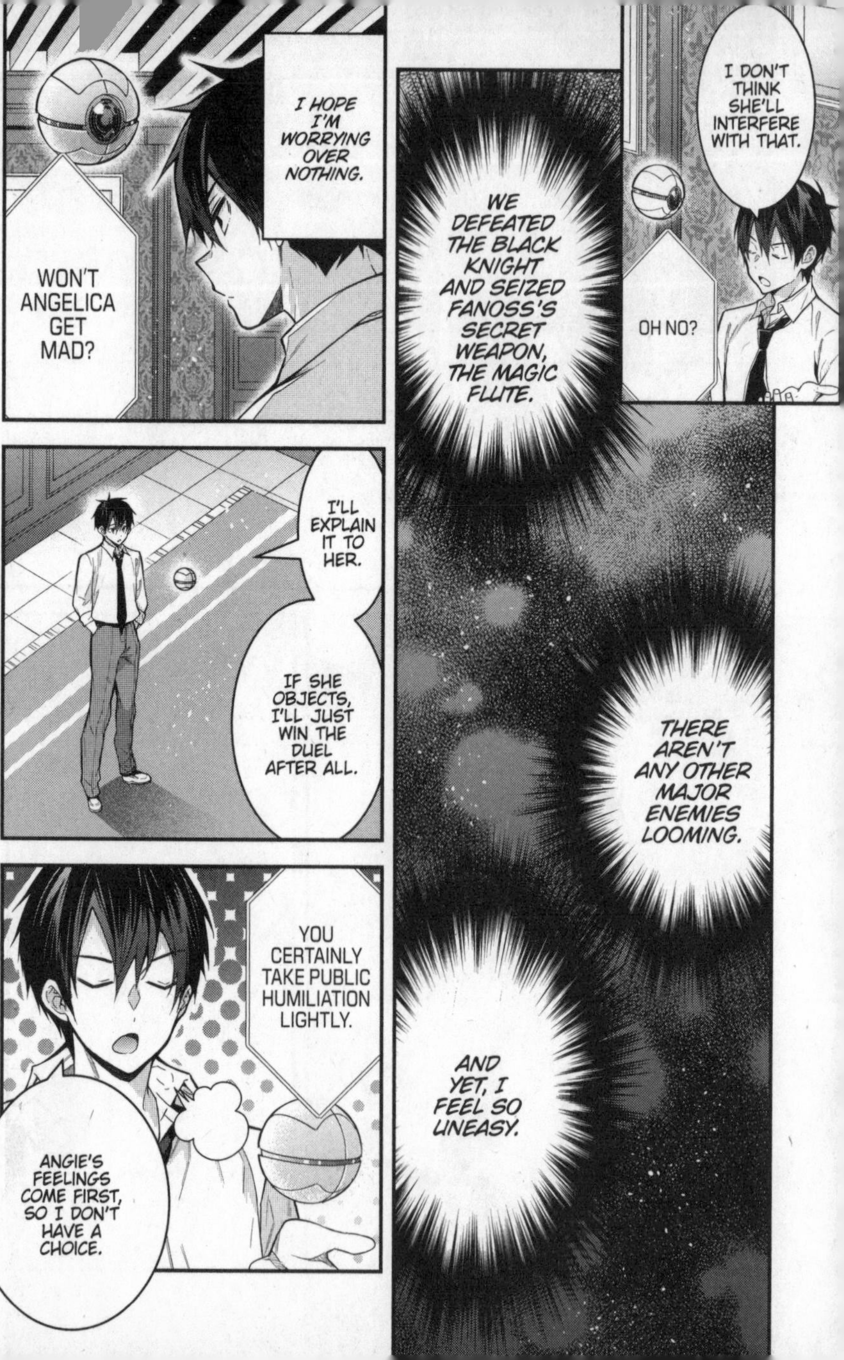
I DON'T THINK SHE'LL INTERFERE WITH THAT.
OH NO?
WE DEFEATED THE BLACK KNIGHT AND SEIZED FANOSS'S SECRET WEAPON, THE MAGIC FLUTE.
THERE AREN'T ANY OTHER MAJOR ENEMIES LOOMING.
AND YET, I FEEL SO UNEASY.
I HOPE I'M WORRYING OVER NOTHING.
WON'T ANGELICA GET MAD?
I'LL EXPLAIN IT TO HER.
IF SHE OBJECTS, I'LL JUST WIN THE DUEL AFTER ALL.
YOU CERTAINLY TAKE PUBLIC HUMILIATION LIGHTLY.
ANGIE'S FEELINGS COME FIRST, SO I DON'T HAVE A CHOICE.

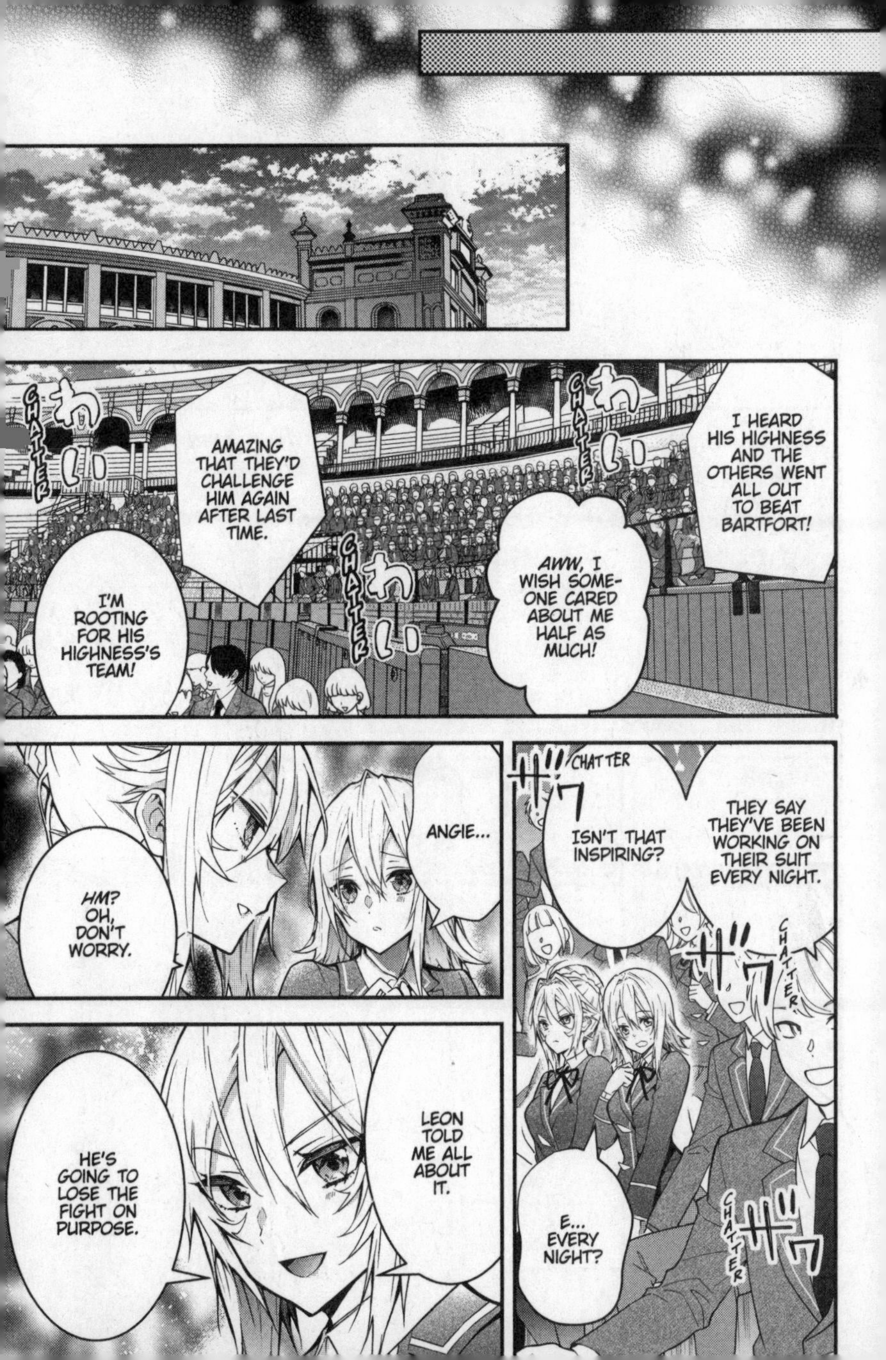
I HEARD HIS HIGHNESS AND THE OTHERS WENT ALL OUT TO BEAT BARTFORT!
わい CHATTER
AWW, I WISH SOME-ONE CARED ABOUT ME HALF AS MUCH!
わい CHATTER
AMAZING THAT THEY'D CHALLENGE HIM AGAIN AFTER LAST TIME.
わい CHATTER
I'M ROOTING FOR HIS HIGHNESS'S TEAM!
THEY SAY THEY'VE BEEN WORKING ON THEIR SUIT EVERY NIGHT.
ザワ CHATTER
ISN'T THAT INSPIRING?
ザワ CHATTER
E... EVERY NIGHT?
ザワ CHATTER
ANGIE...
HM? OH, DON'T WORRY.
LEON TOLD ME ALL ABOUT IT.
HE'S GOING TO LOSE THE FIGHT ON PURPOSE.

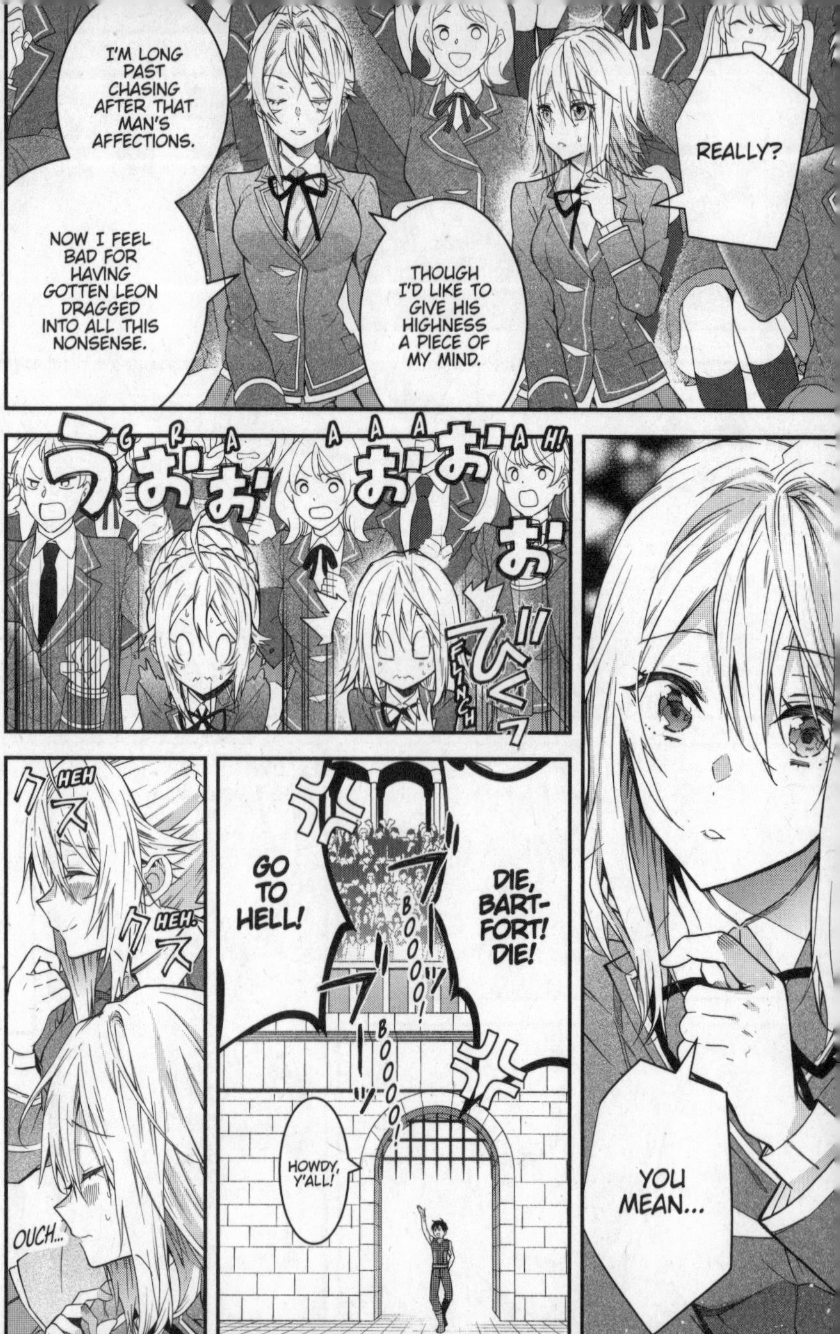

REALLY?
I'M LONG PAST CHASING AFTER THAT MAN'S AFFECTIONS.
THOUGH I'D LIKE TO GIVE HIS HIGHNESS A PIECE OF MY MIND.
NOW I FEEL BAD FOR HAVING GOTTEN LEON DRAGGED INTO ALL THIS NONSENSE.
YOU MEAN...
GRAAAAAAH!
FLINCH
DIE, BART-FORT! DIE!
BOOOOO!
GO TO HELL!
BOOOOO!
HOWDY, Y'ALL!
HEH
HEH.
OUCH...

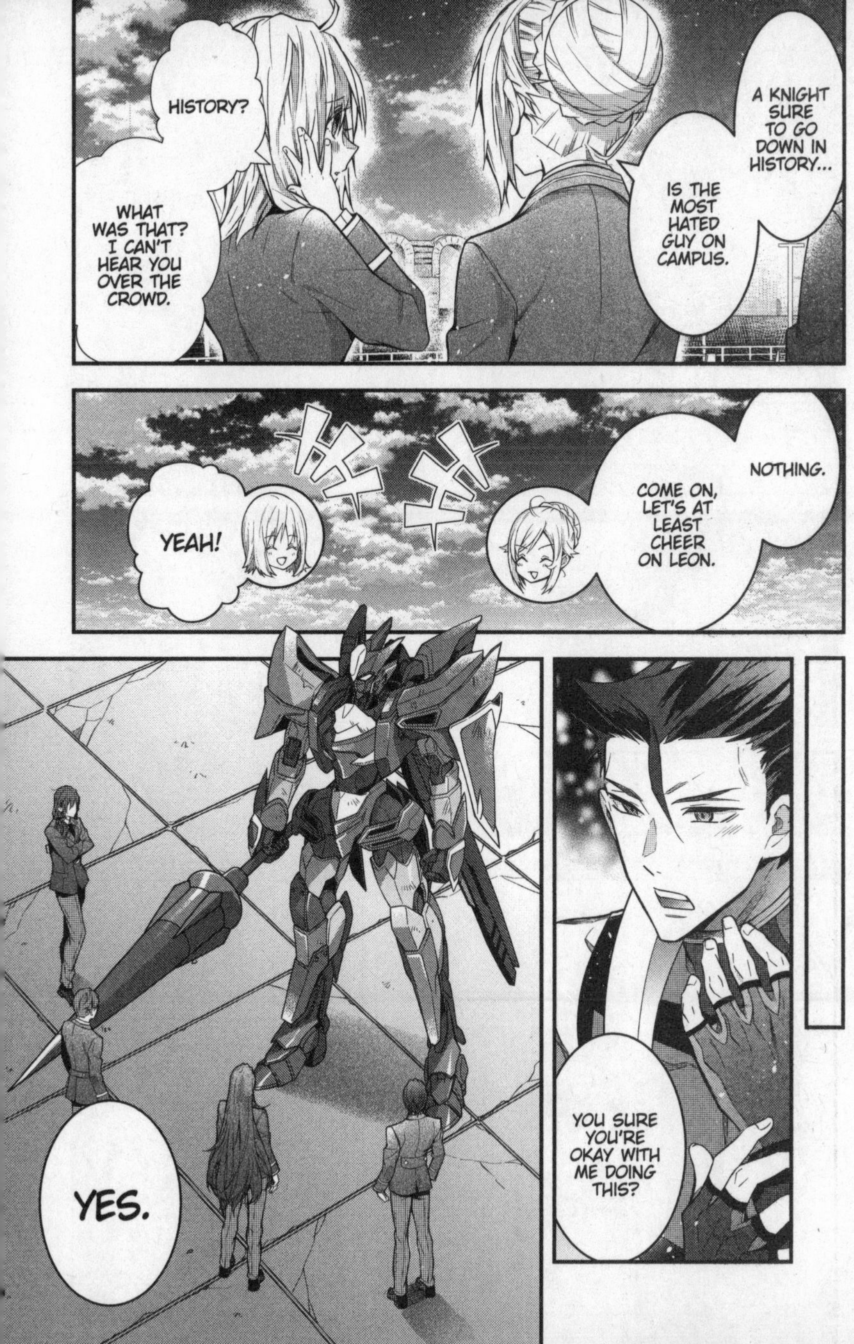
A KNIGHT SURE TO GO DOWN IN HISTORY...
IS THE MOST HATED GUY ON CAMPUS.
HISTORY?
WHAT WAS THAT? I CAN'T HEAR YOU OVER THE CROWD.
NOTHING.
COME ON, LET'S AT LEAST CHEER ON LEON.
YEAH!
YOU SURE YOU'RE OKAY WITH ME DOING THIS?
YES.

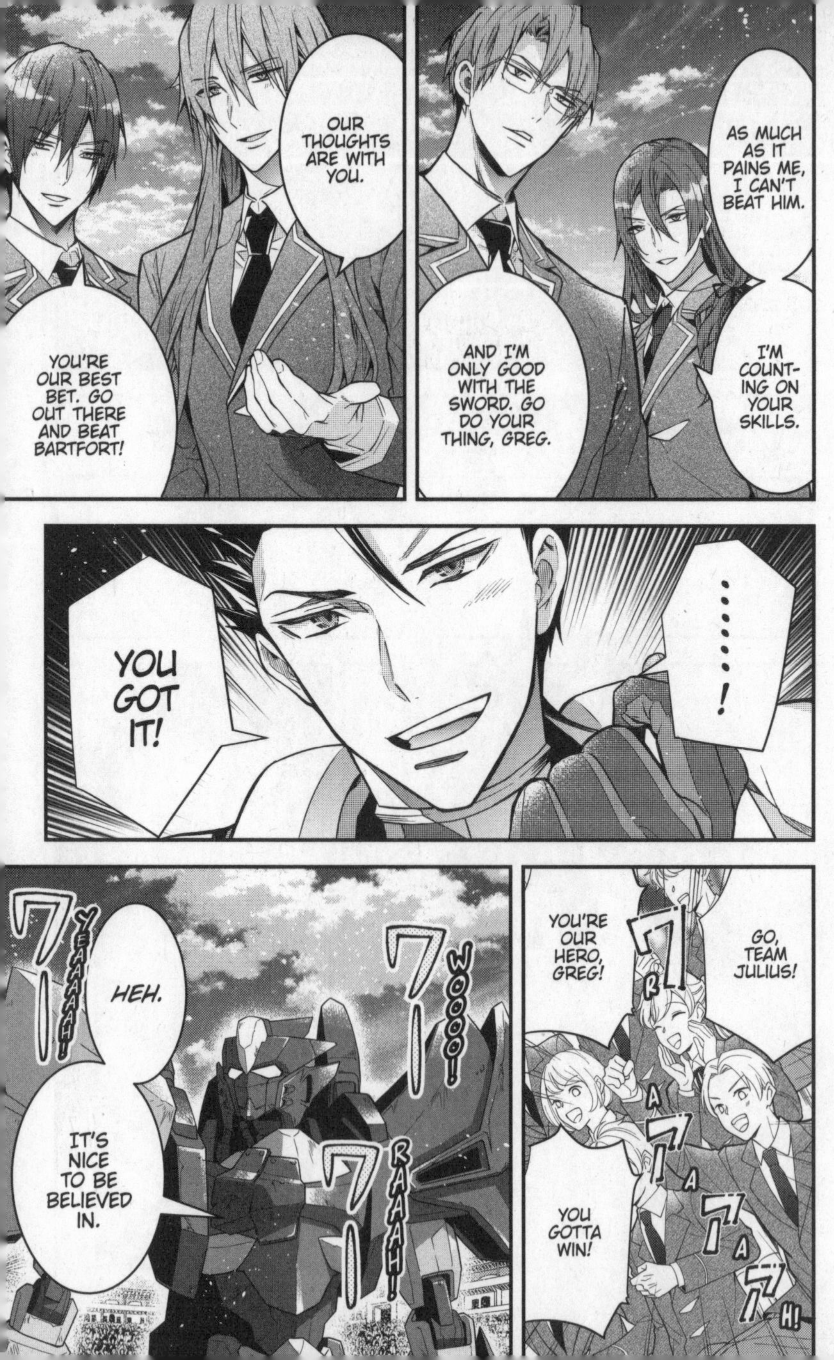
AS MUCH AS IT PAINS ME, I CAN'T BEAT HIM.
I'M COUNTING ON YOUR SKILLS.
AND I'M ONLY GOOD WITH THE SWORD. GO DO YOUR THING, GREG.
OUR THOUGHTS ARE WITH YOU.
YOU'RE OUR BEST BET. GO OUT THERE AND BEAT BARTFORT!
......!
YOU GOT IT!
GO, TEAM JULIUS!
YOU'RE OUR HERO, GREG!
RAAAH!
YOU GOTTA WIN!
WOOOOO!
RAAAAH!
YEAAAAH!
HEH.
IT'S NICE TO BE BELIEVED IN.

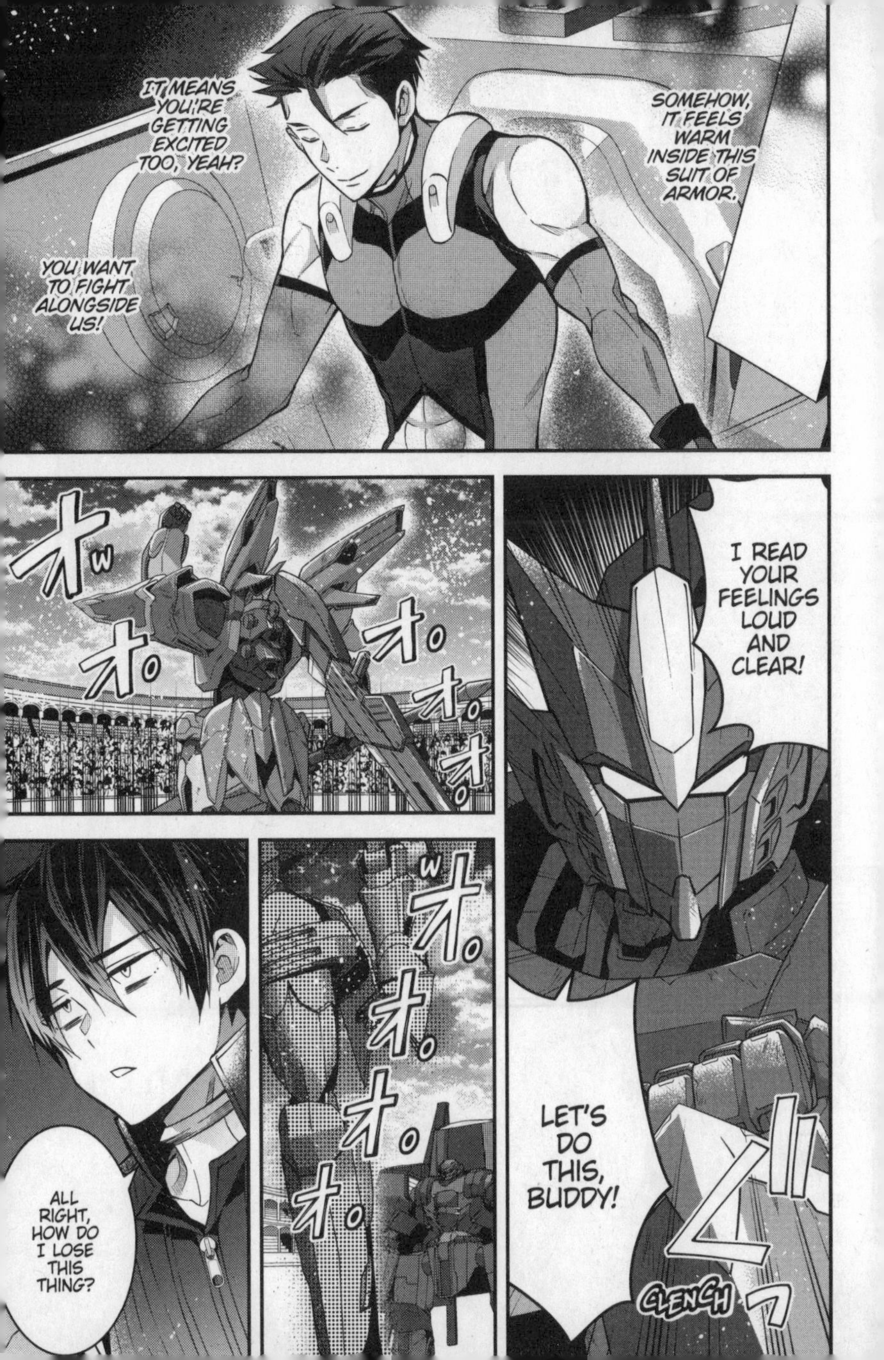
SOMEHOW, IT FEELS WARM INSIDE THIS SUIT OF ARMOR.
IT MEANS YOU'RE GETTING EXCITED TOO, YEAH?
YOU WANT TO FIGHT ALONGSIDE US!
I READ YOUR FEELINGS LOUD AND CLEAR!
LET'S DO THIS, BUDDY!
CLENCH
オw
オ。
オ。
オ。
オ。
wオ。
オ。
オ。
オ。
ALL RIGHT, HOW DO I LOSE THIS THING?

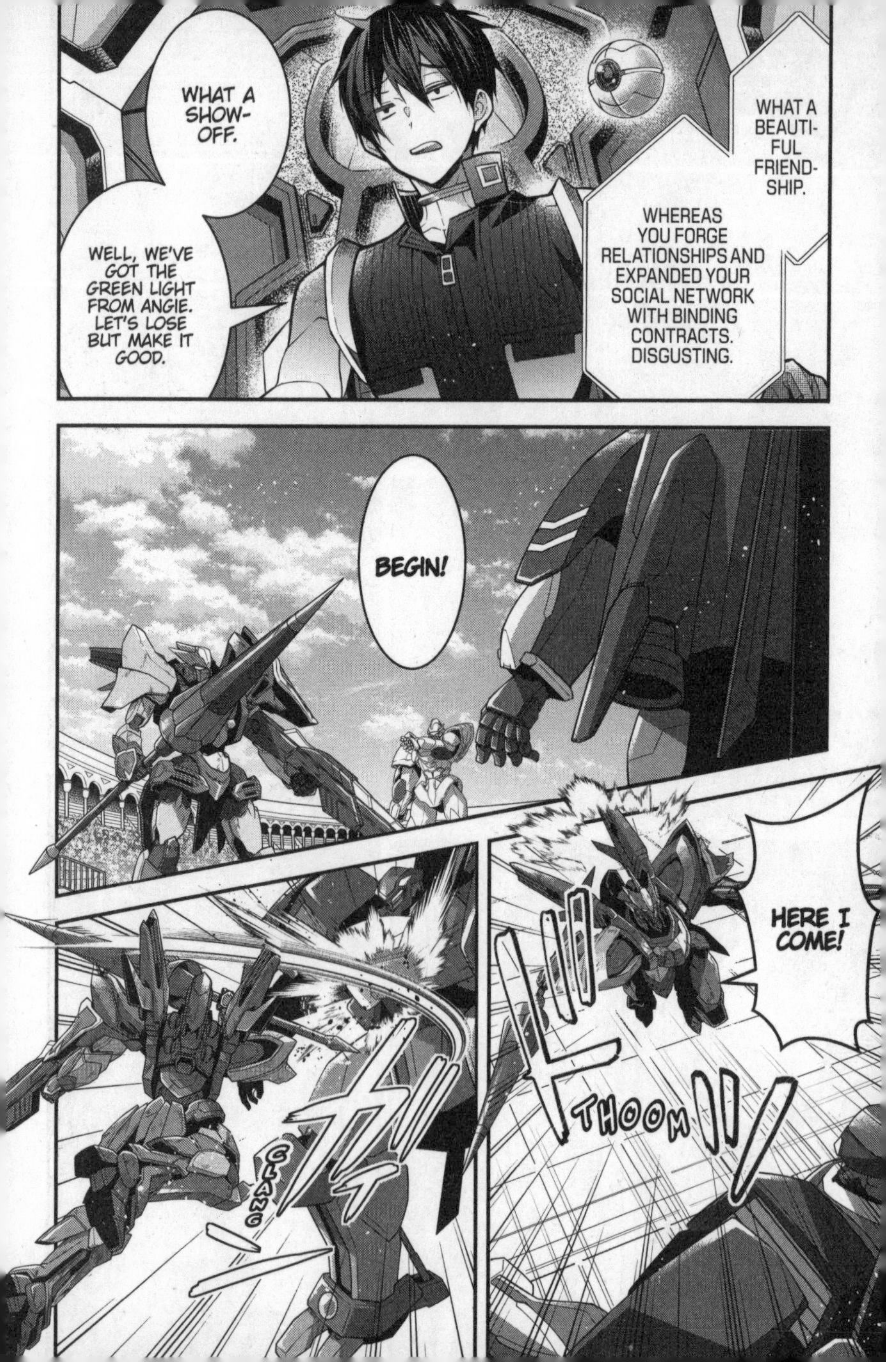
WHAT A BEAUTIFUL FRIENDSHIP.
WHEREAS YOU FORGE RELATIONSHIPS AND EXPANDED YOUR SOCIAL NETWORK WITH BINDING CONTRACTS. DISGUSTING.
WHAT A SHOW-OFF.
WELL, WE'VE GOT THE GREEN LIGHT FROM ANGIE. LET'S LOSE BUT MAKE IT GOOD.
BEGIN!
HERE I COME!
THOOM
SH
CLANG

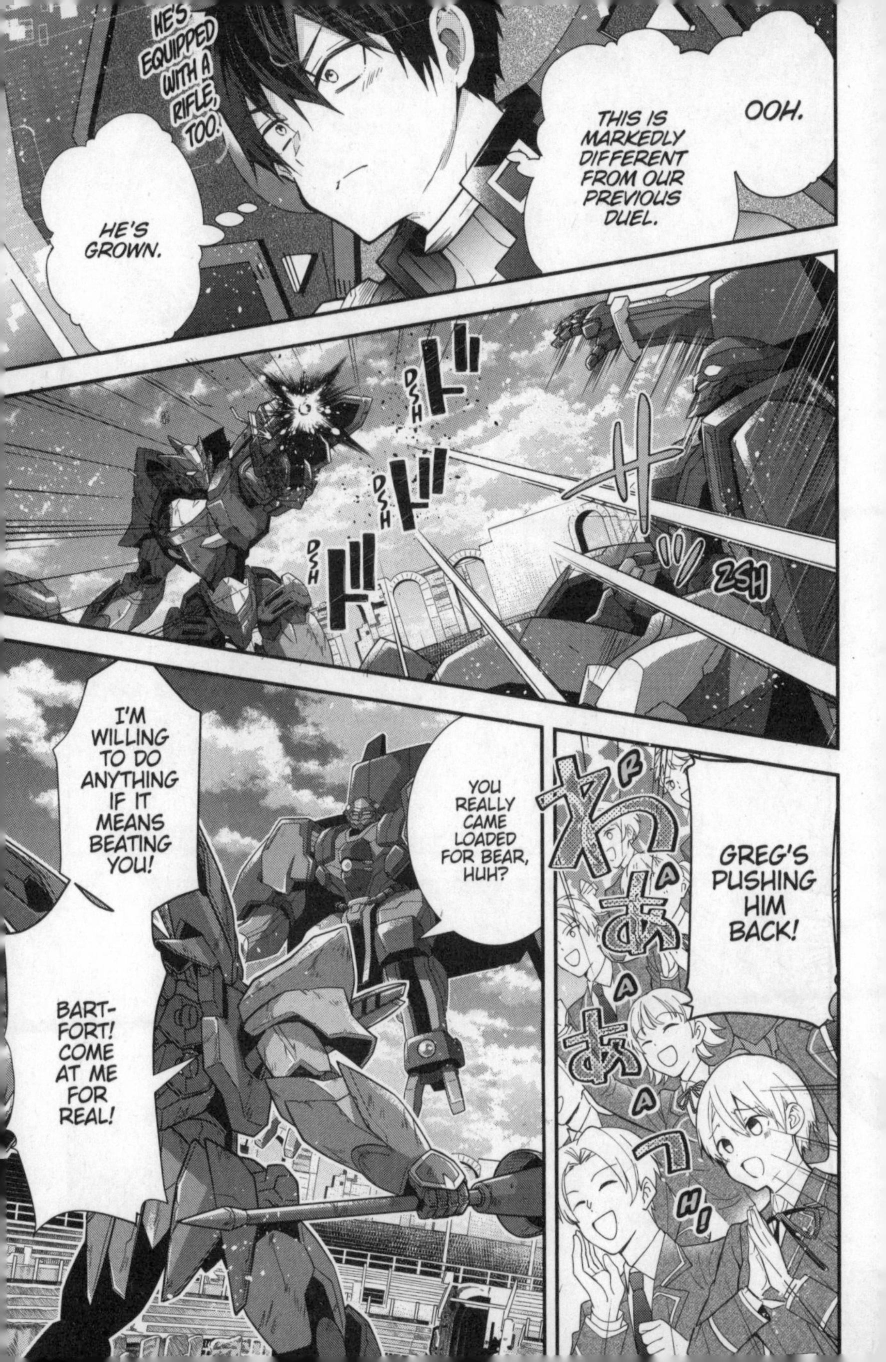
OOH.
THIS IS MARKEDLY DIFFERENT FROM OUR PREVIOUS DUEL.
HE'S EQUIPPED WITH A RIFLE, TOO.
HE'S GROWN.
ZSH
DSH
DSH
DSH
RAAAH!
GREG'S PUSHING HIM BACK!
YOU REALLY CAME LOADED FOR BEAR, HUH?
I'M WILLING TO DO ANYTHING IF IT MEANS BEATING YOU!
BART-FORT! COME AT ME FOR REAL!

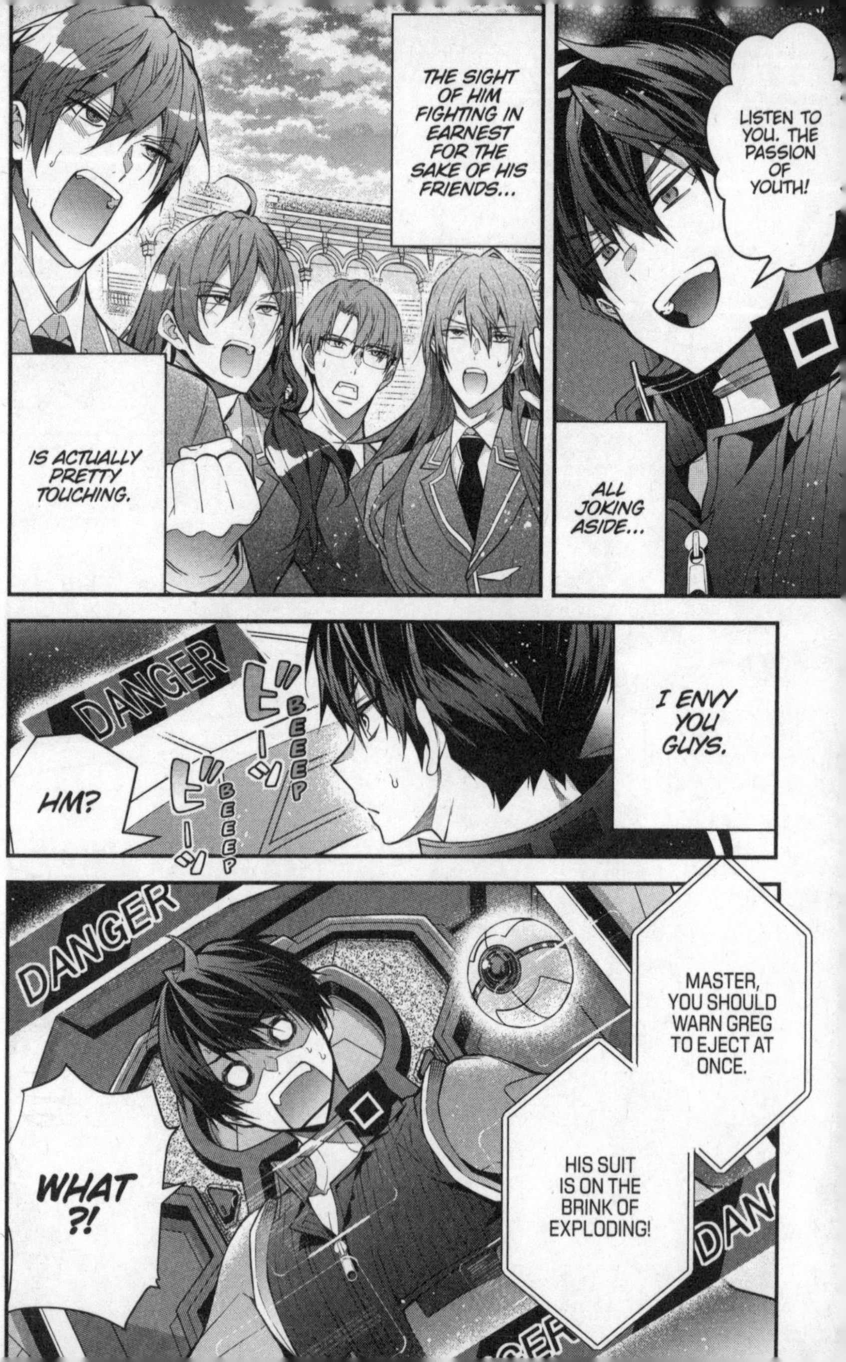
LISTEN TO YOU. THE PASSION OF YOUTH!
ALL JOKING ASIDE...
THE SIGHT OF HIM FIGHTING IN EARNEST FOR THE SAKE OF HIS FRIENDS...
IS ACTUALLY PRETTY TOUCHING.
I ENVY YOU GUYS.
DANGER
BEEEP
BEEEP
HM?
DANGER
MASTER, YOU SHOULD WARN GREG TO EJECT AT ONCE.
HIS SUIT IS ON THE BRINK OF EXPLODING!
WHAT?!
DANG

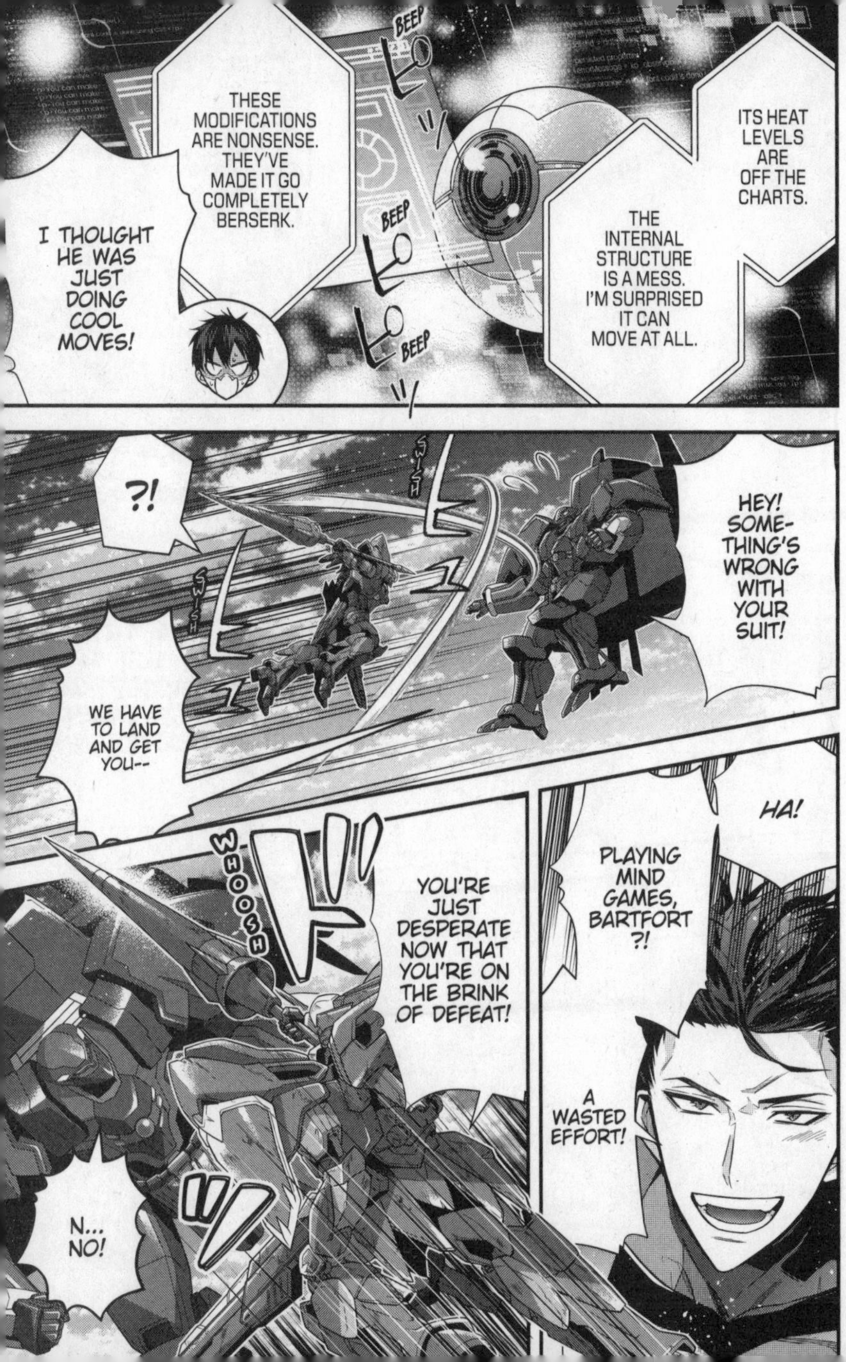
ITS HEAT LEVELS ARE OFF THE CHARTS.
THE INTERNAL STRUCTURE IS A MESS. I'M SURPRISED IT CAN MOVE AT ALL.
BEEP
BEEP
BEEP
THESE MODIFICATIONS ARE NONSENSE. THEY'VE MADE IT GO COMPLETELY BERSERK.
I THOUGHT HE WAS JUST DOING COOL MOVES!
HEY! SOMETHING'S WRONG WITH YOUR SUIT!
WE HAVE TO LAND AND GET YOU--
SWISH
?!
SWISH
HA!
PLAYING MIND GAMES, BARTFORT?!
A WASTED EFFORT!
WHOOSH
YOU'RE JUST DESPERATE NOW THAT YOU'RE ON THE BRINK OF DEFEAT!
N... NO!

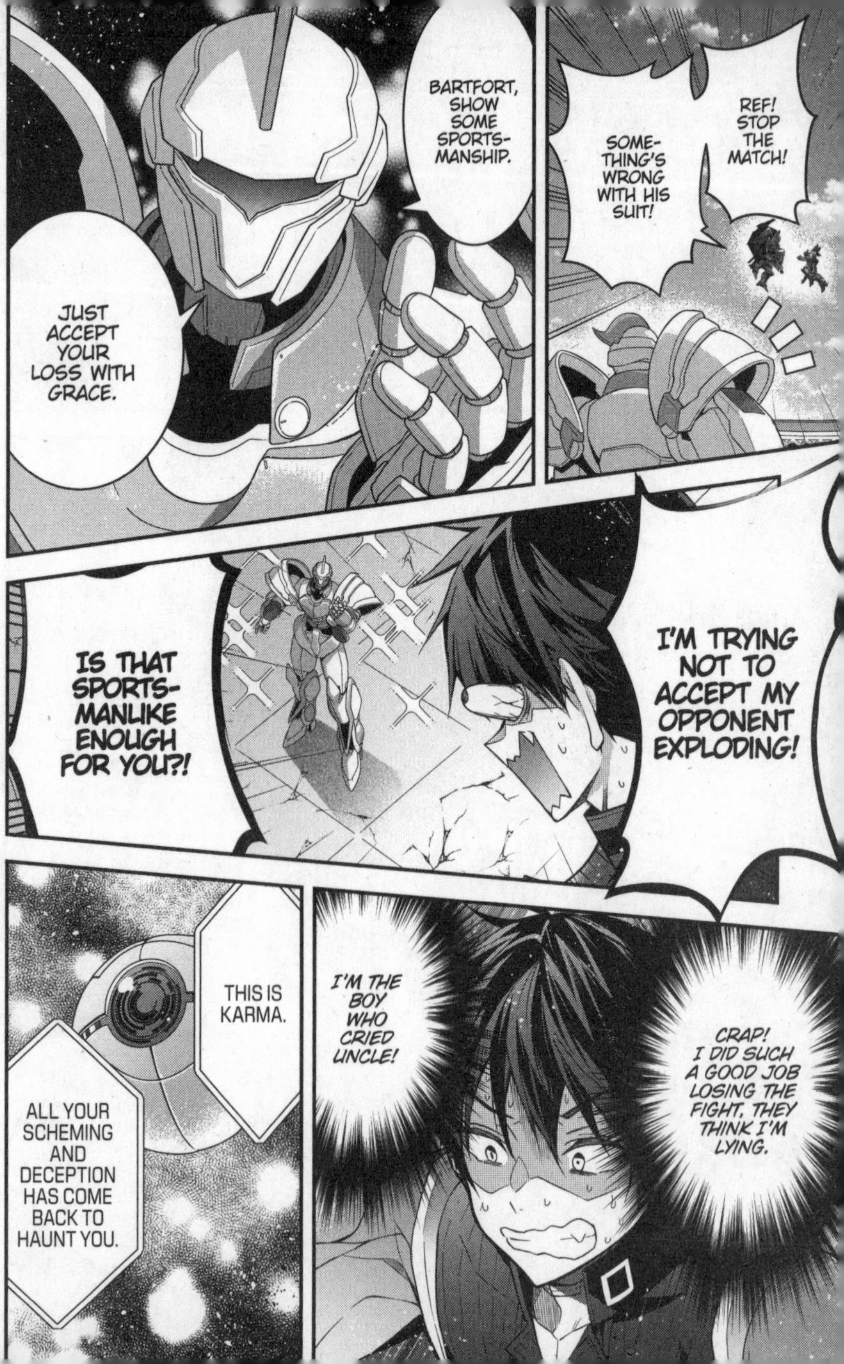
REF! STOP THE MATCH!
SOME-THING'S WRONG WITH HIS SUIT!
BARTFORT, SHOW SOME SPORTS-MANSHIP.
JUST ACCEPT YOUR LOSS WITH GRACE.
I'M TRYING NOT TO ACCEPT MY OPPONENT EXPLODING!
IS THAT SPORTS-MANLIKE ENOUGH FOR YOU?!
CRAP! I DID SUCH A GOOD JOB LOSING THE FIGHT, THEY THINK I'M LYING.
I'M THE BOY WHO CRIED UNCLE!
THIS IS KARMA.
ALL YOUR SCHEMING AND DECEPTION HAS COME BACK TO HAUNT YOU.

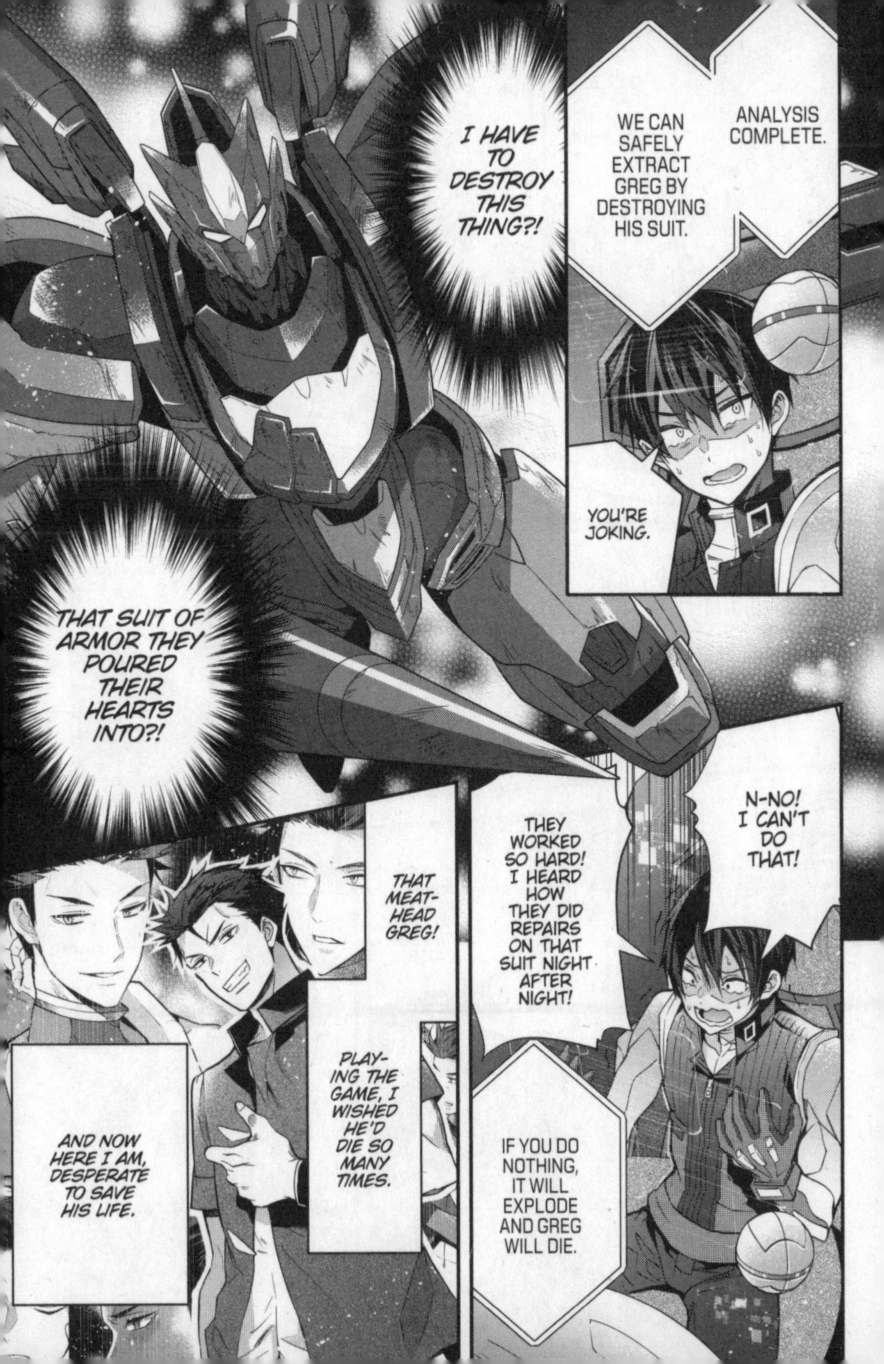
ANALYSIS COMPLETE.
WE CAN SAFELY EXTRACT GREG BY DESTROYING HIS SUIT.
YOU'RE JOKING.
I HAVE TO DESTROY THIS THING?!
THAT SUIT OF ARMOR THEY POURED THEIR HEARTS INTO?!
N-NO! I CAN'T DO THAT!
THEY WORKED SO HARD! I HEARD HOW THEY DID REPAIRS ON THAT SUIT NIGHT AFTER NIGHT!
IF YOU DO NOTHING, IT WILL EXPLODE AND GREG WILL DIE.
THAT MEAT-HEAD GREG!
PLAY-ING THE GAME, I WISHED HE'D DIE SO MANY TIMES.
AND NOW HERE I AM, DESPERATE TO SAVE HIS LIFE.

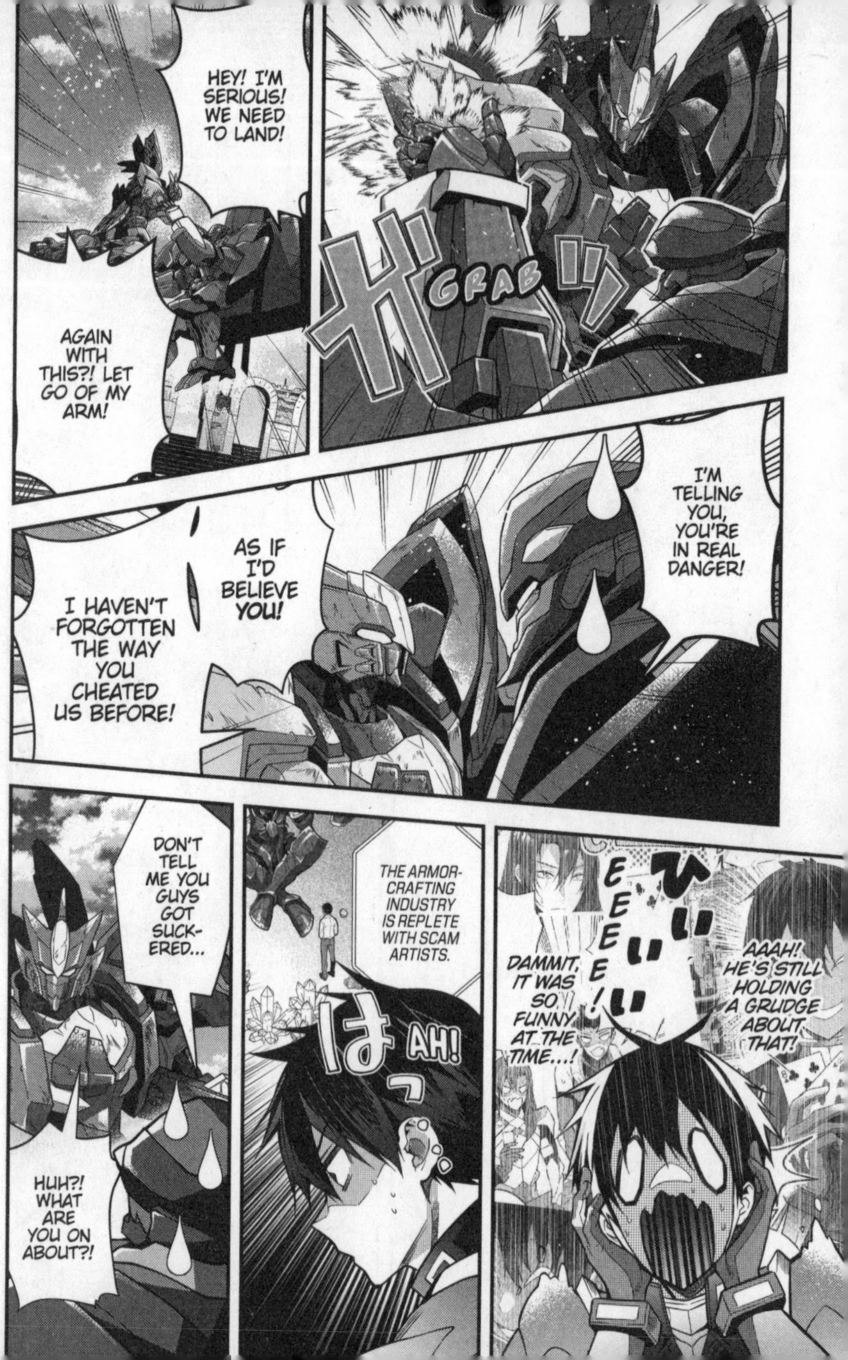
ガ GRAB ッ
HEY! I'M SERIOUS! WE NEED TO LAND!
AGAIN WITH THIS?! LET GO OF MY ARM!
I'M TELLING YOU, YOU'RE IN REAL DANGER!
AS IF I'D BELIEVE YOU!
I HAVEN'T FORGOTTEN THE WAY YOU CHEATED US BEFORE!
ひぃぃぃぃ
EEEEE!
AAAH! HE'S STILL HOLDING A GRUDGE ABOUT THAT!
DAMMIT, IT WAS SO FUNNY AT THE TIME...!
THE ARMOR-CRAFTING INDUSTRY IS REPLETE WITH SCAM ARTISTS.
はっ AH!
DON'T TELL ME YOU GUYS GOT SUCKERED...
HUH?! WHAT ARE YOU ON ABOUT?!

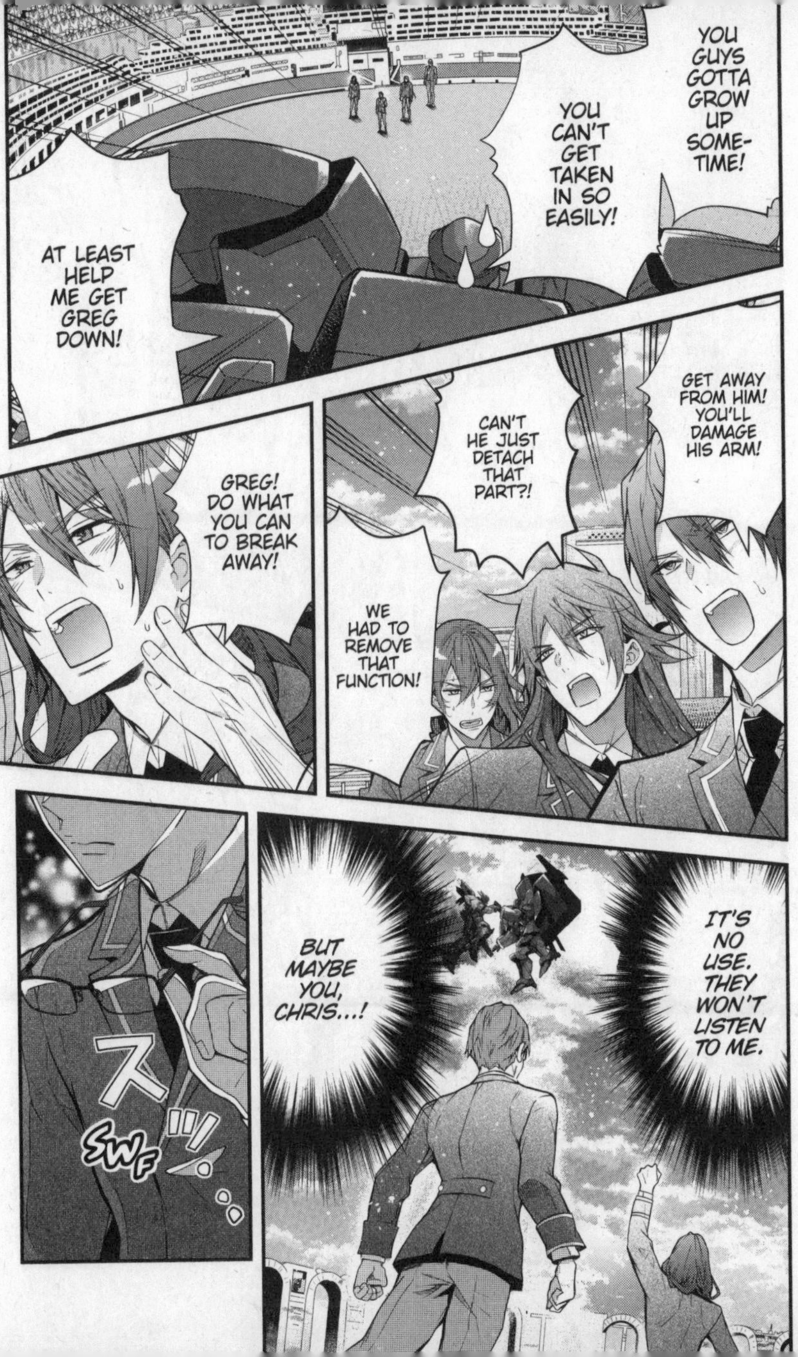
YOU GUYS GOTTA GROW UP SOME-TIME!
YOU CAN'T GET TAKEN IN SO EASILY!
AT LEAST HELP ME GET GREG DOWN!
GET AWAY FROM HIM! YOU'LL DAMAGE HIS ARM!
CAN'T HE JUST DETACH THAT PART?!
WE HAD TO REMOVE THAT FUNCTION!
GREG! DO WHAT YOU CAN TO BREAK AWAY!
IT'S NO USE. THEY WON'T LISTEN TO ME.
BUT MAYBE YOU, CHRIS...!
SWF

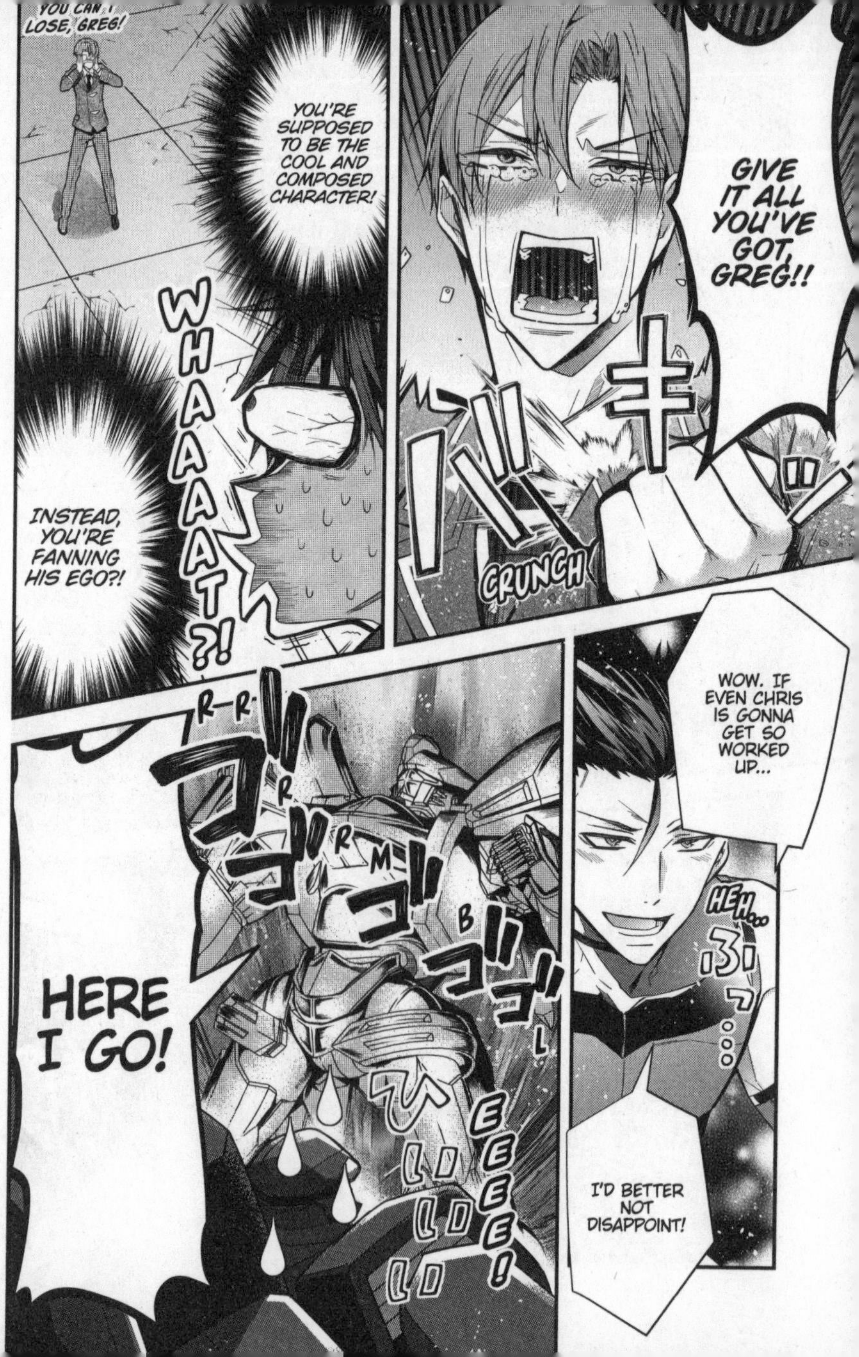
GIVE IT ALL YOU'VE GOT, GREG!!
CRUNCH
YOU CAN'T LOSE, GREG!
YOU'RE SUPPOSED TO BE THE COOL AND COMPOSED CHARACTER!
INSTEAD, YOU'RE FANNING HIS EGO?!
WHAAAAAT?!
WOW. IF EVEN CHRIS IS GONNA GET SO WORKED UP...
HEH...
I'D BETTER NOT DISAPPOINT!
R-R-R-R-M-B-L
HERE I GO!
EEEEE!

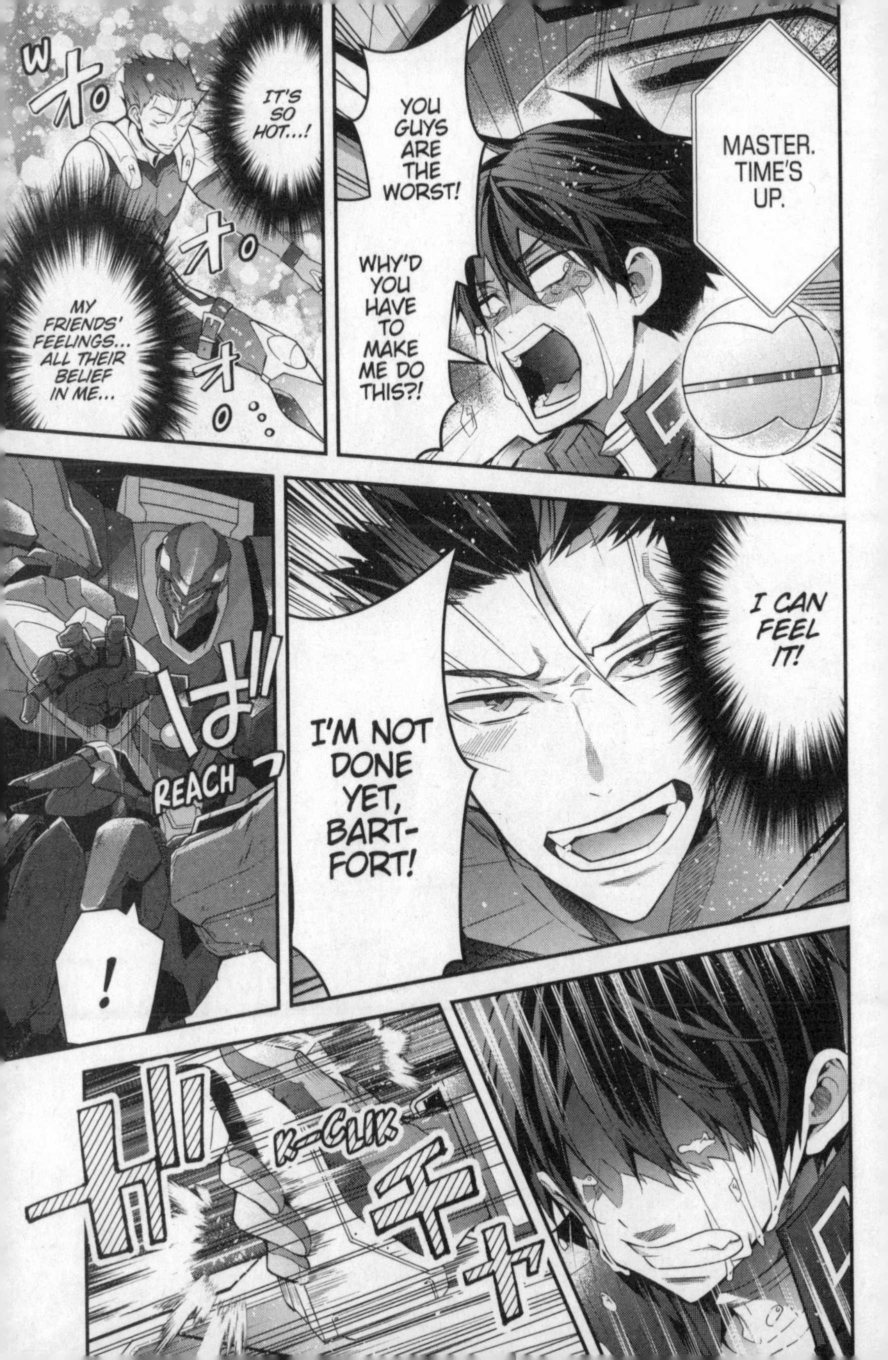
MASTER. TIME'S UP.
YOU GUYS ARE THE WORST!
WHY'D YOU HAVE TO MAKE ME DO THIS?!
W
IT'S SO HOT...!
MY FRIENDS' FEELINGS... ALL THEIR BELIEF IN ME...
I CAN FEEL IT!
I'M NOT DONE YET, BART-FORT!
REACH
!
K-CLIK

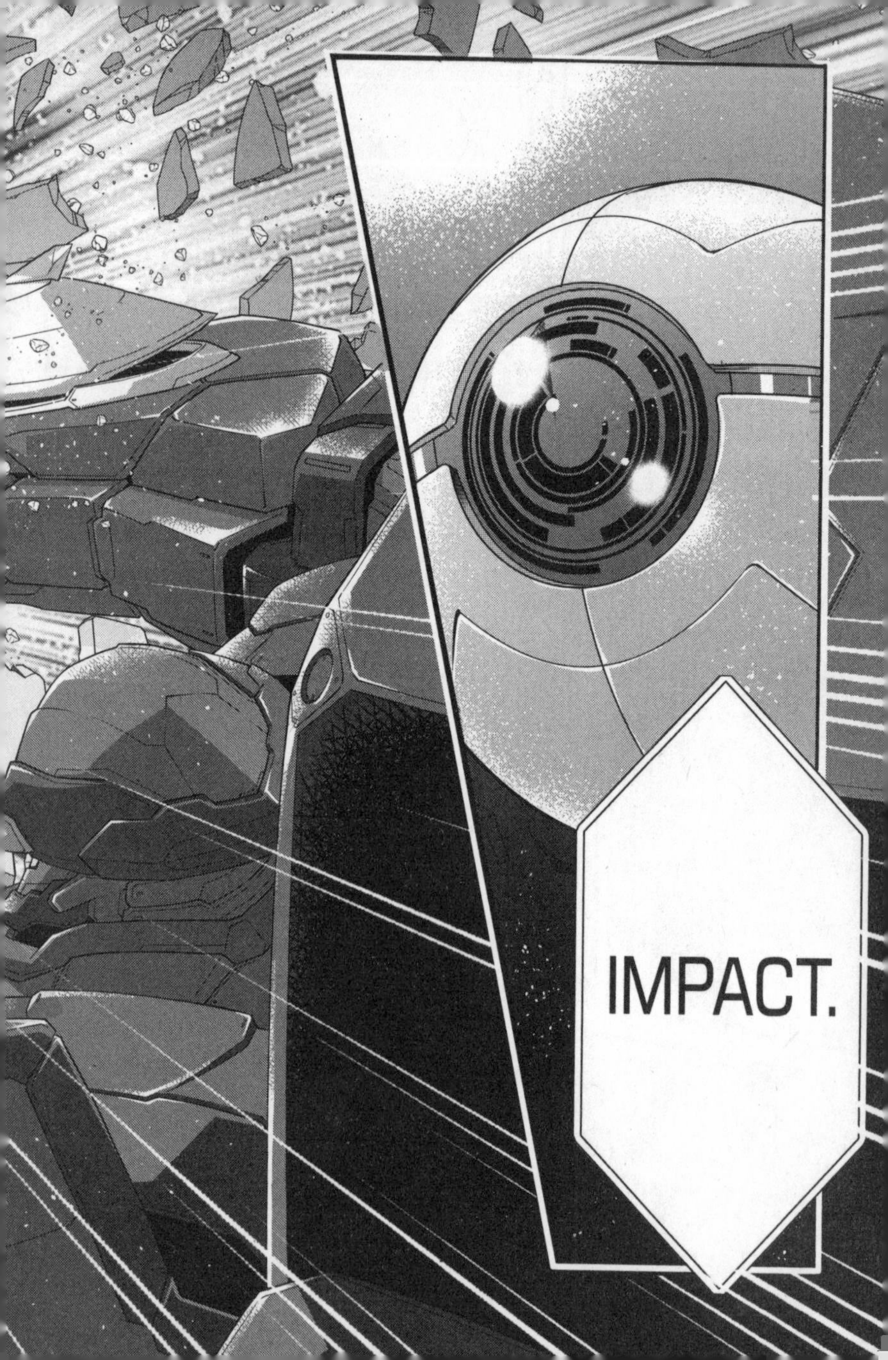
IMPACT.

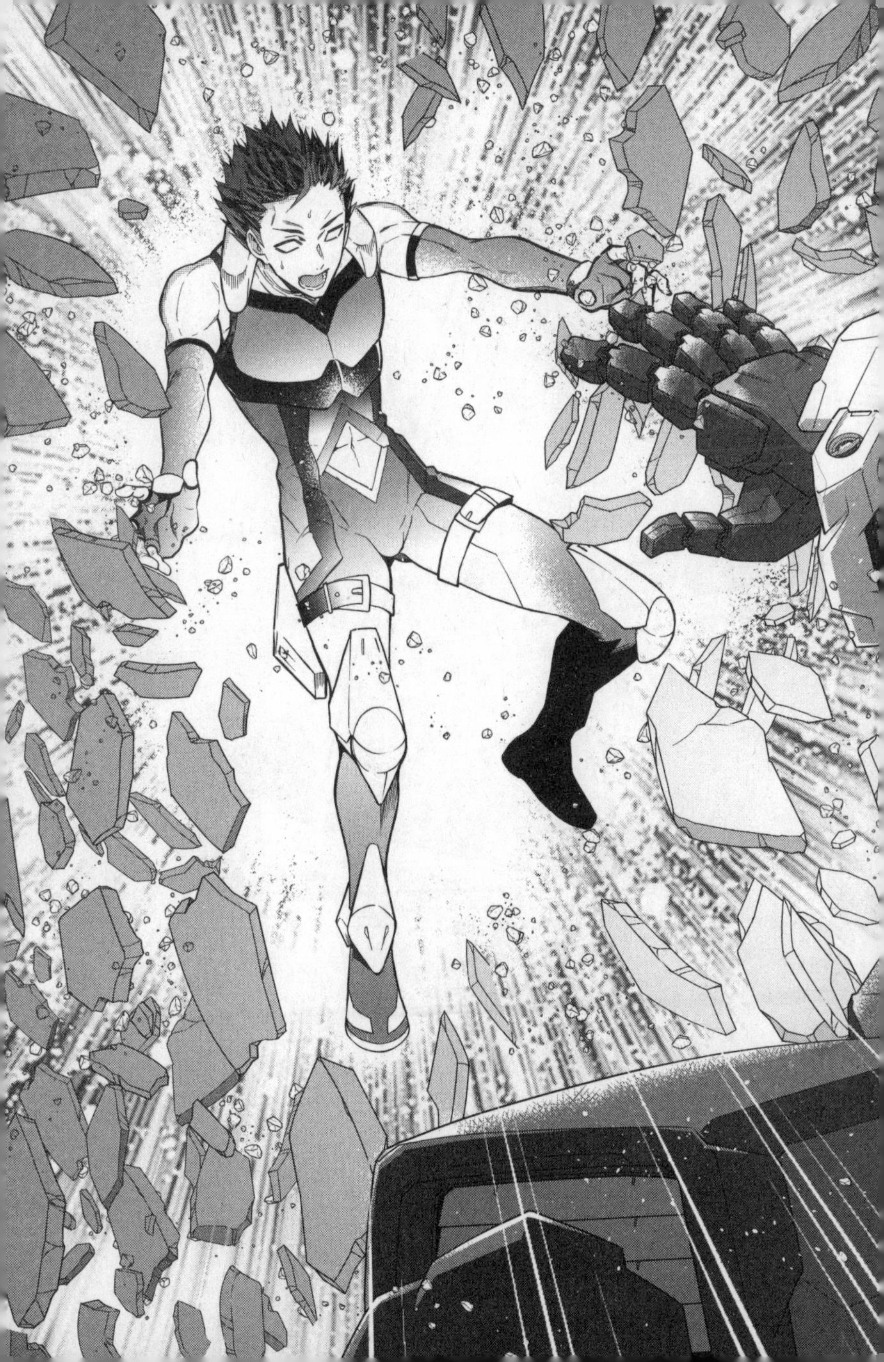

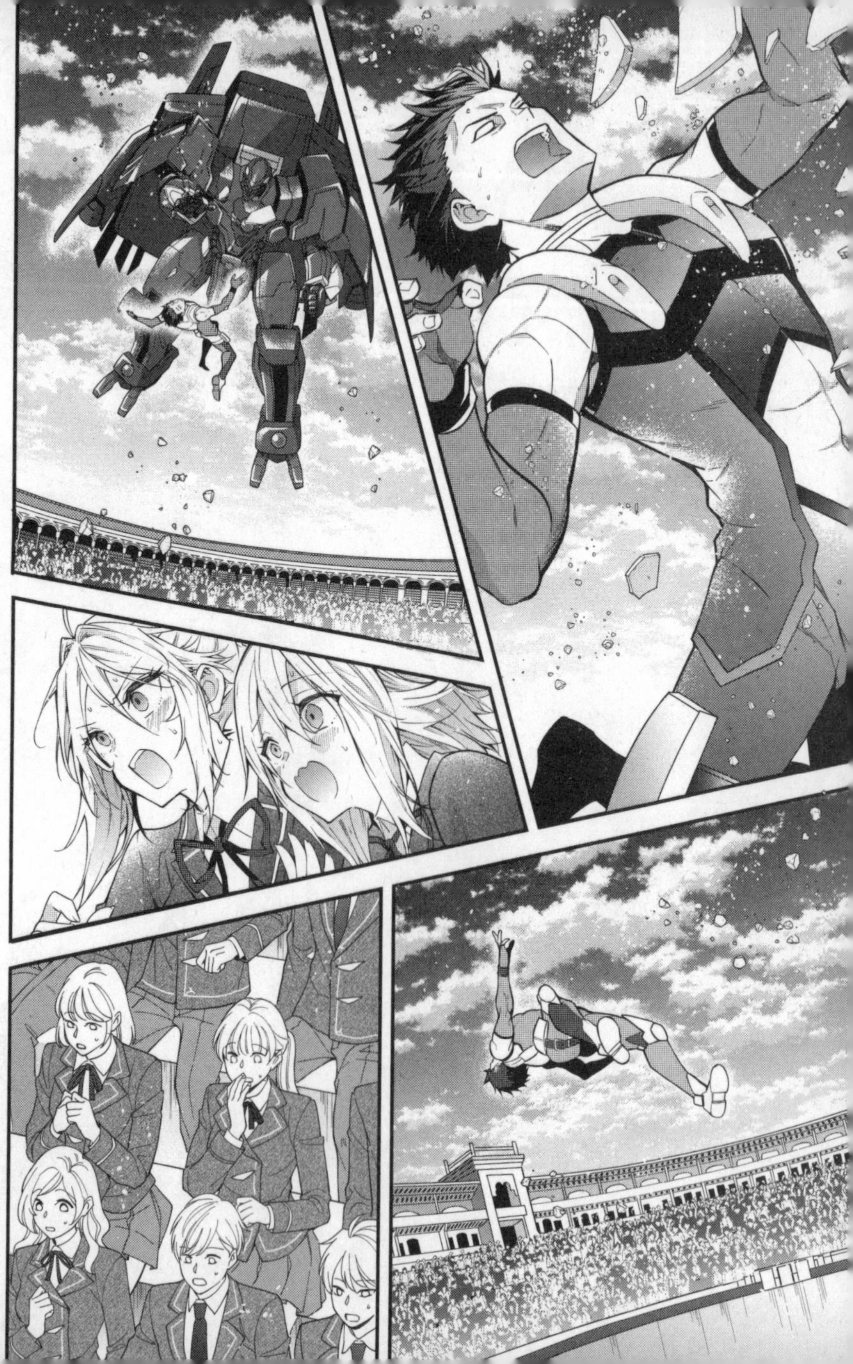

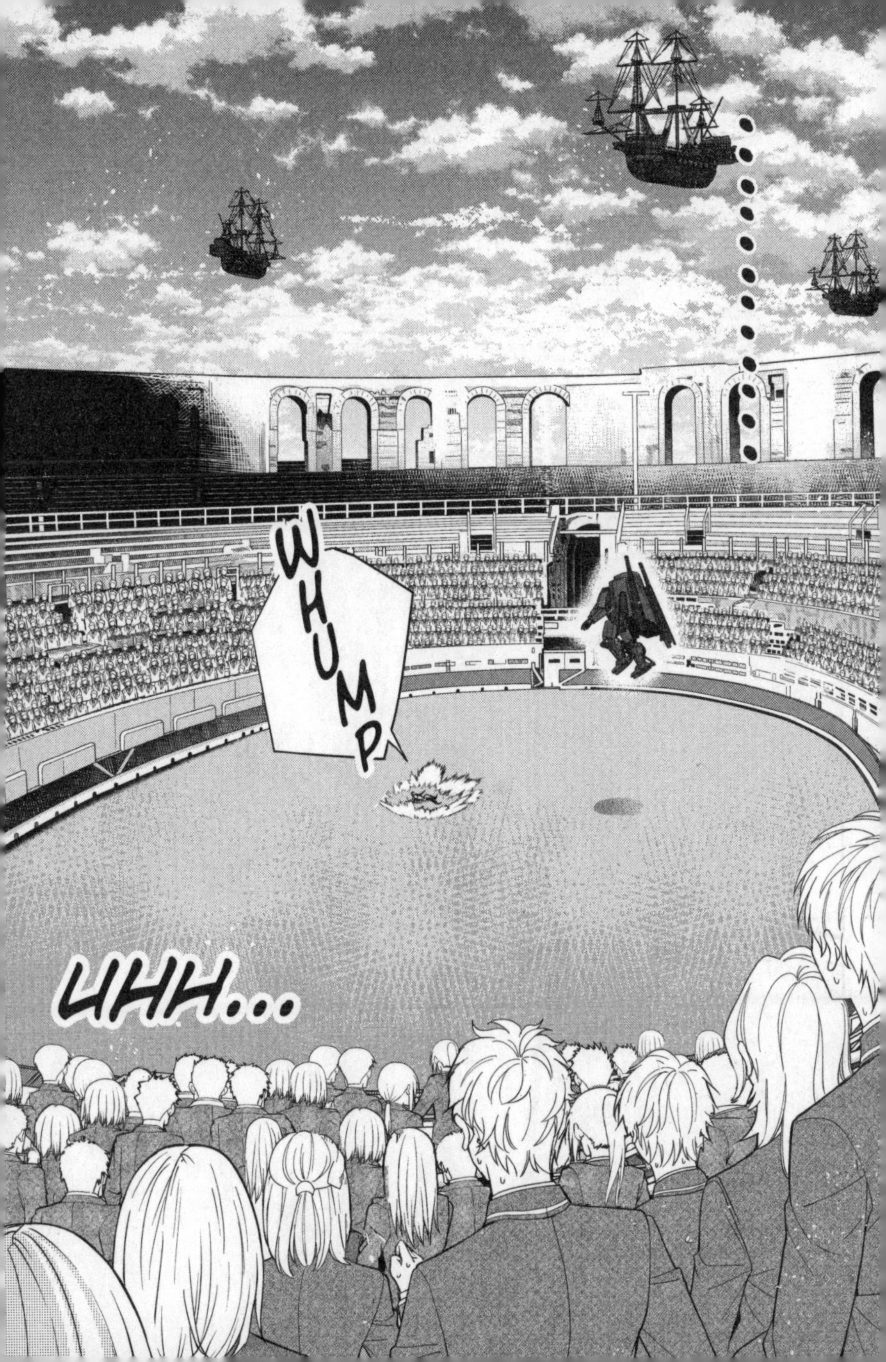

......
WHUMP
UHH...

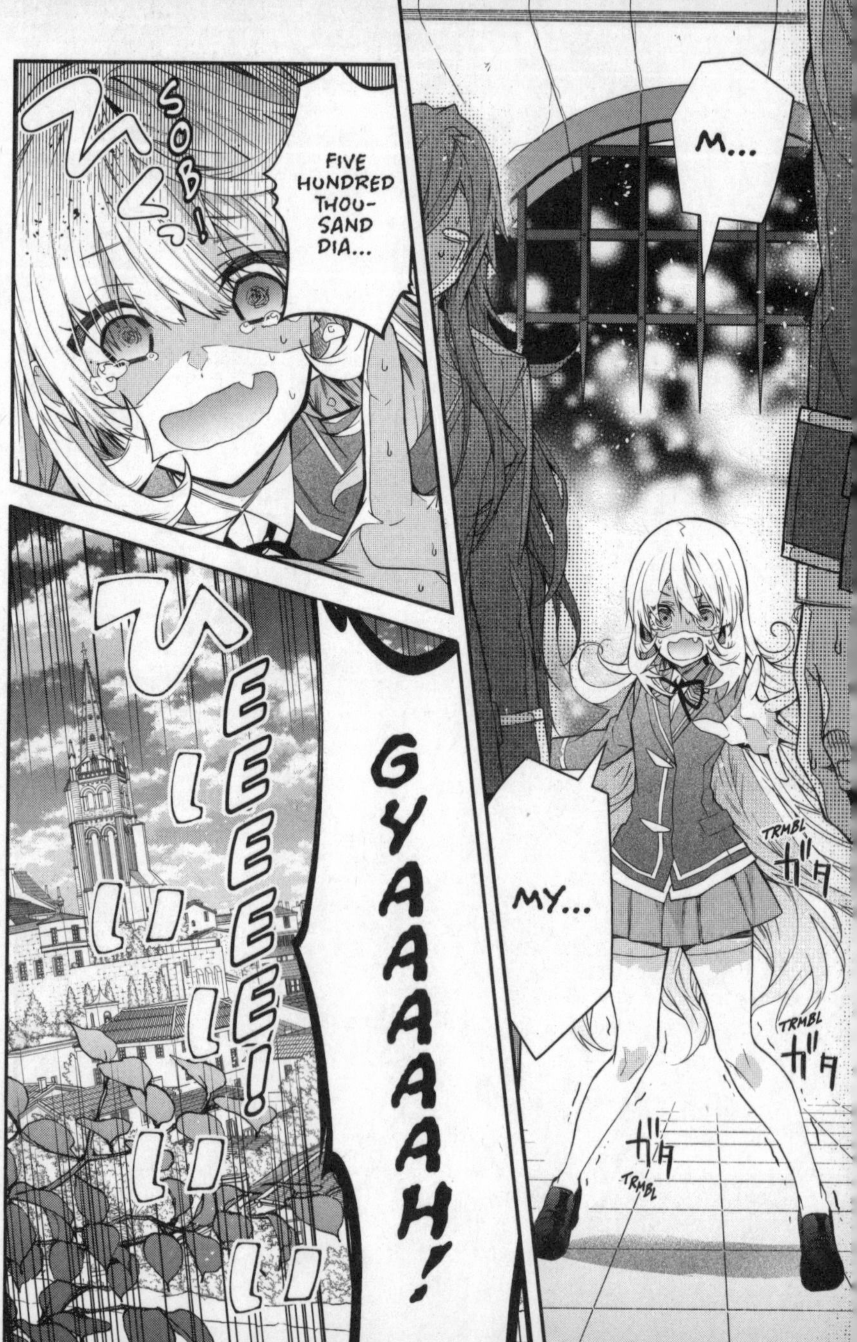

M...
TRMBL
MY...
TRMBL
TRMBL
FIVE HUNDRED THOU-SAND DIA...
SOB!
GYAAAAAH!
EEEEEE!

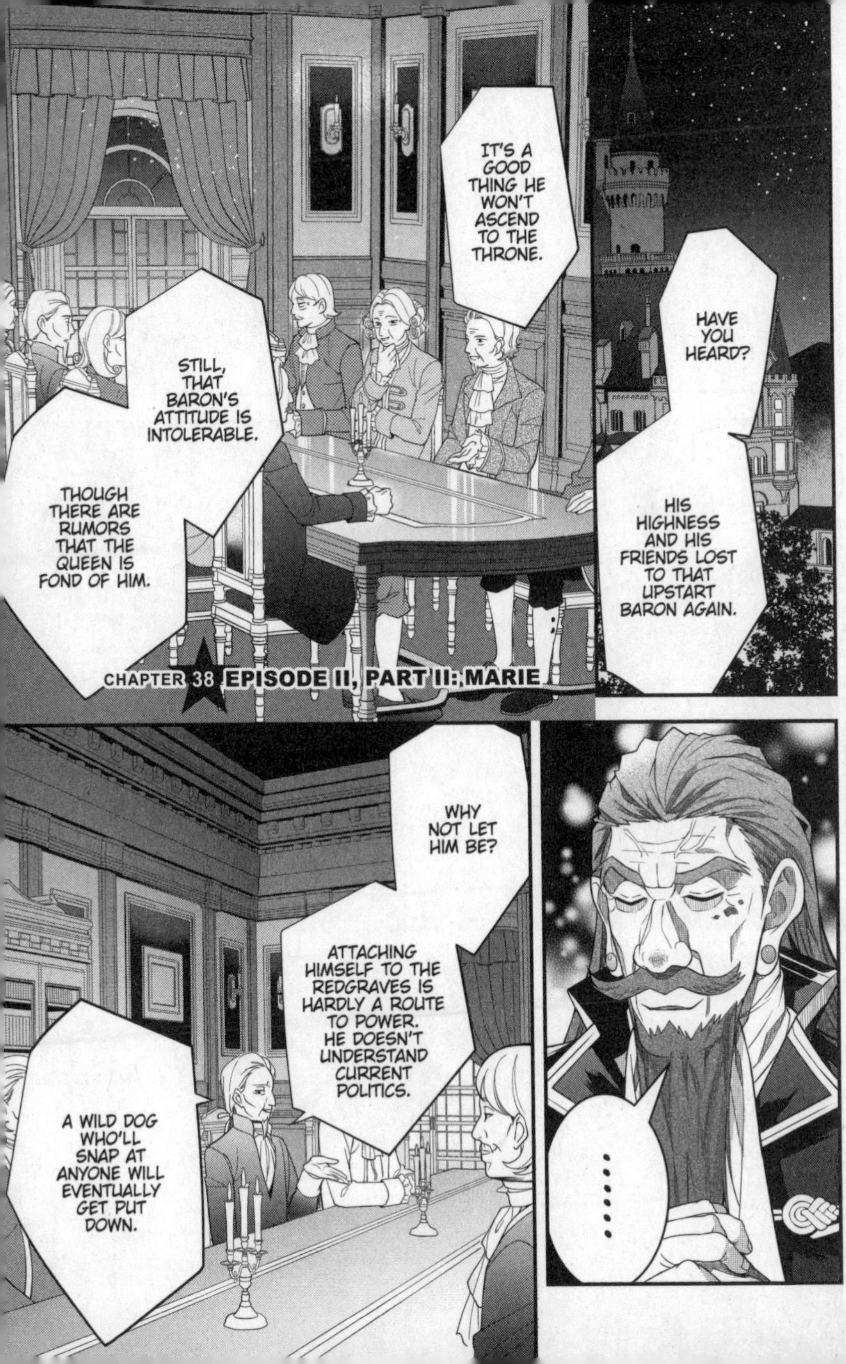
HAVE YOU HEARD?
HIS HIGHNESS AND HIS FRIENDS LOST TO THAT UPSTART BARON AGAIN.
IT'S A GOOD THING HE WON'T ASCEND TO THE THRONE.
STILL, THAT BARON'S ATTITUDE IS INTOLERABLE.
THOUGH THERE ARE RUMORS THAT THE QUEEN IS FOND OF HIM.
CHAPTER 38 EPISODE II, PART II: MARIE
......
WHY NOT LET HIM BE?
ATTACHING HIMSELF TO THE REDGRAVES IS HARDLY A ROUTE TO POWER. HE DOESN'T UNDERSTAND CURRENT POLITICS.
A WILD DOG WHO'LL SNAP AT ANYONE WILL EVENTUALLY GET PUT DOWN.

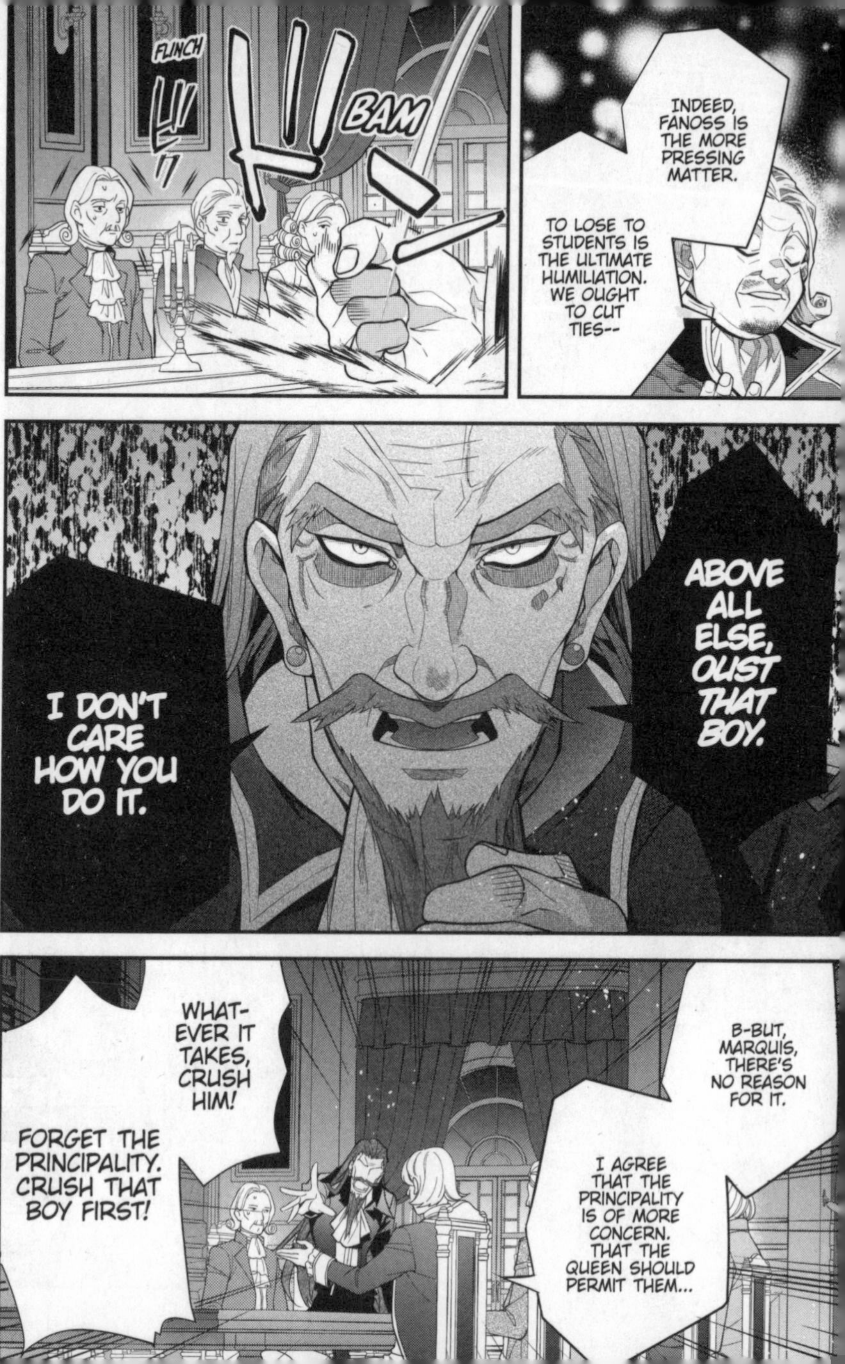
INDEED, FANOSS IS THE MORE PRESSING MATTER.
TO LOSE TO STUDENTS IS THE ULTIMATE HUMILIATION. WE OUGHT TO CUT TIES--
FLINCH
BAM
ABOVE ALL ELSE, OUST THAT BOY.
I DON'T CARE HOW YOU DO IT.
B-BUT, MARQUIS, THERE'S NO REASON FOR IT.
I AGREE THAT THE PRINCIPALITY IS OF MORE CONCERN. THAT THE QUEEN SHOULD PERMIT THEM...
WHAT-EVER IT TAKES, CRUSH HIM!
FORGET THE PRINCIPALITY. CRUSH THAT BOY FIRST!

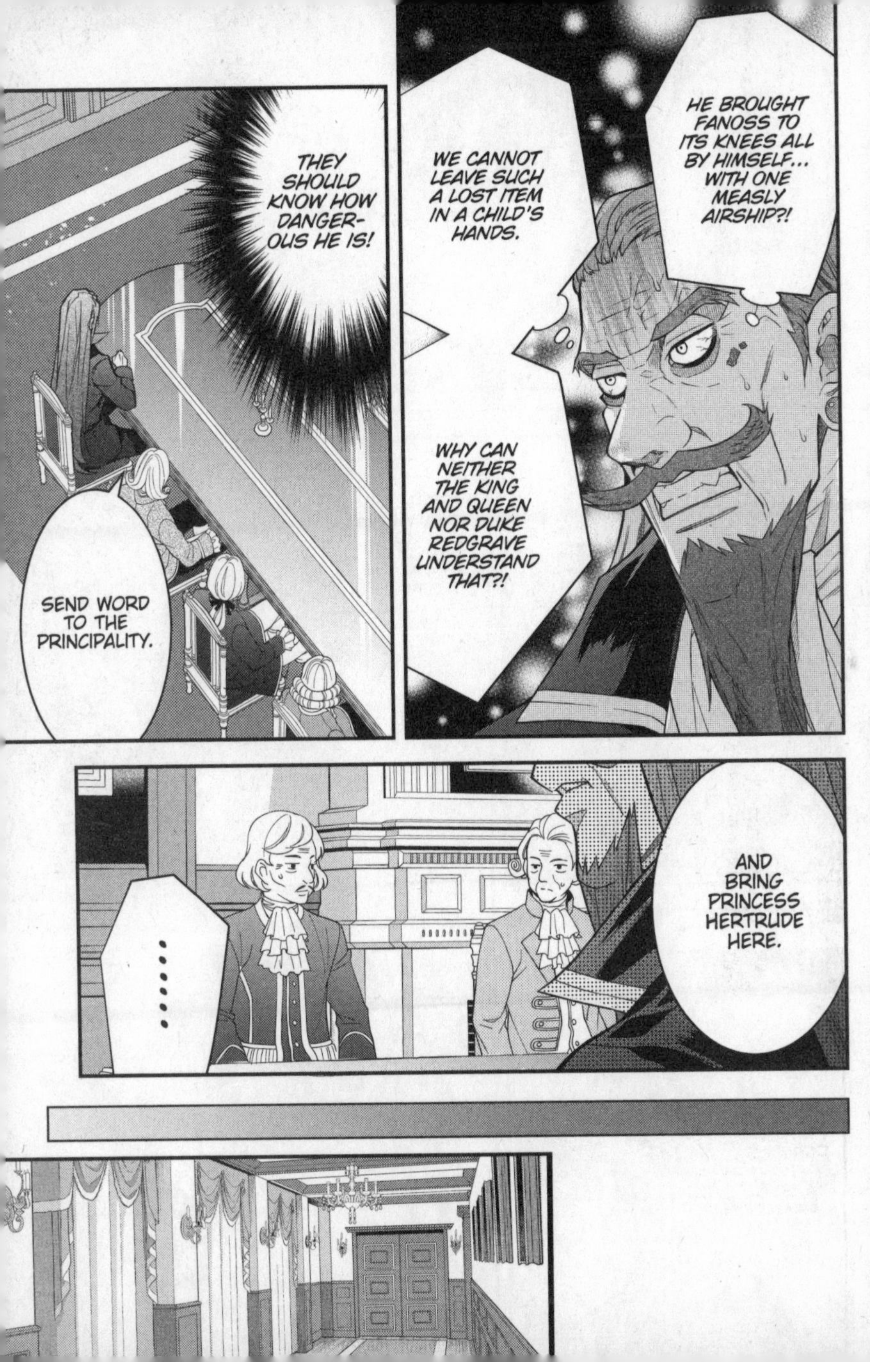
HE BROUGHT FANOSS TO ITS KNEES ALL BY HIMSELF... WITH ONE MEASLY AIRSHIP?!
WE CANNOT LEAVE SUCH A LOST ITEM IN A CHILD'S HANDS.
WHY CAN NEITHER THE KING AND QUEEN NOR DUKE REDGRAVE UNDERSTAND THAT?!
THEY SHOULD KNOW HOW DANGER-OUS HE IS!
SEND WORD TO THE PRINCIPALITY.
AND BRING PRINCESS HERTRUDE HERE.
......

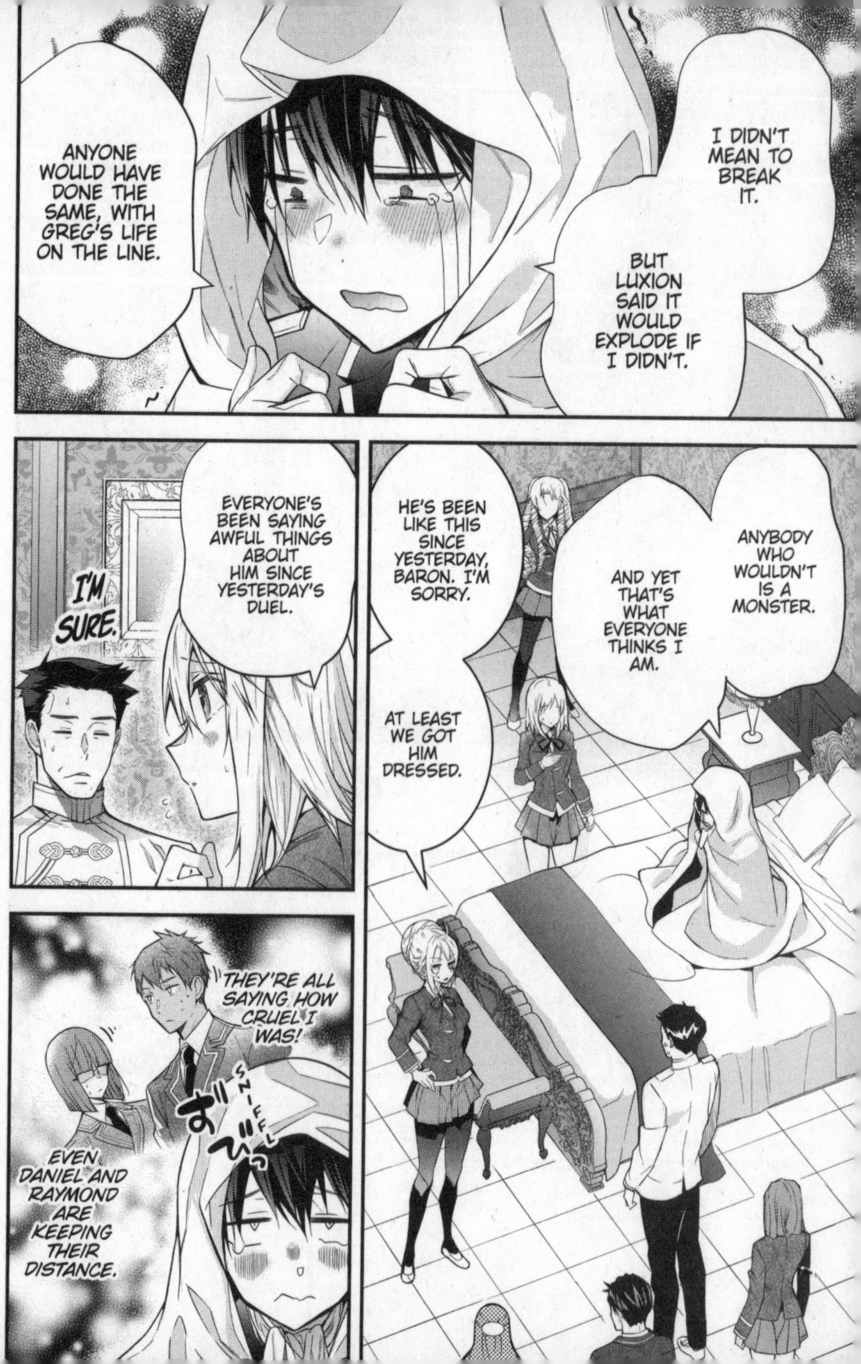
I DIDN'T MEAN TO BREAK IT.
BUT LUXION SAID IT WOULD EXPLODE IF I DIDN'T.
ANYONE WOULD HAVE DONE THE SAME, WITH GREG'S LIFE ON THE LINE.
ANYBODY WHO WOULDN'T IS A MONSTER.
AND YET THAT'S WHAT EVERYONE THINKS I AM.
HE'S BEEN LIKE THIS SINCE YESTERDAY, BARON. I'M SORRY.
AT LEAST WE GOT HIM DRESSED.
EVERYONE'S BEEN SAYING AWFUL THINGS ABOUT HIM SINCE YESTERDAY'S DUEL.
I'M SURE.
THEY'RE ALL SAYING HOW CRUEL I WAS!
SNIFFL
すびっ
EVEN DANIEL AND RAYMOND ARE KEEPING THEIR DISTANCE.

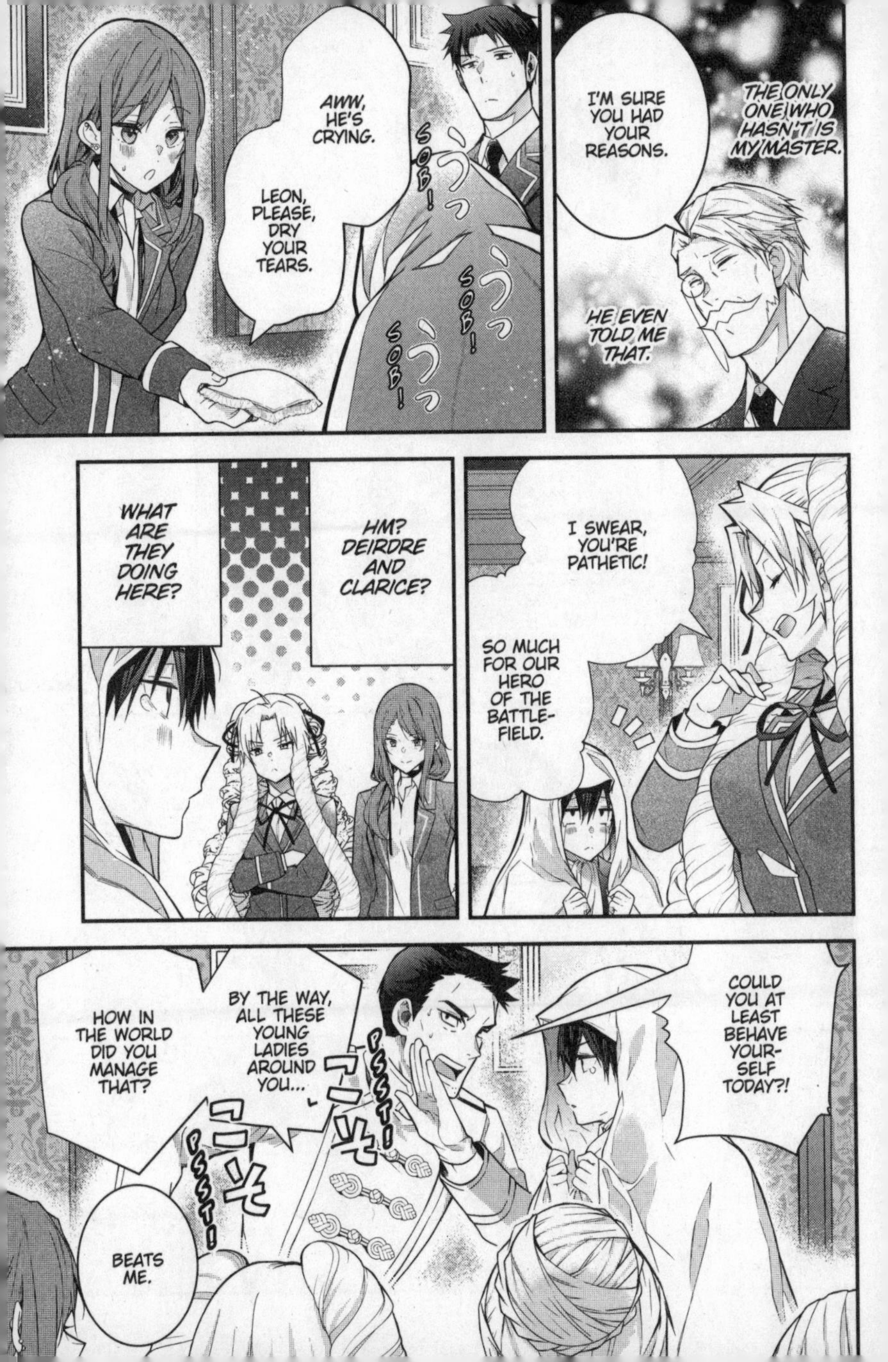
THE ONLY ONE WHO HASN'T IS MY MASTER.
I'M SURE YOU HAD YOUR REASONS.
HE EVEN TOLD ME THAT.
AWW, HE'S CRYING.
SOB!
SOB!
SOB!
LEON, PLEASE, DRY YOUR TEARS.
I SWEAR, YOU'RE PATHETIC!
SO MUCH FOR OUR HERO OF THE BATTLE-FIELD.
HM? DEIRDRE AND CLARICE?
WHAT ARE THEY DOING HERE?
COULD YOU AT LEAST BEHAVE YOUR-SELF TODAY?!
BY THE WAY, ALL THESE YOUNG LADIES AROUND YOU...
PSST!
HOW IN THE WORLD DID YOU MANAGE THAT?
PSST!
BEATS ME.

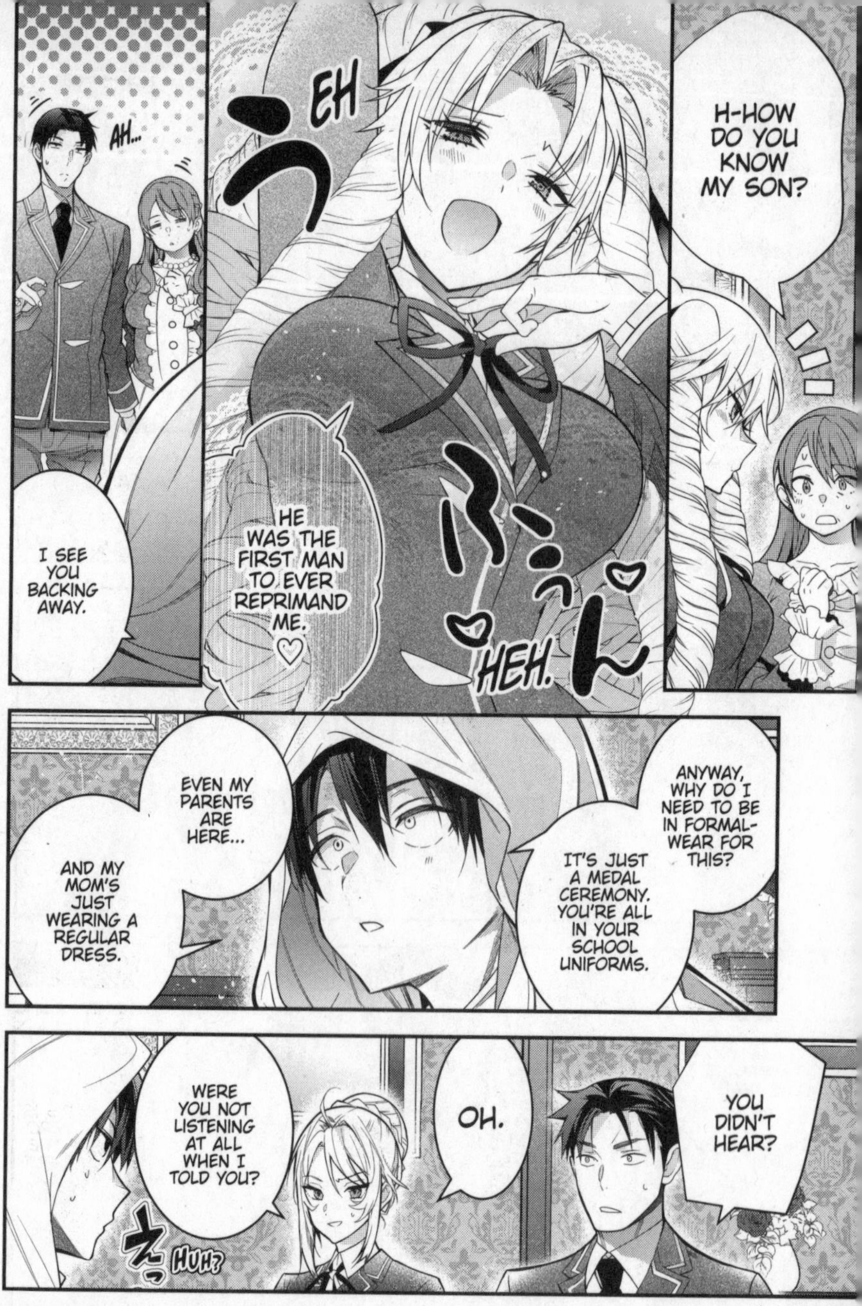
H-HOW DO YOU KNOW MY SON?
EH
HE WAS THE FIRST MAN TO EVER REPRIMAND ME. ♡
HEH.
AH...
I SEE YOU BACKING AWAY.
ANYWAY, WHY DO I NEED TO BE IN FORMAL-WEAR FOR THIS?
IT'S JUST A MEDAL CEREMONY. YOU'RE ALL IN YOUR SCHOOL UNIFORMS.
EVEN MY PARENTS ARE HERE...
AND MY MOM'S JUST WEARING A REGULAR DRESS.
YOU DIDN'T HEAR?
OH.
WERE YOU NOT LISTENING AT ALL WHEN I TOLD YOU?
HUH?

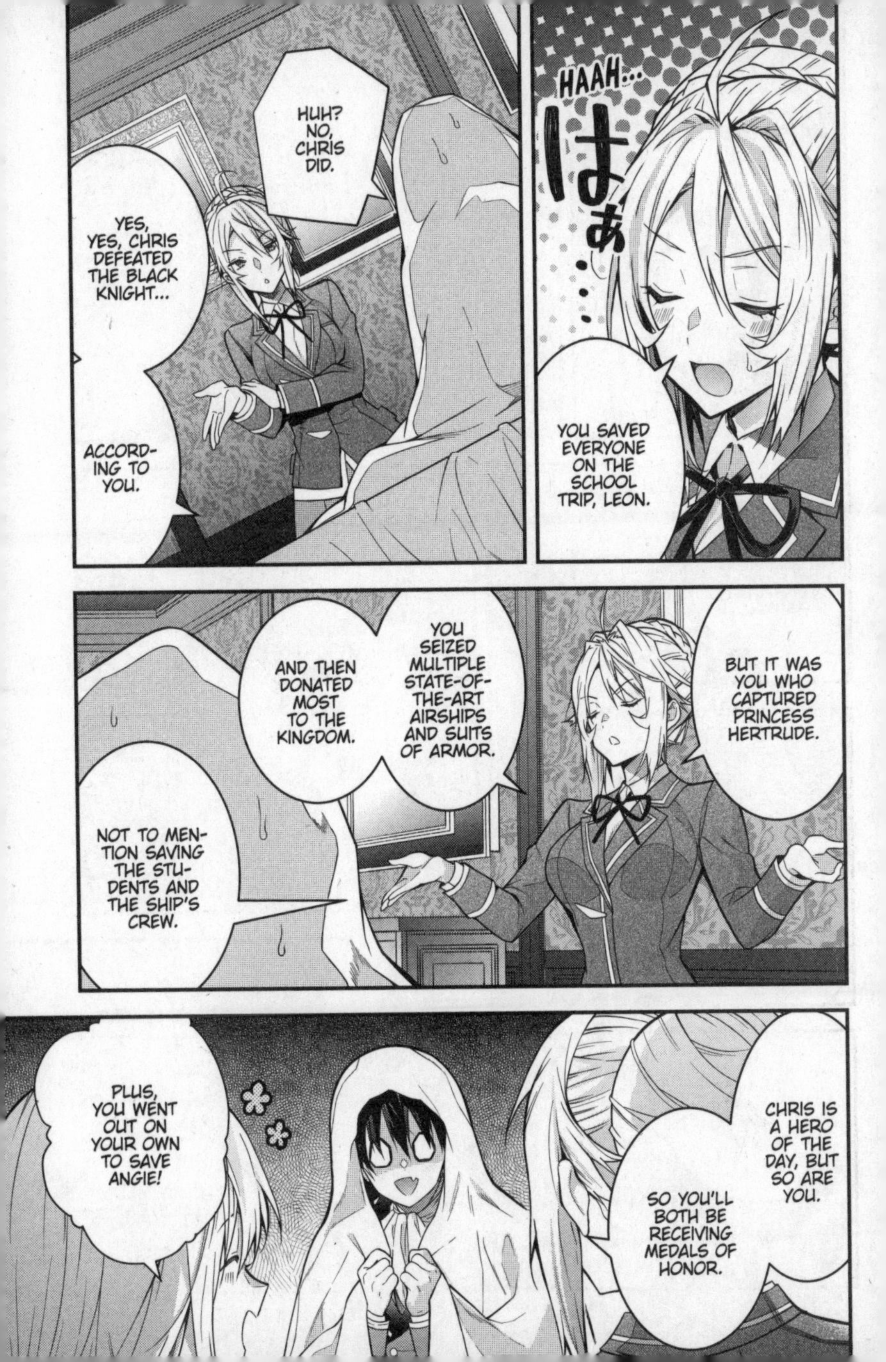
HAAH...
はぁ...
YOU SAVED EVERYONE ON THE SCHOOL TRIP, LEON.
HUH? NO, CHRIS DID.
YES, YES, CHRIS DEFEATED THE BLACK KNIGHT...
ACCORDING TO YOU.
BUT IT WAS YOU WHO CAPTURED PRINCESS HERTRUDE.
YOU SEIZED MULTIPLE STATE-OF-THE-ART AIRSHIPS AND SUITS OF ARMOR.
AND THEN DONATED MOST TO THE KINGDOM.
NOT TO MENTION SAVING THE STUDENTS AND THE SHIP'S CREW.
CHRIS IS A HERO OF THE DAY, BUT SO ARE YOU.
SO YOU'LL BOTH BE RECEIVING MEDALS OF HONOR.
PLUS, YOU WENT OUT ON YOUR OWN TO SAVE ANGIE!

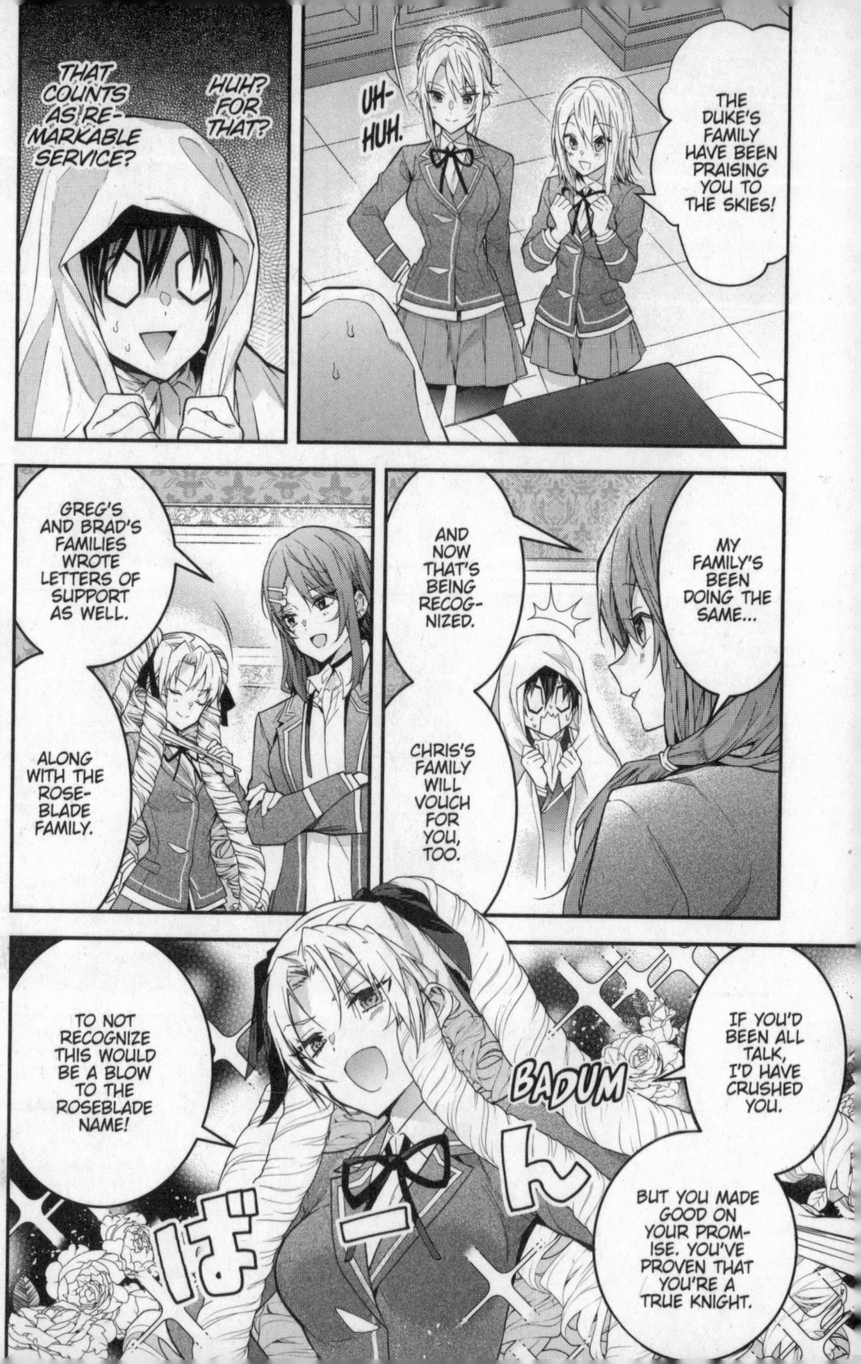
THE DUKE'S FAMILY HAVE BEEN PRAISING YOU TO THE SKIES!
UH-HUH.
HUH? FOR THAT?
THAT COUNTS AS REMARKABLE SERVICE?
MY FAMILY'S BEEN DOING THE SAME...
AND NOW THAT'S BEING RECOGNIZED.
CHRIS'S FAMILY WILL VOUCH FOR YOU, TOO.
GREG'S AND BRAD'S FAMILIES WROTE LETTERS OF SUPPORT AS WELL.
ALONG WITH THE ROSEBLADE FAMILY.
IF YOU'D BEEN ALL TALK, I'D HAVE CRUSHED YOU.
BADUM
ばーん
BUT YOU MADE GOOD ON YOUR PROMISE. YOU'VE PROVEN THAT YOU'RE A TRUE KNIGHT.
TO NOT RECOGNIZE THIS WOULD BE A BLOW TO THE ROSEBLADE NAME!

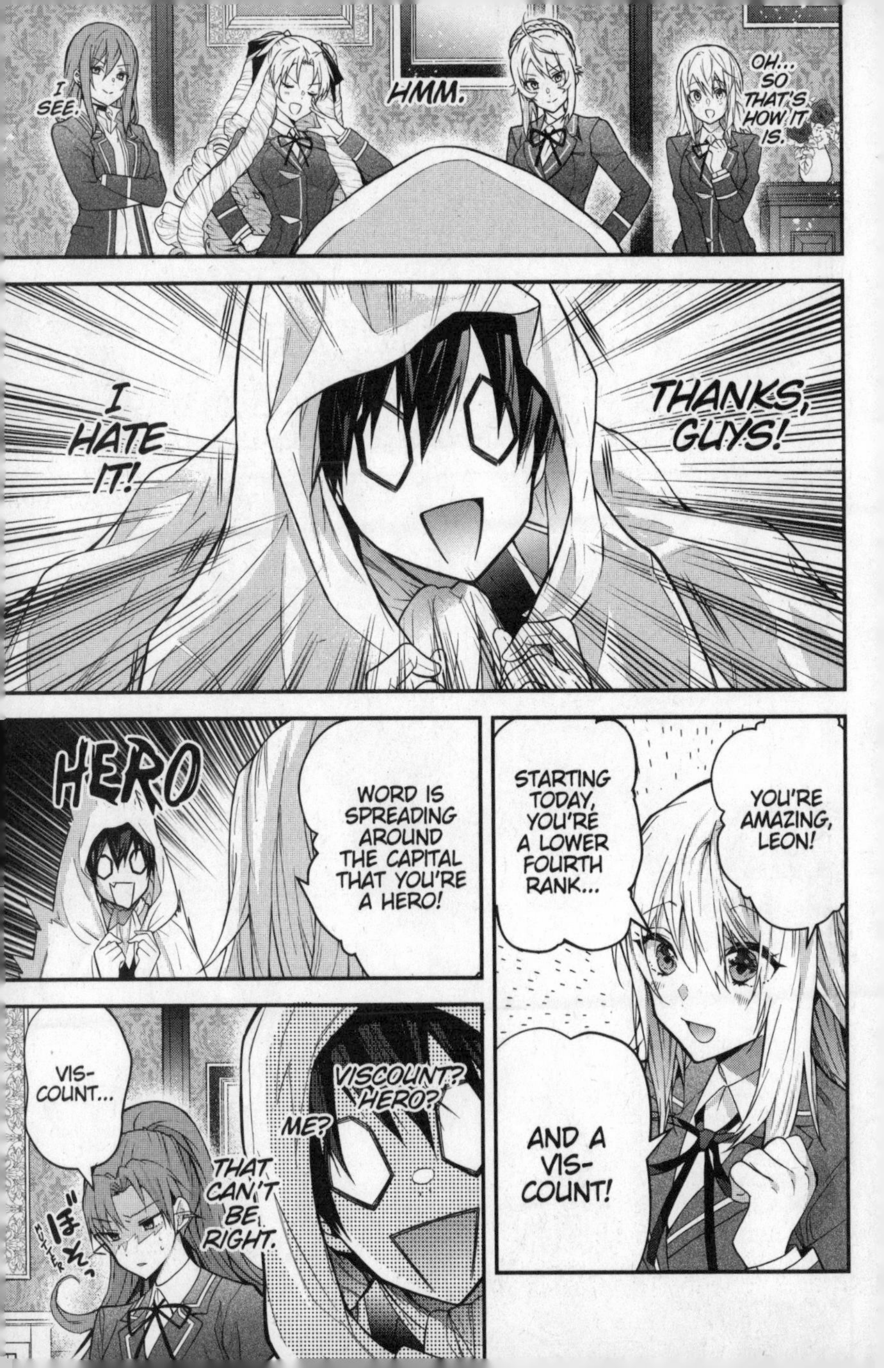
OH... SO THAT'S HOW IT IS.
HMM.
I SEE.
THANKS, GUYS!
I HATE IT!
YOU'RE AMAZING, LEON!
STARTING TODAY, YOU'RE A LOWER FOURTH RANK...
AND A VIS-COUNT!
WORD IS SPREADING AROUND THE CAPITAL THAT YOU'RE A HERO!
HERO
VISCOUNT? HERO?
ME?
THAT CAN'T BE RIGHT.
VIS-COUNT...
MUTTER

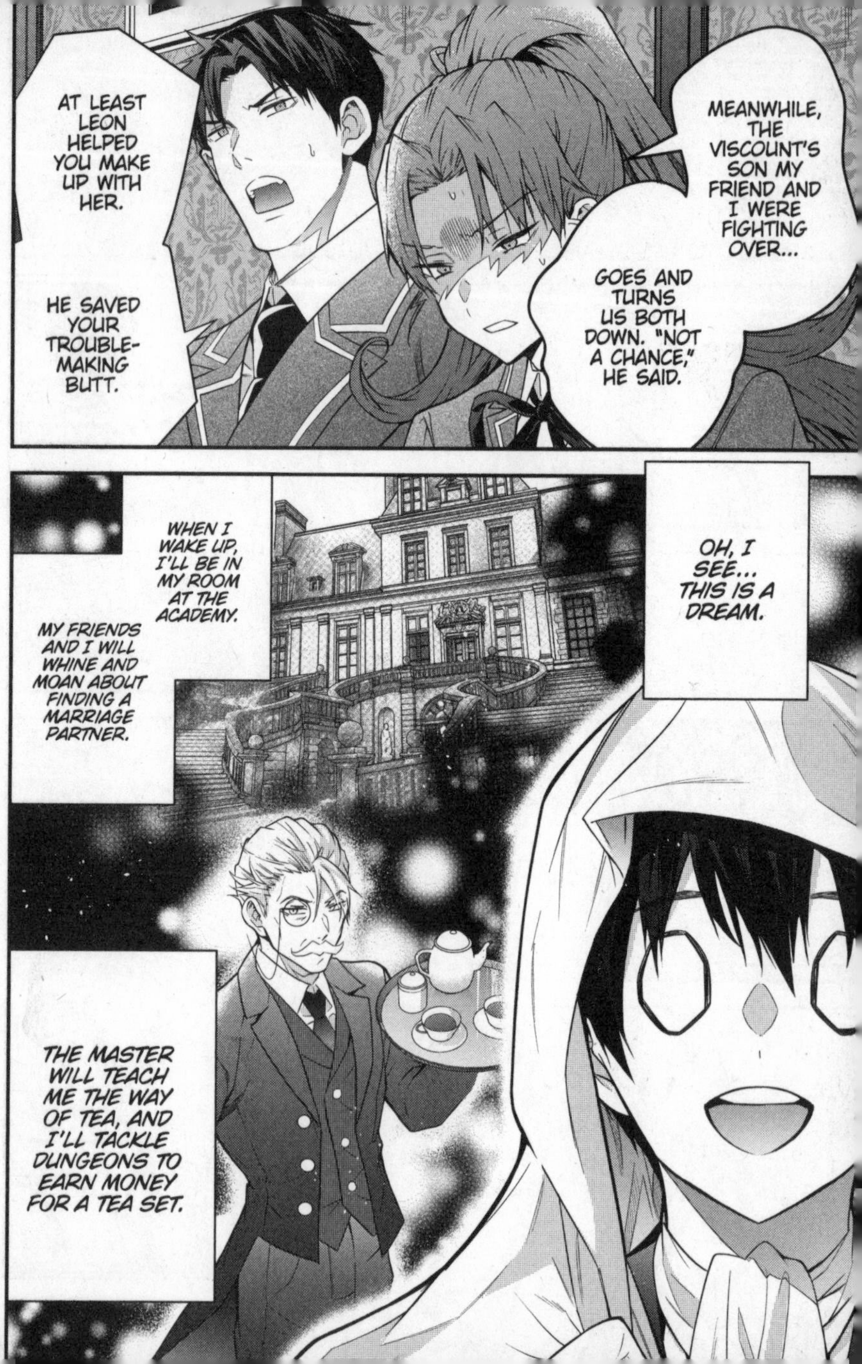
MEANWHILE, THE VISCOUNT'S SON MY FRIEND AND I WERE FIGHTING OVER...
GOES AND TURNS US BOTH DOWN. "NOT A CHANCE," HE SAID.
AT LEAST LEON HELPED YOU MAKE UP WITH HER.
HE SAVED YOUR TROUBLE-MAKING BUTT.
OH, I SEE... THIS IS A DREAM.
WHEN I WAKE UP, I'LL BE IN MY ROOM AT THE ACADEMY.
MY FRIENDS AND I WILL WHINE AND MOAN ABOUT FINDING A MARRIAGE PARTNER.
THE MASTER WILL TEACH ME THE WAY OF TEA, AND I'LL TACKLE DUNGEONS TO EARN MONEY FOR A TEA SET.

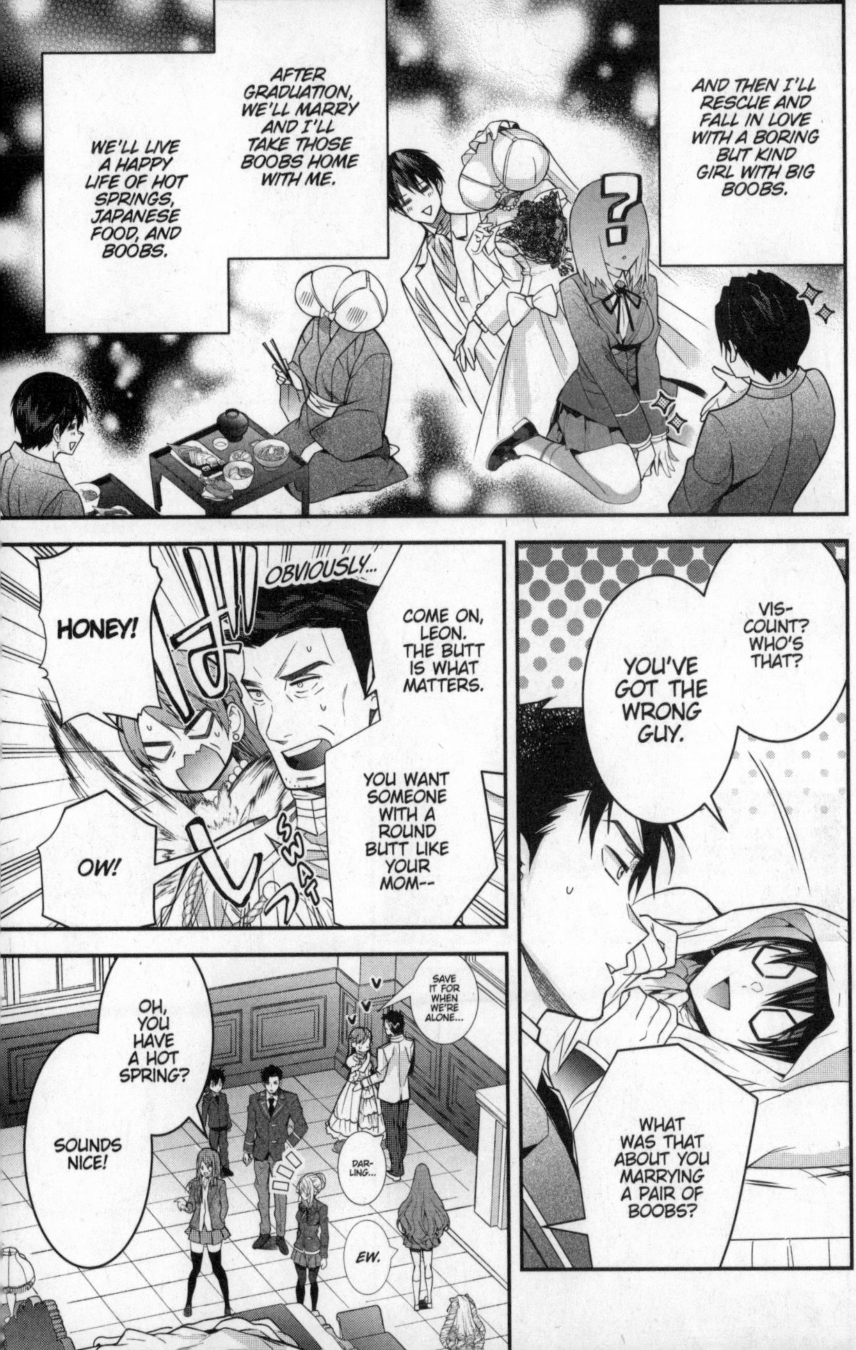
AND THEN I'LL RESCUE AND FALL IN LOVE WITH A BORING BUT KIND GIRL WITH BIG BOOBS.
AFTER GRADUATION, WE'LL MARRY AND I'LL TAKE THOSE BOOBS HOME WITH ME.
WE'LL LIVE A HAPPY LIFE OF HOT SPRINGS, JAPANESE FOOD, AND BOOBS.
VIS-COUNT? WHO'S THAT?
YOU'VE GOT THE WRONG GUY.
WHAT WAS THAT ABOUT YOU MARRYING A PAIR OF BOOBS?
OBVIOUSLY...
COME ON, LEON. THE BUTT IS WHAT MATTERS.
HONEY!
YOU WANT SOMEONE WITH A ROUND BUTT LIKE YOUR MOM--
SWAT
OW!
SAVE IT FOR WHEN WE'RE ALONE...
OH, YOU HAVE A HOT SPRING?
DAR-LING...
SOUNDS NICE!
EW.

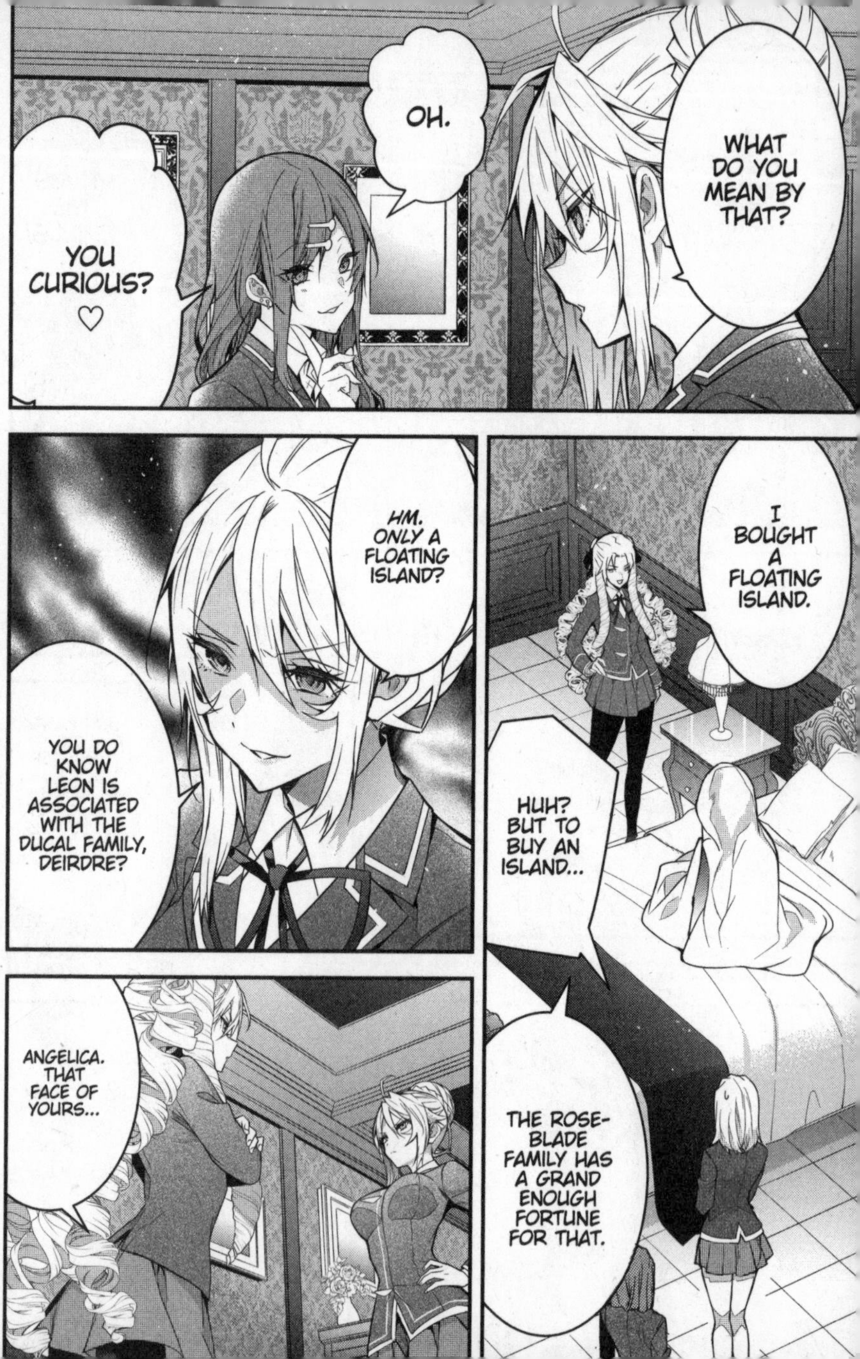

WHAT DO YOU MEAN BY THAT?
OH.
YOU CURIOUS? ♡
I BOUGHT A FLOATING ISLAND.
HUH? BUT TO BUY AN ISLAND...
THE ROSE-BLADE FAMILY HAS A GRAND ENOUGH FORTUNE FOR THAT.
HM. ONLY A FLOATING ISLAND?
YOU DO KNOW LEON IS ASSOCIATED WITH THE DUCAL FAMILY, DEIRDRE?
ANGELICA. THAT FACE OF YOURS...

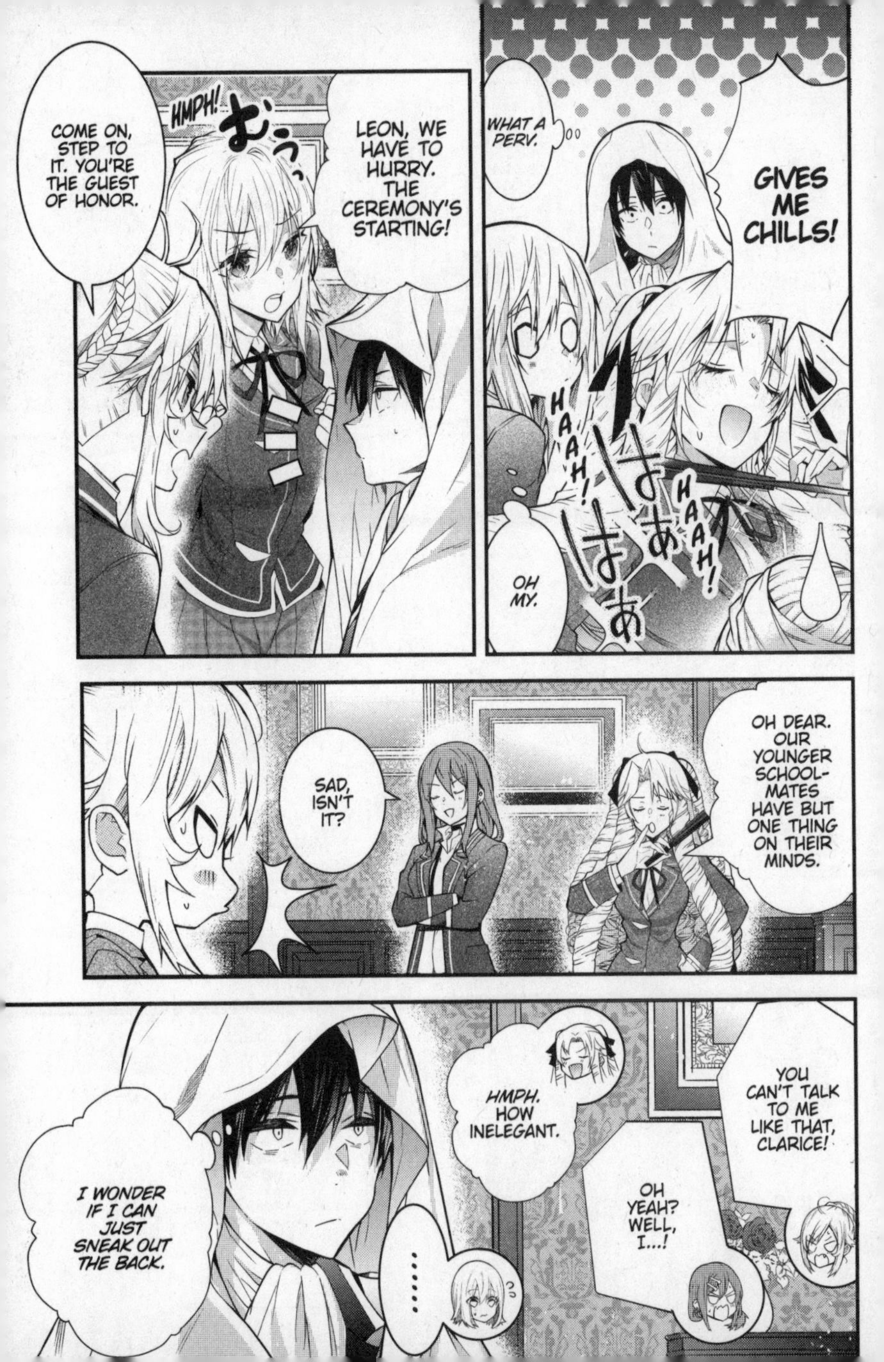
GIVES ME CHILLS!
WHAT A PERV.
HAAH! HAAH!
はあはあ
HAAH! HAAH!
OH MY.
LEON, WE HAVE TO HURRY. THE CEREMONY'S STARTING!
HMPH!
むっ
COME ON, STEP TO IT. YOU'RE THE GUEST OF HONOR.
OH DEAR. OUR YOUNGER SCHOOL-MATES HAVE BUT ONE THING ON THEIR MINDS.
SAD, ISN'T IT?
YOU CAN'T TALK TO ME LIKE THAT, CLARICE!
HMPH. HOW INELEGANT.
OH YEAH? WELL, I...!
......
I WONDER IF I CAN JUST SNEAK OUT THE BACK.

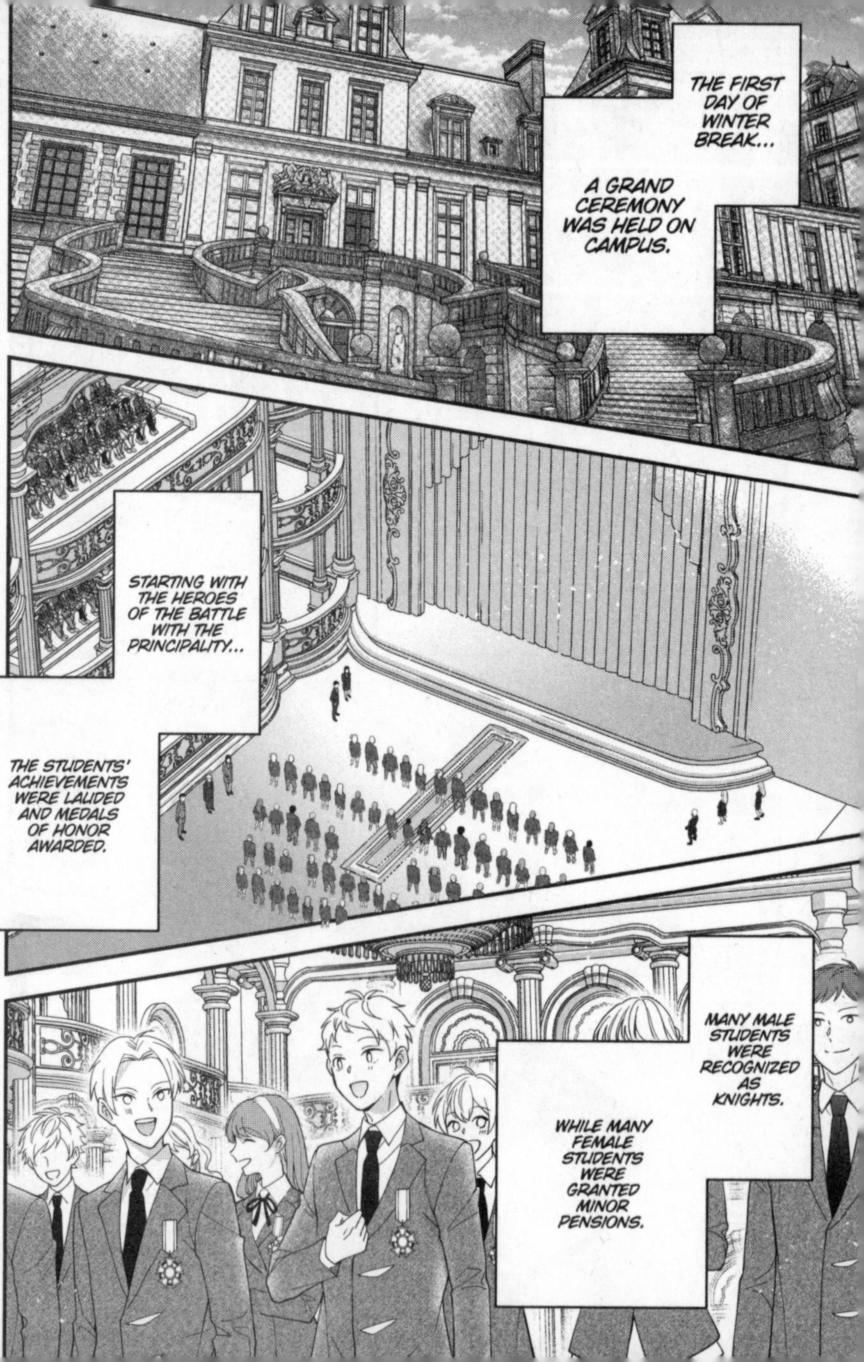
THE FIRST DAY OF WINTER BREAK...
A GRAND CEREMONY WAS HELD ON CAMPUS.
STARTING WITH THE HEROES OF THE BATTLE WITH THE PRINCIPALITY...
THE STUDENTS' ACHIEVEMENTS WERE LAUDED AND MEDALS OF HONOR AWARDED.
MANY MALE STUDENTS WERE RECOGNIZED AS KNIGHTS.
WHILE MANY FEMALE STUDENTS WERE GRANTED MINOR PENSIONS.

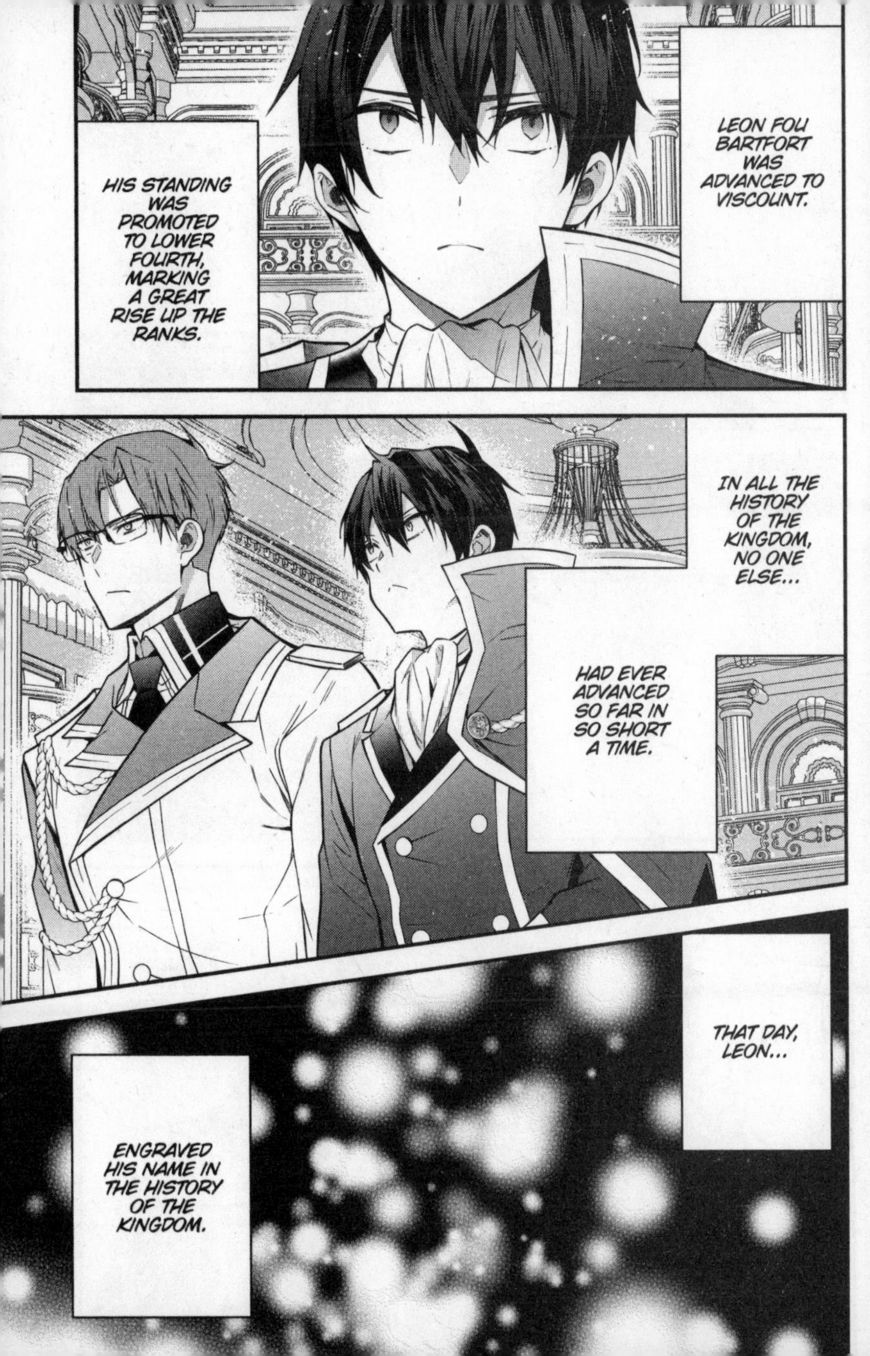
LEON FOU BARTFORT WAS ADVANCED TO VISCOUNT.
HIS STANDING WAS PROMOTED TO LOWER FOURTH, MARKING A GREAT RISE UP THE RANKS.
IN ALL THE HISTORY OF THE KINGDOM, NO ONE ELSE...
HAD EVER ADVANCED SO FAR IN SO SHORT A TIME.
THAT DAY, LEON...
ENGRAVED HIS NAME IN THE HISTORY OF THE KINGDOM.

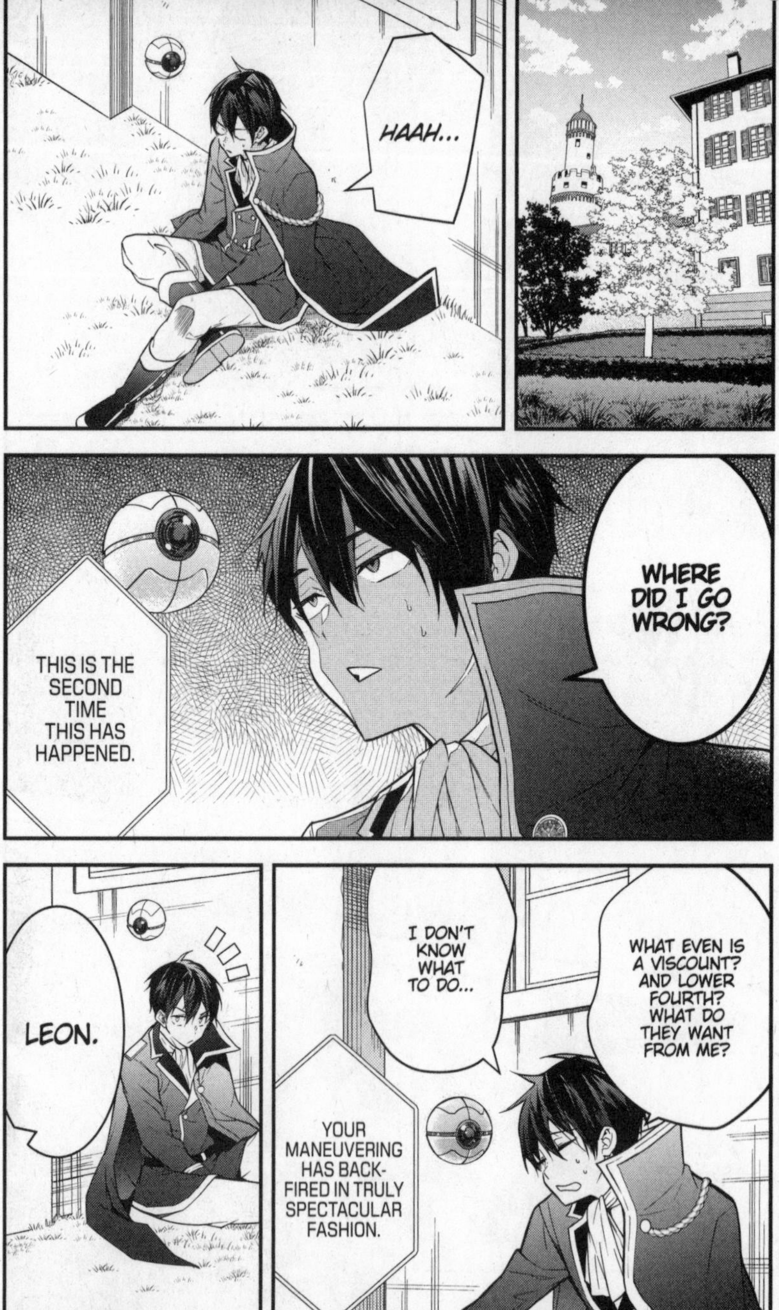
HAAH...
WHERE DID I GO WRONG?
THIS IS THE SECOND TIME THIS HAS HAPPENED.
WHAT EVEN IS A VISCOUNT? AND LOWER FOURTH? WHAT DO THEY WANT FROM ME?
I DON'T KNOW WHAT TO DO...
YOUR MANEUVERING HAS BACK-FIRED IN TRULY SPECTACULAR FASHION.
LEON.

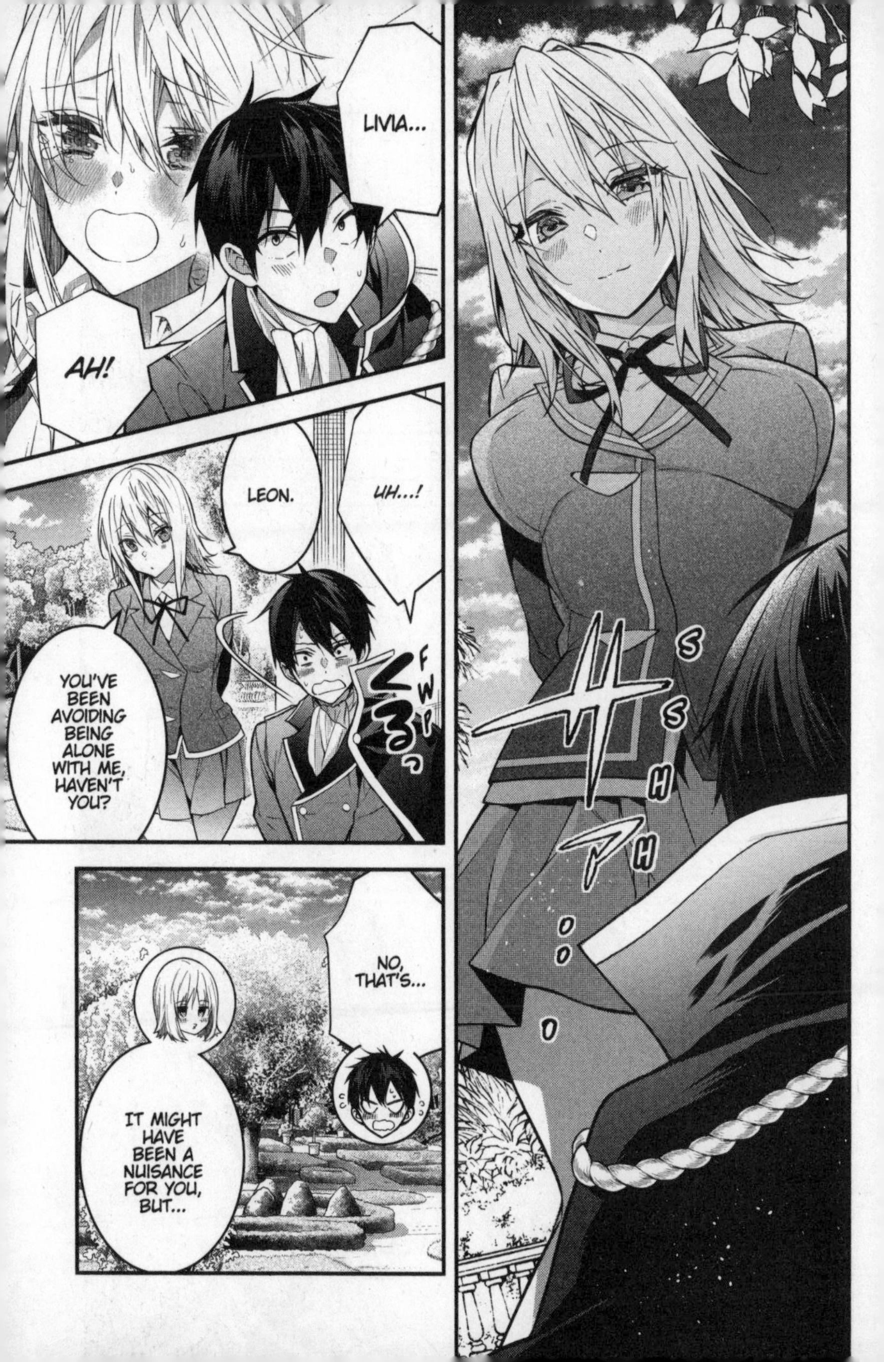
SSHHH
OOO
LIVIA...
AH!
UH...!
LEON.
FWP
YOU'VE BEEN AVOIDING BEING ALONE WITH ME, HAVEN'T YOU?
NO, THAT'S...
IT MIGHT HAVE BEEN A NUISANCE FOR YOU, BUT...

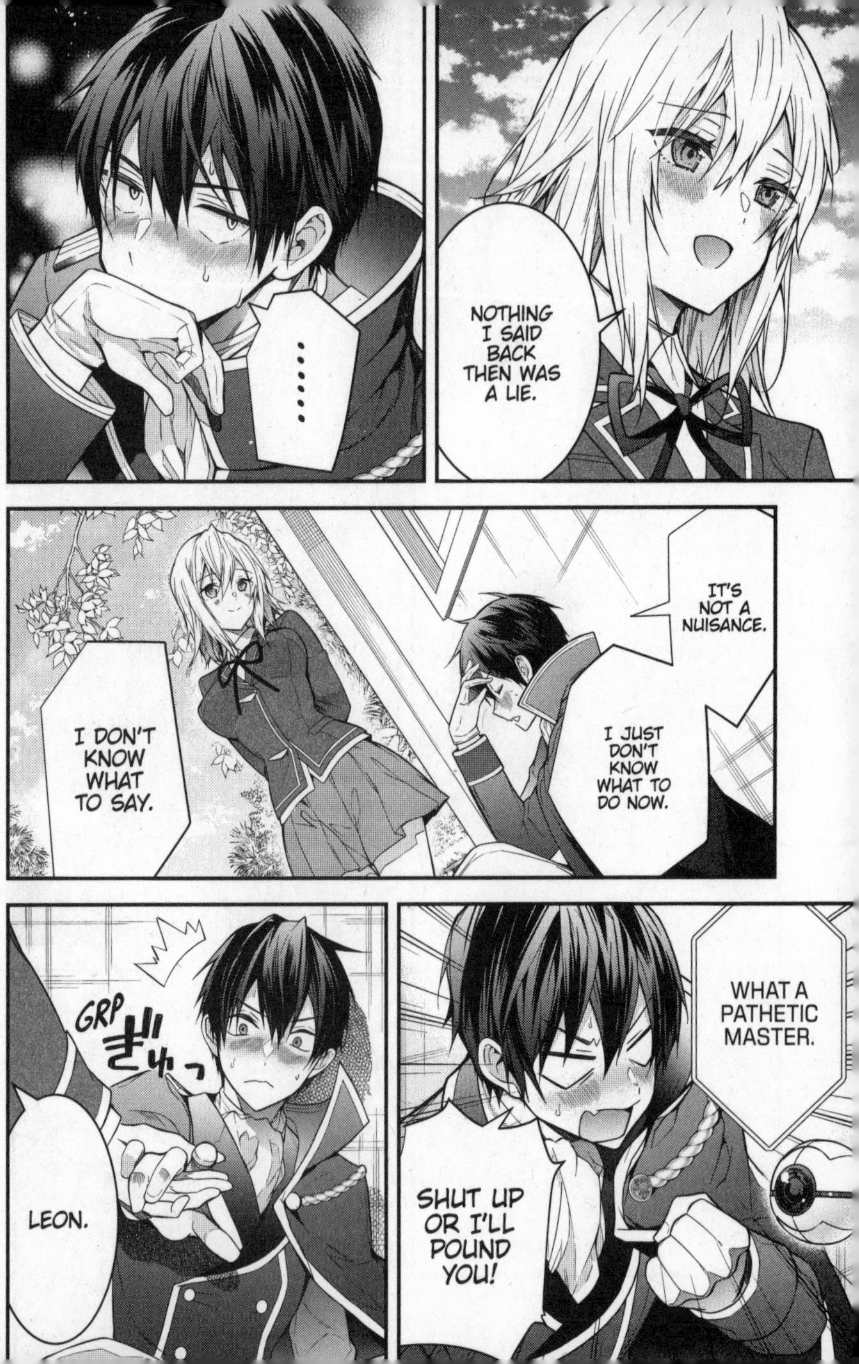
NOTHING I SAID BACK THEN WAS A LIE.
......
IT'S NOT A NUISANCE.
I JUST DON'T KNOW WHAT TO DO NOW.
I DON'T KNOW WHAT TO SAY.
WHAT A PATHETIC MASTER.
SHUT UP OR I'LL POUND YOU!
GRP
ぎゅっ
LEON.

LET ME HEAR YOUR ANSWER SOMETIME.

I'LL BE WAITING.

LIVIA...

NOW LET'S GET GOING.

EVERY-ONE'S WAITING.

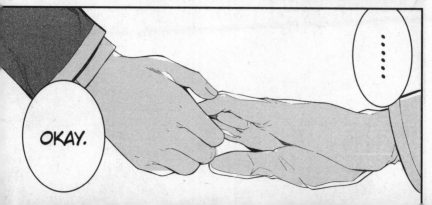

. . . . . .

OKAY.

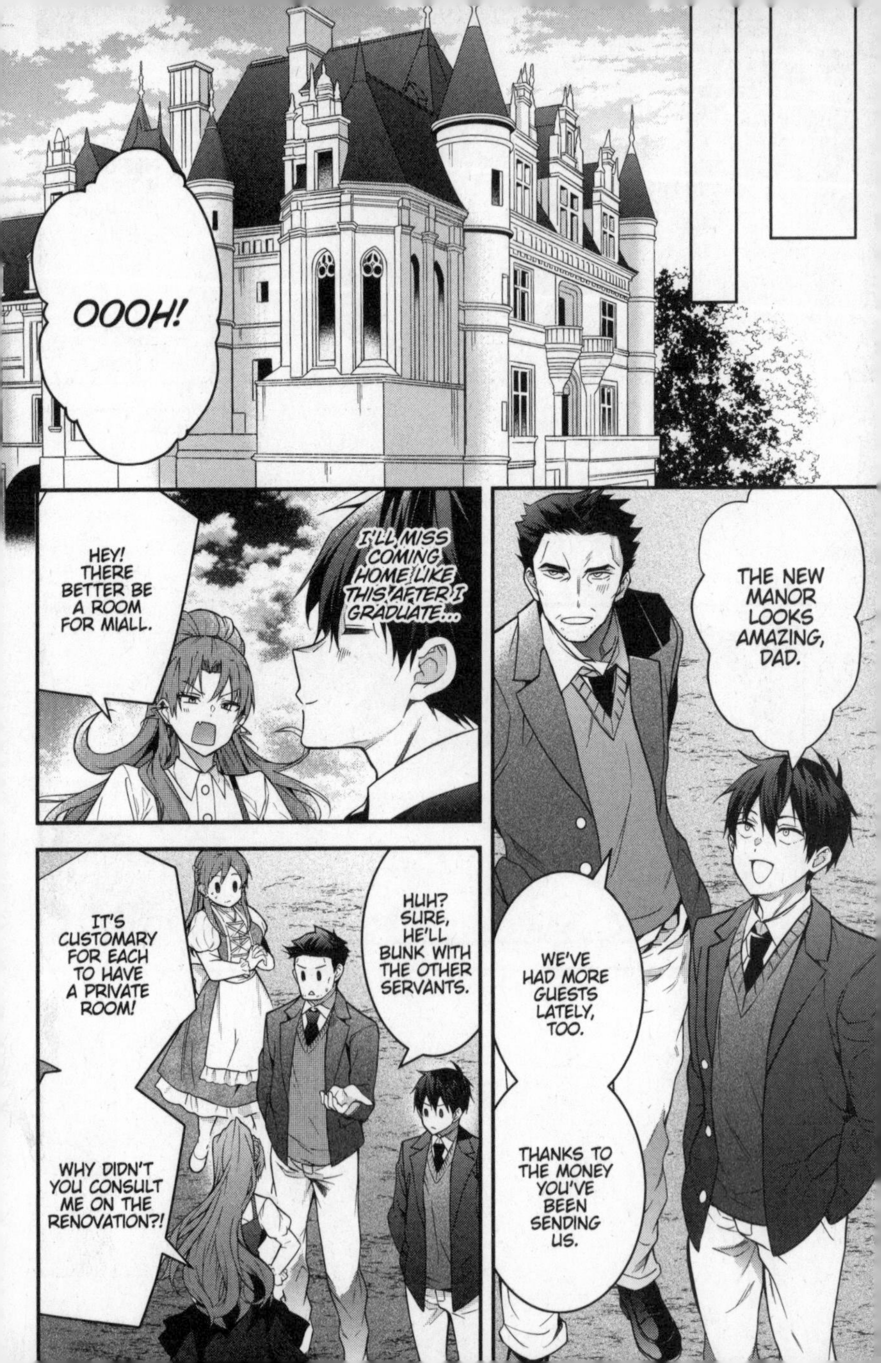
OOOH!
THE NEW MANOR LOOKS AMAZING, DAD.
WE'VE HAD MORE GUESTS LATELY, TOO.
THANKS TO THE MONEY YOU'VE BEEN SENDING US.
I'LL MISS COMING HOME LIKE THIS AFTER I GRADUATE...
HEY! THERE BETTER BE A ROOM FOR MIALL.
HUH? SURE, HE'LL BUNK WITH THE OTHER SERVANTS.
IT'S CUSTOMARY FOR EACH TO HAVE A PRIVATE ROOM!
WHY DIDN'T YOU CONSULT ME ON THE RENOVATION?!

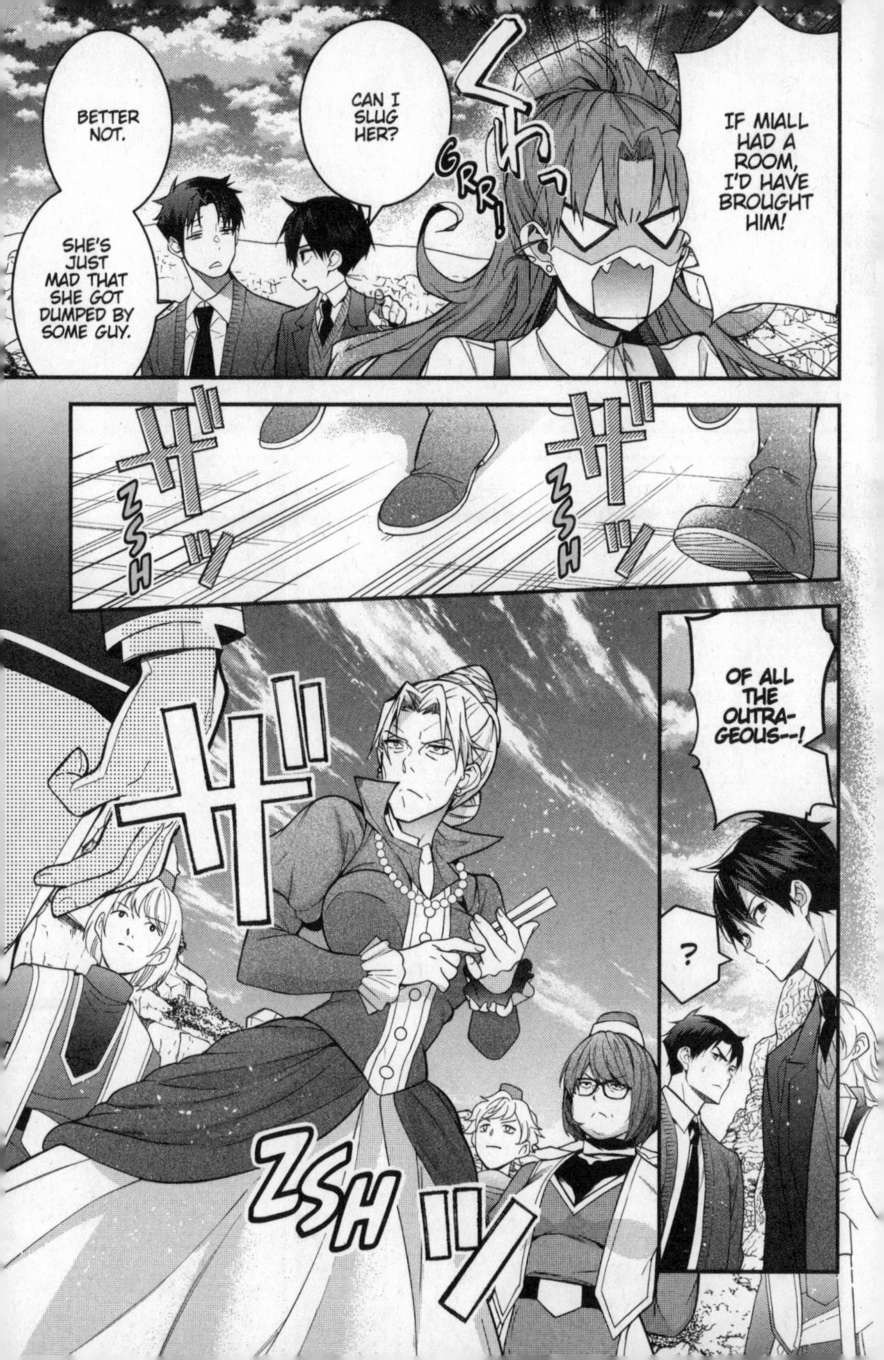
IF MIALL HAD A ROOM, I'D HAVE BROUGHT HIM!
GRR!
CAN I SLUG HER?
BETTER NOT.
SHE'S JUST MAD THAT SHE GOT DUMPED BY SOME GUY.
ZSH
ZSH
OF ALL THE OUTRAGEOUS--!
?
ZSH

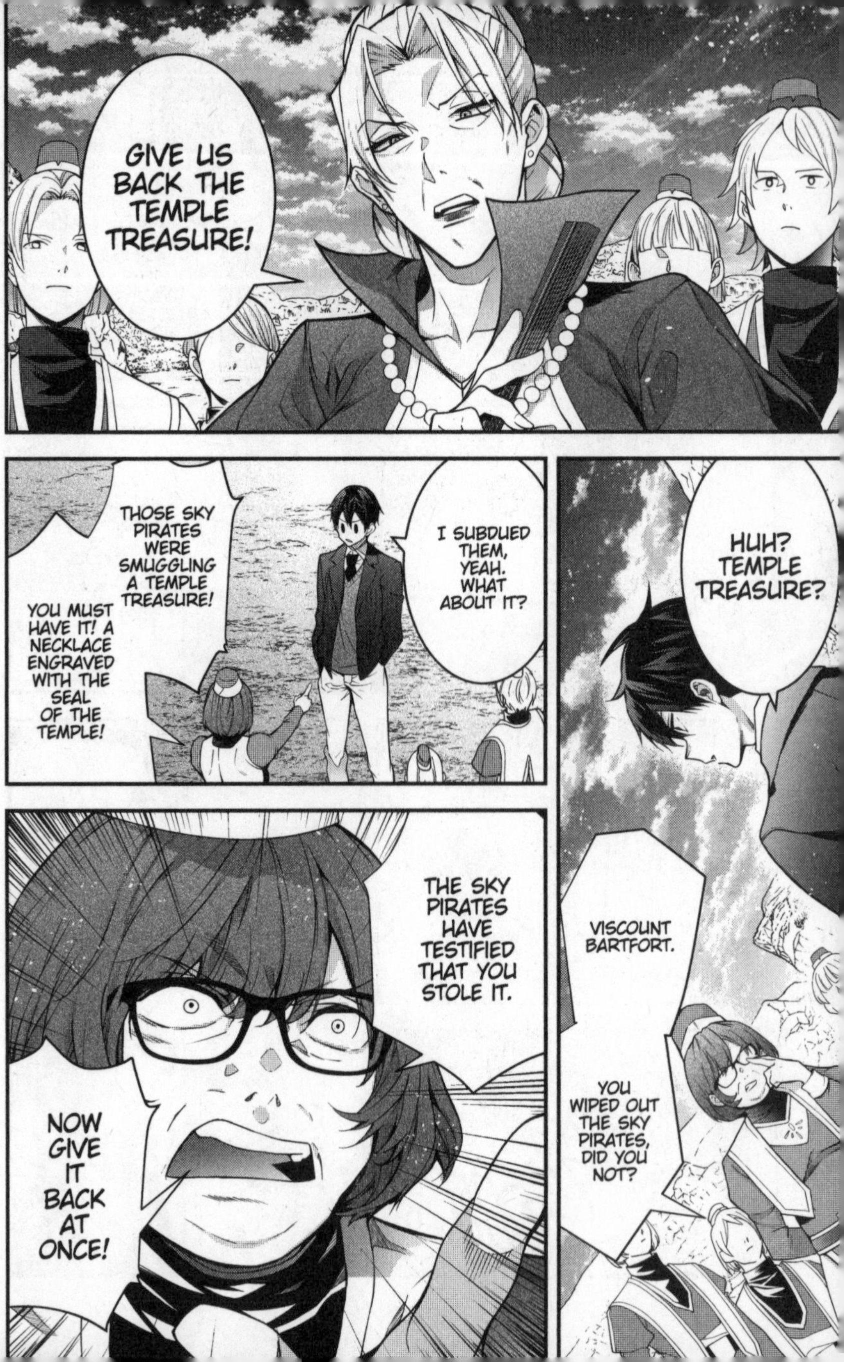
GIVE US BACK THE TEMPLE TREASURE!
HUH? TEMPLE TREASURE?
VISCOUNT BARTFORT.
YOU WIPED OUT THE SKY PIRATES, DID YOU NOT?
I SUBDUED THEM, YEAH. WHAT ABOUT IT?
THOSE SKY PIRATES WERE SMUGGLING A TEMPLE TREASURE!
YOU MUST HAVE IT! A NECKLACE ENGRAVED WITH THE SEAL OF THE TEMPLE!
THE SKY PIRATES HAVE TESTIFIED THAT YOU STOLE IT.
NOW GIVE IT BACK AT ONCE!

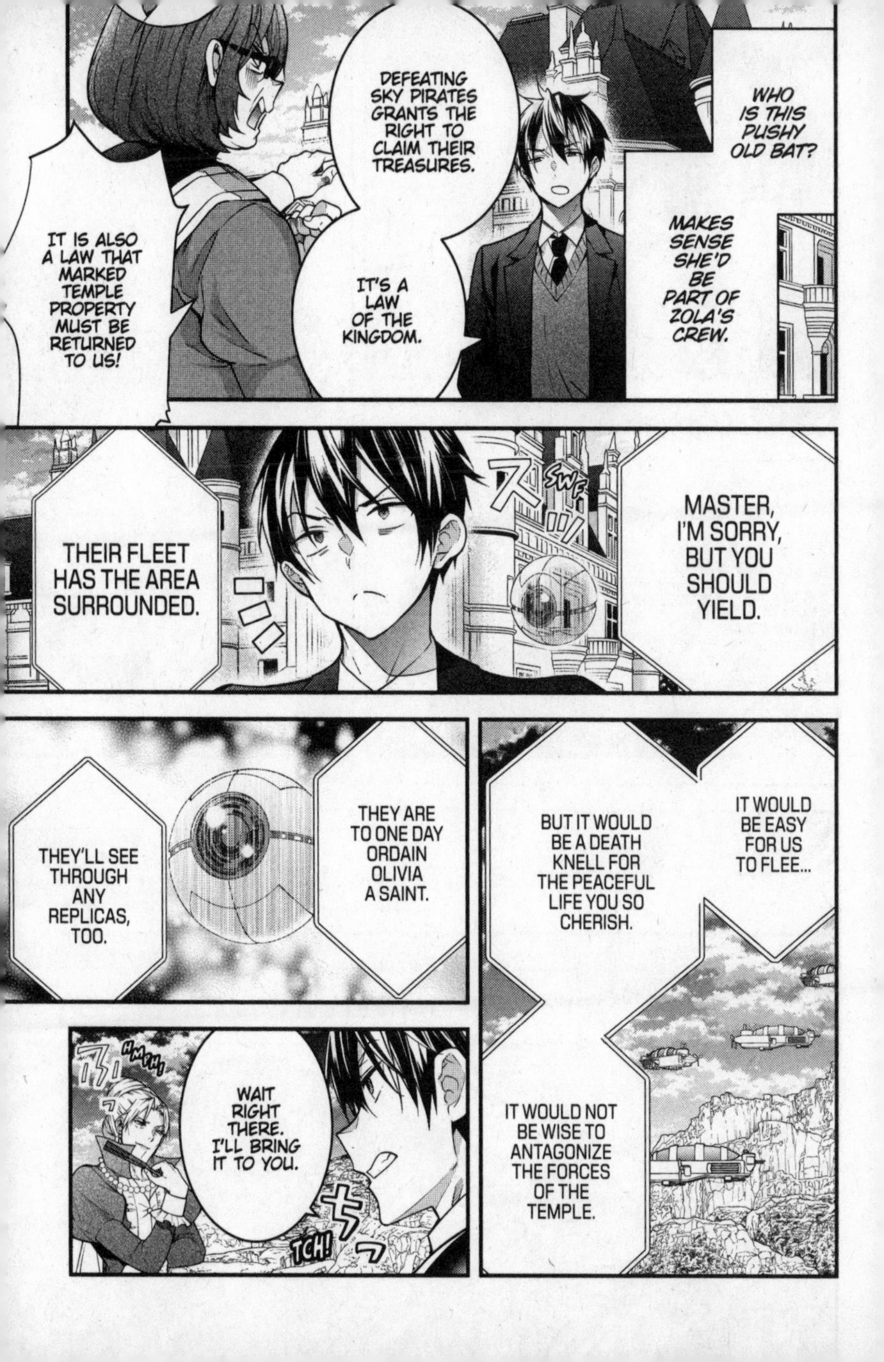

WHO IS THIS PUSHY OLD BAT?
MAKES SENSE SHE'D BE PART OF ZOLA'S CREW.
DEFEATING SKY PIRATES GRANTS THE RIGHT TO CLAIM THEIR TREASURES.
IT'S A LAW OF THE KINGDOM.
IT IS ALSO A LAW THAT MARKED TEMPLE PROPERTY MUST BE RETURNED TO US!
MASTER, I'M SORRY, BUT YOU SHOULD YIELD.
SWF
THEIR FLEET HAS THE AREA SURROUNDED.
IT WOULD BE EASY FOR US TO FLEE...
BUT IT WOULD BE A DEATH KNELL FOR THE PEACEFUL LIFE YOU SO CHERISH.
IT WOULD NOT BE WISE TO ANTAGONIZE THE FORCES OF THE TEMPLE.
THEY ARE TO ONE DAY ORDAIN OLIVIA A SAINT.
THEY'LL SEE THROUGH ANY REPLICAS, TOO.
WAIT RIGHT THERE. I'LL BRING IT TO YOU.
TCH!
HMPH!

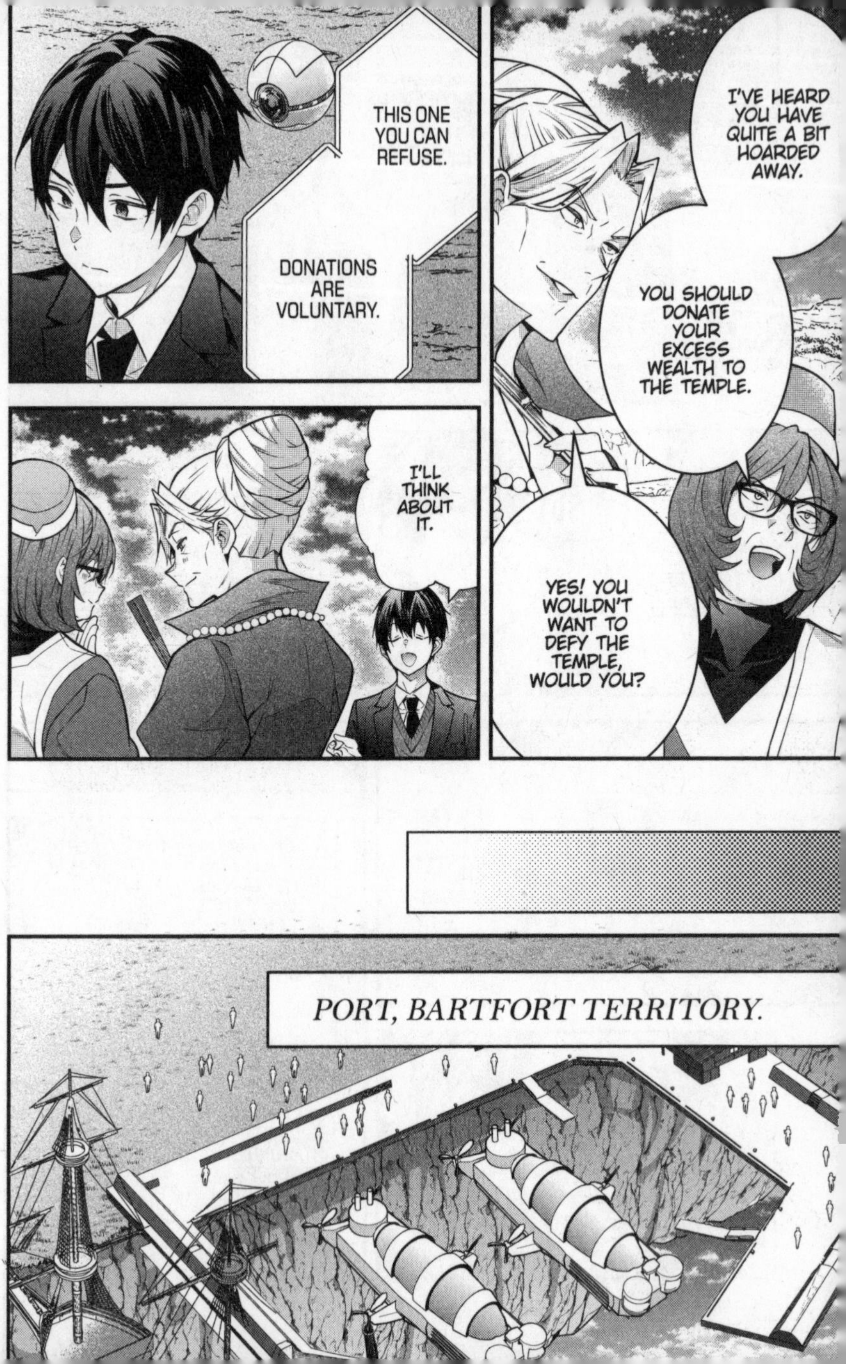
I'VE HEARD YOU HAVE QUITE A BIT HOARDED AWAY.
YOU SHOULD DONATE YOUR EXCESS WEALTH TO THE TEMPLE.
YES! YOU WOULDN'T WANT TO DEFY THE TEMPLE, WOULD YOU?
THIS ONE YOU CAN REFUSE.
DONATIONS ARE VOLUNTARY.
I'LL THINK ABOUT IT.
PORT, BARTFORT TERRITORY.

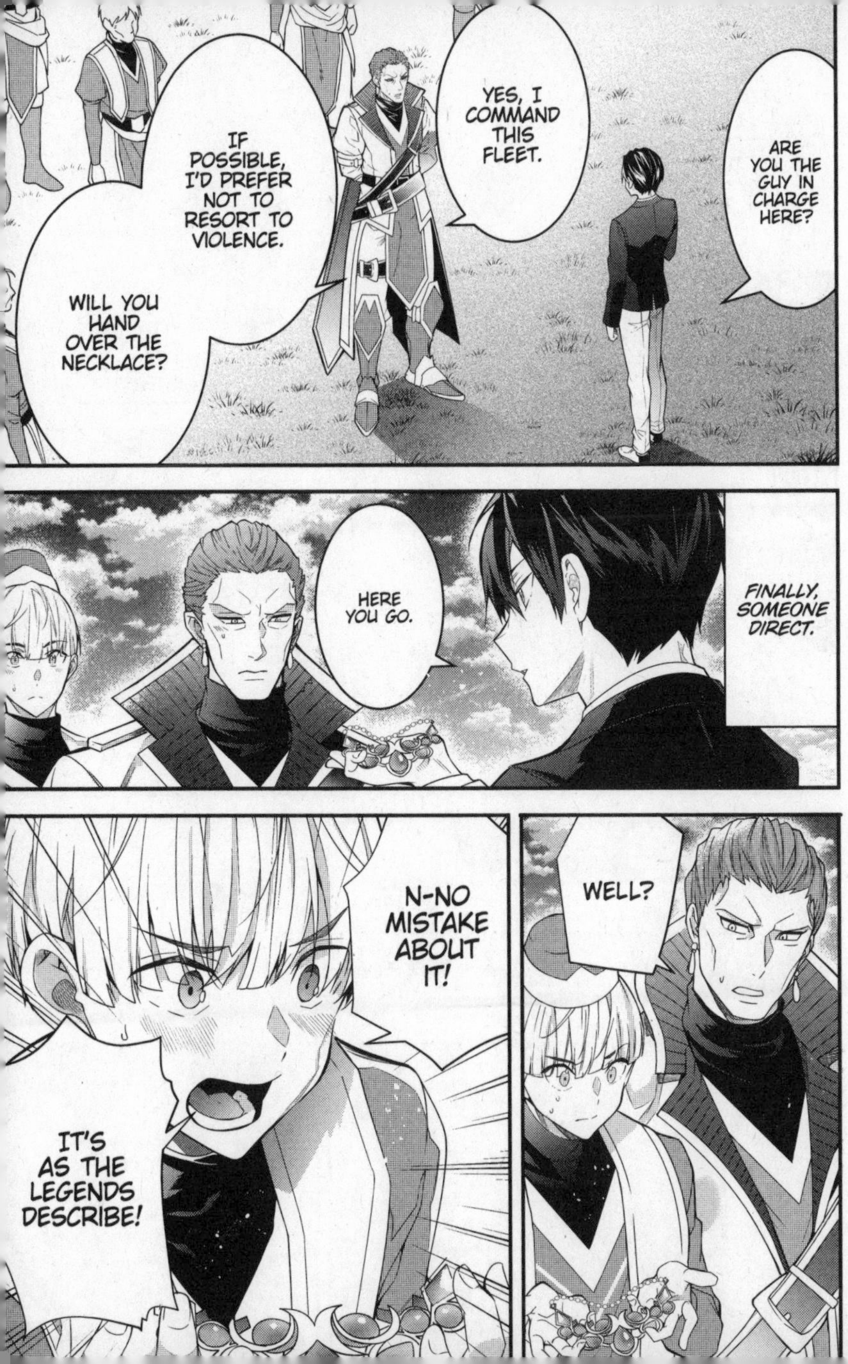
ARE YOU THE GUY IN CHARGE HERE?
YES, I COMMAND THIS FLEET.
IF POSSIBLE, I'D PREFER NOT TO RESORT TO VIOLENCE.
WILL YOU HAND OVER THE NECKLACE?
FINALLY, SOMEONE DIRECT.
HERE YOU GO.
WELL?
N-NO MISTAKE ABOUT IT!
IT'S AS THE LEGENDS DESCRIBE!

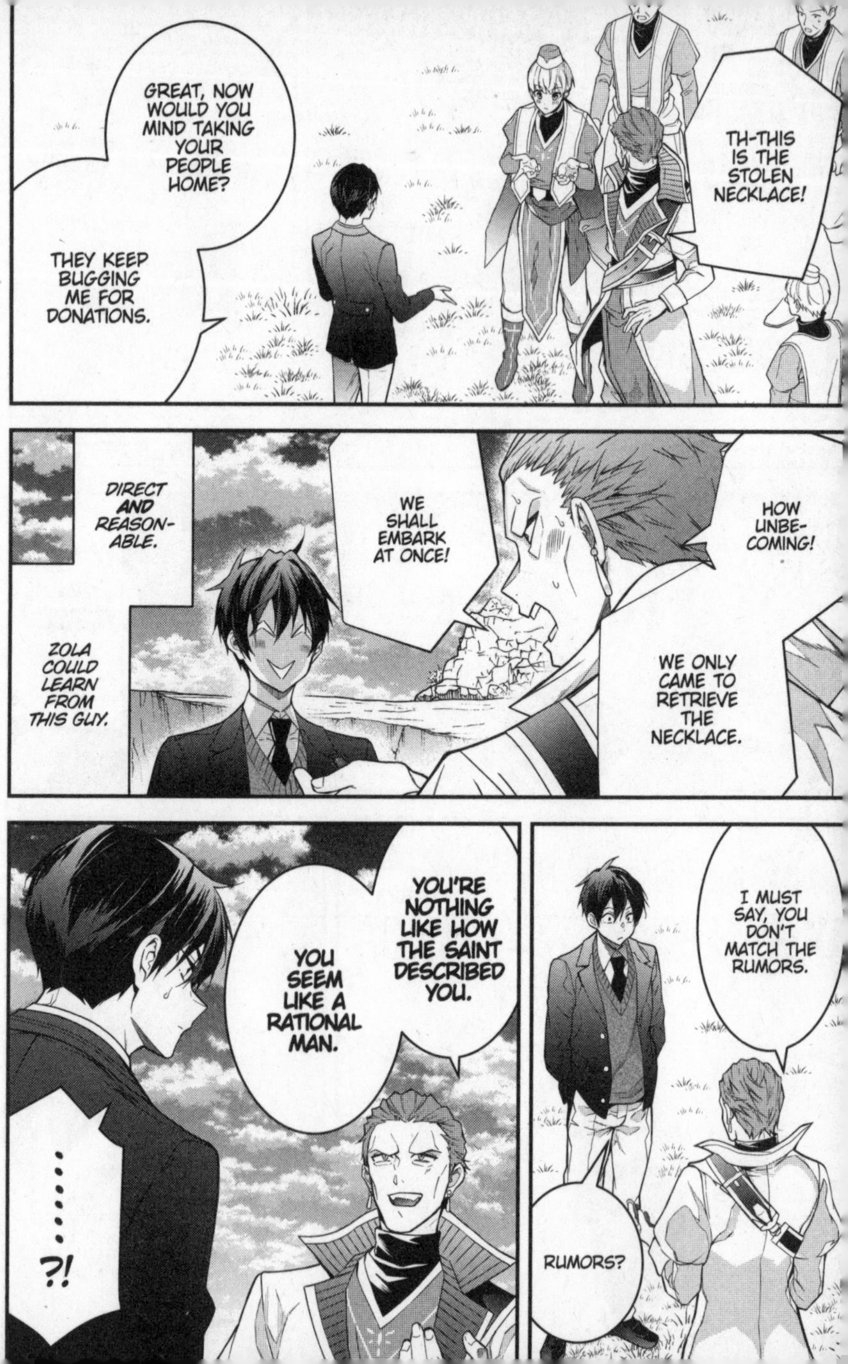
TH-THIS IS THE STOLEN NECKLACE!
GREAT, NOW WOULD YOU MIND TAKING YOUR PEOPLE HOME?
THEY KEEP BUGGING ME FOR DONATIONS.
HOW UNBE-COMING!
WE ONLY CAME TO RETRIEVE THE NECKLACE.
WE SHALL EMBARK AT ONCE!
DIRECT AND REASON-ABLE.
ZOLA COULD LEARN FROM THIS GUY.
I MUST SAY, YOU DON'T MATCH THE RUMORS.
RUMORS?
YOU'RE NOTHING LIKE HOW THE SAINT DESCRIBED YOU.
YOU SEEM LIKE A RATIONAL MAN.
......?!

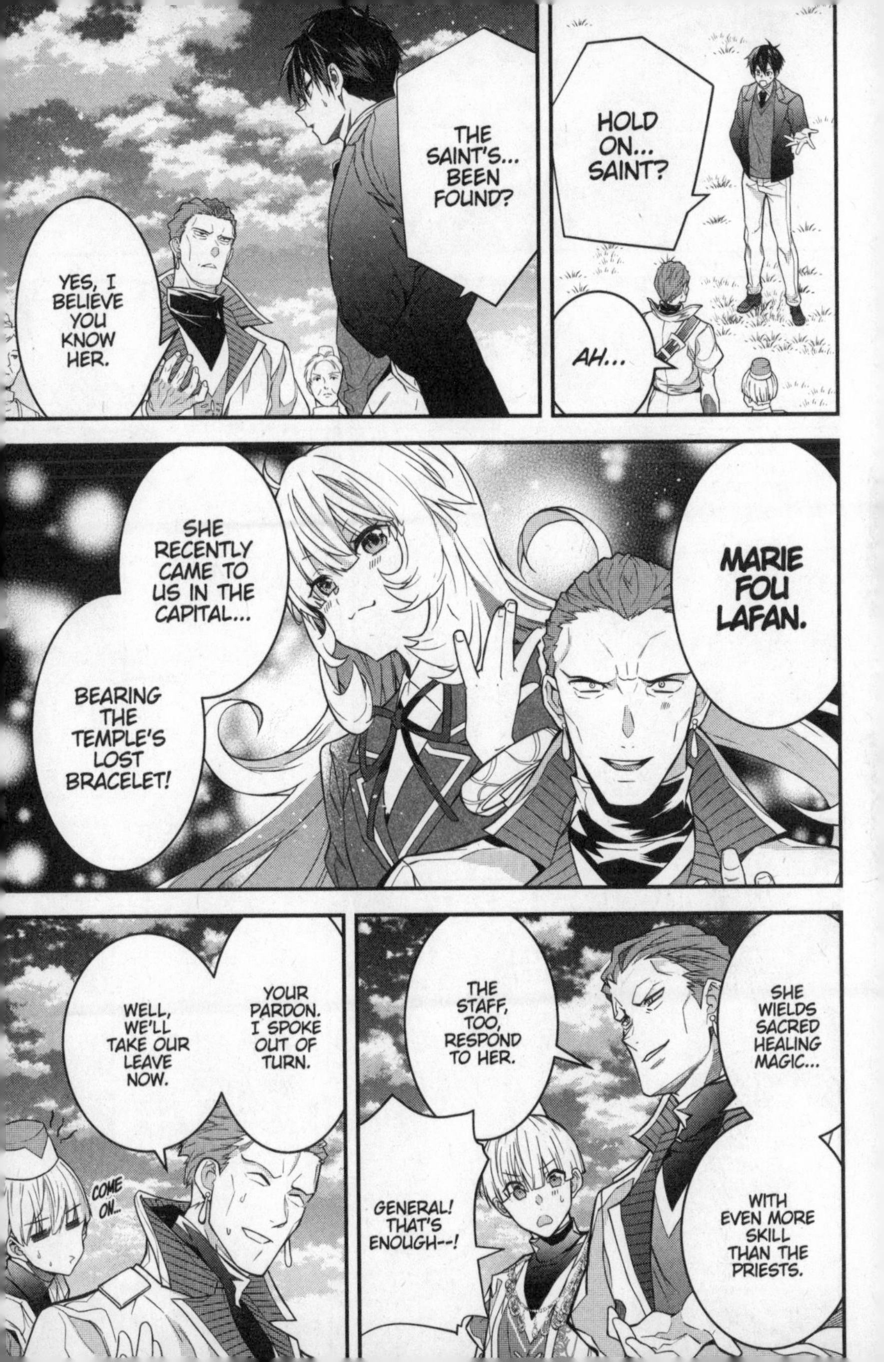

HOLD ON... SAINT?
AH...
THE SAINT'S... BEEN FOUND?
YES, I BELIEVE YOU KNOW HER.
MARIE FOU LAFAN.
SHE RECENTLY CAME TO US IN THE CAPITAL...
BEARING THE TEMPLE'S LOST BRACELET!
SHE WIELDS SACRED HEALING MAGIC...
THE STAFF, TOO, RESPOND TO HER.
WITH EVEN MORE SKILL THAN THE PRIESTS.
GENERAL! THAT'S ENOUGH--!
YOUR PARDON. I SPOKE OUT OF TURN.
WELL, WE'LL TAKE OUR LEAVE NOW.
COME ON...

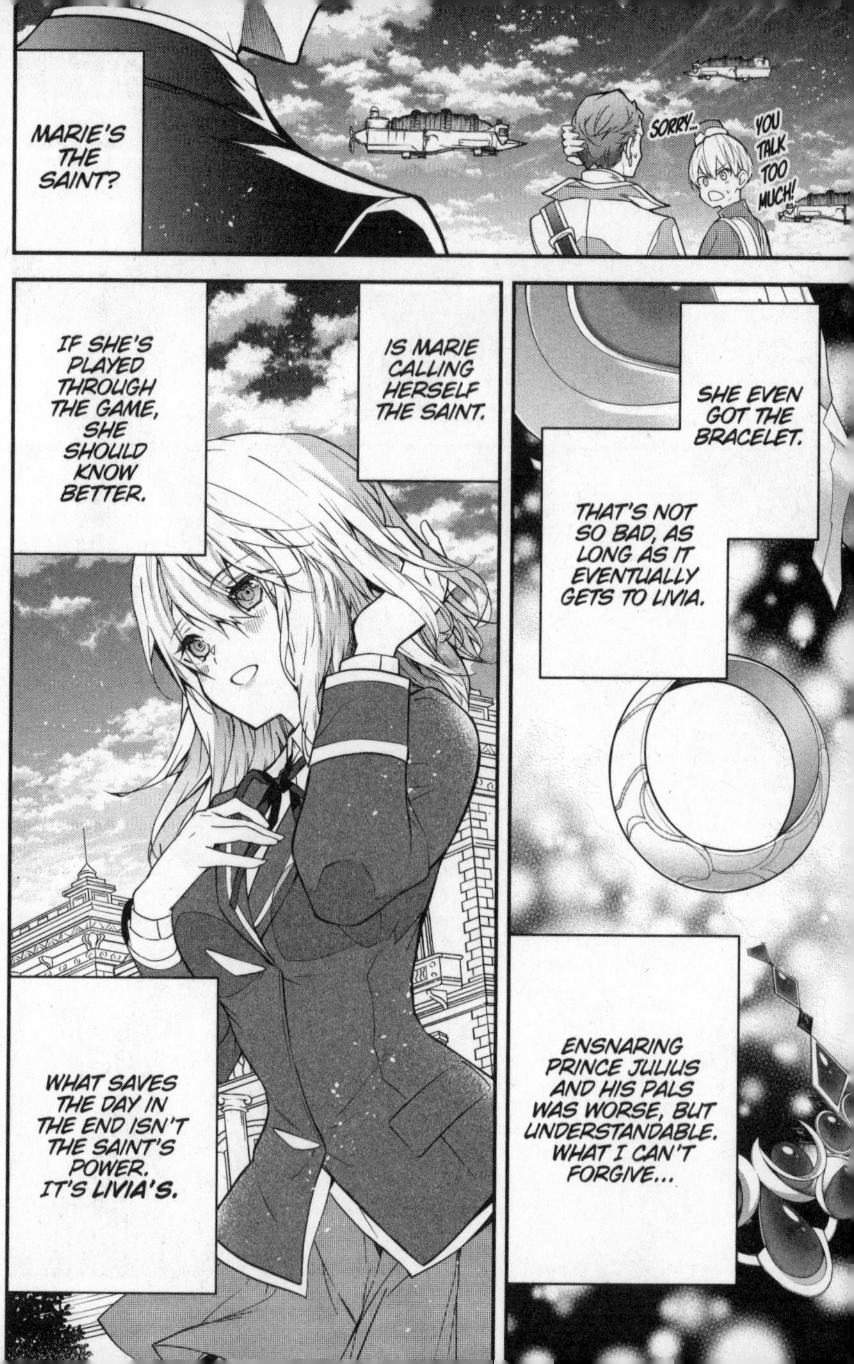
YOU TALK TOO MUCH!
SORRY...
MARIE'S THE SAINT?
SHE EVEN GOT THE BRACELET.
THAT'S NOT SO BAD, AS LONG AS IT EVENTUALLY GETS TO LIVIA.
ENSNARING PRINCE JULIUS AND HIS PALS WAS WORSE, BUT UNDERSTANDABLE. WHAT I CAN'T FORGIVE...
IS MARIE CALLING HERSELF THE SAINT.
IF SHE'S PLAYED THROUGH THE GAME, SHE SHOULD KNOW BETTER.
WHAT SAVES THE DAY IN THE END ISN'T THE SAINT'S POWER. IT'S LIVIA'S.

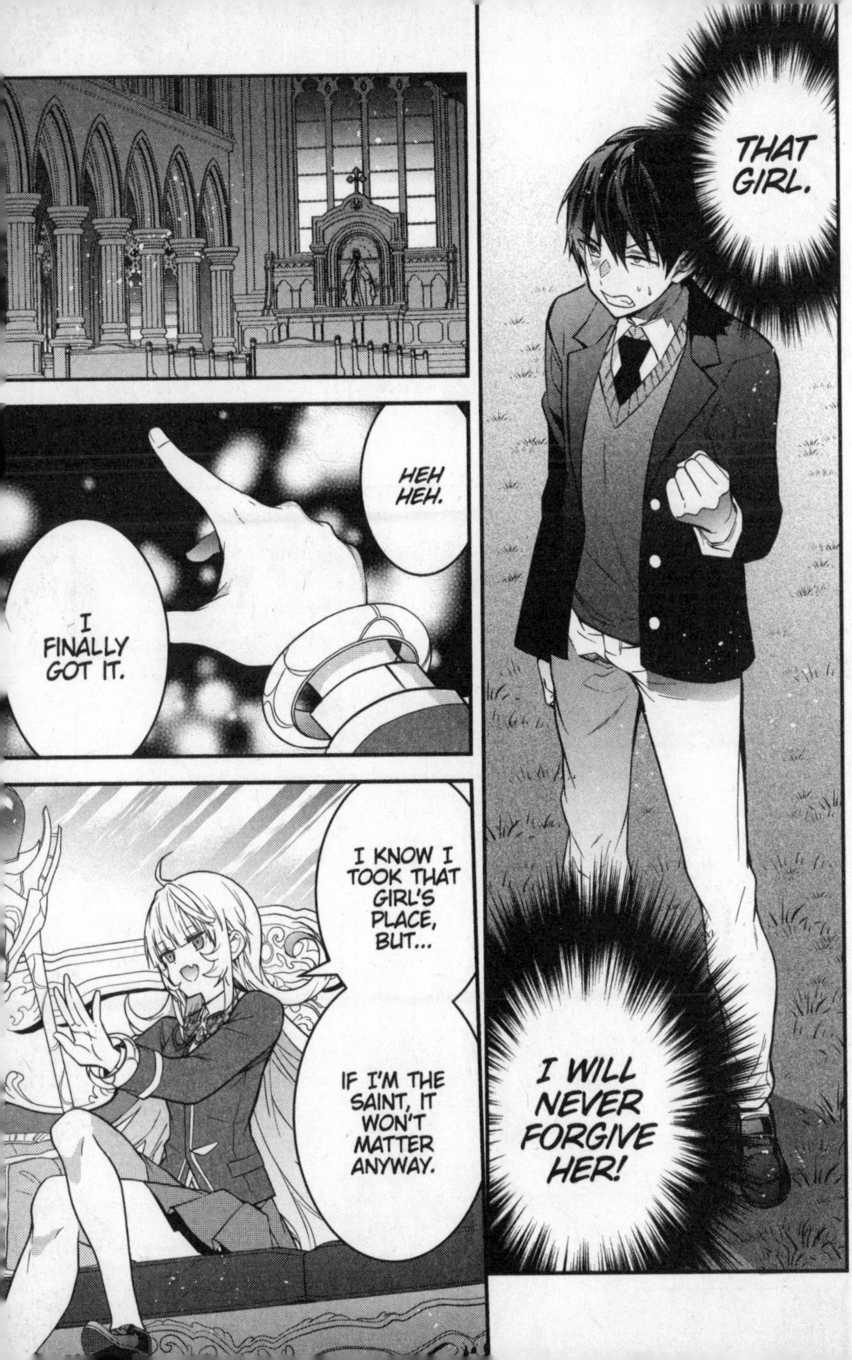
THAT GIRL.
I WILL NEVER FORGIVE HER!
HEH HEH.
I FINALLY GOT IT.
I KNOW I TOOK THAT GIRL'S PLACE, BUT...
IF I'M THE SAINT, IT WON'T MATTER ANYWAY.

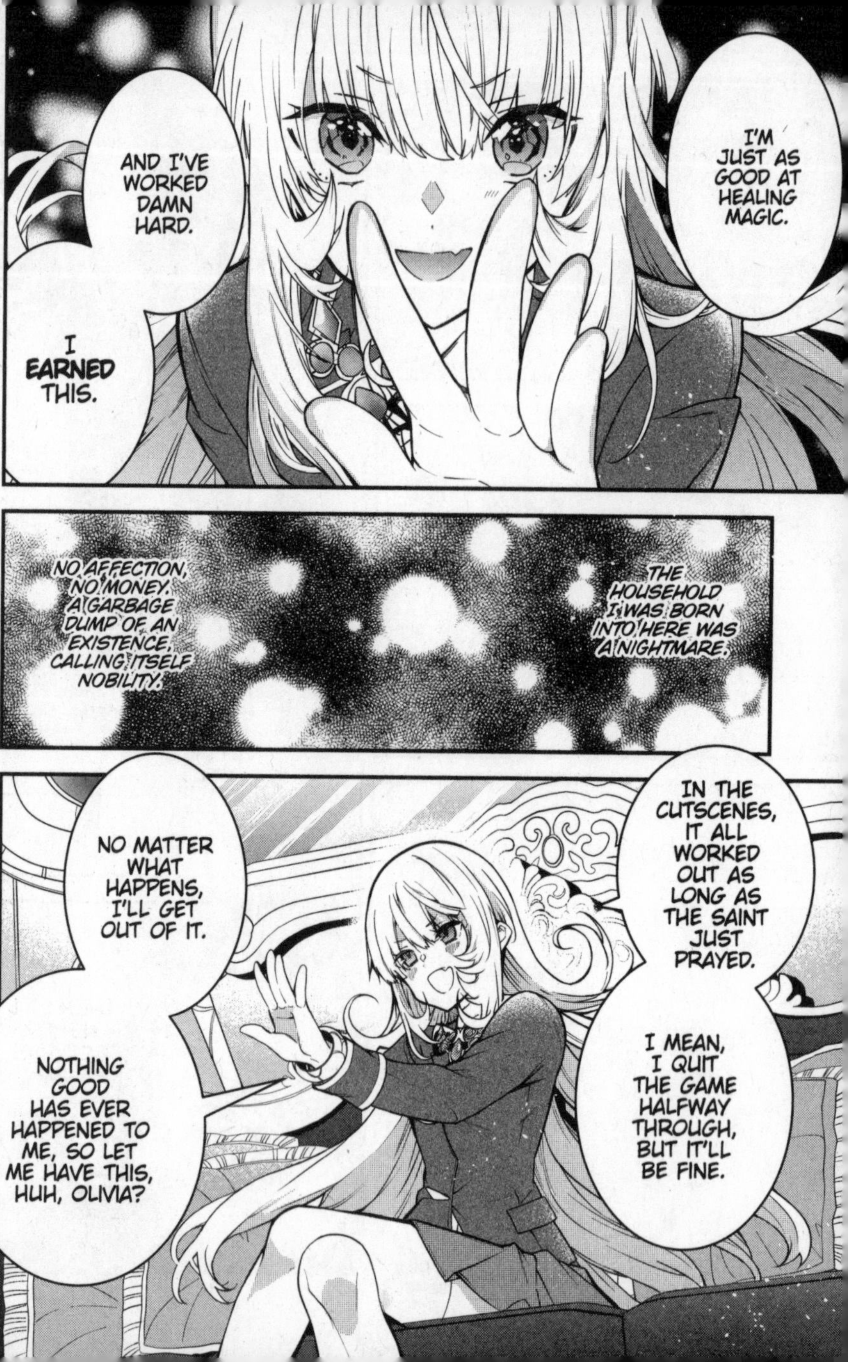
I'M JUST AS GOOD AT HEALING MAGIC.
AND I'VE WORKED DAMN HARD.
I EARNED THIS.
THE HOUSEHOLD I WAS BORN INTO HERE WAS A NIGHTMARE.
NO AFFECTION, NO MONEY. A GARBAGE DUMP OF AN EXISTENCE, CALLING ITSELF NOBILITY.
IN THE CUTSCENES, IT ALL WORKED OUT AS LONG AS THE SAINT JUST PRAYED.
NO MATTER WHAT HAPPENS, I'LL GET OUT OF IT.
I MEAN, I QUIT THE GAME HALFWAY THROUGH, BUT IT'LL BE FINE.
NOTHING GOOD HAS EVER HAPPENED TO ME, SO LET ME HAVE THIS, HUH, OLIVIA?

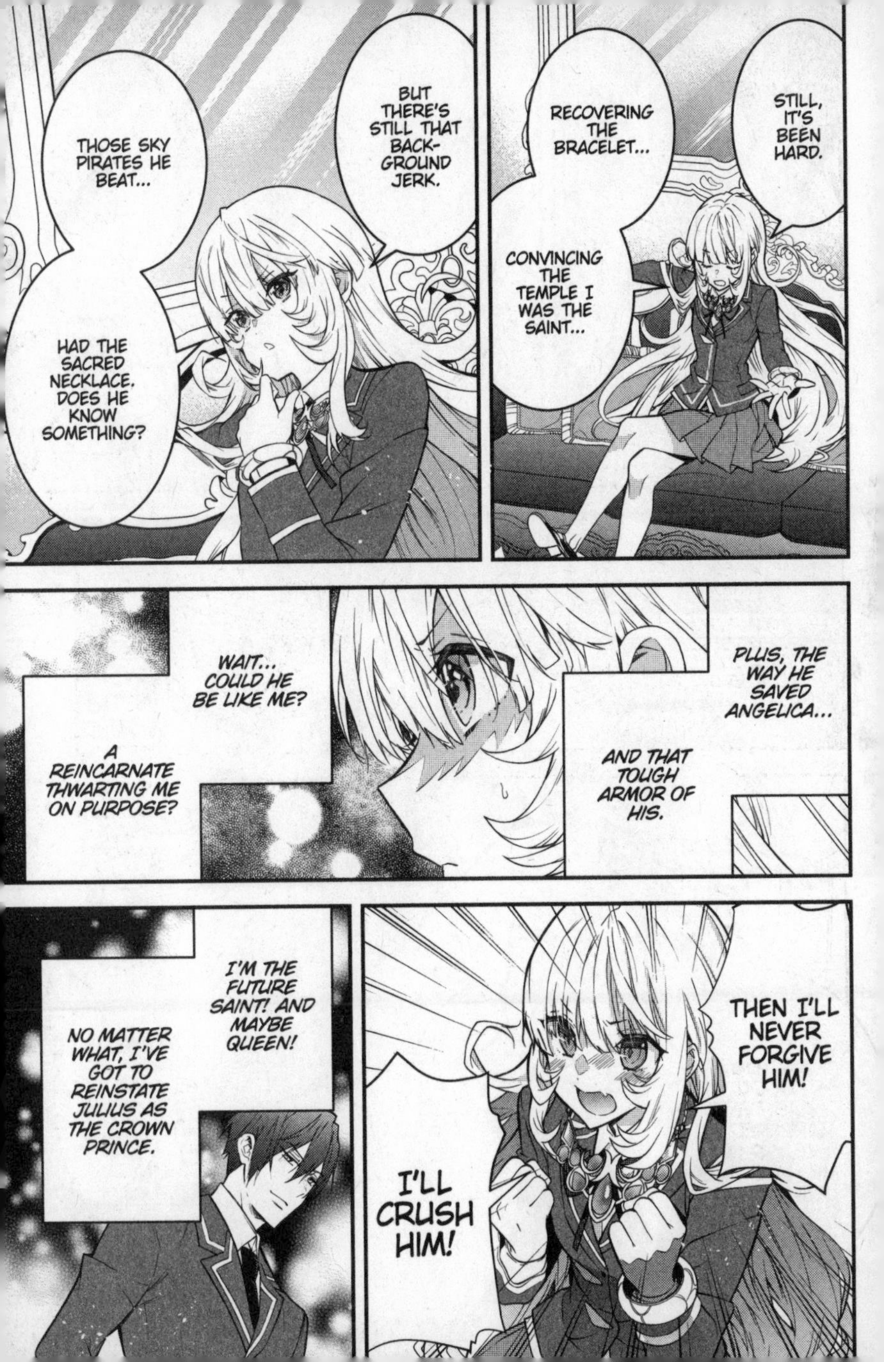
STILL, IT'S BEEN HARD.
RECOVERING THE BRACELET...
CONVINCING THE TEMPLE I WAS THE SAINT...
BUT THERE'S STILL THAT BACK-GROUND JERK.
THOSE SKY PIRATES HE BEAT...
HAD THE SACRED NECKLACE. DOES HE KNOW SOMETHING?
PLUS, THE WAY HE SAVED ANGELICA...
AND THAT TOUGH ARMOR OF HIS.
WAIT... COULD HE BE LIKE ME?
A REINCARNATE THWARTING ME ON PURPOSE?
THEN I'LL NEVER FORGIVE HIM!
I'LL CRUSH HIM!
I'M THE FUTURE SAINT! AND MAYBE QUEEN!
NO MATTER WHAT, I'VE GOT TO REINSTATE JULIUS AS THE CROWN PRINCE.

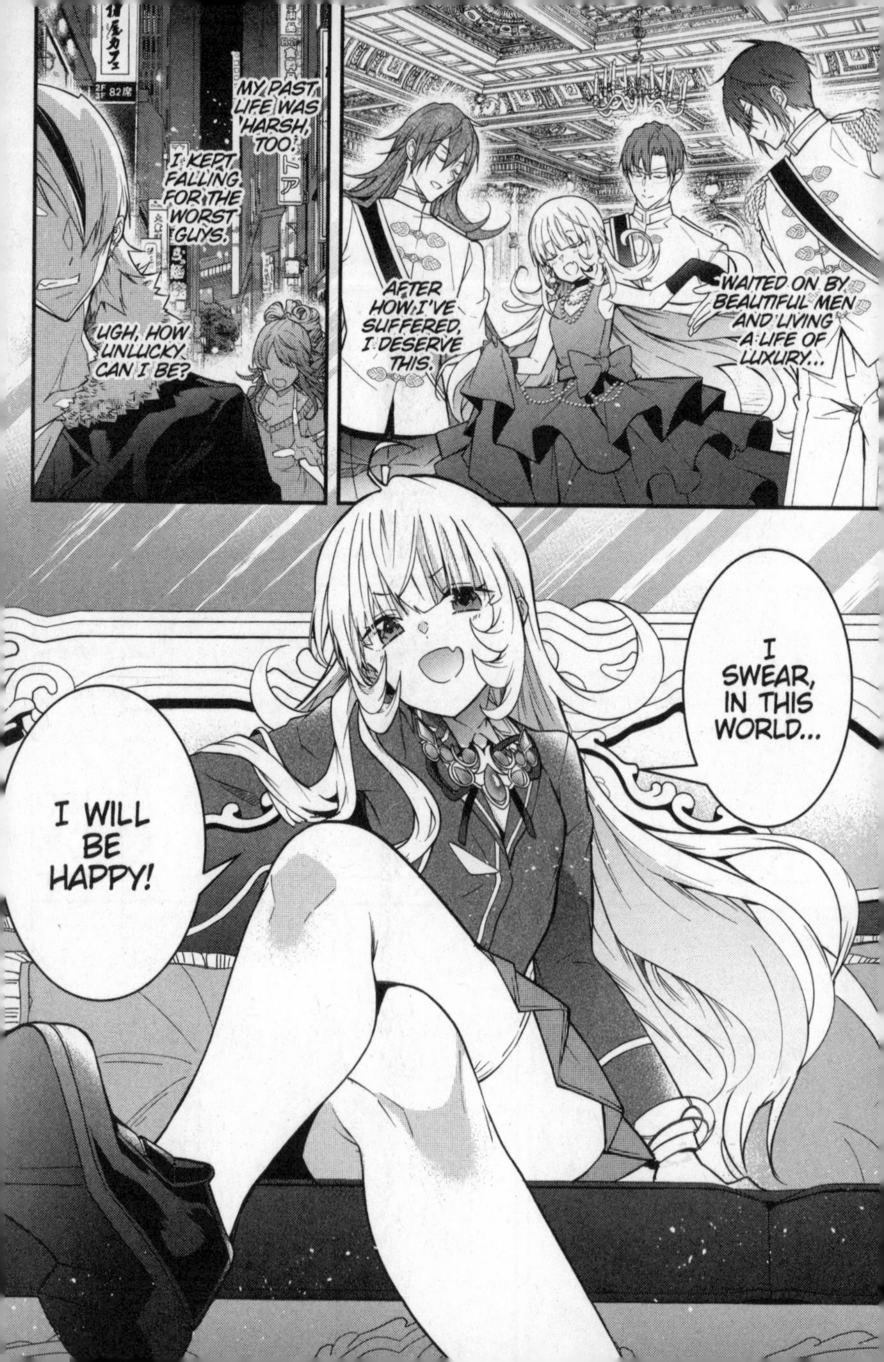
WAITED ON BY BEAUTIFUL MEN AND LIVING A LIFE OF LUXURY...
AFTER HOW I'VE SUFFERED, I DESERVE THIS.
MY PAST LIFE WAS HARSH, TOO.
I KEPT FALLING FOR THE WORST GUYS.
UGH, HOW UNLUCKY CAN I BE?
I SWEAR, IN THIS WORLD...
I WILL BE HAPPY!

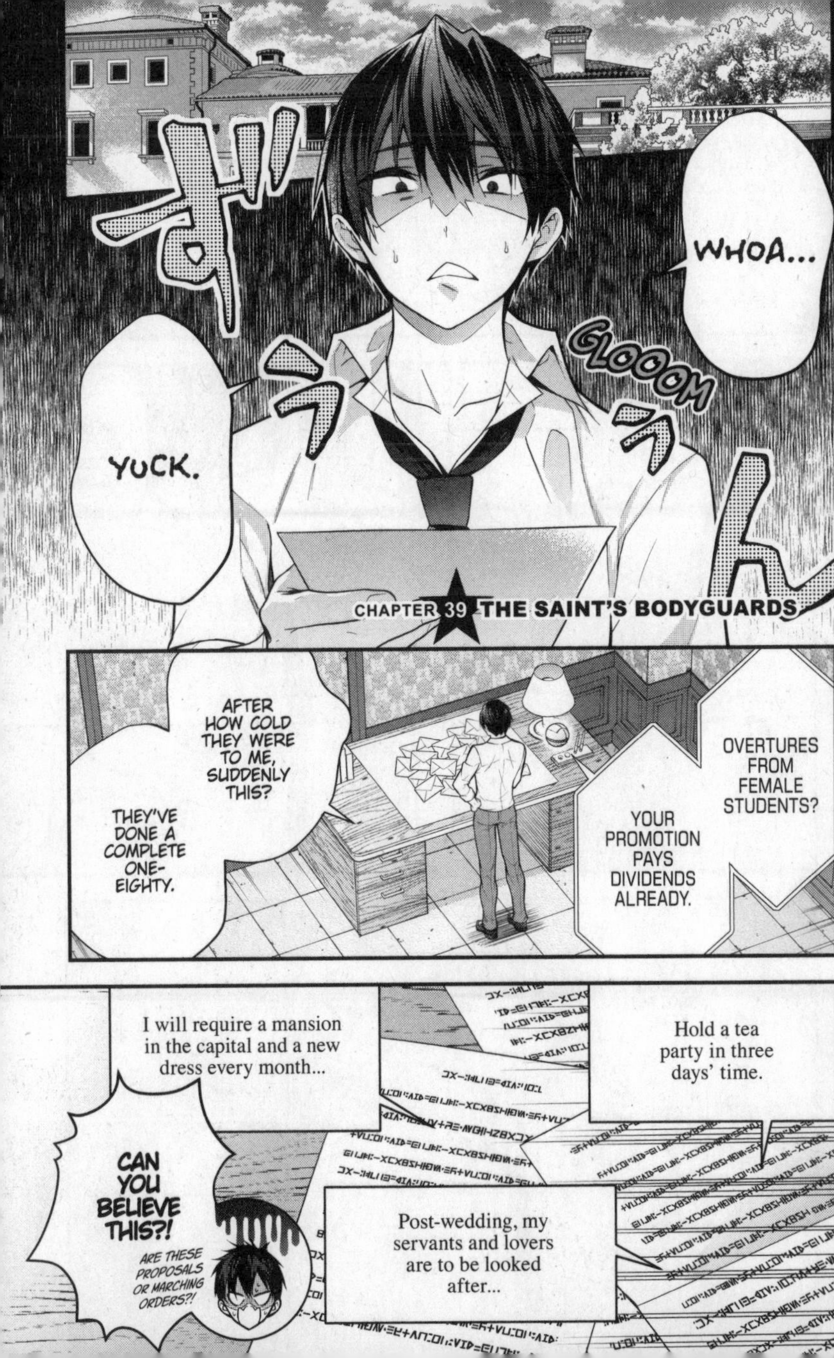
WHOA...
GLOOOM
YUCK.
CHAPTER 39 THE SAINT'S BODYGUARDS
OVERTURES FROM FEMALE STUDENTS?
YOUR PROMOTION PAYS DIVIDENDS ALREADY.
AFTER HOW COLD THEY WERE TO ME, SUDDENLY THIS?
THEY'VE DONE A COMPLETE ONE-EIGHTY.
Hold a tea party in three days' time.
I will require a mansion in the capital and a new dress every month...
Post-wedding, my servants and lovers are to be looked after...
CAN YOU BELIEVE THIS?!
ARE THESE PROPOSALS OR MARCHING ORDERS?!

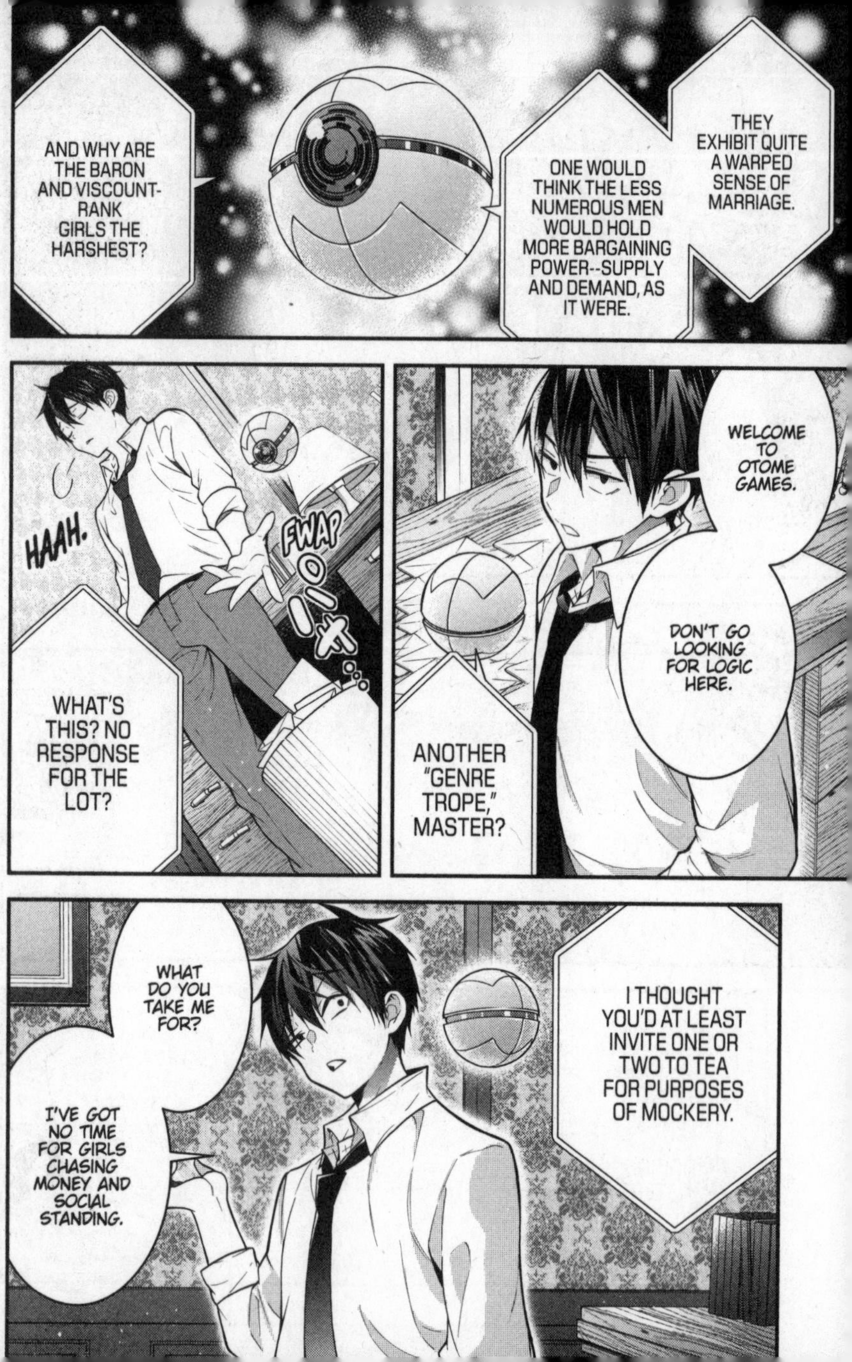
THEY EXHIBIT QUITE A WARPED SENSE OF MARRIAGE.
ONE WOULD THINK THE LESS NUMEROUS MEN WOULD HOLD MORE BARGAINING POWER--SUPPLY AND DEMAND, AS IT WERE.
AND WHY ARE THE BARON AND VISCOUNT-RANK GIRLS THE HARSHEST?
WELCOME TO OTOME GAMES.
DON'T GO LOOKING FOR LOGIC HERE.
ANOTHER "GENRE TROPE," MASTER?
FWAP
HAAH.
WHAT'S THIS? NO RESPONSE FOR THE LOT?
I THOUGHT YOU'D AT LEAST INVITE ONE OR TWO TO TEA FOR PURPOSES OF MOCKERY.
WHAT DO YOU TAKE ME FOR?
I'VE GOT NO TIME FOR GIRLS CHASING MONEY AND SOCIAL STANDING.

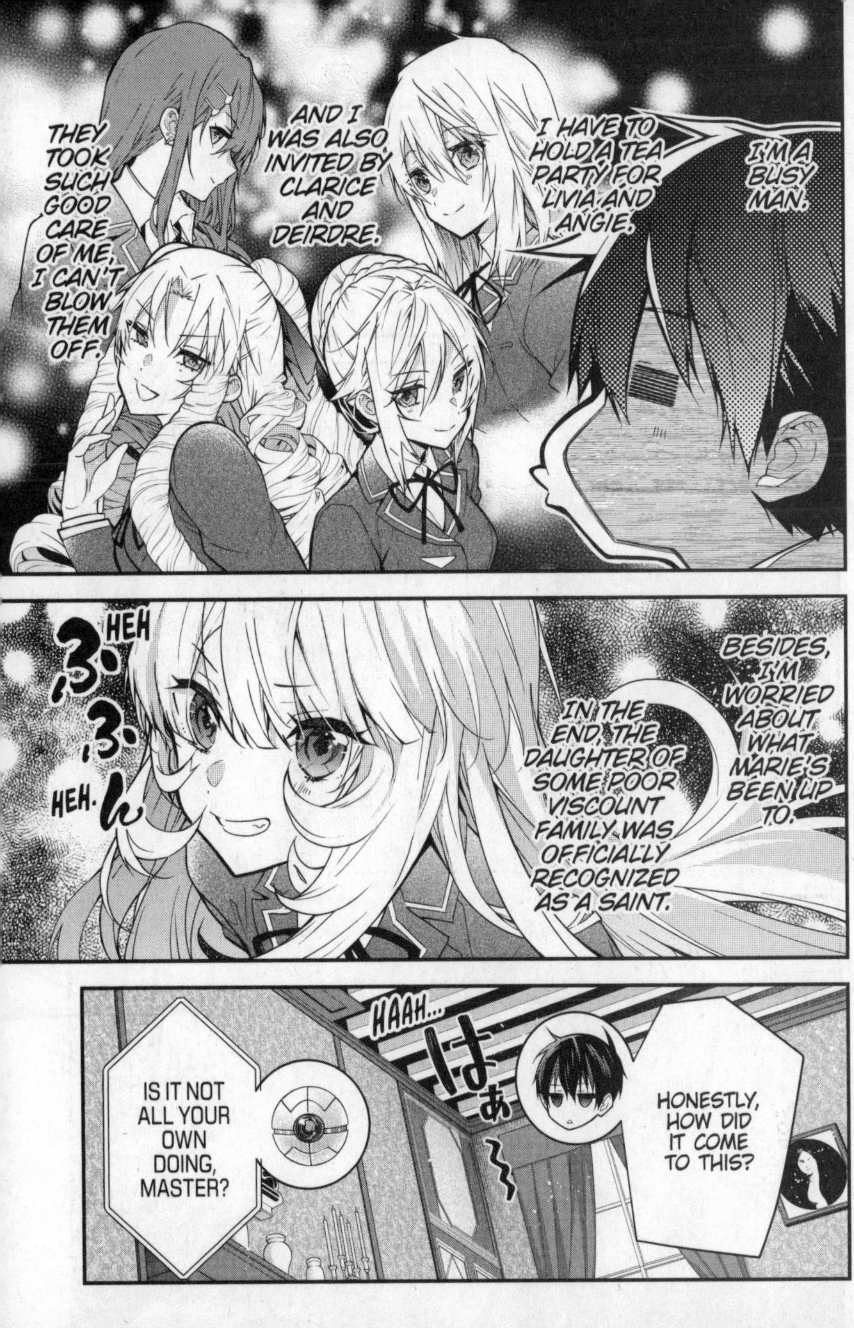
I'M A BUSY MAN.
I HAVE TO HOLD A TEA PARTY FOR LIVIA AND ANGIE.
AND I WAS ALSO INVITED BY CLARICE AND DEIRDRE.
THEY TOOK SUCH GOOD CARE OF ME, I CAN'T BLOW THEM OFF.
BESIDES, I'M WORRIED ABOUT WHAT MARIE'S BEEN UP TO.
IN THE END, THE DAUGHTER OF SOME POOR VISCOUNT FAMILY WAS OFFICIALLY RECOGNIZED AS A SAINT.
ふふん
HEH HEH.
HONESTLY, HOW DID IT COME TO THIS?
はぁ~
HAAH...
IS IT NOT ALL YOUR OWN DOING, MASTER?

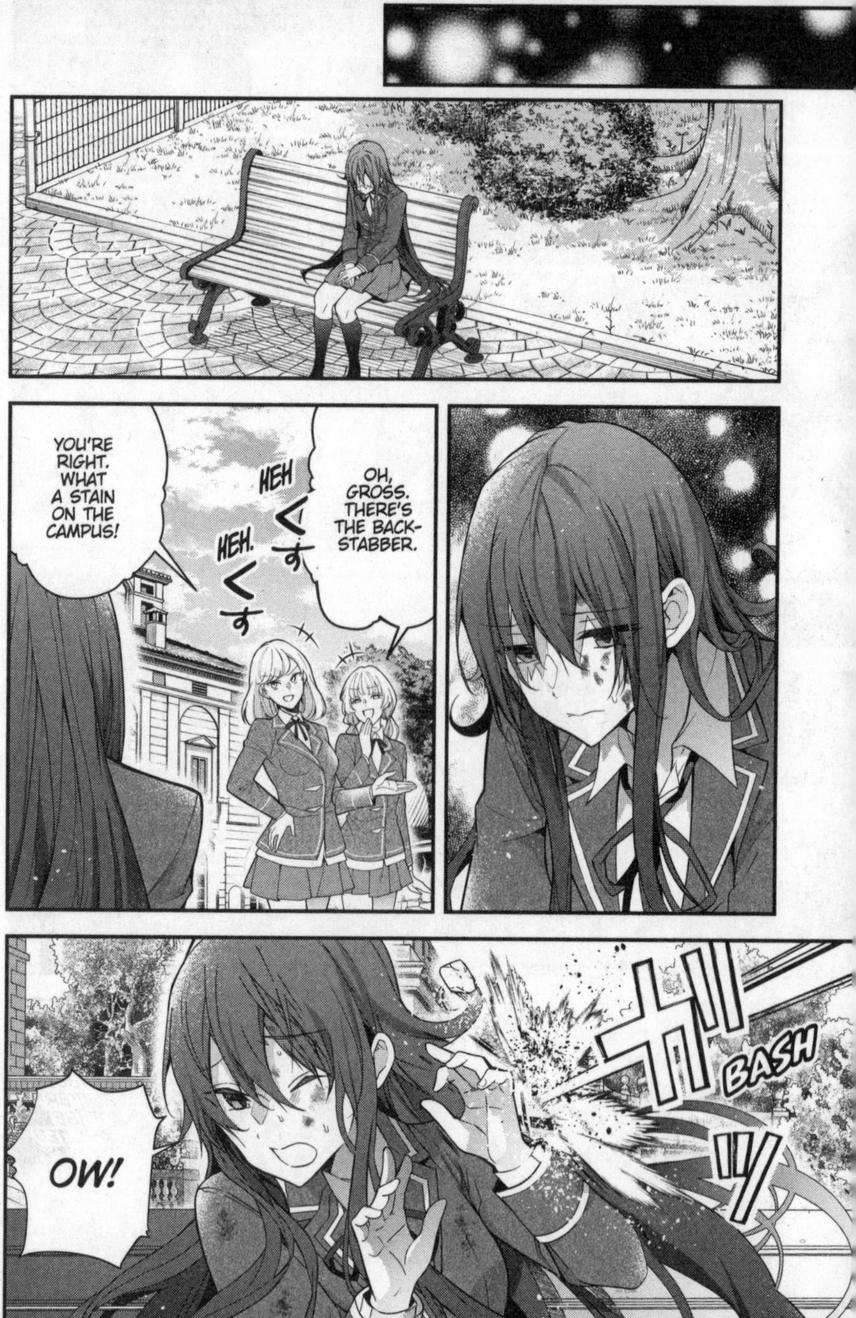
OH, GROSS. THERE'S THE BACK-STABBER.
HEH HEH.
くすくす
YOU'RE RIGHT. WHAT A STAIN ON THE CAMPUS!
ガッ
BASH
OW!

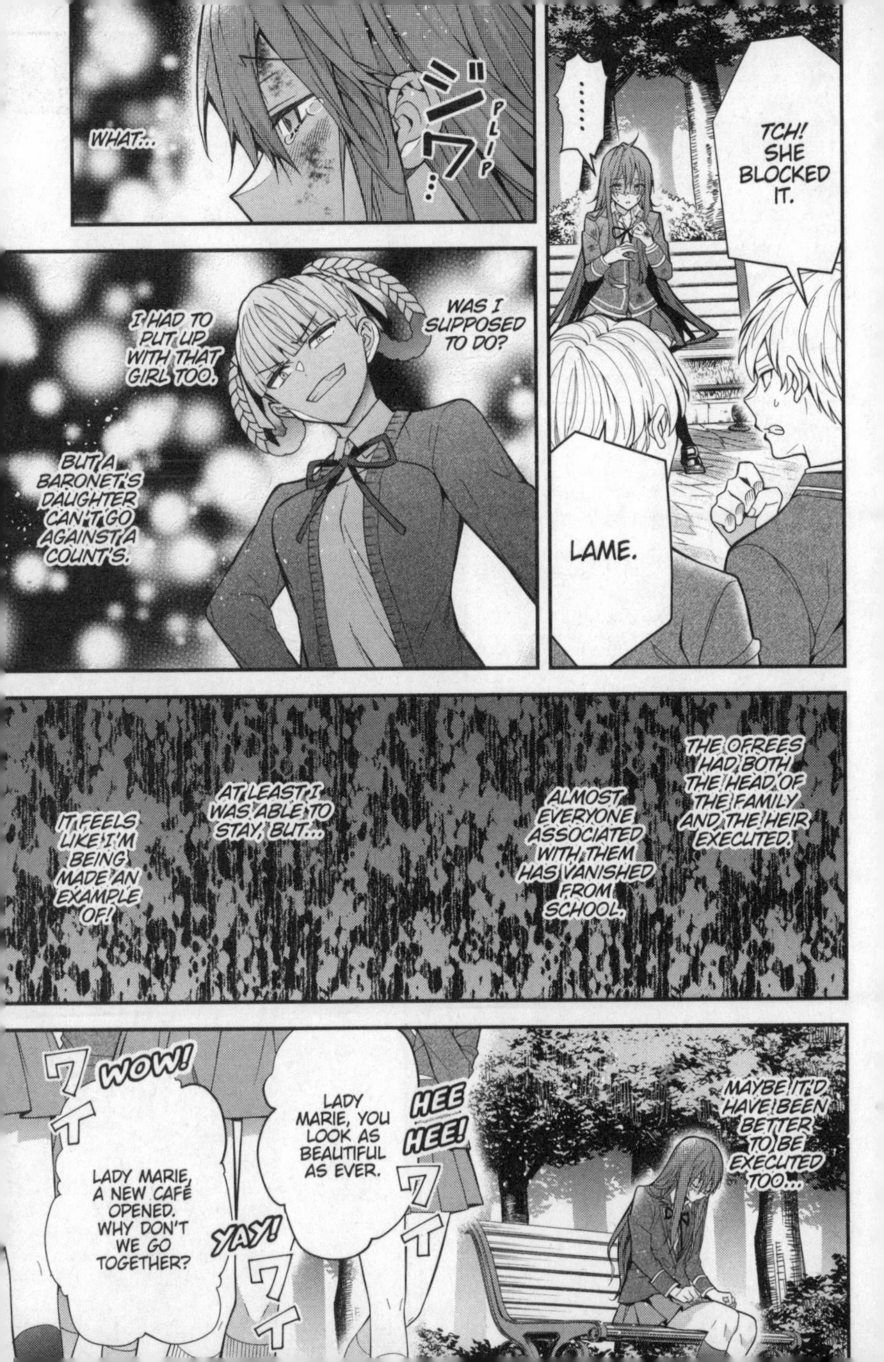
TCH! SHE BLOCKED IT.
......
LAME.
WHAT...
PLIP
WAS I SUPPOSED TO DO?
I HAD TO PUT UP WITH THAT GIRL TOO.
BUT A BARONET'S DAUGHTER CAN'T GO AGAINST A COUNT'S.
THE OFREES HAD BOTH THE HEAD OF THE FAMILY AND THE HEIR EXECUTED.
ALMOST EVERYONE ASSOCIATED WITH THEM HAS VANISHED FROM SCHOOL.
AT LEAST I WAS ABLE TO STAY, BUT...
IT FEELS LIKE I'M BEING MADE AN EXAMPLE OF!
MAYBE IT'D HAVE BEEN BETTER TO BE EXECUTED TOO...
HEE HEE!
LADY MARIE, YOU LOOK AS BEAUTIFUL AS EVER.
WOW!
YAY!
LADY MARIE, A NEW CAFÉ OPENED. WHY DON'T WE GO TOGETHER?

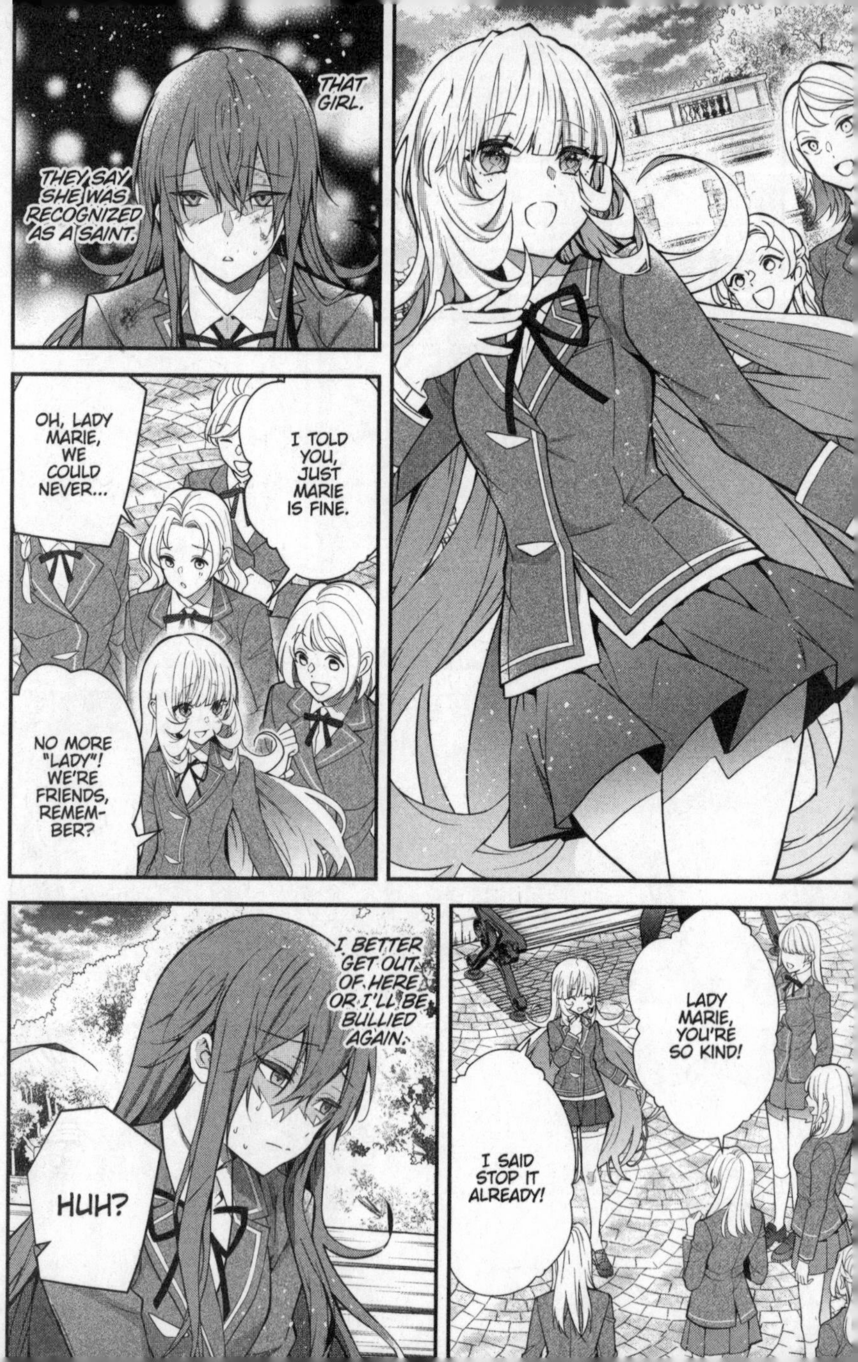

THAT GIRL.
THEY SAY SHE WAS RECOGNIZED AS A SAINT.
I TOLD YOU, JUST MARIE IS FINE.
OH, LADY MARIE, WE COULD NEVER...
NO MORE "LADY"! WE'RE FRIENDS, REMEMBER?
LADY MARIE, YOU'RE SO KIND!
I SAID STOP IT ALREADY!
I BETTER GET OUT OF HERE OR I'LL BE BULLIED AGAIN.
HUH?

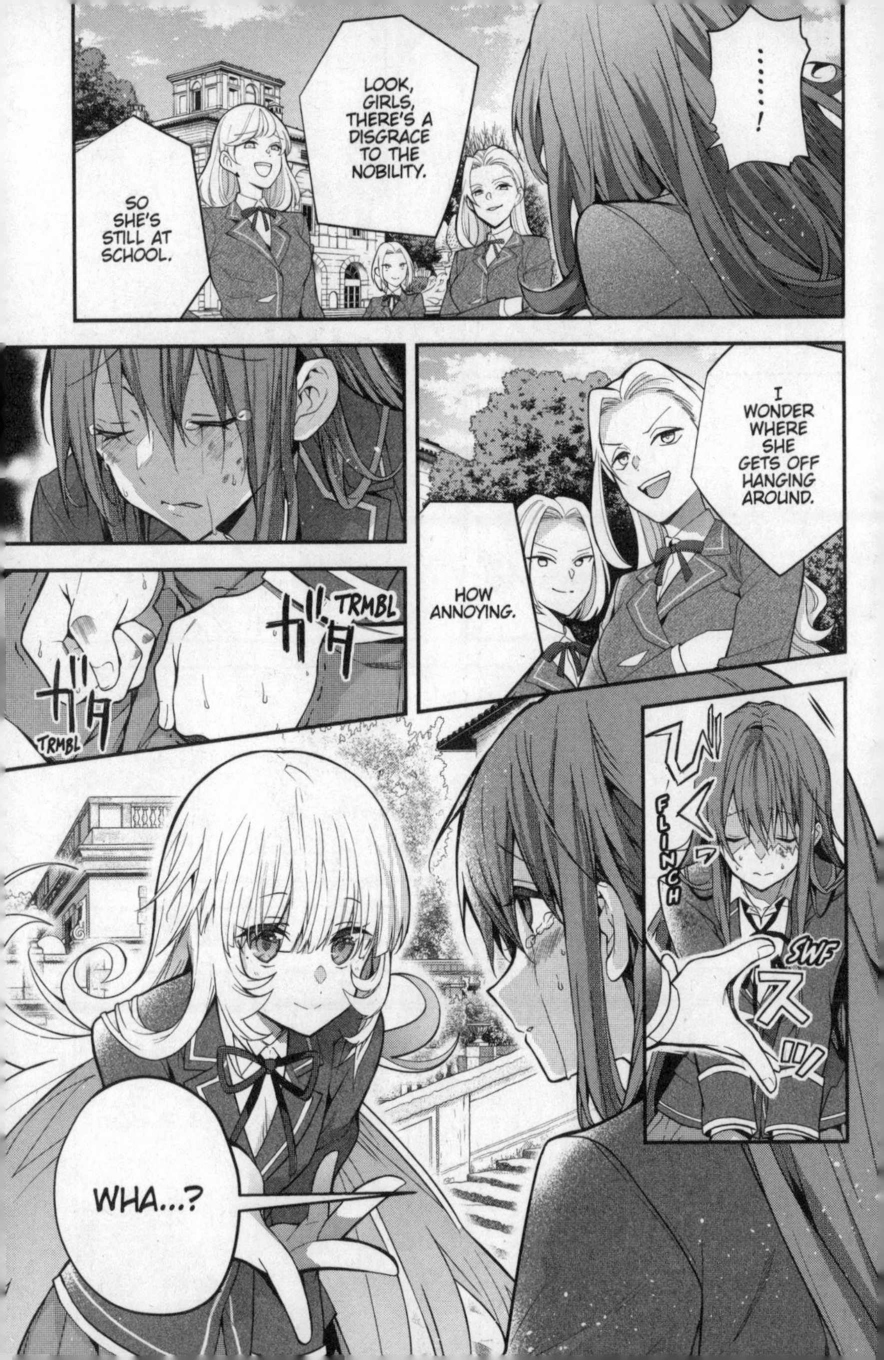
......!
LOOK, GIRLS, THERE'S A DISGRACE TO THE NOBILITY.
SO SHE'S STILL AT SCHOOL.
I WONDER WHERE SHE GETS OFF HANGING AROUND.
HOW ANNOYING.
TRMBL
TRMBL
FLINCH
SWF
WHA...?

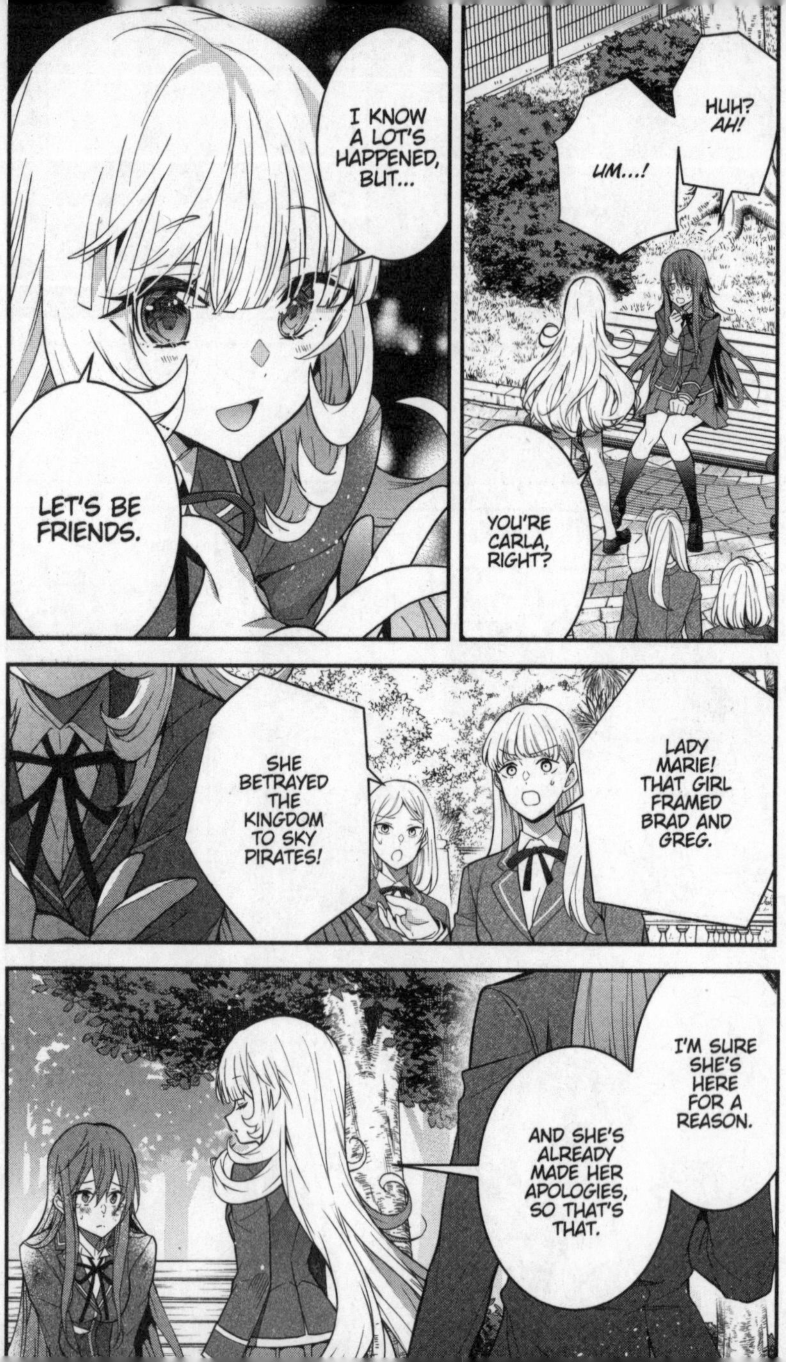
HUH? AH!
UM...!
YOU'RE CARLA, RIGHT?
I KNOW A LOT'S HAPPENED, BUT...
LET'S BE FRIENDS.
LADY MARIE! THAT GIRL FRAMED BRAD AND GREG.
SHE BETRAYED THE KINGDOM TO SKY PIRATES!
I'M SURE SHE'S HERE FOR A REASON.
AND SHE'S ALREADY MADE HER APOLOGIES, SO THAT'S THAT.

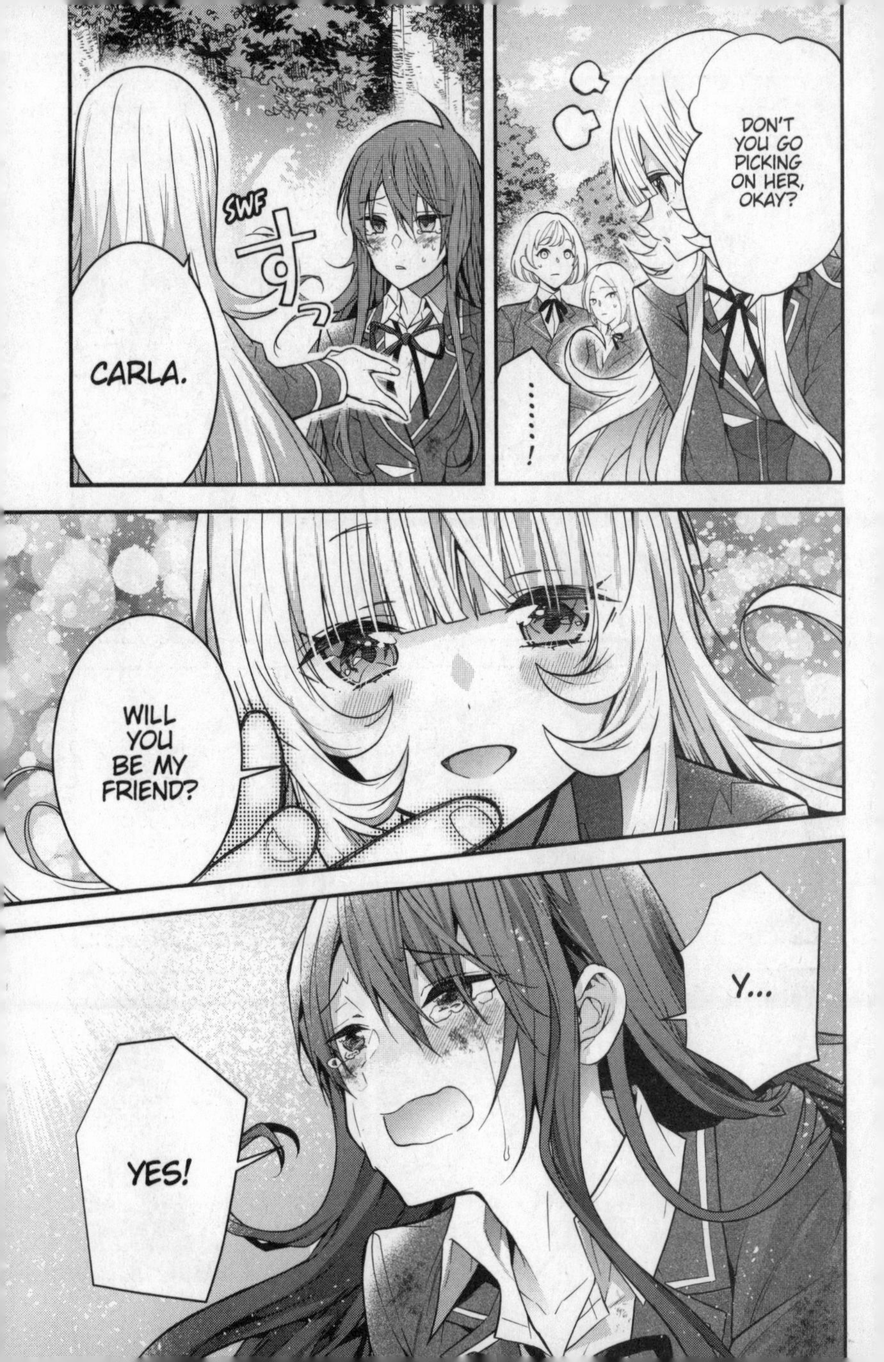
DON'T YOU GO PICKING ON HER, OKAY?
......!
SWF
すっ
CARLA.
WILL YOU BE MY FRIEND?
Y...
YES!

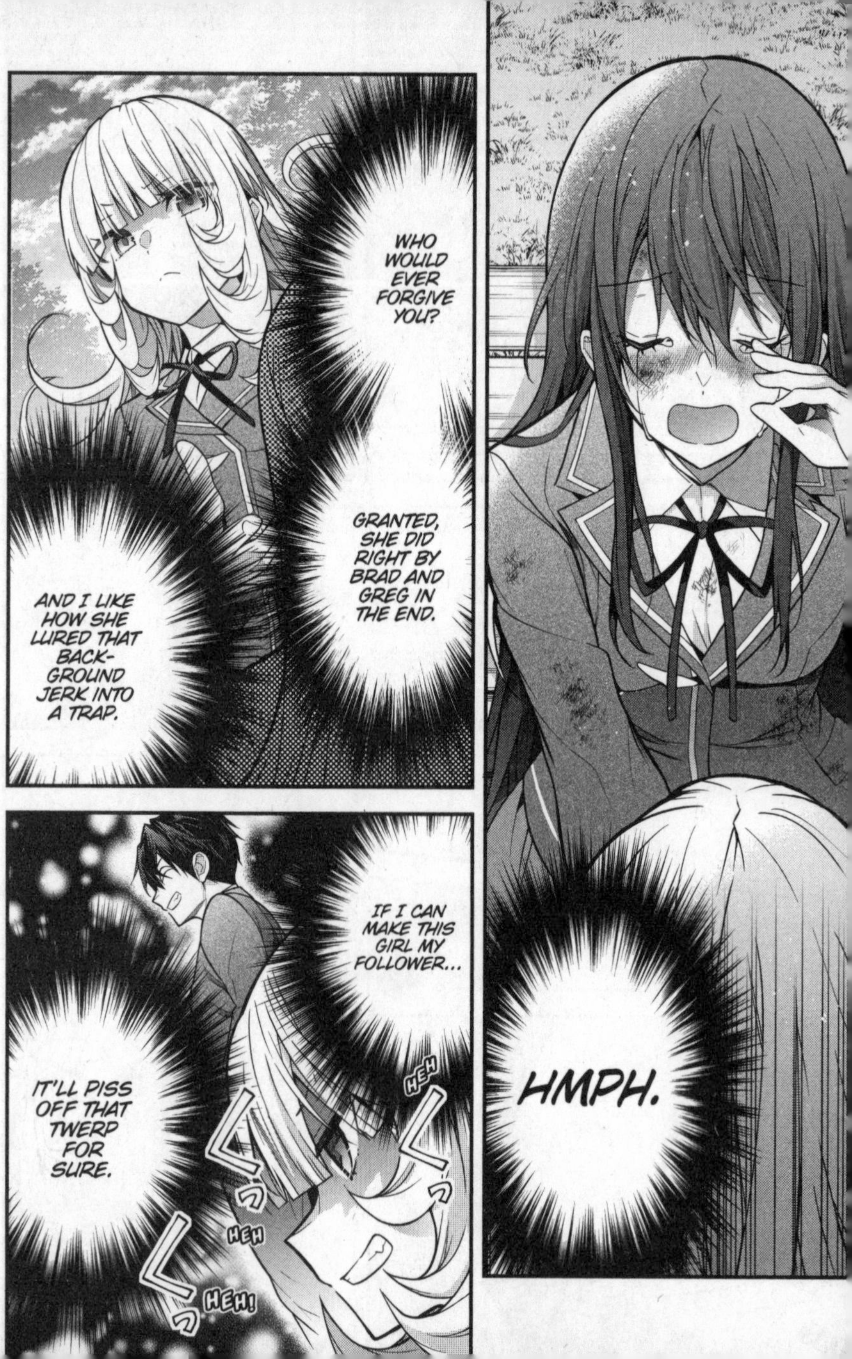
HMPH.
WHO WOULD EVER FORGIVE YOU?
GRANTED, SHE DID RIGHT BY BRAD AND GREG IN THE END.
AND I LIKE HOW SHE LURED THAT BACK-GROUND JERK INTO A TRAP.
IF I CAN MAKE THIS GIRL MY FOLLOWER...
HEH
IT'LL PISS OFF THAT TWERP FOR SURE.
HEH
HEH!

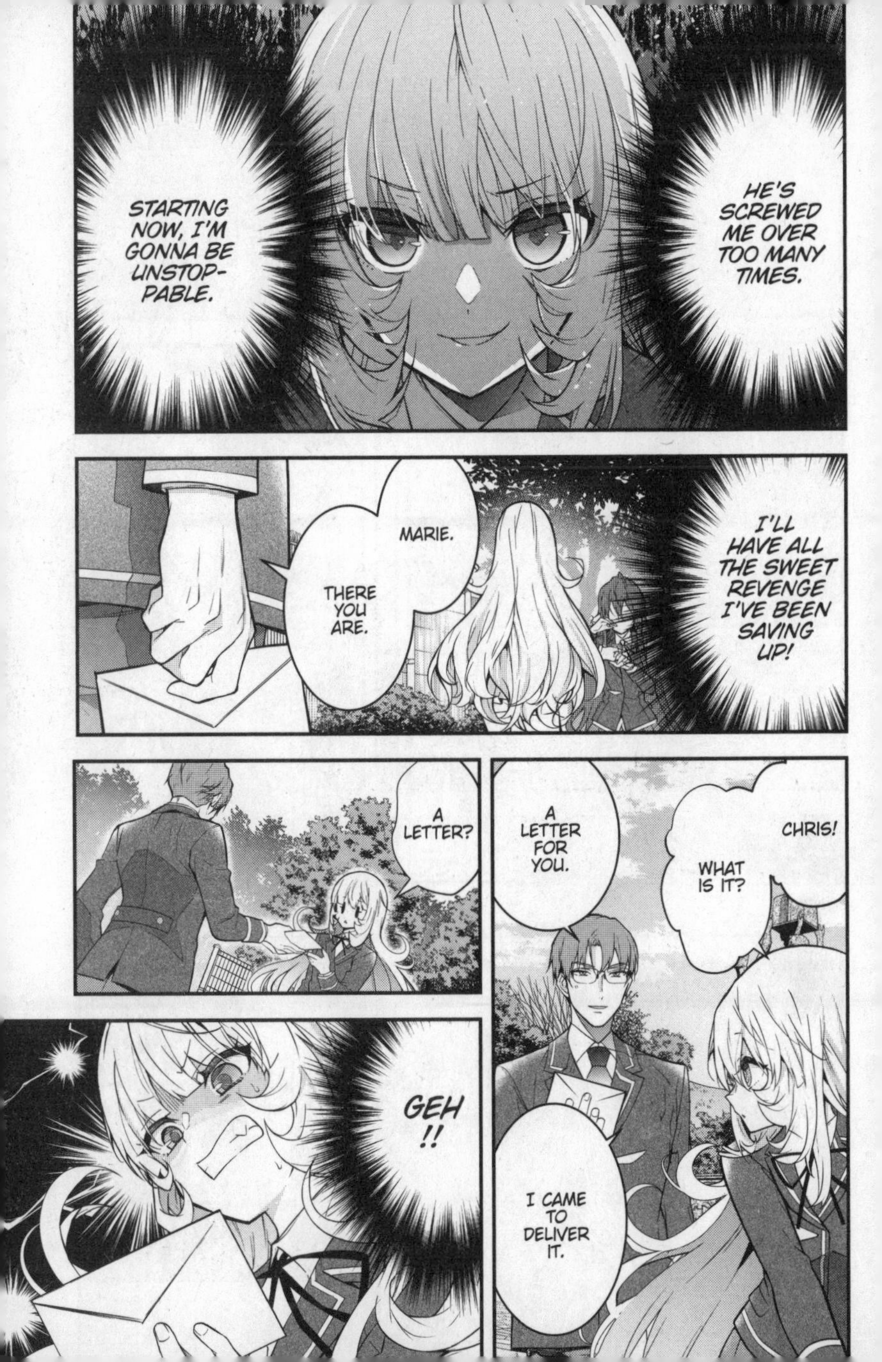
HE'S SCREWED ME OVER TOO MANY TIMES.
STARTING NOW, I'M GONNA BE UNSTOP-PABLE.
I'LL HAVE ALL THE SWEET REVENGE I'VE BEEN SAVING UP!
MARIE.
THERE YOU ARE.
CHRIS!
WHAT IS IT?
A LETTER FOR YOU.
I CAME TO DELIVER IT.
A LETTER?
GEH!!

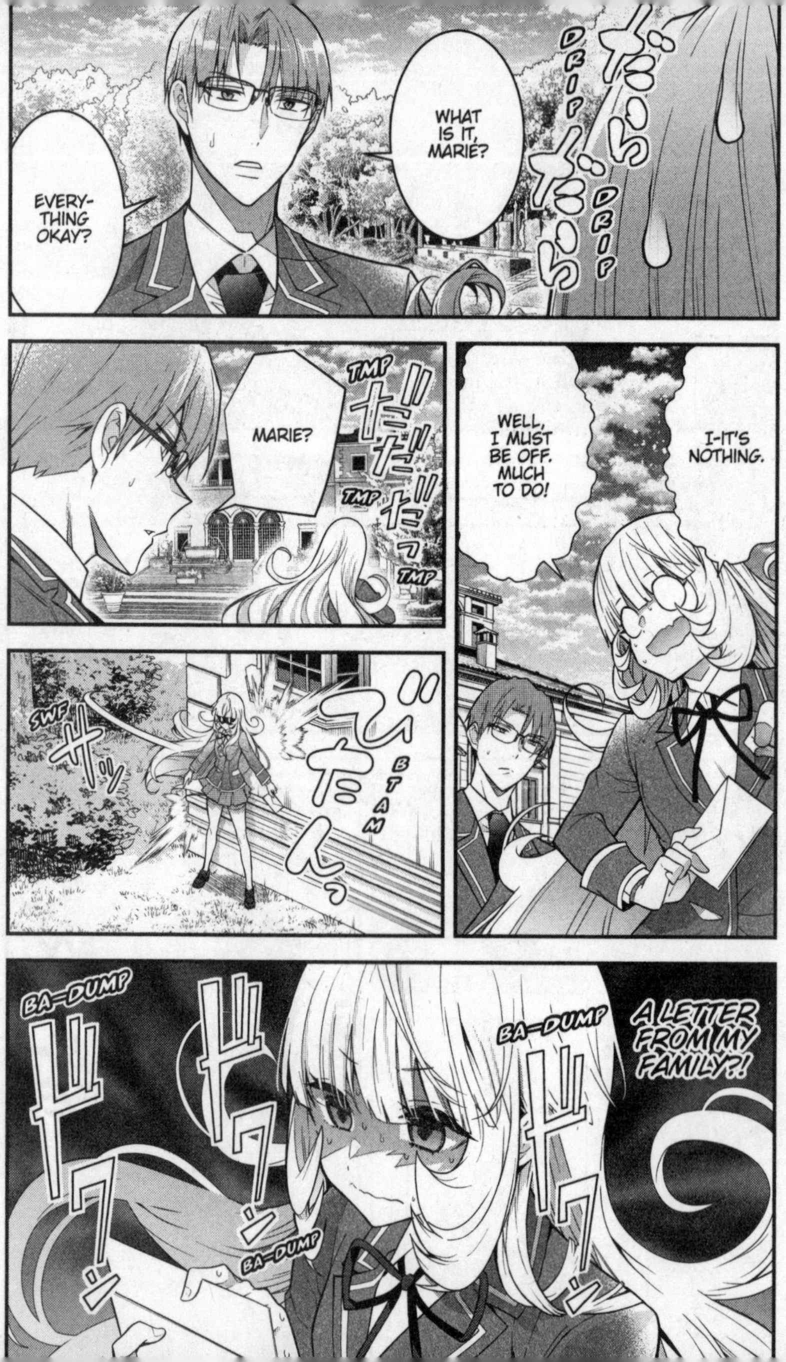
DRIP
DRIP
WHAT IS IT, MARIE?
EVERY-THING OKAY?
I-IT'S NOTHING.
WELL, I MUST BE OFF. MUCH TO DO!
TMP
TMP
TMP
MARIE?
BTAM
SWF
A LETTER FROM MY FAMILY?!
BA-DUMP
BA-DUMP
BA-DUMP

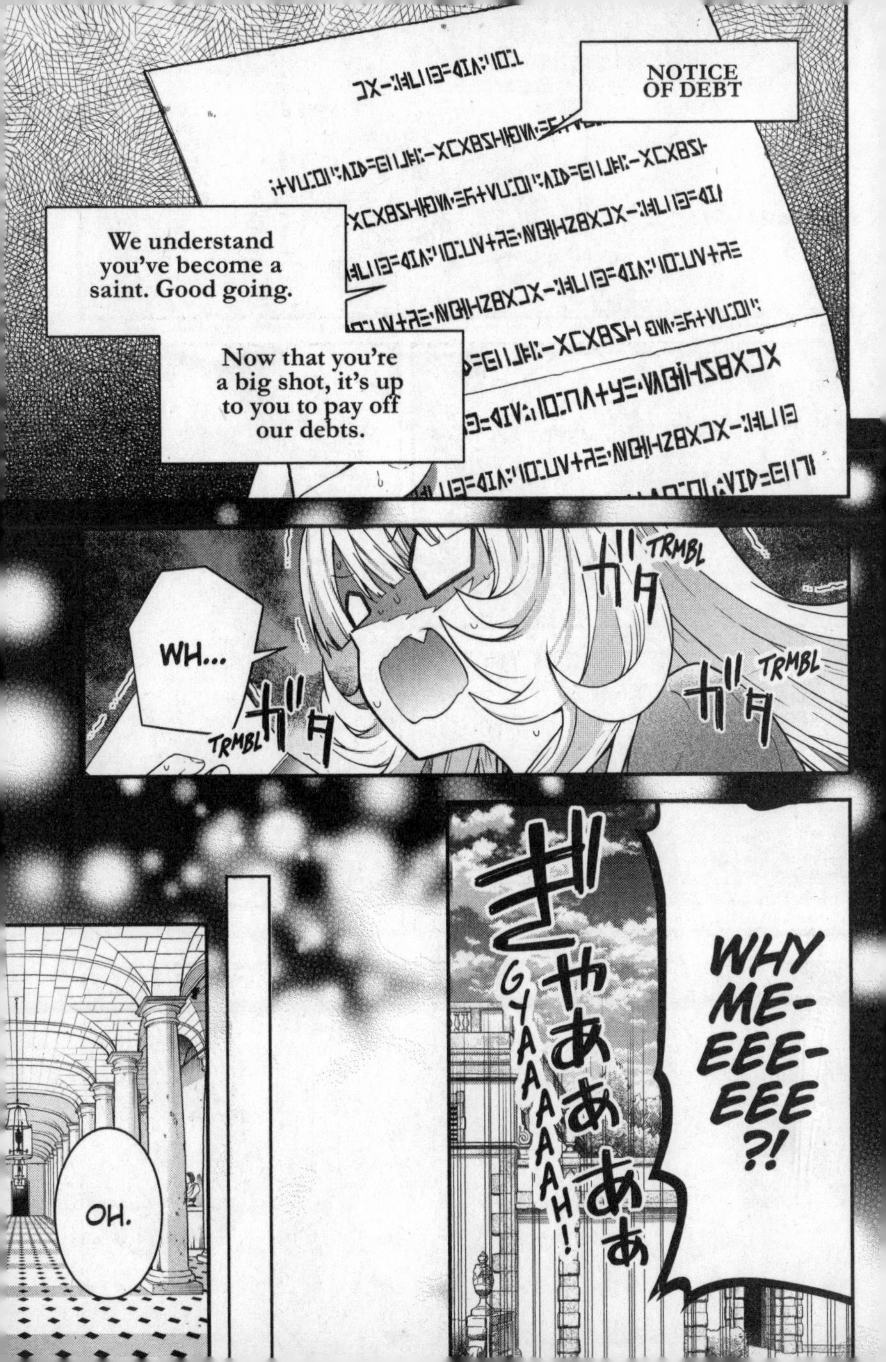
NOTICE OF DEBT
We understand you've become a saint. Good going.
Now that you're a big shot, it's up to you to pay off our debts.
ガタ TRMBL
ガタ TRMBL
WH...
ガタ TRMBL
WHY ME-EEE-EEE?!
ぎゃあああああ GYAAAAAH!
OH.

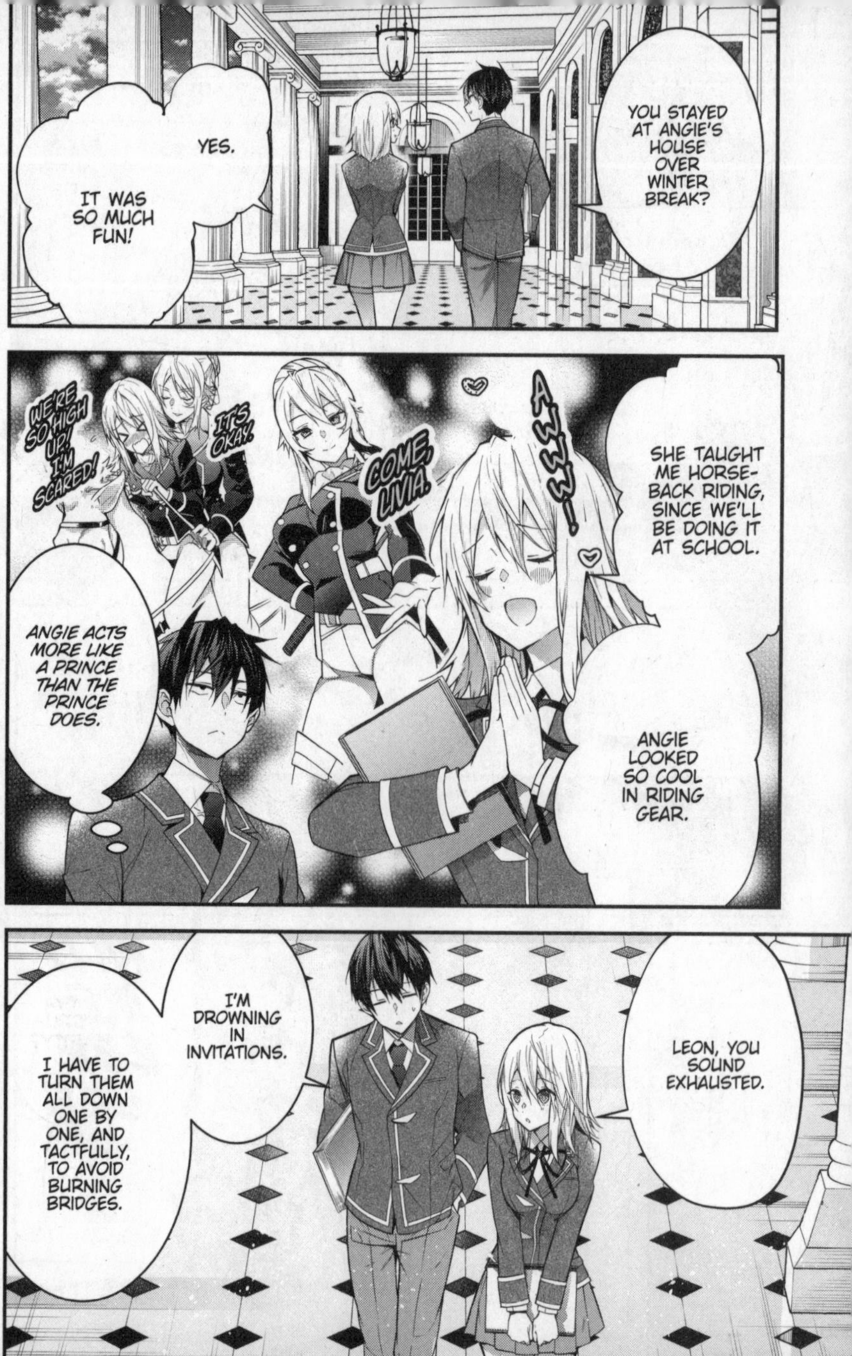
YOU STAYED AT ANGIE'S HOUSE OVER WINTER BREAK?
YES.
IT WAS SO MUCH FUN!
AWWW!
SHE TAUGHT ME HORSE-BACK RIDING, SINCE WE'LL BE DOING IT AT SCHOOL.
COME, LIVIA.
IT'S OKAY.
WE'RE SO HIGH UP! I'M SCARED!
ANGIE LOOKED SO COOL IN RIDING GEAR.
ANGIE ACTS MORE LIKE A PRINCE THAN THE PRINCE DOES.
LEON, YOU SOUND EXHAUSTED.
I'M DROWNING IN INVITATIONS.
I HAVE TO TURN THEM ALL DOWN ONE BY ONE, AND TACTFULLY, TO AVOID BURNING BRIDGES.

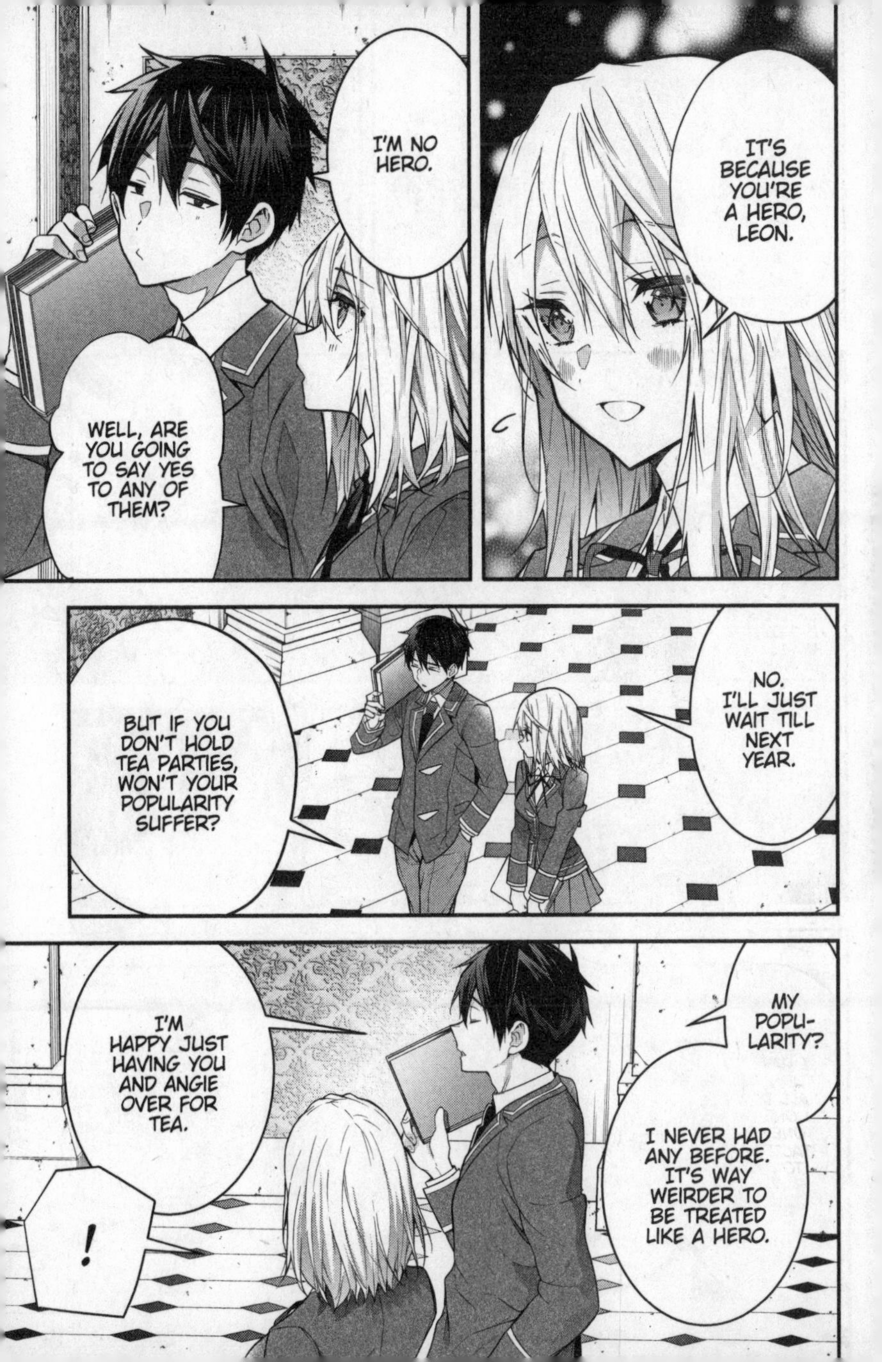
IT'S BECAUSE YOU'RE A HERO, LEON.
I'M NO HERO.
WELL, ARE YOU GOING TO SAY YES TO ANY OF THEM?
NO. I'LL JUST WAIT TILL NEXT YEAR.
BUT IF YOU DON'T HOLD TEA PARTIES, WON'T YOUR POPULARITY SUFFER?
MY POPULARITY?
I NEVER HAD ANY BEFORE. IT'S WAY WEIRDER TO BE TREATED LIKE A HERO.
I'M HAPPY JUST HAVING YOU AND ANGIE OVER FOR TEA.
!

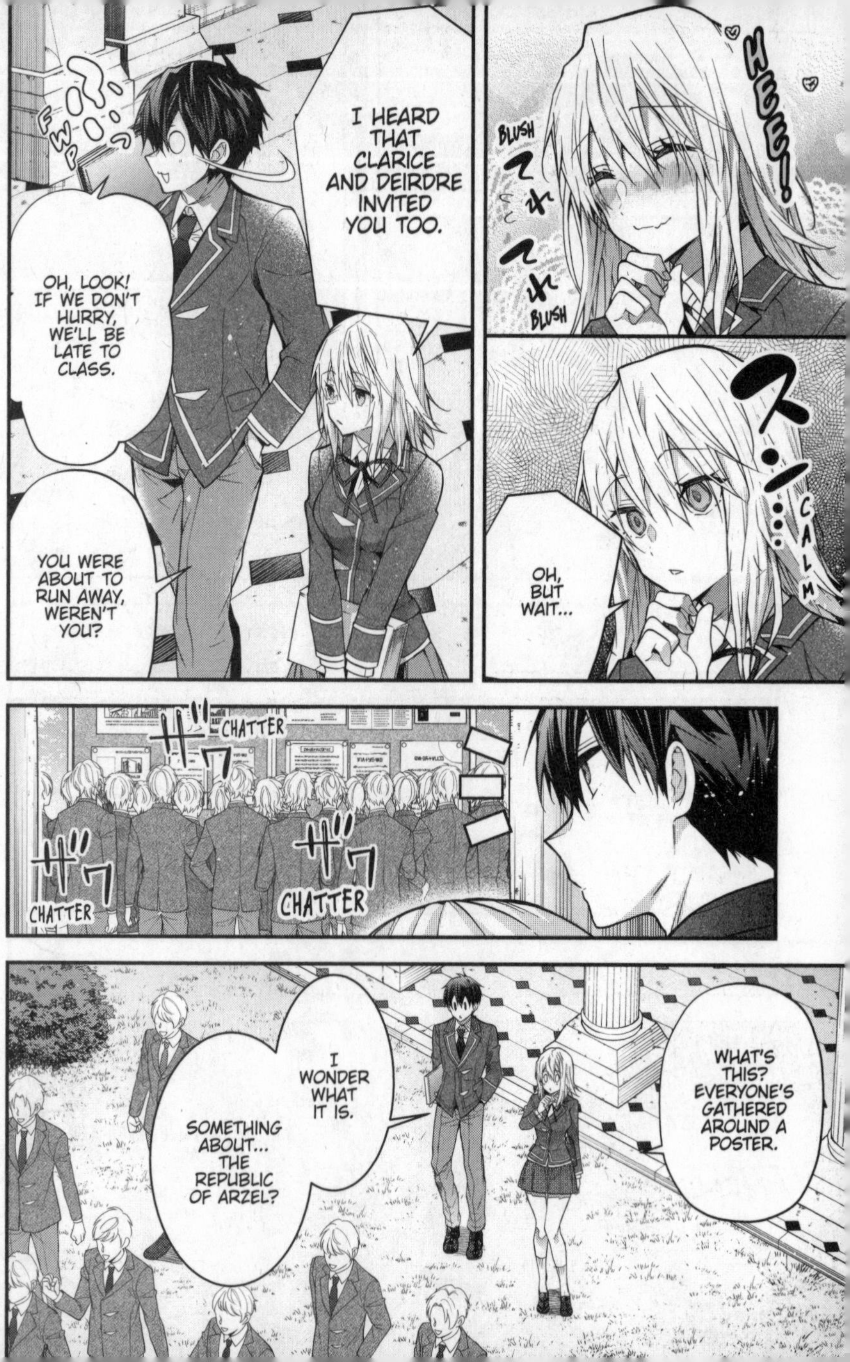

HEEE!
BLUSH
BLUSH
CALM
OH, BUT WAIT...
I HEARD THAT CLARICE AND DEIRDRE INVITED YOU TOO.
FWP
OH, LOOK! IF WE DON'T HURRY, WE'LL BE LATE TO CLASS.
YOU WERE ABOUT TO RUN AWAY, WEREN'T YOU?
CHATTER
CHATTER
CHATTER
WHAT'S THIS? EVERYONE'S GATHERED AROUND A POSTER.
I WONDER WHAT IT IS.
SOMETHING ABOUT... THE REPUBLIC OF ARZEL?

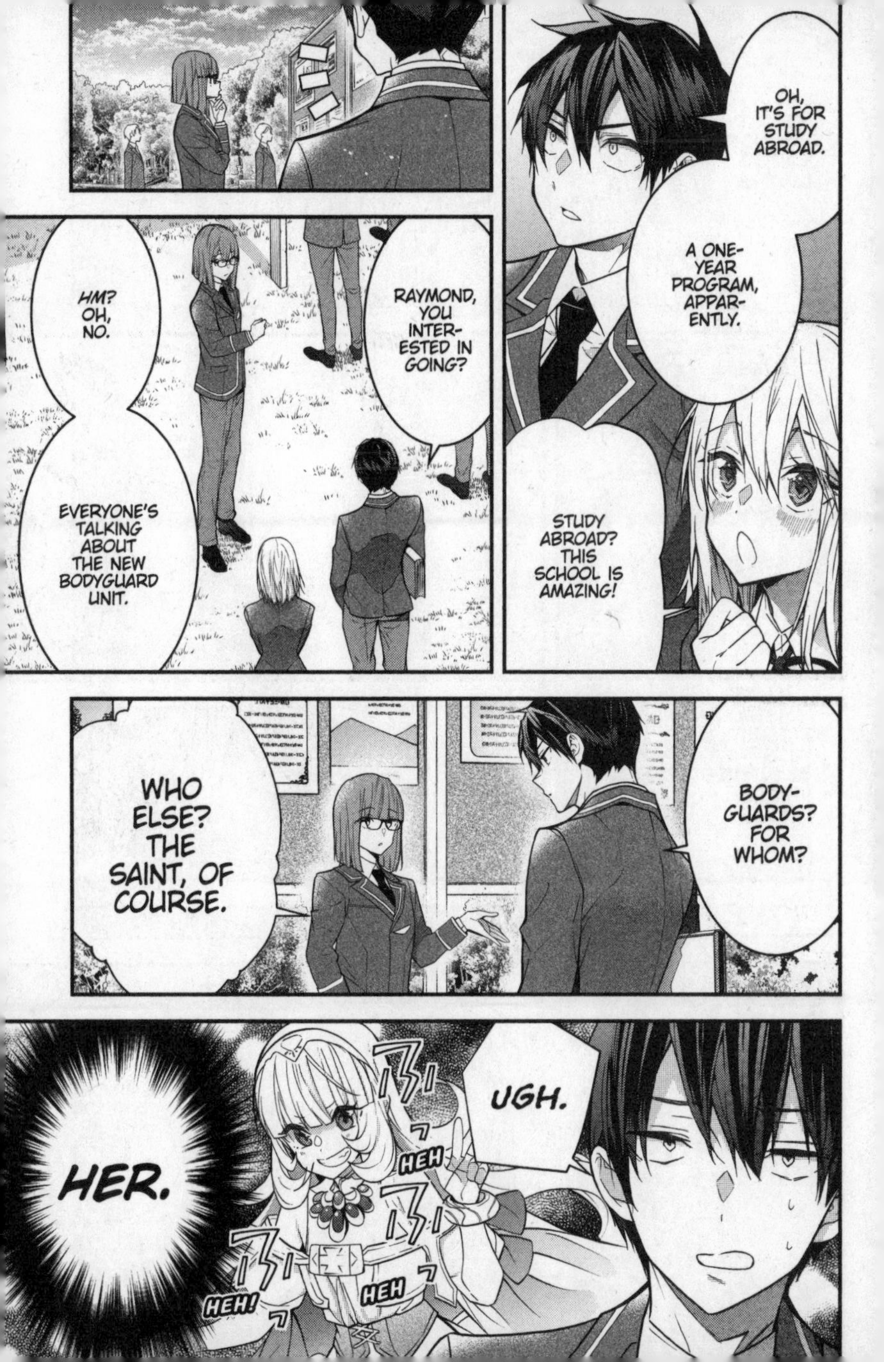
OH, IT'S FOR STUDY ABROAD.
A ONE-YEAR PROGRAM, APPARENTLY.
STUDY ABROAD? THIS SCHOOL IS AMAZING!
RAYMOND, YOU INTERESTED IN GOING?
HM? OH, NO.
EVERYONE'S TALKING ABOUT THE NEW BODYGUARD UNIT.
BODY-GUARDS? FOR WHOM?
WHO ELSE? THE SAINT, OF COURSE.
UGH.
HEH
HEH
HEH!
HER.

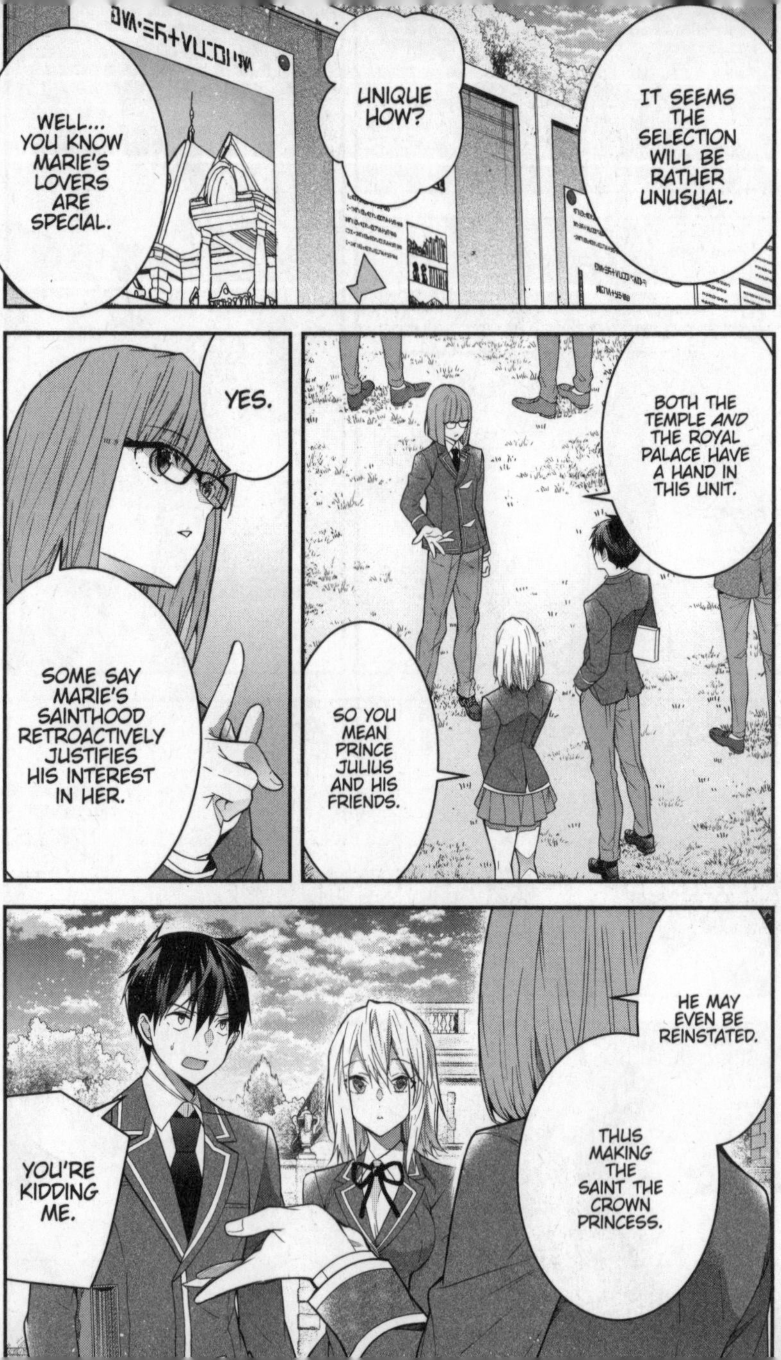
IT SEEMS THE SELECTION WILL BE RATHER UNUSUAL.
UNIQUE HOW?
WELL... YOU KNOW MARIE'S LOVERS ARE SPECIAL.
BOTH THE TEMPLE *AND* THE ROYAL PALACE HAVE A HAND IN THIS UNIT.
SO YOU MEAN PRINCE JULIUS AND HIS FRIENDS.
YES.
SOME SAY MARIE'S SAINTHOOD RETROACTIVELY JUSTIFIES HIS INTEREST IN HER.
HE MAY EVEN BE REINSTATED.
THUS MAKING THE SAINT THE CROWN PRINCESS.
YOU'RE KIDDING ME.

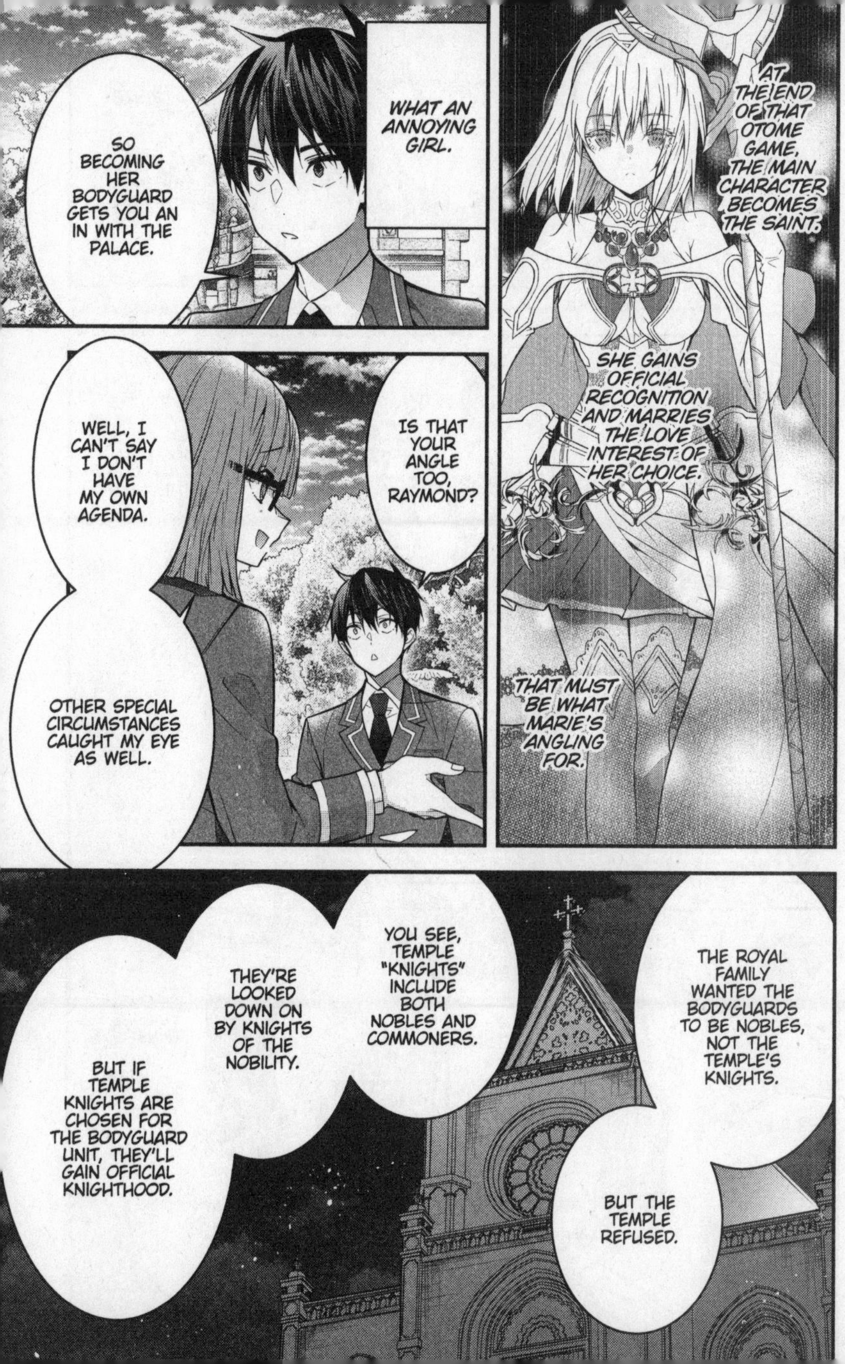
AT THE END OF THAT OTOME GAME, THE MAIN CHARACTER BECOMES THE SAINT.
SHE GAINS OFFICIAL RECOGNITION AND MARRIES THE LOVE INTEREST OF HER CHOICE.
THAT MUST BE WHAT MARIE'S ANGLING FOR.
WHAT AN ANNOYING GIRL.
SO BECOMING HER BODYGUARD GETS YOU AN IN WITH THE PALACE.
IS THAT YOUR ANGLE TOO, RAYMOND?
WELL, I CAN'T SAY I DON'T HAVE MY OWN AGENDA.
OTHER SPECIAL CIRCUMSTANCES CAUGHT MY EYE AS WELL.
THE ROYAL FAMILY WANTED THE BODYGUARDS TO BE NOBLES, NOT THE TEMPLE'S KNIGHTS.
BUT THE TEMPLE REFUSED.
YOU SEE, TEMPLE "KNIGHTS" INCLUDE BOTH NOBLES AND COMMONERS.
THEY'RE LOOKED DOWN ON BY KNIGHTS OF THE NOBILITY.
BUT IF TEMPLE KNIGHTS ARE CHOSEN FOR THE BODYGUARD UNIT, THEY'LL GAIN OFFICIAL KNIGHTHOOD.

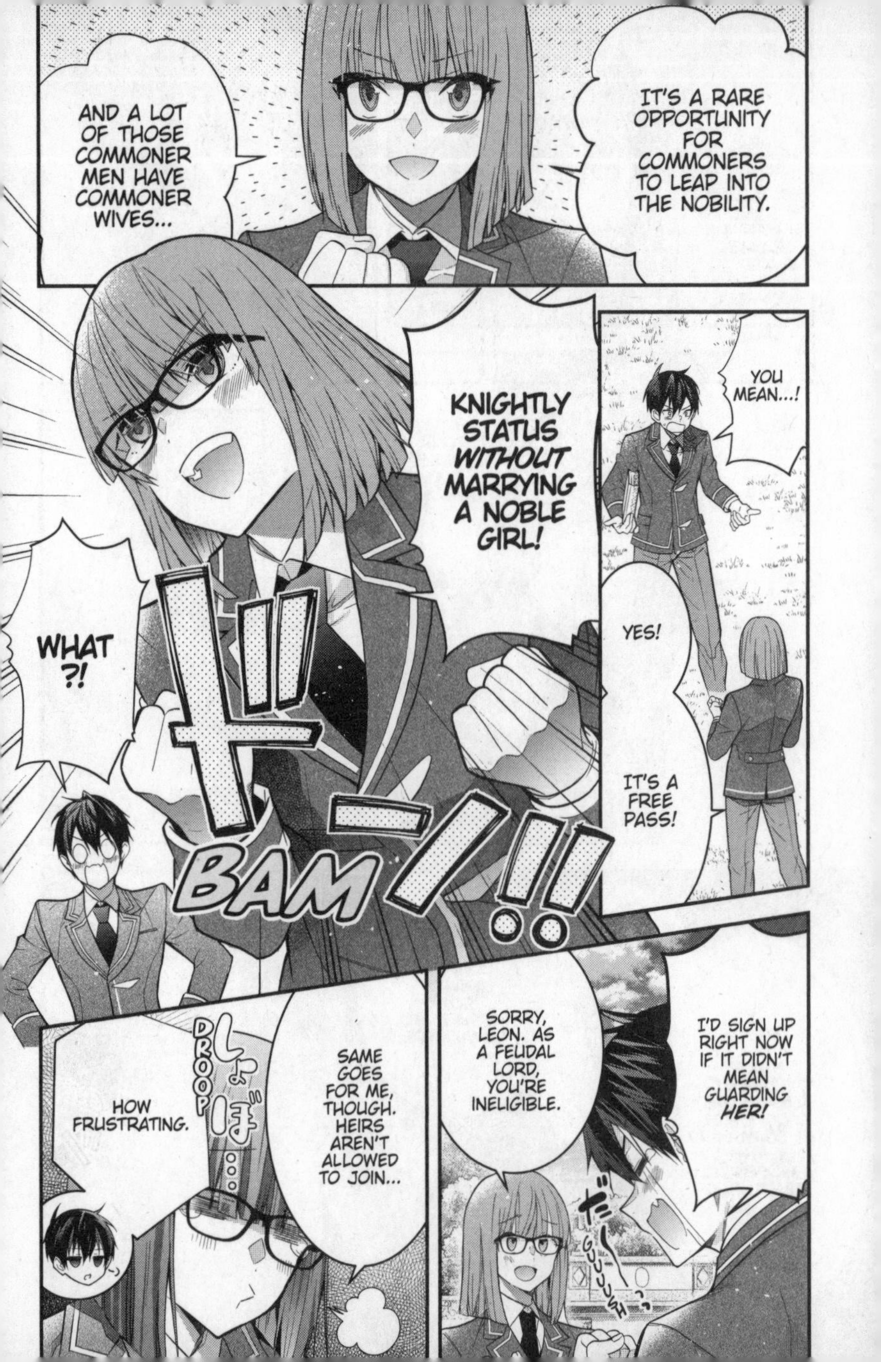
IT'S A RARE OPPORTUNITY FOR COMMONERS TO LEAP INTO THE NOBILITY.
AND A LOT OF THOSE COMMONER MEN HAVE COMMONER WIVES...
YOU MEAN...!
YES!
IT'S A FREE PASS!
KNIGHTLY STATUS *WITHOUT* MARRYING A NOBLE GIRL!
BAM!!!
WHAT?!
I'D SIGN UP RIGHT NOW IF IT DIDN'T MEAN GUARDING *HER!*
GUUUUSH
SORRY, LEON. AS A FEUDAL LORD, YOU'RE INELIGIBLE.
SAME GOES FOR ME, THOUGH. HEIRS AREN'T ALLOWED TO JOIN...
DROOP
HOW FRUSTRATING.

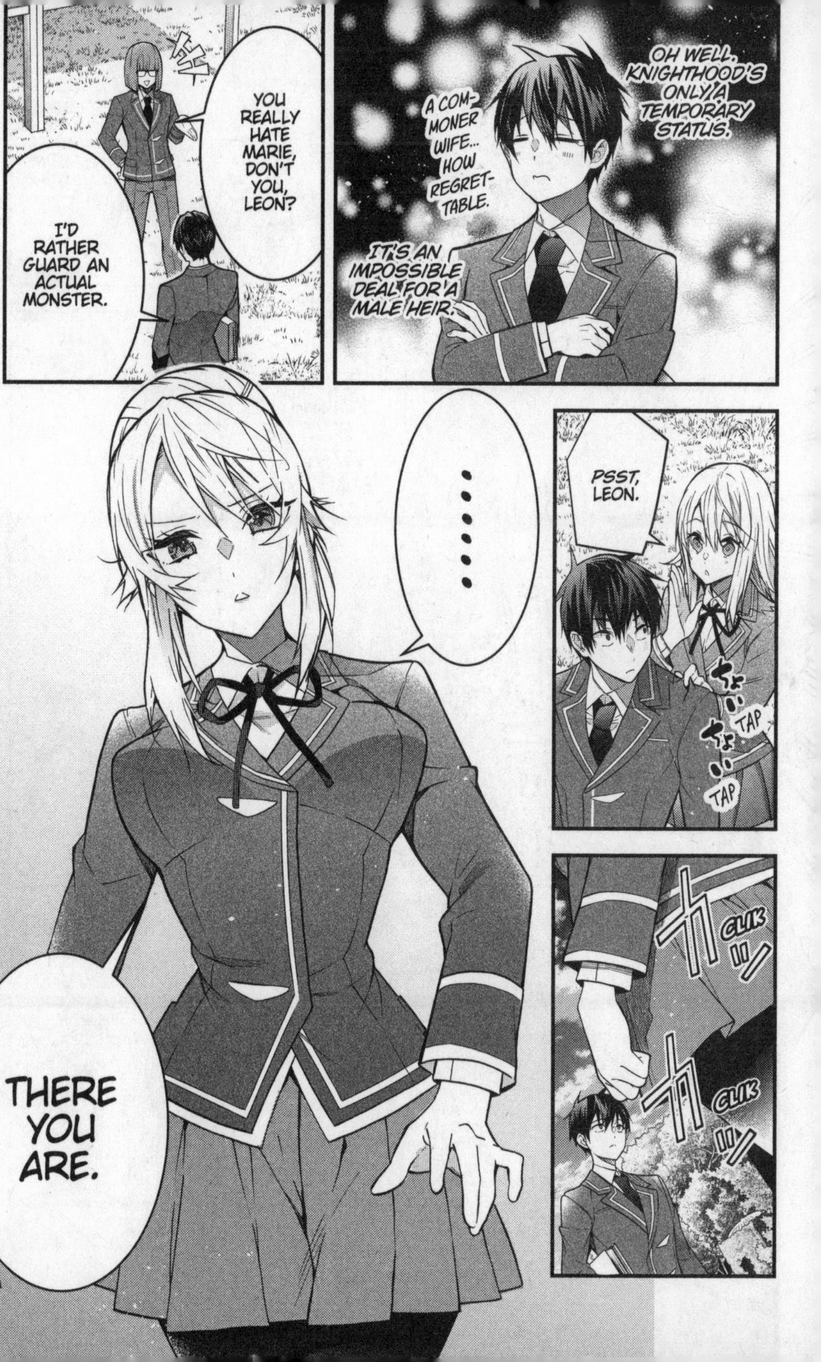
OH WELL. KNIGHTHOOD'S ONLY A TEMPORARY STATUS.
A COM-MONER WIFE... HOW REGRET-TABLE.
IT'S AN IMPOSSIBLE DEAL FOR A MALE HEIR.
YOU REALLY HATE MARIE, DON'T YOU, LEON?
I'D RATHER GUARD AN ACTUAL MONSTER.
PSST, LEON.
ちょい
TAP
ちょい
TAP
CLIK
CLIK
......
THERE YOU ARE.

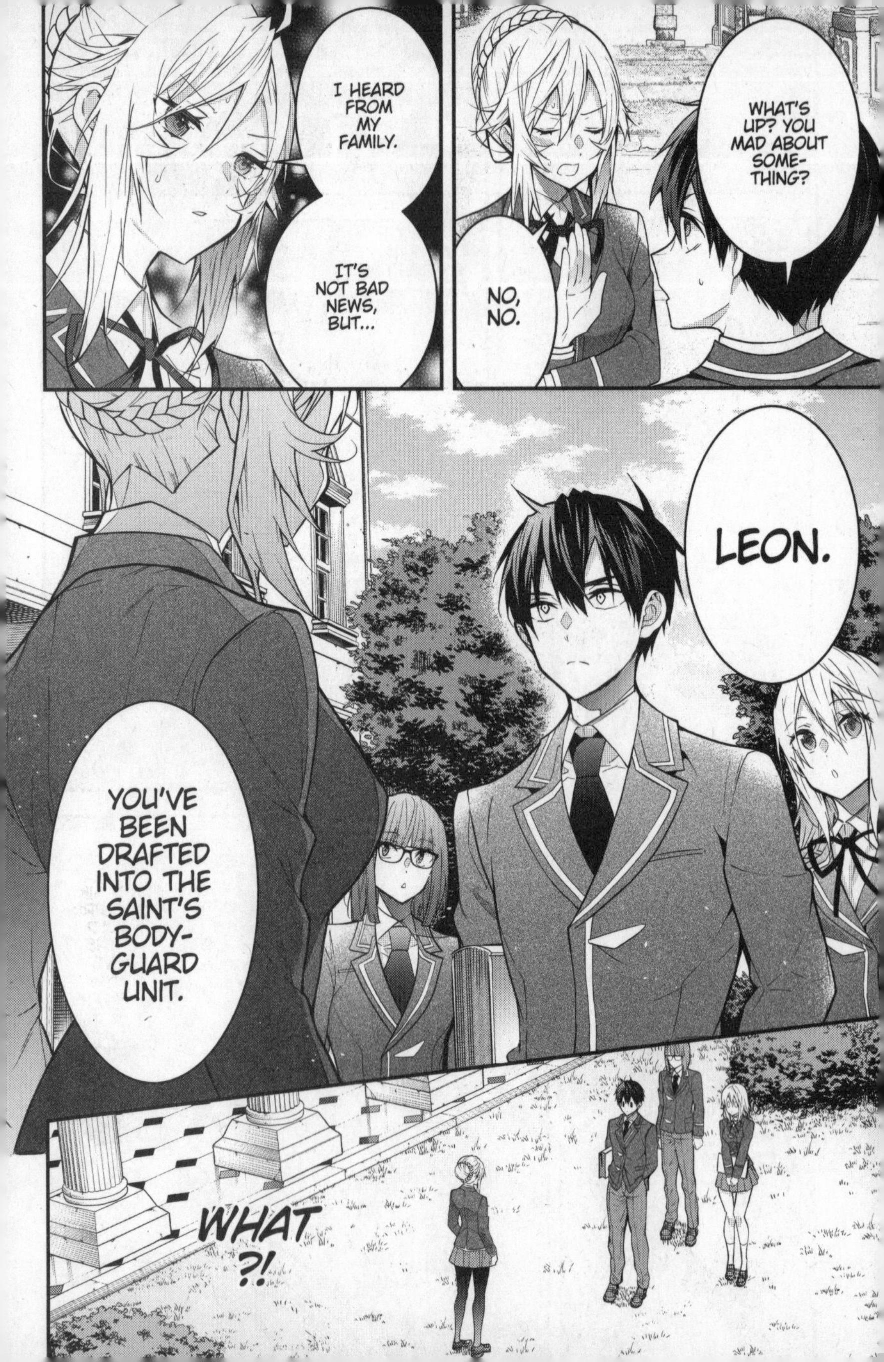
WHAT'S UP? YOU MAD ABOUT SOME-THING?
NO, NO.
I HEARD FROM MY FAMILY.
IT'S NOT BAD NEWS, BUT...
LEON.
YOU'VE BEEN DRAFTED INTO THE SAINT'S BODY-GUARD UNIT.
WHAT?!

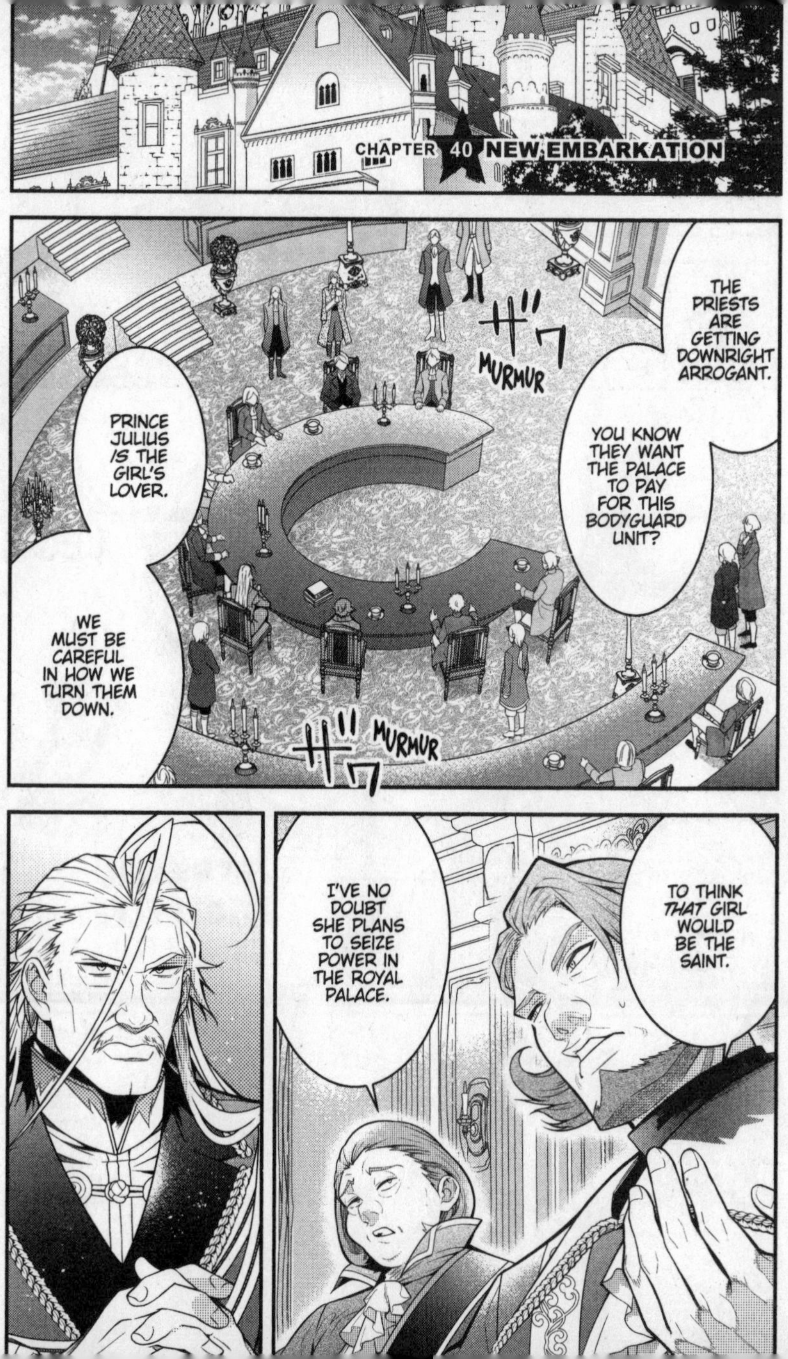
CHAPTER 40 NEW EMBARKATION
THE PRIESTS ARE GETTING DOWNRIGHT ARROGANT.
YOU KNOW THEY WANT THE PALACE TO PAY FOR THIS BODYGUARD UNIT?
ザワ MURMUR
PRINCE JULIUS IS THE GIRL'S LOVER.
WE MUST BE CAREFUL IN HOW WE TURN THEM DOWN.
ザワ MURMUR
TO THINK *THAT* GIRL WOULD BE THE SAINT.
I'VE NO DOUBT SHE PLANS TO SEIZE POWER IN THE ROYAL PALACE.

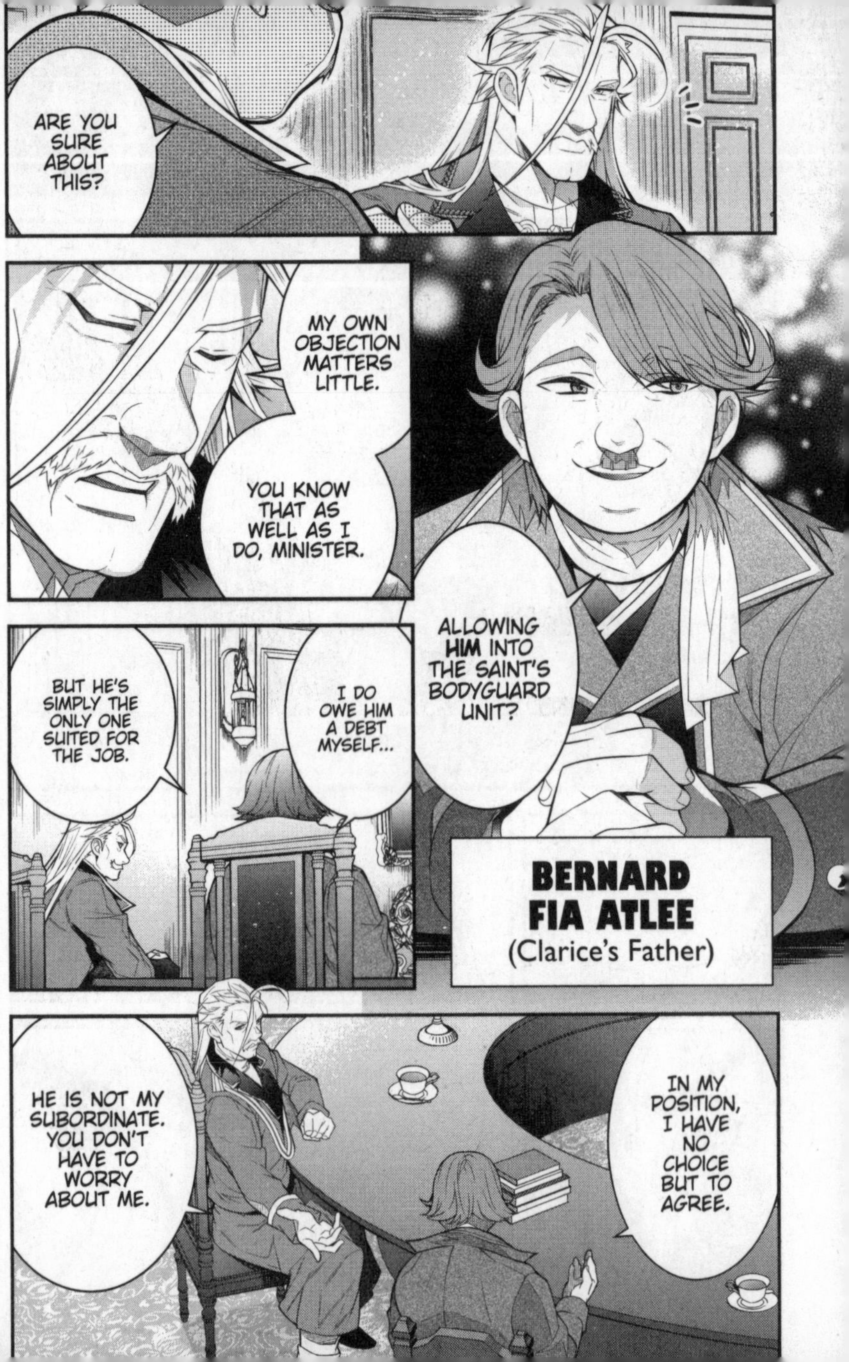
ARE YOU SURE ABOUT THIS?
ALLOWING HIM INTO THE SAINT'S BODYGUARD UNIT?
BERNARD FIA ATLEE
(Clarice's Father)
MY OWN OBJECTION MATTERS LITTLE.
YOU KNOW THAT AS WELL AS I DO, MINISTER.
I DO OWE HIM A DEBT MYSELF...
BUT HE'S SIMPLY THE ONLY ONE SUITED FOR THE JOB.
IN MY POSITION, I HAVE NO CHOICE BUT TO AGREE.
HE IS NOT MY SUBORDINATE. YOU DON'T HAVE TO WORRY ABOUT ME.

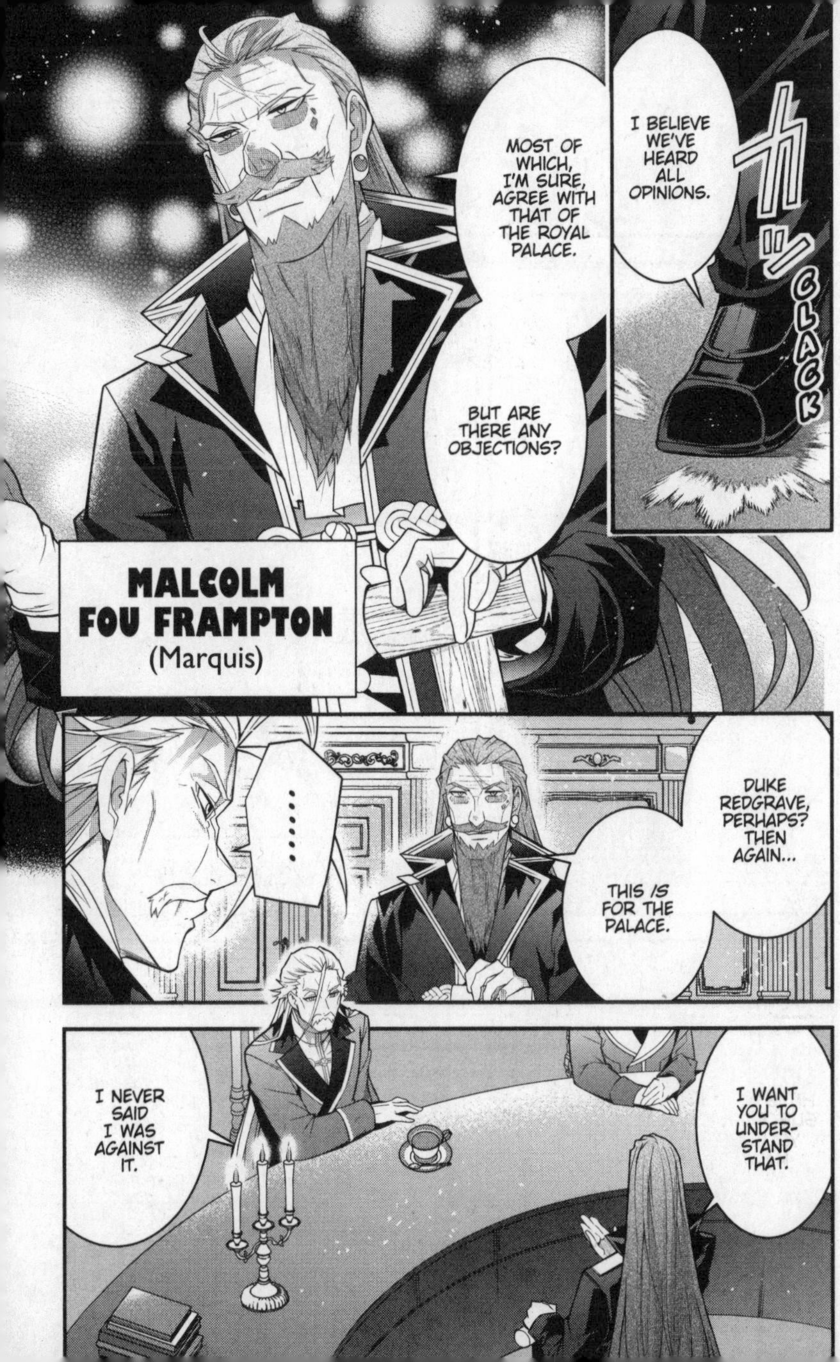
I BELIEVE WE'VE HEARD ALL OPINIONS.
CLACK
MOST OF WHICH, I'M SURE, AGREE WITH THAT OF THE ROYAL PALACE.
BUT ARE THERE ANY OBJECTIONS?
MALCOLM FOU FRAMPTON (Marquis)
DUKE REDGRAVE, PERHAPS? THEN AGAIN...
THIS *IS* FOR THE PALACE.
......
I WANT YOU TO UNDER-STAND THAT.
I NEVER SAID I WAS AGAINST IT.

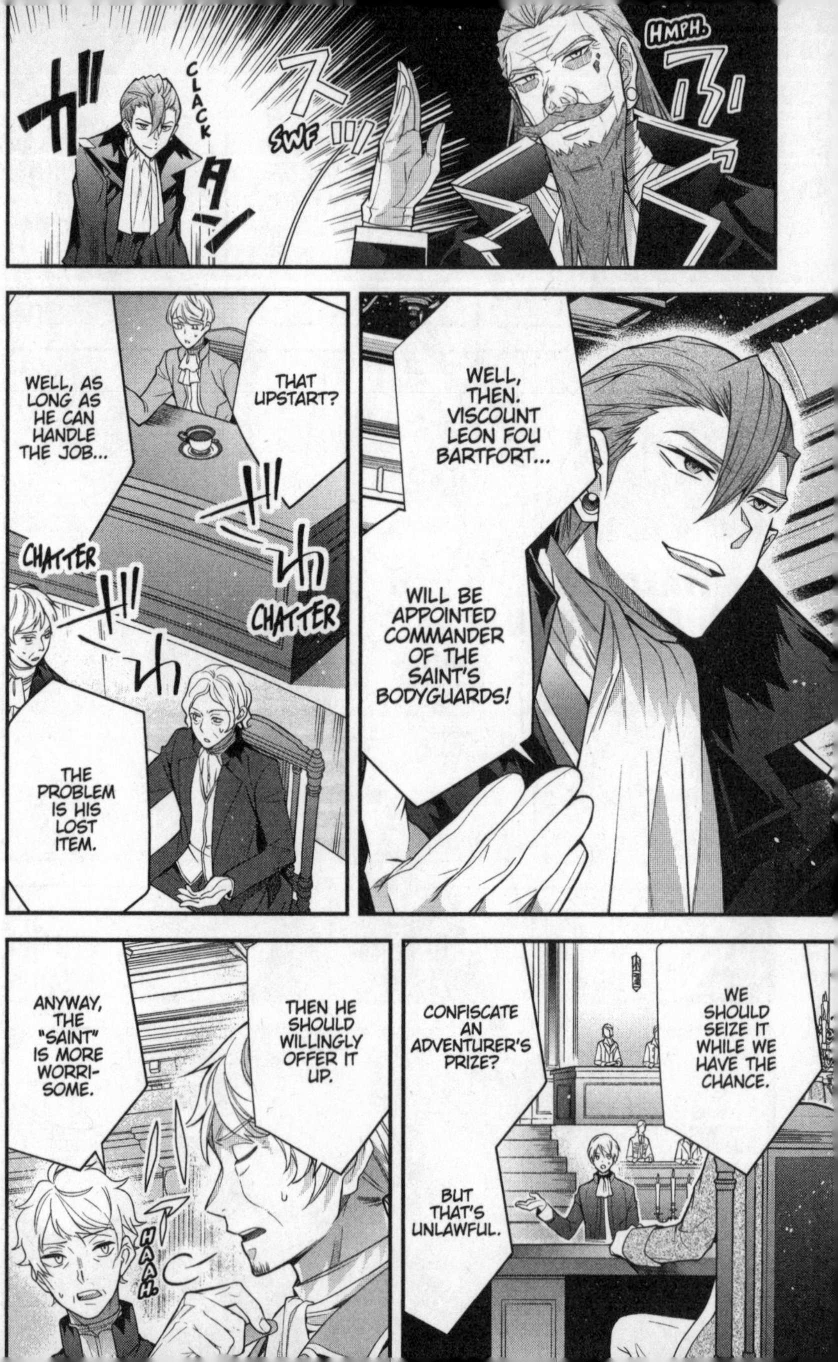
HMPH.
SWF
CLACK
WELL, THEN. VISCOUNT LEON FOU BARTFORT...
WILL BE APPOINTED COMMANDER OF THE SAINT'S BODYGUARDS!
THAT UPSTART?
WELL, AS LONG AS HE CAN HANDLE THE JOB...
CHATTER
CHATTER
THE PROBLEM IS HIS LOST ITEM.
WE SHOULD SEIZE IT WHILE WE HAVE THE CHANCE.
CONFISCATE AN ADVENTURER'S PRIZE?
BUT THAT'S UNLAWFUL.
THEN HE SHOULD WILLINGLY OFFER IT UP.
ANYWAY, THE "SAINT" IS MORE WORRI-SOME.
HAAAH.

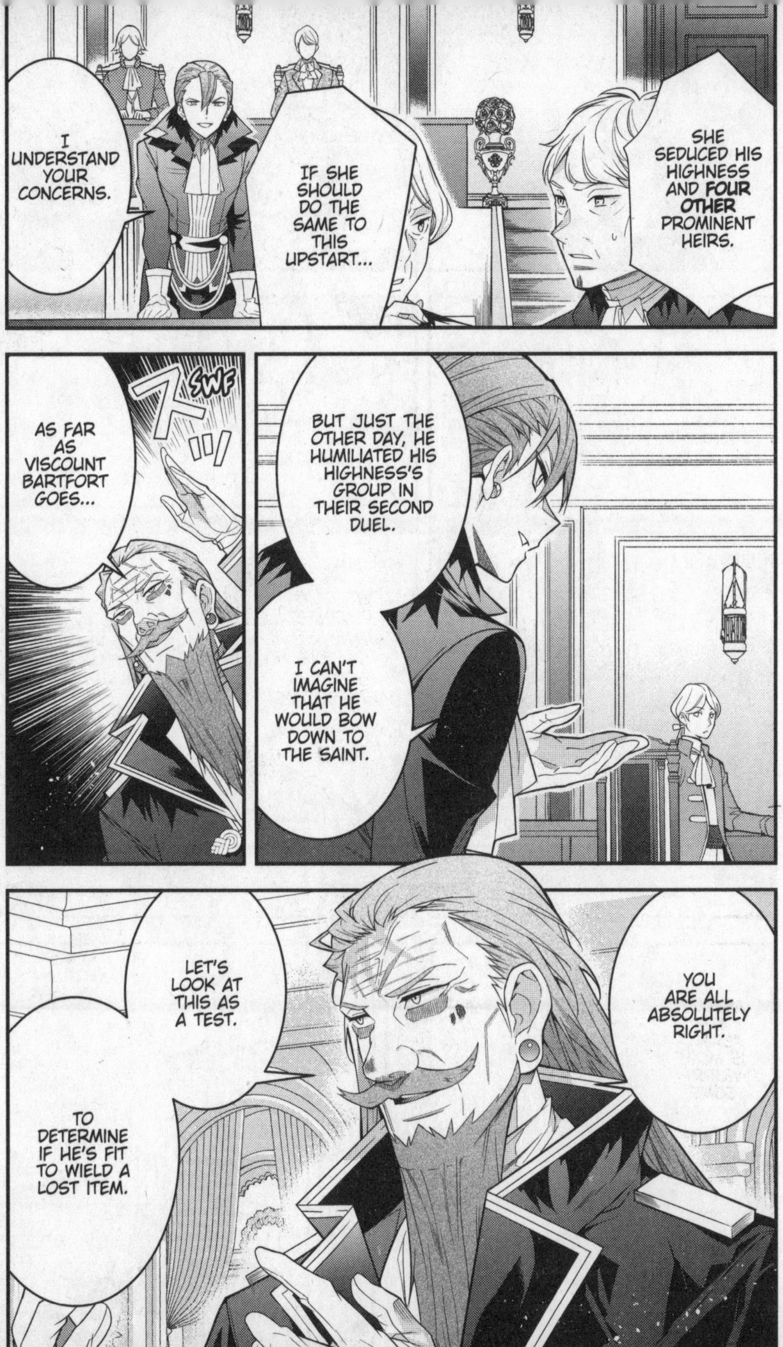
SHE SEDUCED HIS HIGHNESS AND **FOUR OTHER** PROMINENT HEIRS.
IF SHE SHOULD DO THE SAME TO THIS UPSTART...
I UNDERSTAND YOUR CONCERNS.
BUT JUST THE OTHER DAY, HE HUMILIATED HIS HIGHNESS'S GROUP IN THEIR SECOND DUEL.
I CAN'T IMAGINE THAT HE WOULD BOW DOWN TO THE SAINT.
SWF
AS FAR AS VISCOUNT BARTFORT GOES...
YOU ARE ALL ABSOLUTLY RIGHT.
LET'S LOOK AT THIS AS A TEST.
TO DETERMINE IF HE'S FIT TO WIELD A LOST ITEM.

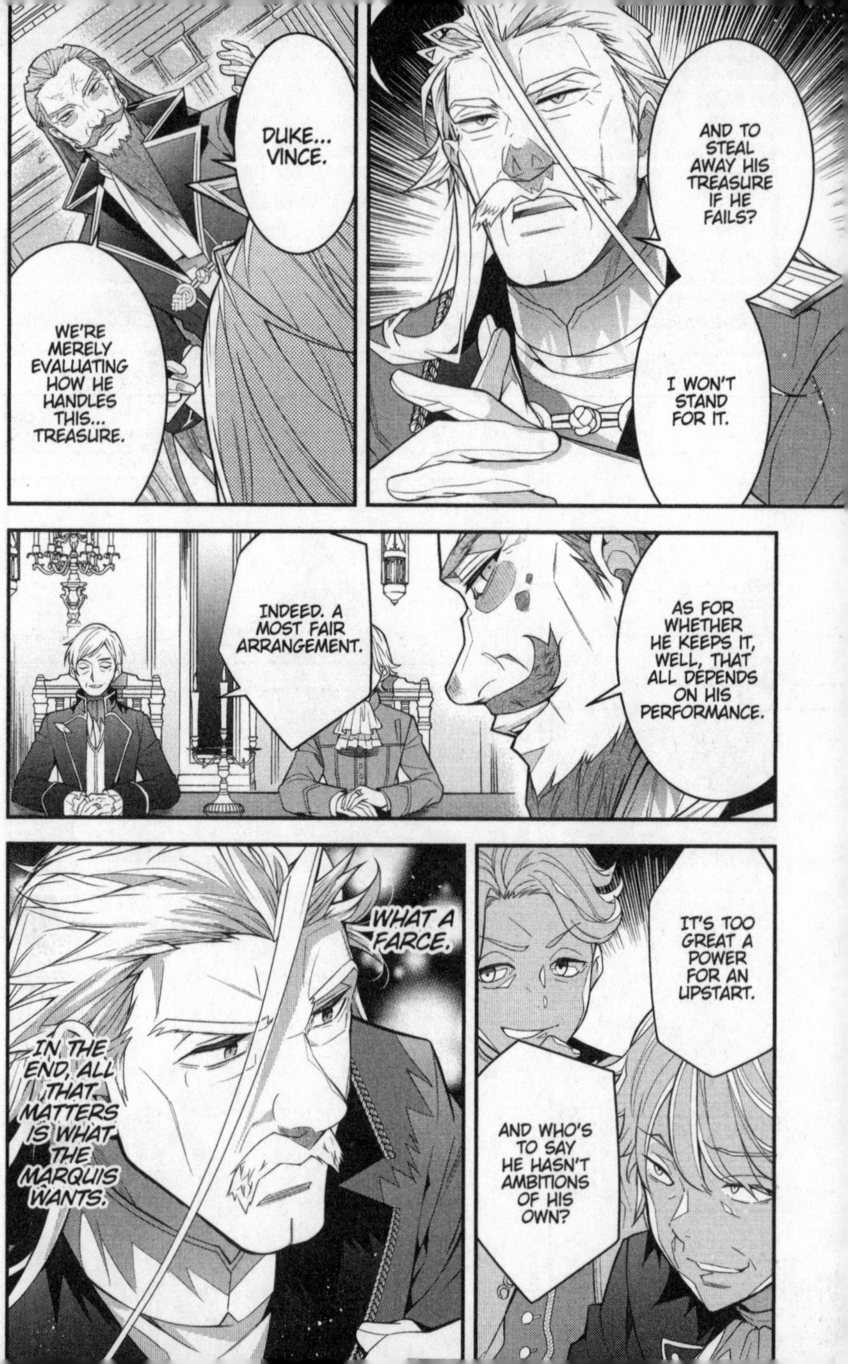
AND TO STEAL AWAY HIS TREASURE IF HE FAILS?
I WON'T STAND FOR IT.
DUKE... VINCE.
WE'RE MERELY EVALUATING HOW HE HANDLES THIS... TREASURE.
AS FOR WHETHER HE KEEPS IT, WELL, THAT ALL DEPENDS ON HIS PERFORMANCE.
INDEED. A MOST FAIR ARRANGEMENT.
IT'S TOO GREAT A POWER FOR AN UPSTART.
AND WHO'S TO SAY HE HASN'T AMBITIONS OF HIS OWN?
WHAT A FARCE.
IN THE END, ALL THAT MATTERS IS WHAT THE MARQUIS WANTS.

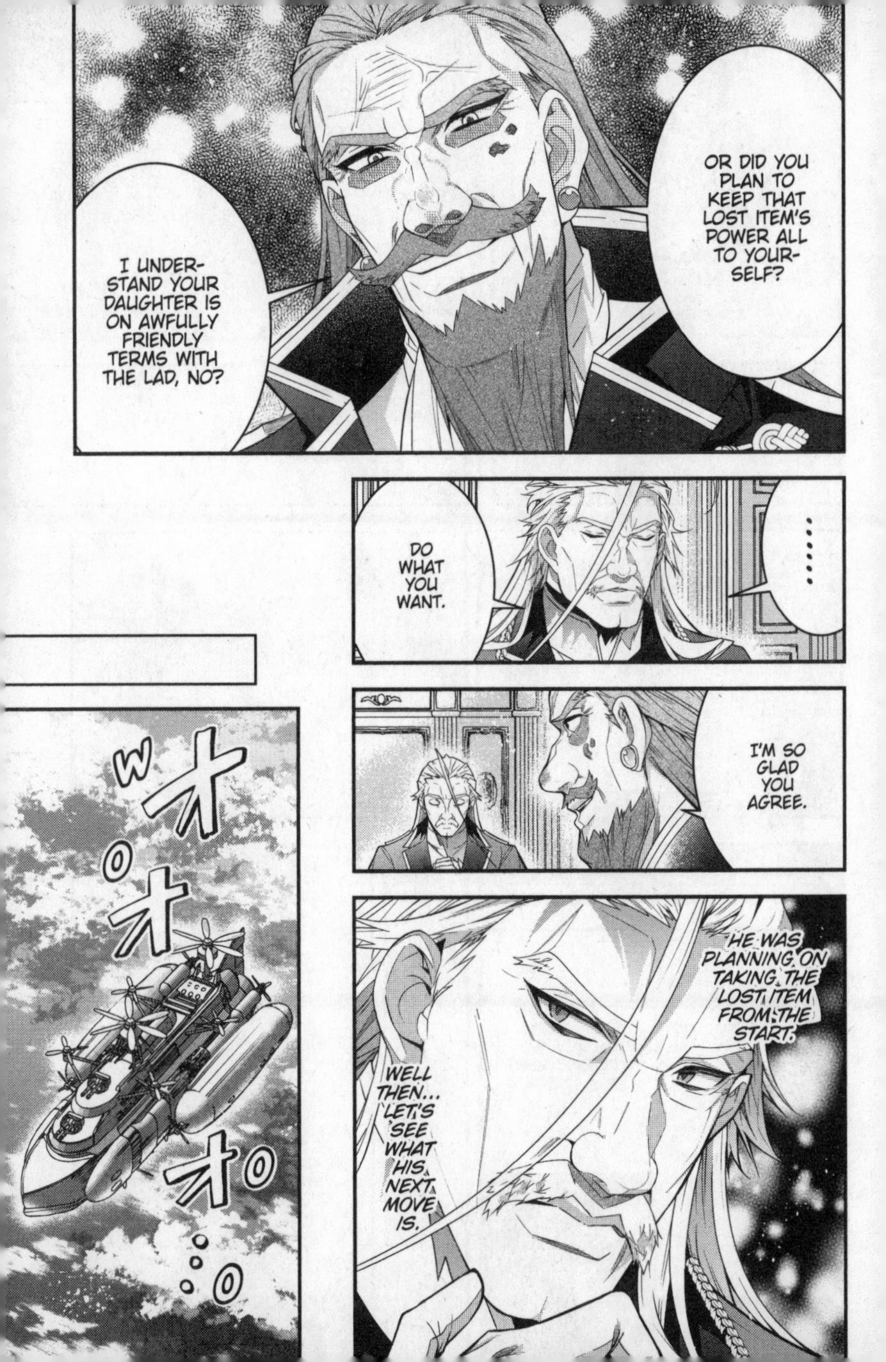
OR DID YOU PLAN TO KEEP THAT LOST ITEM'S POWER ALL TO YOUR-SELF?
I UNDER-STAND YOUR DAUGHTER IS ON AWFULLY FRIENDLY TERMS WITH THE LAD, NO?
......
DO WHAT YOU WANT.
I'M SO GLAD YOU AGREE.
HE WAS PLANNING ON TAKING THE LOST ITEM FROM THE START.
WELL THEN... LET'S SEE WHAT HIS NEXT MOVE IS.
WOOOO

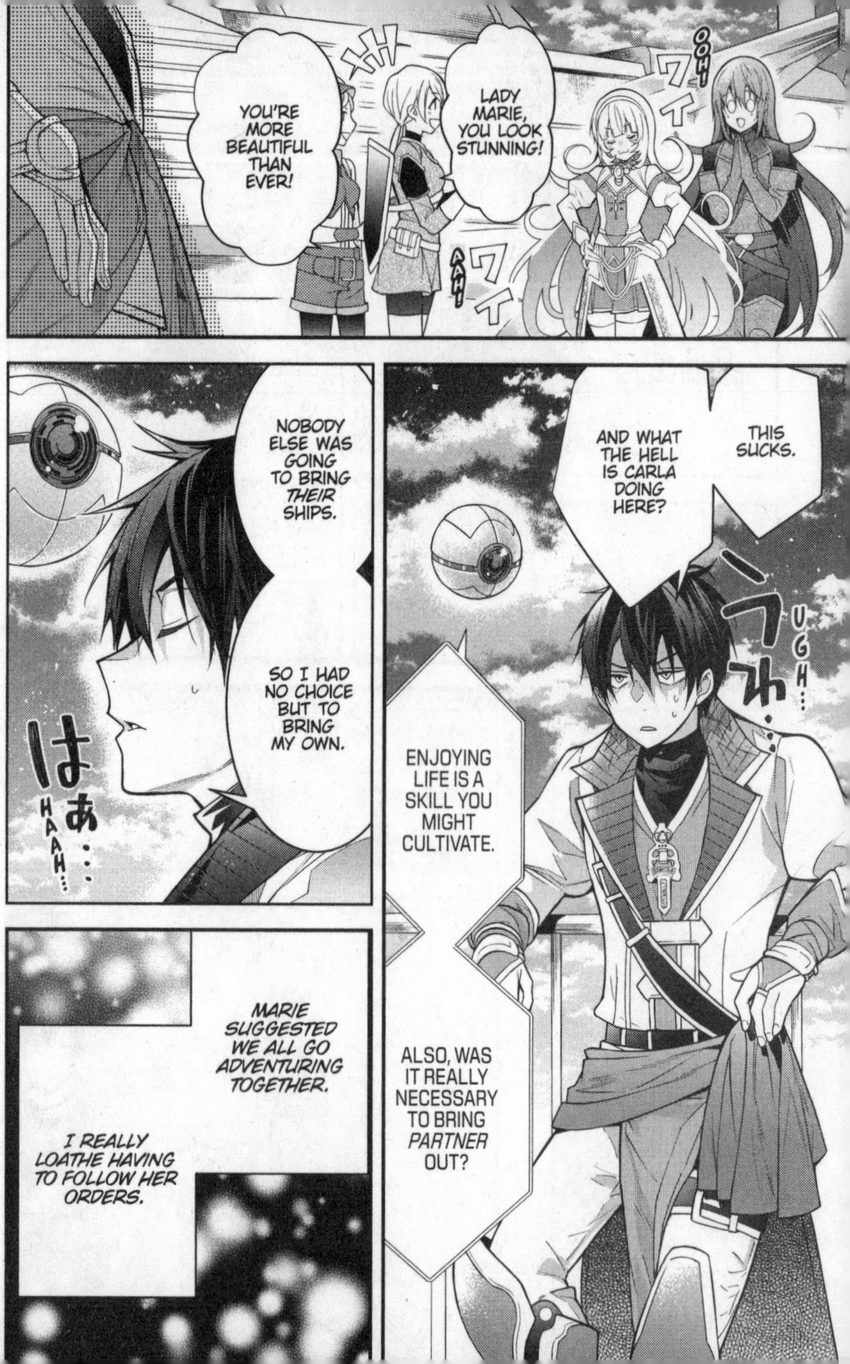
OOOH!
AAH!
LADY MARIE, YOU LOOK STUNNING!
YOU'RE MORE BEAUTIFUL THAN EVER!
THIS SUCKS.
AND WHAT THE HELL IS CARLA DOING HERE?
UGH...
ENJOYING LIFE IS A SKILL YOU MIGHT CULTIVATE.
ALSO, WAS IT REALLY NECESSARY TO BRING *PARTNER* OUT?
NOBODY ELSE WAS GOING TO BRING *THEIR* SHIPS.
SO I HAD NO CHOICE BUT TO BRING MY OWN.
HAAAH...
MARIE SUGGESTED WE ALL GO ADVENTURING TOGETHER.
I REALLY LOATHE HAVING TO FOLLOW HER ORDERS.

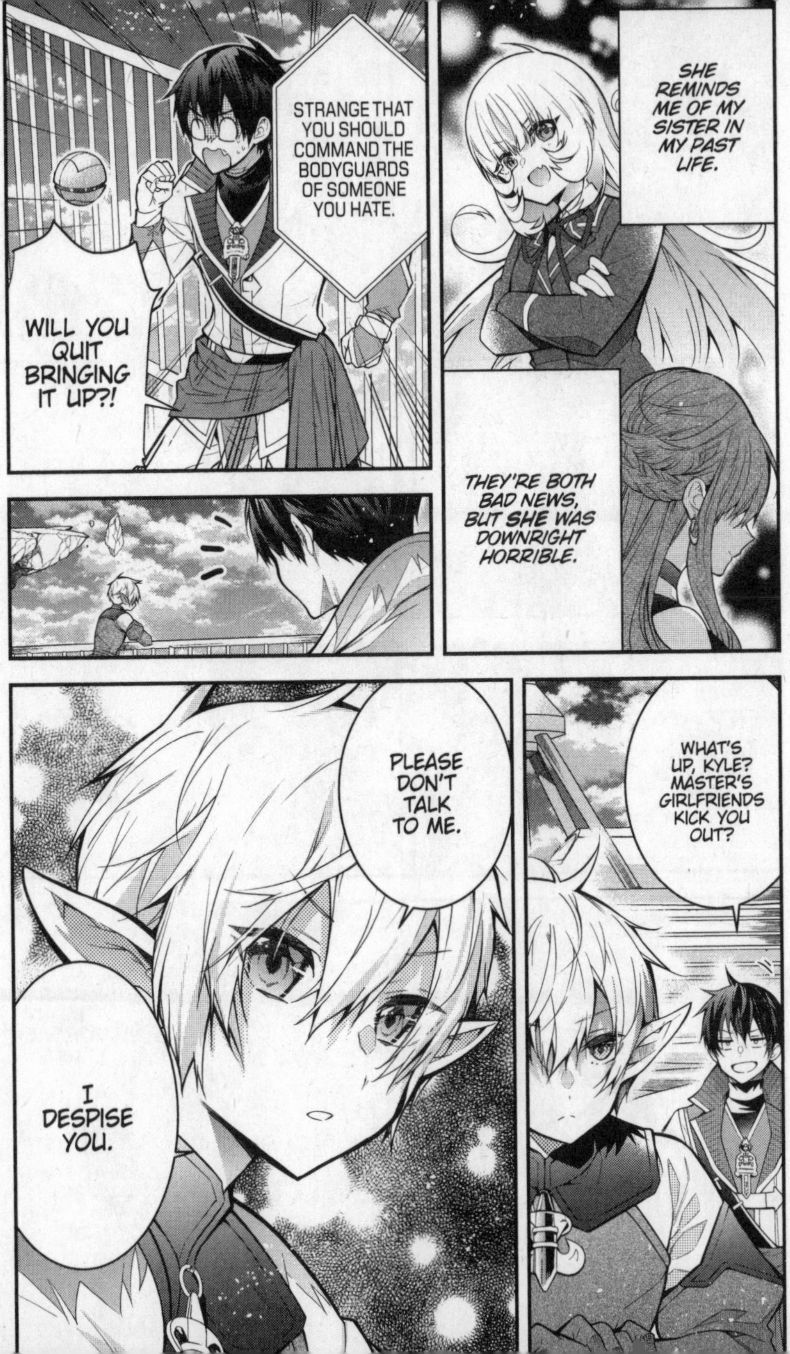
SHE REMINDS ME OF MY SISTER IN MY PAST LIFE.
STRANGE THAT YOU SHOULD COMMAND THE BODYGUARDS OF SOMEONE YOU HATE.
WILL YOU QUIT BRINGING IT UP?!
THEY'RE BOTH BAD NEWS, BUT SHE WAS DOWNRIGHT HORRIBLE.
WHAT'S UP, KYLE? MASTER'S GIRLFRIENDS KICK YOU OUT?
PLEASE DON'T TALK TO ME.
I DESPISE YOU.

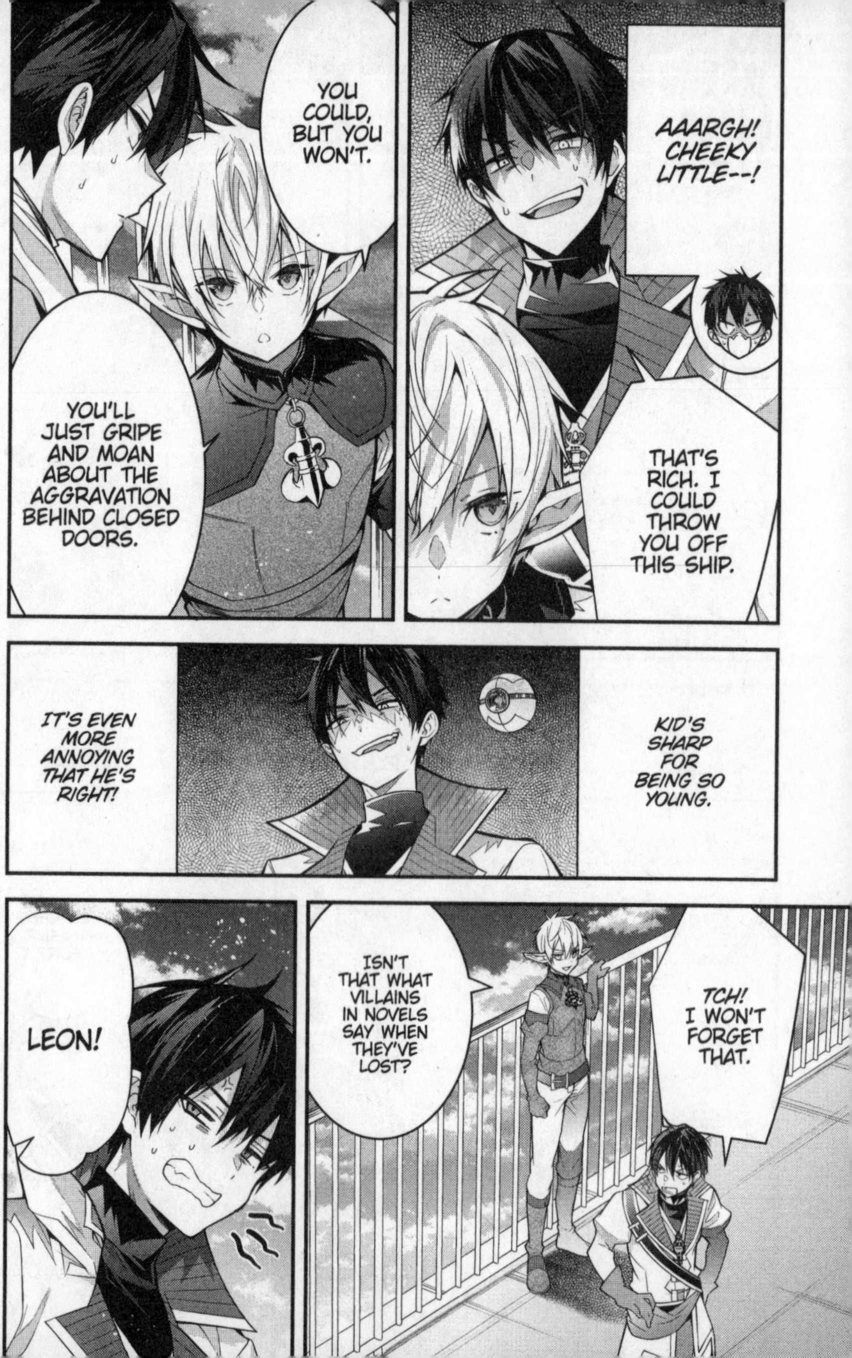
AAARGH! CHEEKY LITTLE--!
THAT'S RICH. I COULD THROW YOU OFF THIS SHIP.
YOU COULD, BUT YOU WON'T.
YOU'LL JUST GRIPE AND MOAN ABOUT THE AGGRAVATION BEHIND CLOSED DOORS.
KID'S SHARP FOR BEING SO YOUNG.
IT'S EVEN MORE ANNOYING THAT HE'S RIGHT!
TCH! I WON'T FORGET THAT.
ISN'T THAT WHAT VILLAINS IN NOVELS SAY WHEN THEY'VE LOST?
LEON!

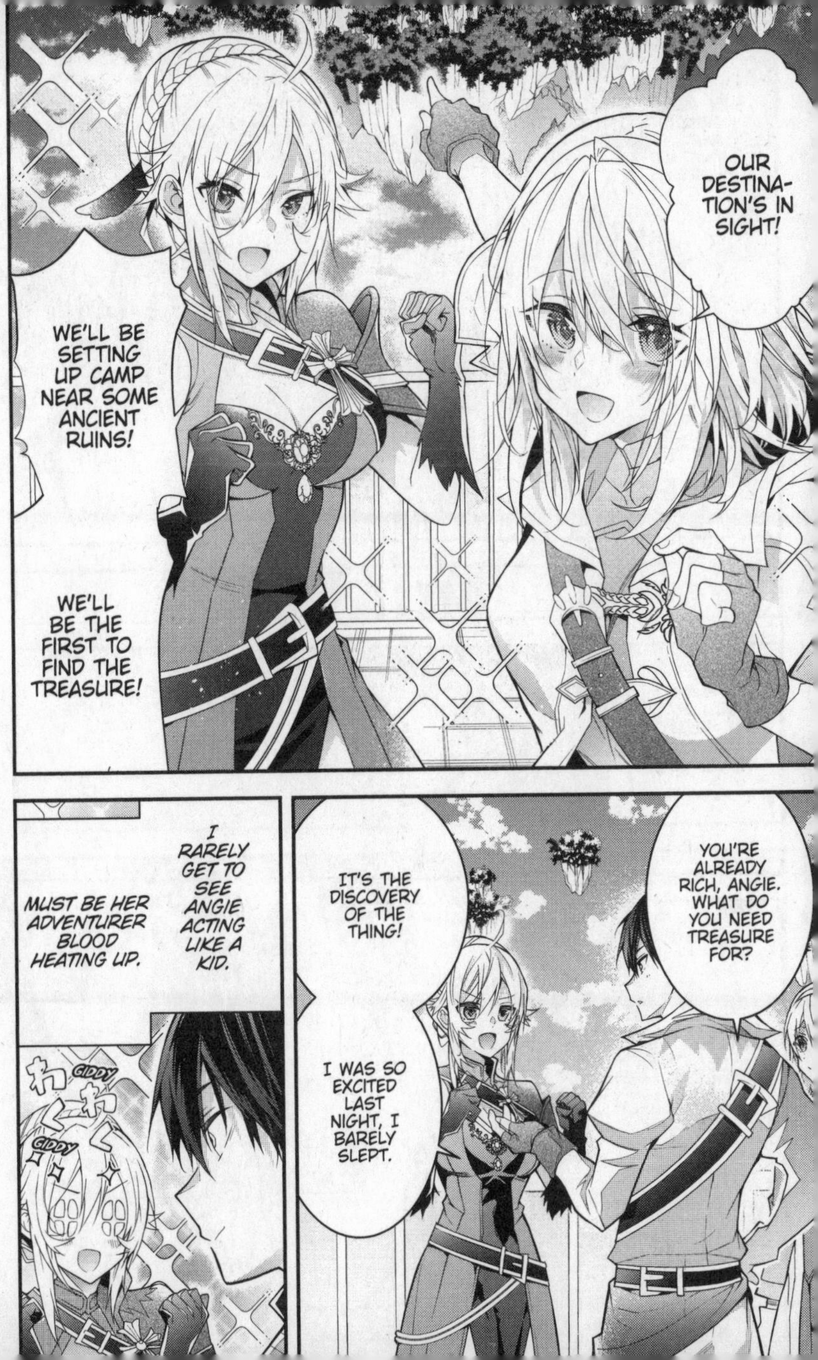
OUR DESTINATION'S IN SIGHT!
WE'LL BE SETTING UP CAMP NEAR SOME ANCIENT RUINS!
WE'LL BE THE FIRST TO FIND THE TREASURE!
YOU'RE ALREADY RICH, ANGIE. WHAT DO YOU NEED TREASURE FOR?
IT'S THE DISCOVERY OF THE THING!
I WAS SO EXCITED LAST NIGHT, I BARELY SLEPT.
I RARELY GET TO SEE ANGIE ACTING LIKE A KID.
MUST BE HER ADVENTURER BLOOD HEATING UP.
わくわく
GIDDY
GIDDY

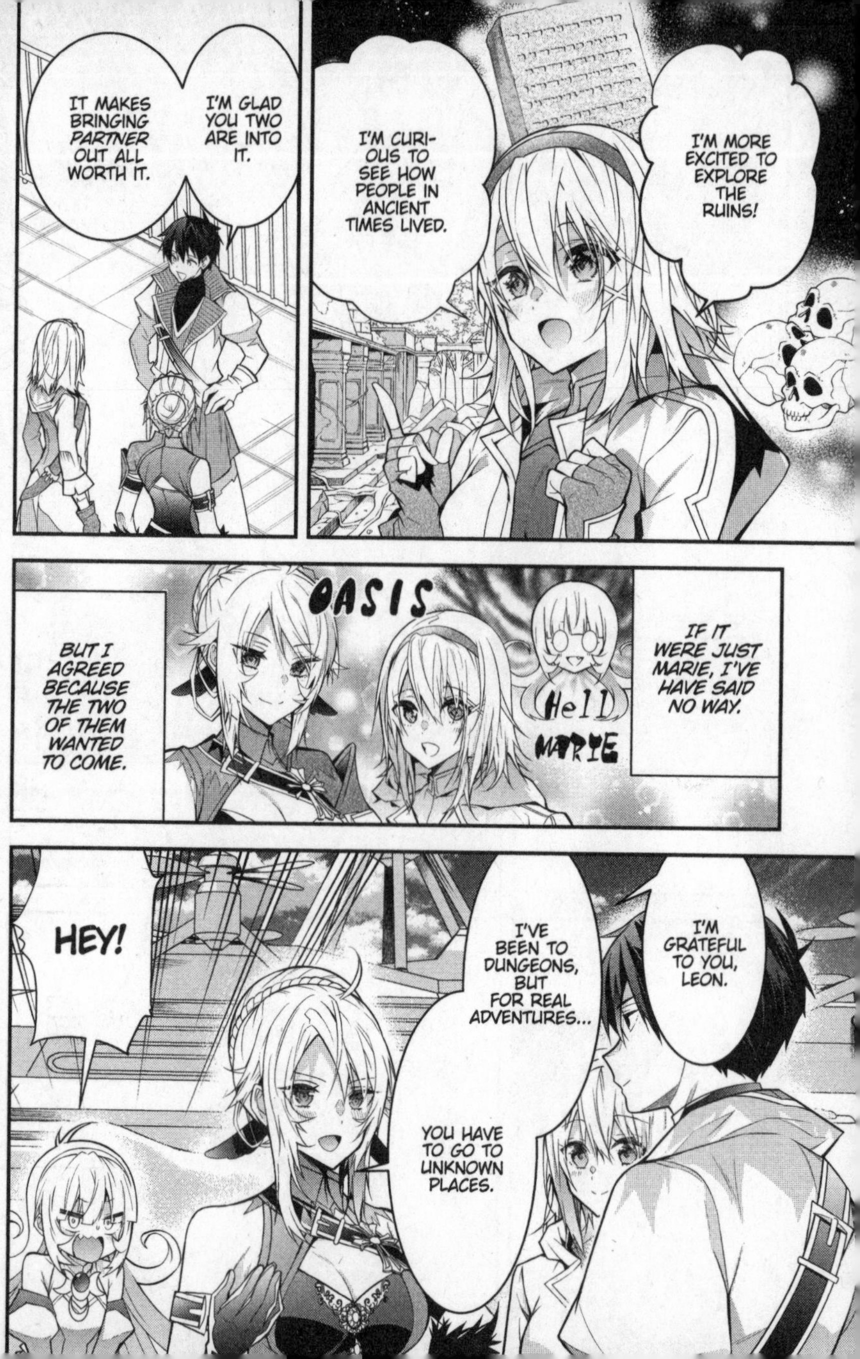
I'M MORE EXCITED TO EXPLORE THE RUINS!
I'M CURI-OUS TO SEE HOW PEOPLE IN ANCIENT TIMES LIVED.
I'M GLAD YOU TWO ARE INTO IT.
IT MAKES BRINGING PARTNER OUT ALL WORTH IT.
IF IT WERE JUST MARIE, I'VE HAVE SAID NO WAY.
OASIS
Hell
MARIE
BUT I AGREED BECAUSE THE TWO OF THEM WANTED TO COME.
I'M GRATEFUL TO YOU, LEON.
I'VE BEEN TO DUNGEONS, BUT FOR REAL ADVENTURES...
YOU HAVE TO GO TO UNKNOWN PLACES.
HEY!

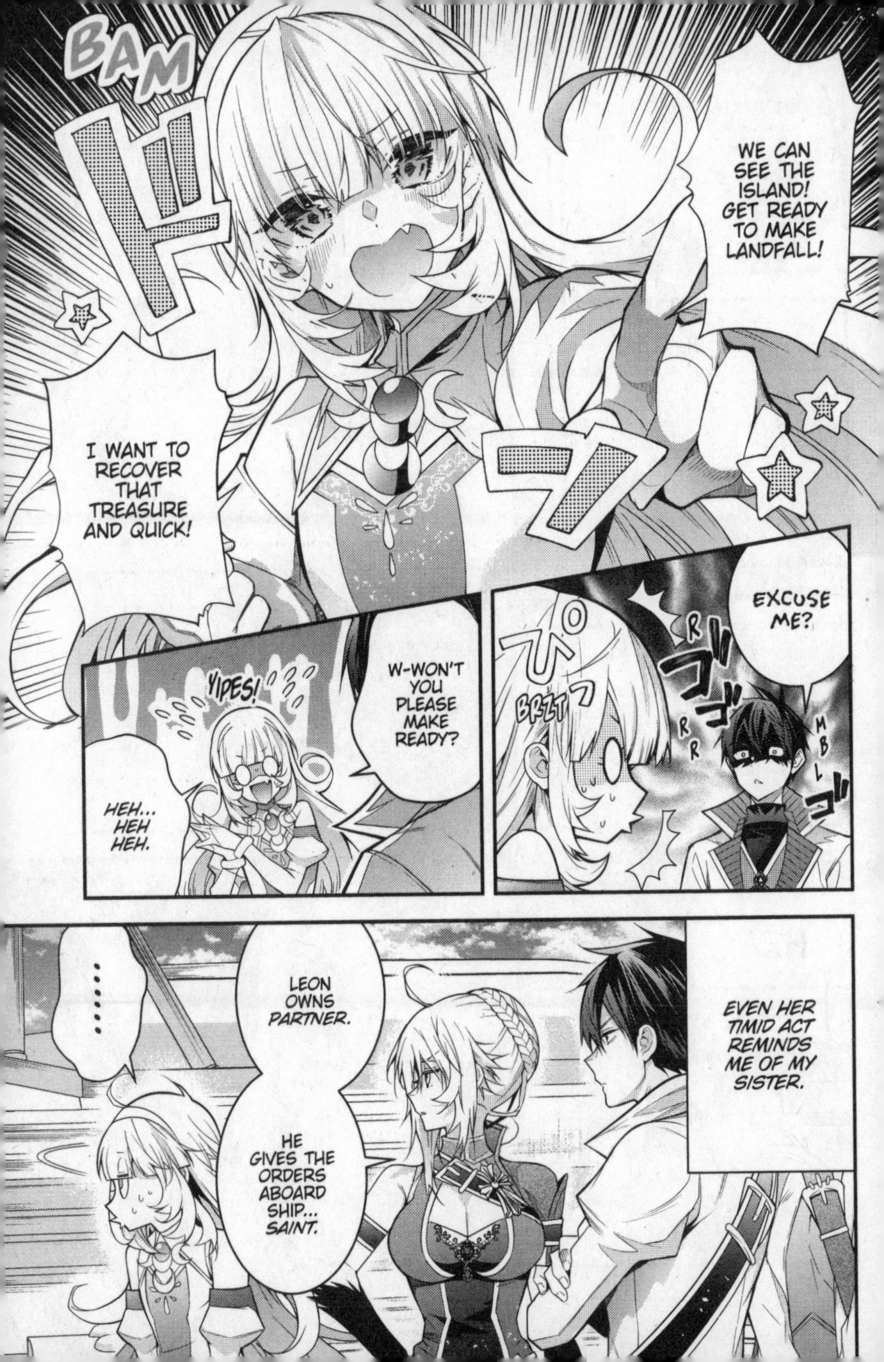
BAM
WE CAN SEE THE ISLAND! GET READY TO MAKE LANDFALL!
I WANT TO RECOVER THAT TREASURE AND QUICK!
EXCUSE ME?
RRR
MBL
BRZT
W-WON'T YOU PLEASE MAKE READY?
YIPES!
HEH... HEH HEH.
EVEN HER TIMID ACT REMINDS ME OF MY SISTER.
LEON OWNS PARTNER.
HE GIVES THE ORDERS ABOARD SHIP... SAINT.
......

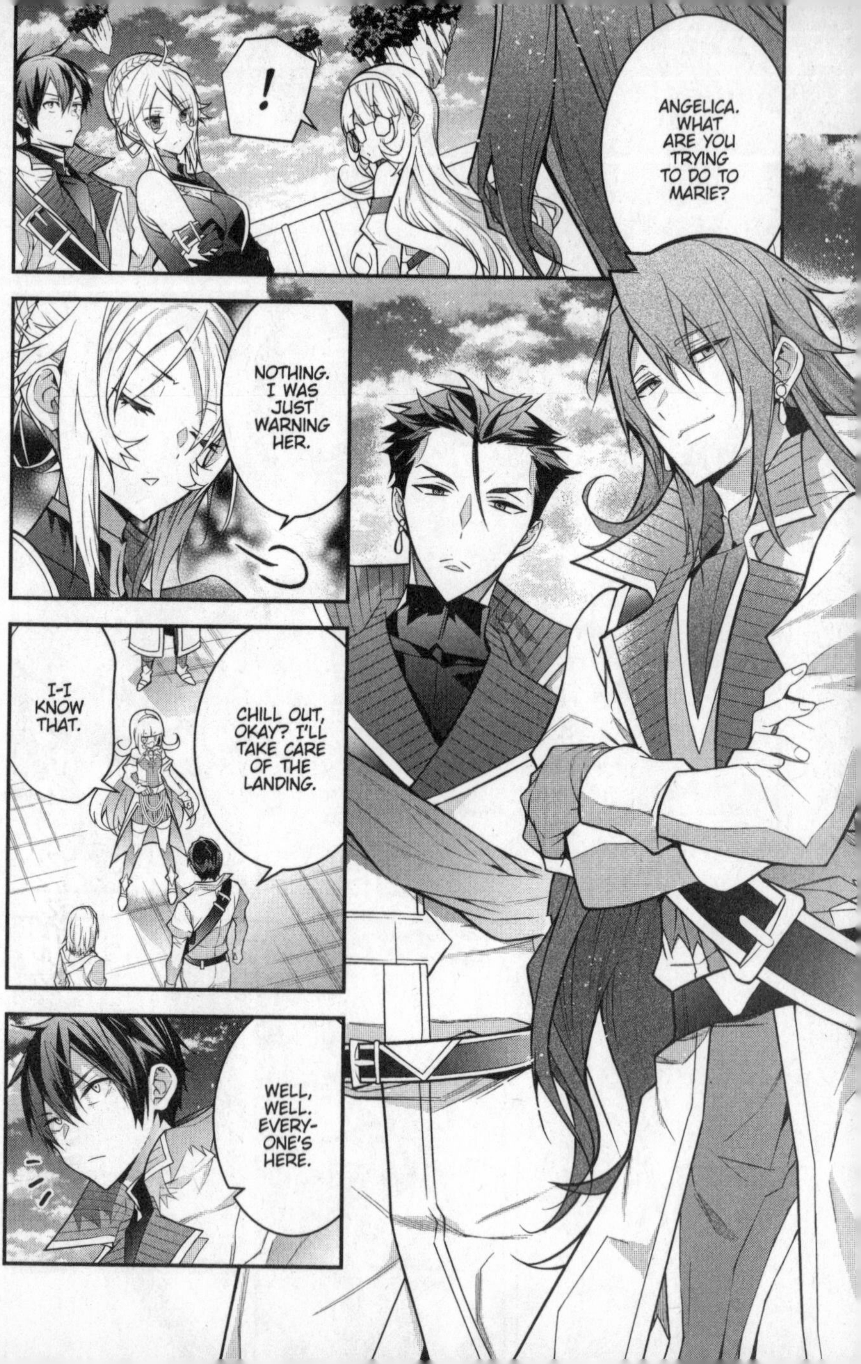
ANGELICA. WHAT ARE YOU TRYING TO DO TO MARIE?
!
NOTHING. I WAS JUST WARNING HER.
CHILL OUT, OKAY? I'LL TAKE CARE OF THE LANDING.
I-I KNOW THAT.
WELL, WELL. EVERY-ONE'S HERE.

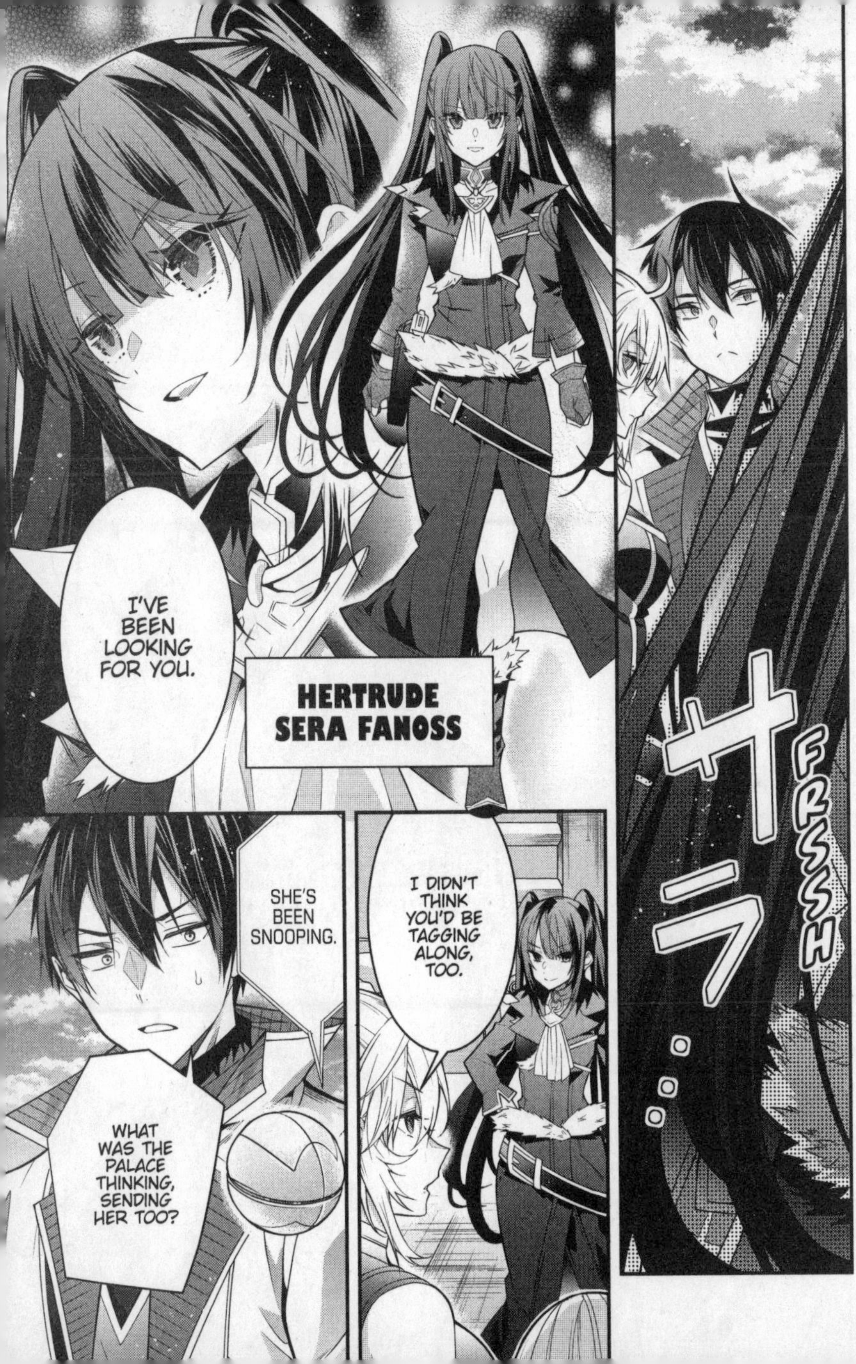
サラ...
FRSSH
I'VE BEEN LOOKING FOR YOU.
HERTRUDE SERA FANOSS
I DIDN'T THINK YOU'D BE TAGGING ALONG, TOO.
SHE'S BEEN SNOOPING.
WHAT WAS THE PALACE THINKING, SENDING HER TOO?

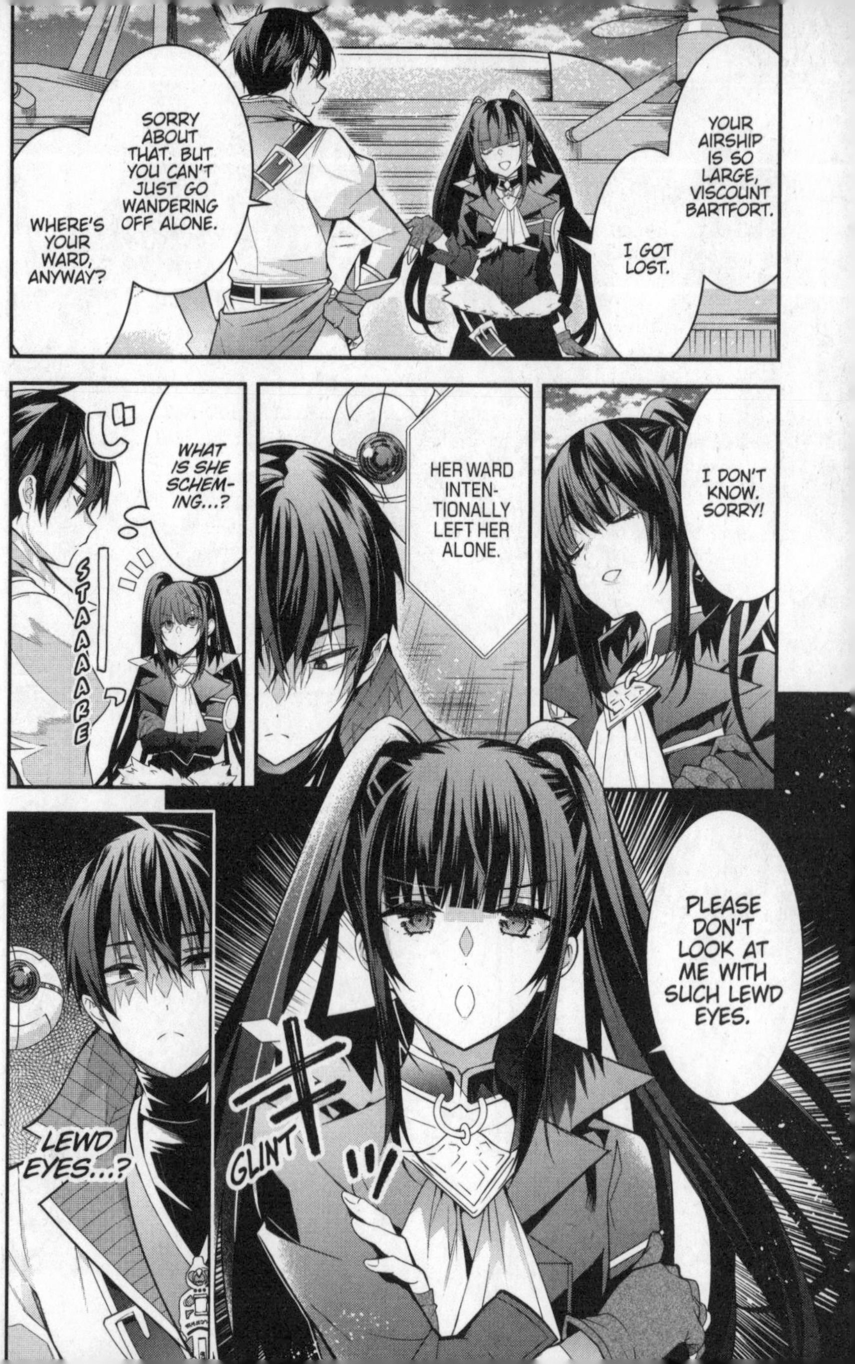
YOUR AIRSHIP IS SO LARGE, VISCOUNT BARTFORT.
I GOT LOST.
SORRY ABOUT THAT. BUT YOU CAN'T JUST GO WANDERING OFF ALONE.
WHERE'S YOUR WARD, ANYWAY?
I DON'T KNOW. SORRY!
HER WARD INTENTIONALLY LEFT HER ALONE.
WHAT IS SHE SCHEMING...?
STAAAAARE
PLEASE DON'T LOOK AT ME WITH SUCH LEWD EYES.
GLINT
LEWD EYES...?

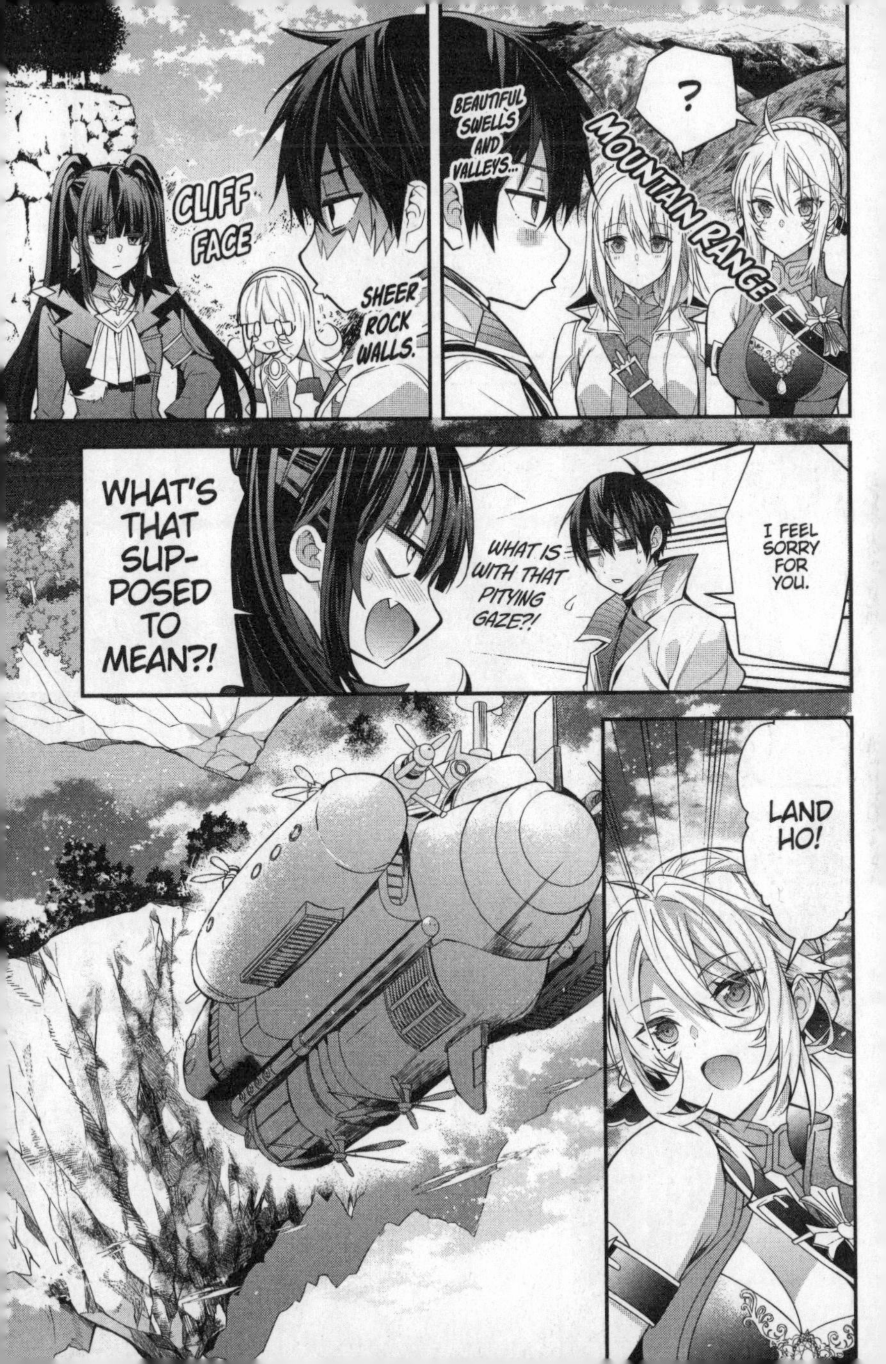
?
MOUNTAIN RANGE
BEAUTIFUL SWELLS AND VALLEYS...
SHEER ROCK WALLS.
CLIFF FACE
I FEEL SORRY FOR YOU.
WHAT IS WITH THAT PITYING GAZE?!
WHAT'S THAT SUP-POSED TO MEAN?!
LAND HO!

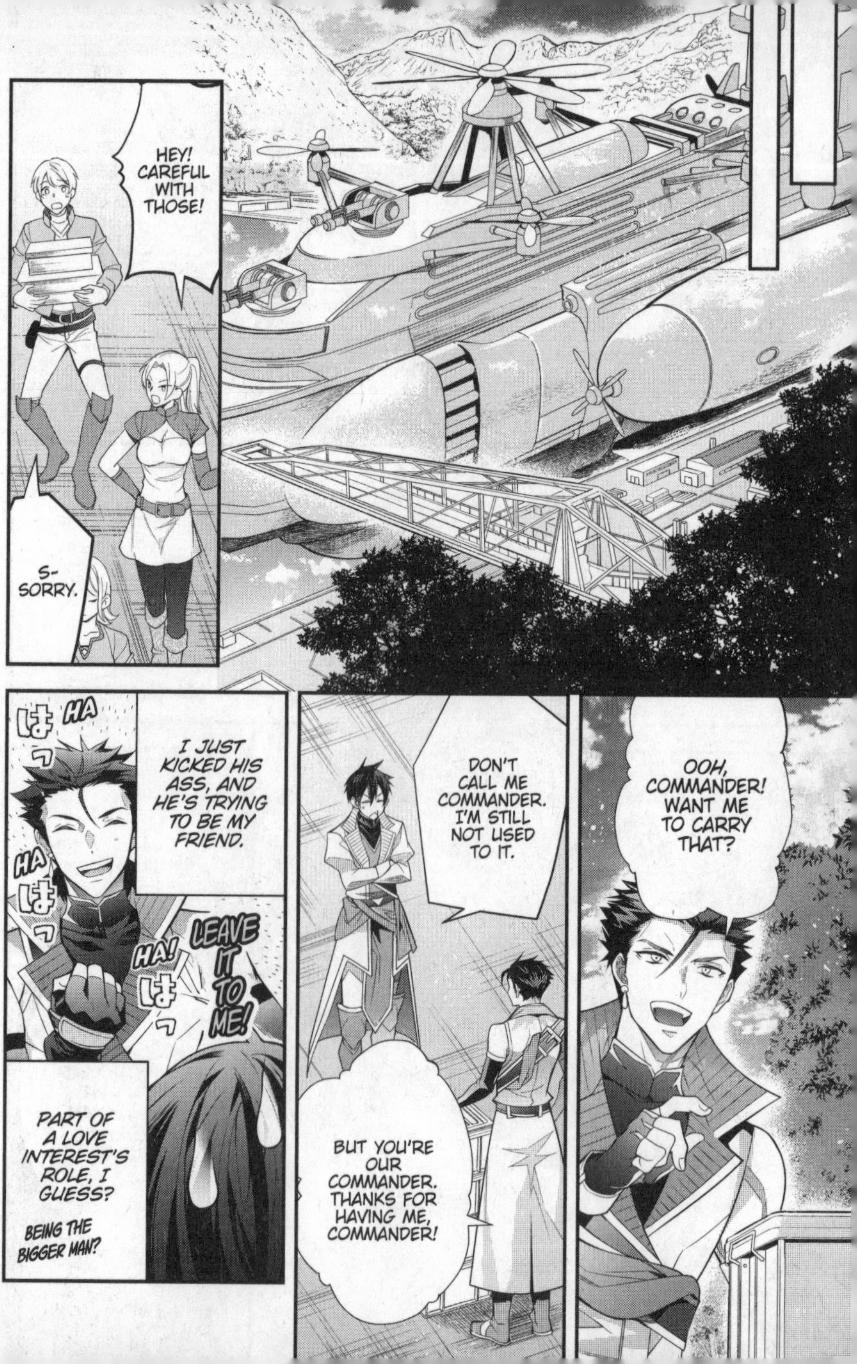
HEY! CAREFUL WITH THOSE!
S-SORRY.
OOH, COMMANDER! WANT ME TO CARRY THAT?
DON'T CALL ME COMMANDER. I'M STILL NOT USED TO IT.
BUT YOU'RE OUR COMMANDER. THANKS FOR HAVING ME, COMMANDER!
I JUST KICKED HIS ASS, AND HE'S TRYING TO BE MY FRIEND.
HA はっ
HA はっ
LEAVE IT TO ME!
HA! はっ
PART OF A LOVE INTEREST'S ROLE, I GUESS?
BEING THE BIGGER MAN?

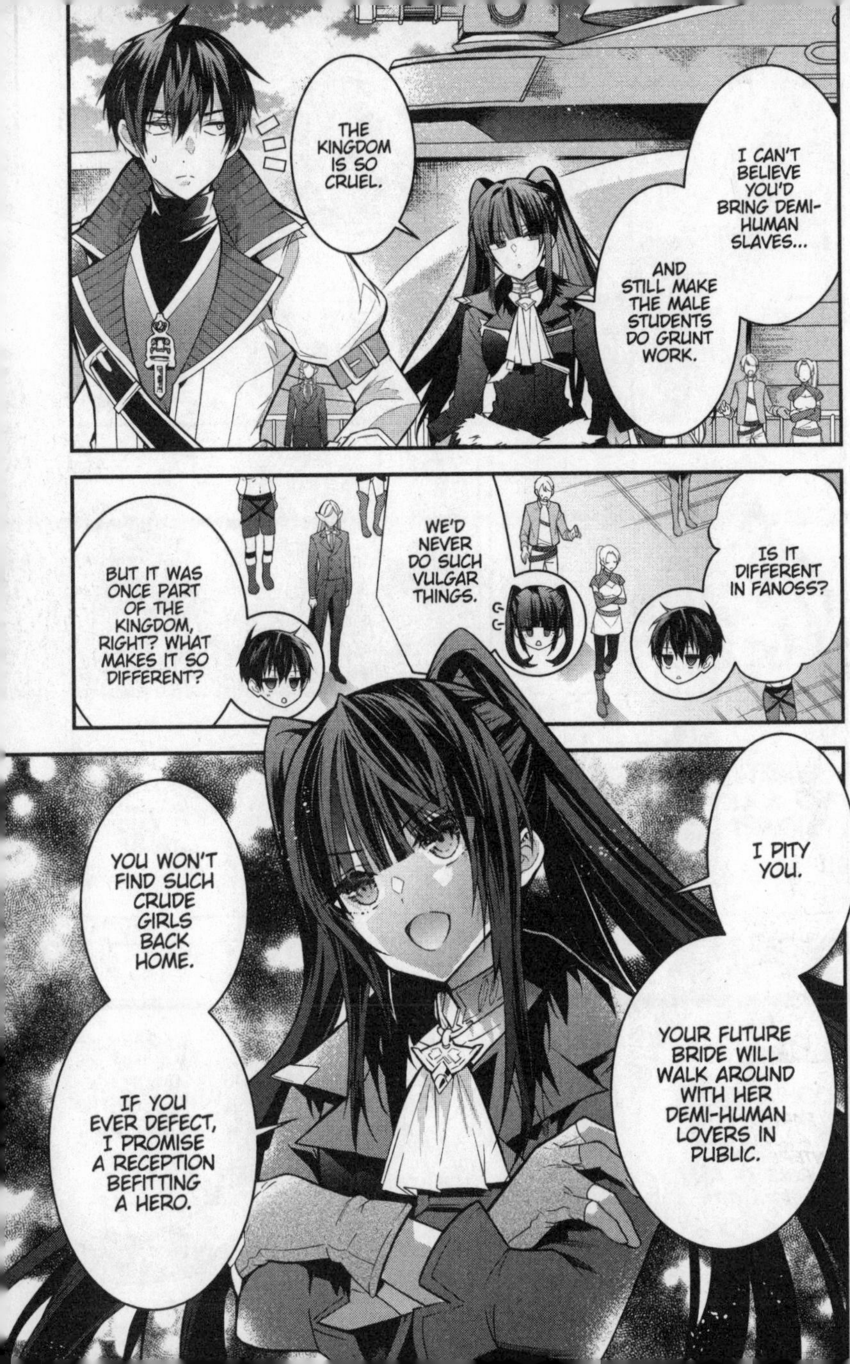
I CAN'T BELIEVE YOU'D BRING DEMI-HUMAN SLAVES...
AND STILL MAKE THE MALE STUDENTS DO GRUNT WORK.
THE KINGDOM IS SO CRUEL.
IS IT DIFFERENT IN FANOSS?
WE'D NEVER DO SUCH VULGAR THINGS.
BUT IT WAS ONCE PART OF THE KINGDOM, RIGHT? WHAT MAKES IT SO DIFFERENT?
I PITY YOU.
YOUR FUTURE BRIDE WILL WALK AROUND WITH HER DEMI-HUMAN LOVERS IN PUBLIC.
YOU WON'T FIND SUCH CRUDE GIRLS BACK HOME.
IF YOU EVER DEFECT, I PROMISE A RECEPTION BEFITTING A HERO.

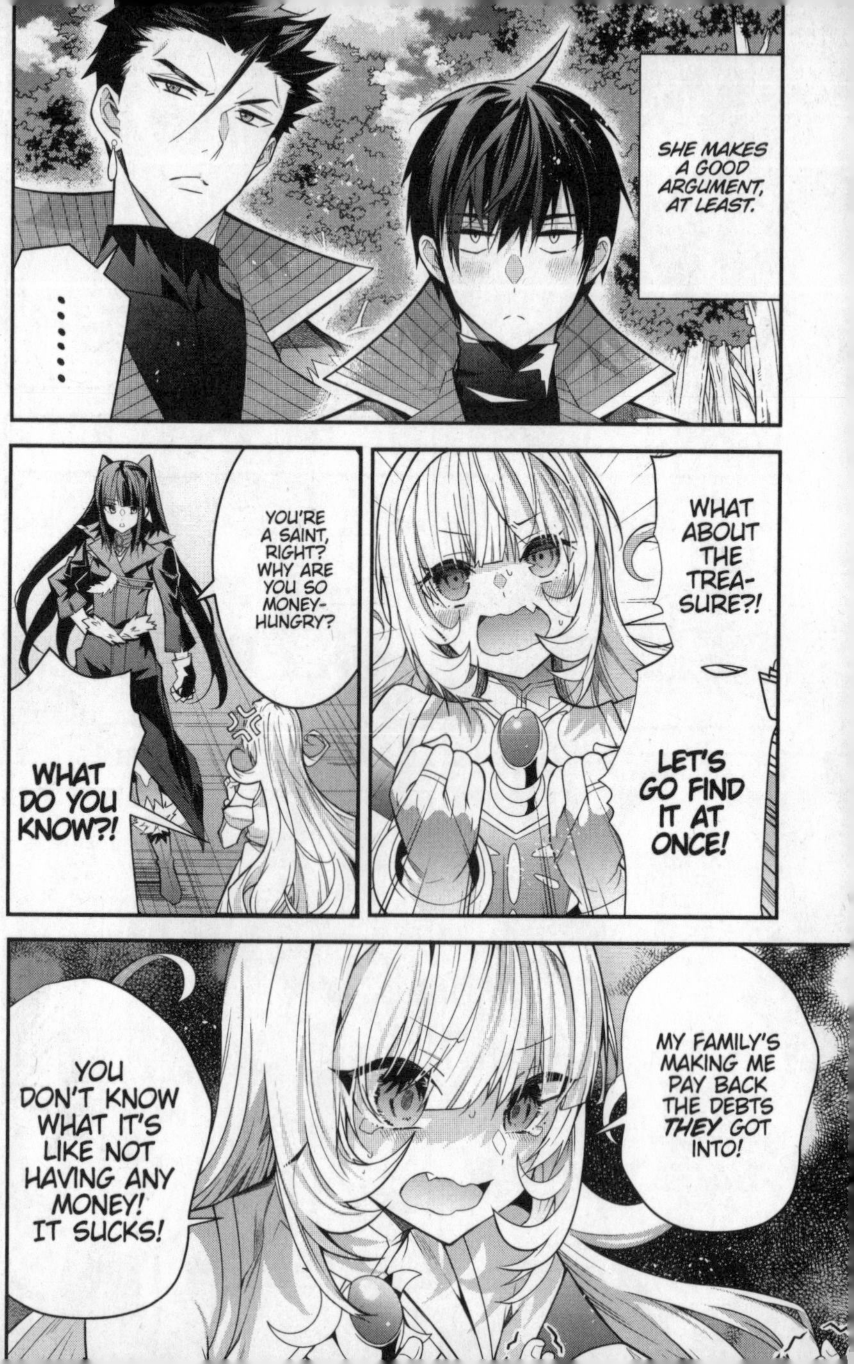
SHE MAKES A GOOD ARGUMENT, AT LEAST.
......
WHAT ABOUT THE TREASURE?!
LET'S GO FIND IT AT ONCE!
YOU'RE A SAINT, RIGHT? WHY ARE YOU SO MONEY-HUNGRY?
WHAT DO YOU KNOW?!
MY FAMILY'S MAKING ME PAY BACK THE DEBTS *THEY* GOT INTO!
YOU DON'T KNOW WHAT IT'S LIKE NOT HAVING ANY MONEY! IT SUCKS!

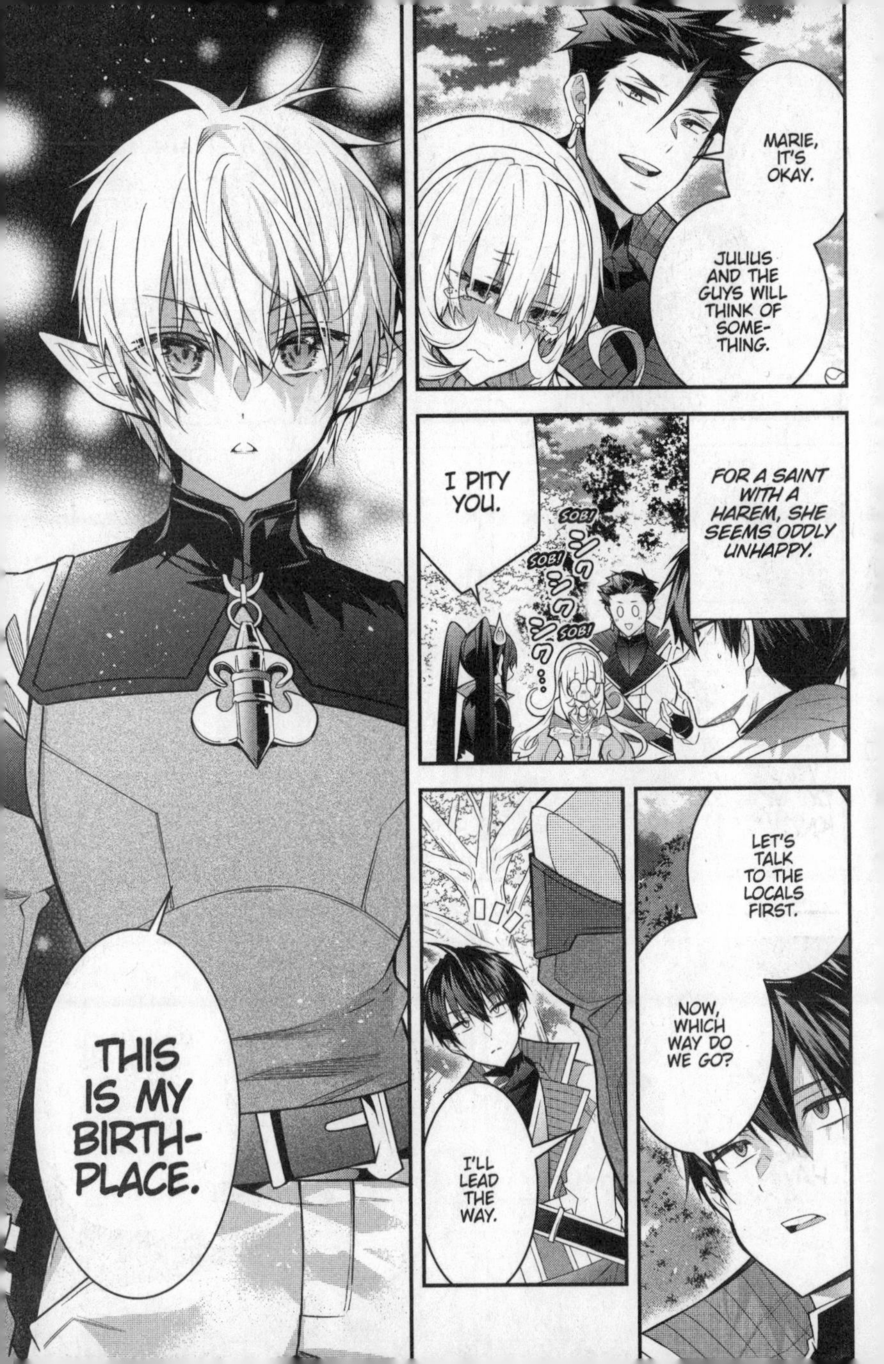

MARIE, IT'S OKAY.
JULIUS AND THE GUYS WILL THINK OF SOME-THING.
FOR A SAINT WITH A HAREM, SHE SEEMS ODDLY UNHAPPY.
I PITY YOU.
SOB!
SOB!
SOB!
LET'S TALK TO THE LOCALS FIRST.
NOW, WHICH WAY DO WE GO?
I'LL LEAD THE WAY.
THIS IS MY BIRTH-PLACE.

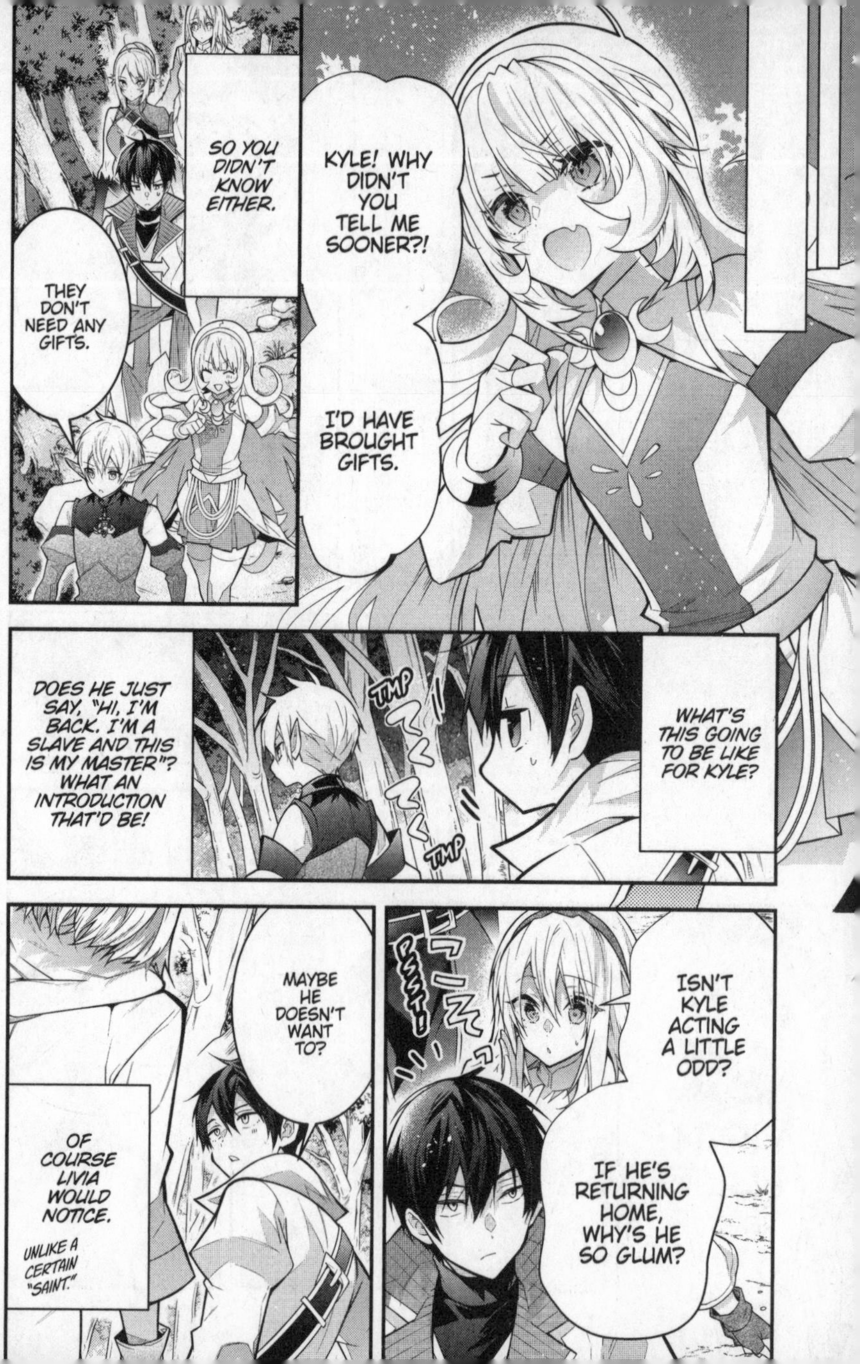
KYLE! WHY DIDN'T YOU TELL ME SOONER?!
I'D HAVE BROUGHT GIFTS.
SO YOU DIDN'T KNOW EITHER.
THEY DON'T NEED ANY GIFTS.
WHAT'S THIS GOING TO BE LIKE FOR KYLE?
TMP
TMP
DOES HE JUST SAY, "HI, I'M BACK. I'M A SLAVE AND THIS IS MY MASTER"? WHAT AN INTRODUCTION THAT'D BE!
PSST!
ISN'T KYLE ACTING A LITTLE ODD?
IF HE'S RETURNING HOME, WHY'S HE SO GLUM?
MAYBE HE DOESN'T WANT TO?
OF COURSE LIVIA WOULD NOTICE.
UNLIKE A CERTAIN "SAINT."

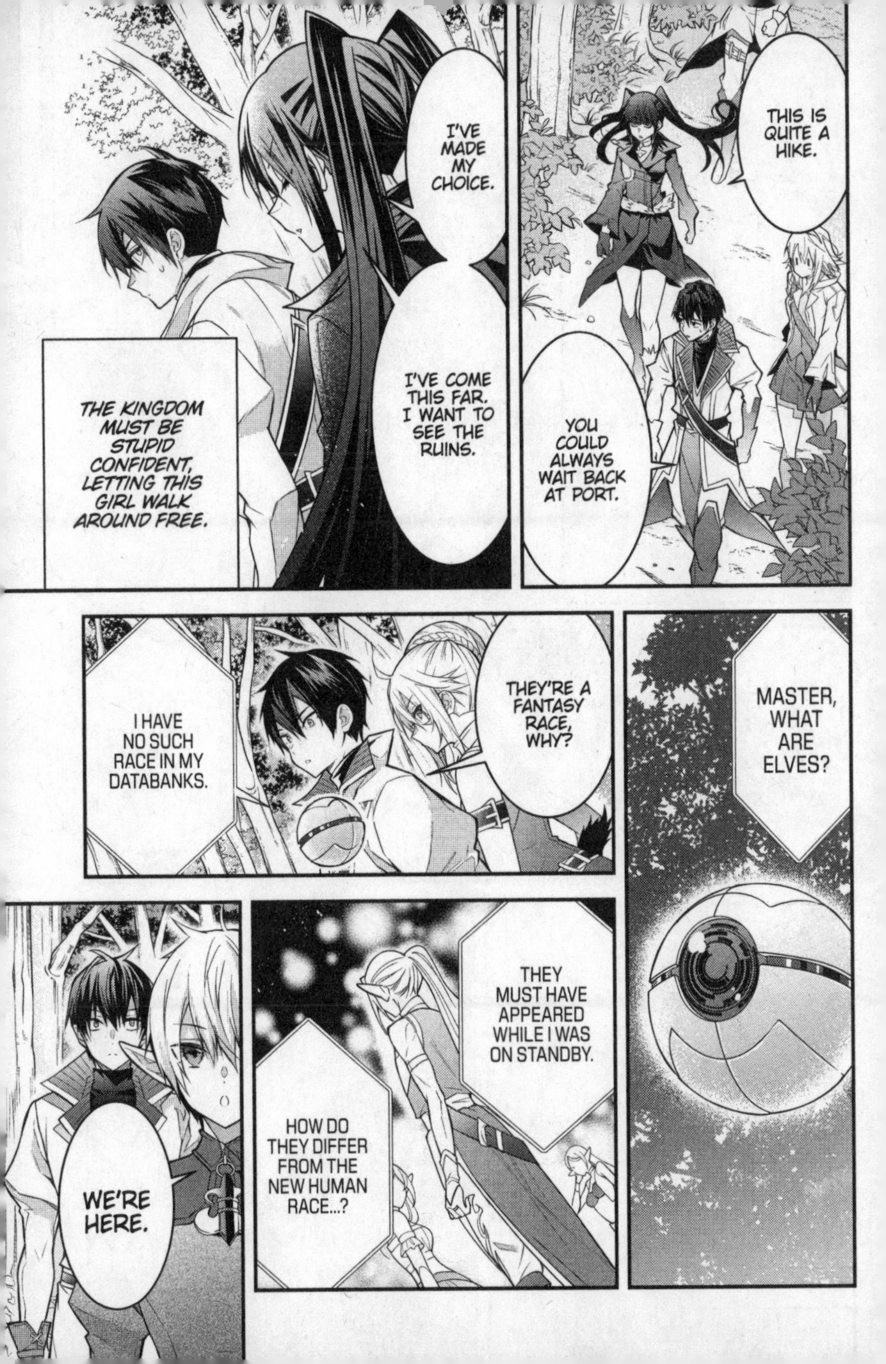
THIS IS QUITE A HIKE.
YOU COULD ALWAYS WAIT BACK AT PORT.
I'VE MADE MY CHOICE.
I'VE COME THIS FAR. I WANT TO SEE THE RUINS.
THE KINGDOM MUST BE STUPID CONFIDENT, LETTING THIS GIRL WALK AROUND FREE.
MASTER, WHAT ARE ELVES?
THEY'RE A FANTASY RACE, WHY?
I HAVE NO SUCH RACE IN MY DATABANKS.
THEY MUST HAVE APPEARED WHILE I WAS ON STANDBY.
HOW DO THEY DIFFER FROM THE NEW HUMAN RACE...?
WE'RE HERE.

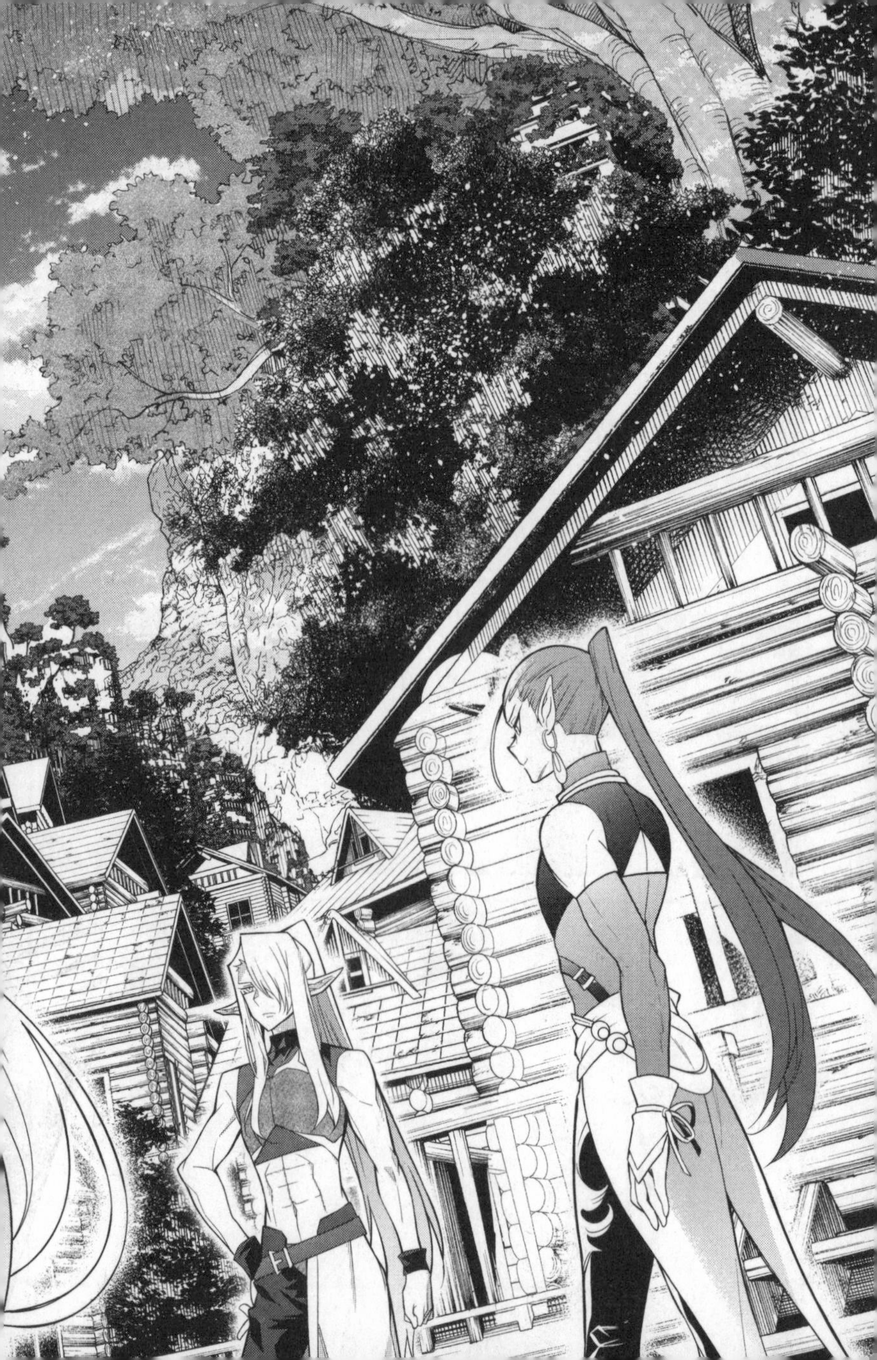

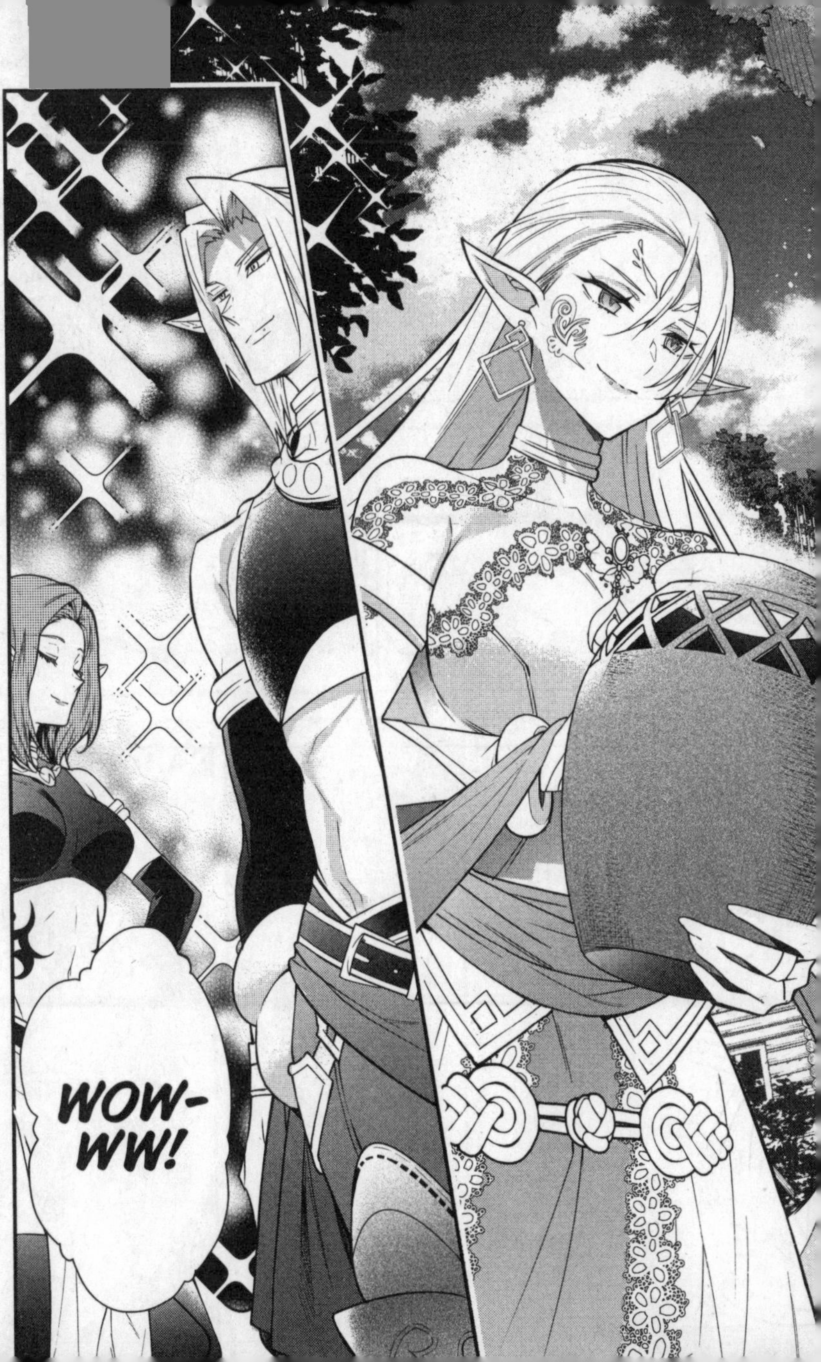
WOW-
WW!

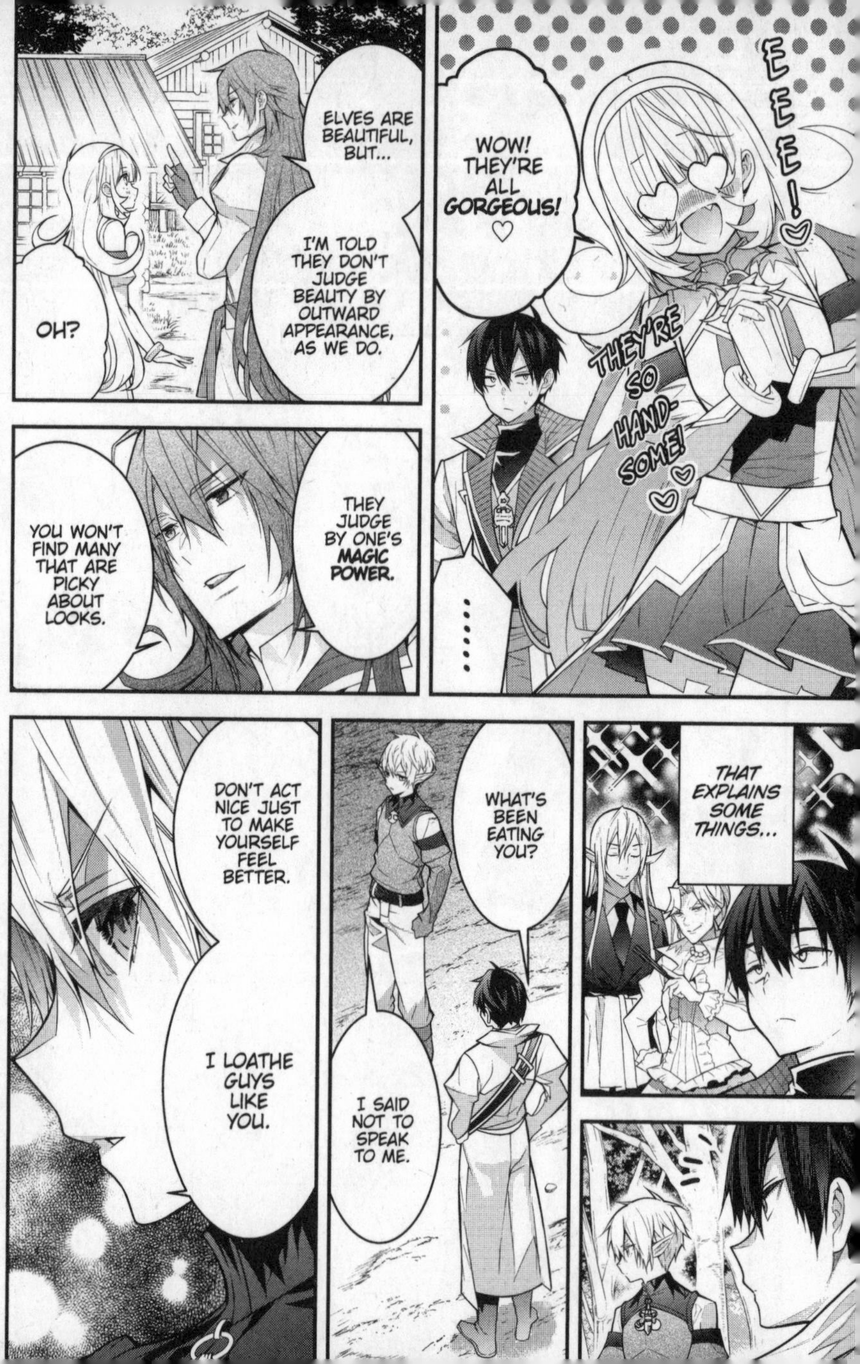

EEEE!♡
WOW! THEY'RE ALL GORGEOUS! ♡
THEY'RE SO HANDSOME! ♡
......
ELVES ARE BEAUTIFUL, BUT...
I'M TOLD THEY DON'T JUDGE BEAUTY BY OUTWARD APPEARANCE, AS WE DO.
OH?
THEY JUDGE BY ONE'S MAGIC POWER.
YOU WON'T FIND MANY THAT ARE PICKY ABOUT LOOKS.
THAT EXPLAINS SOME THINGS...
WHAT'S BEEN EATING YOU?
I SAID NOT TO SPEAK TO ME.
DON'T ACT NICE JUST TO MAKE YOURSELF FEEL BETTER.
I LOATHE GUYS LIKE YOU.

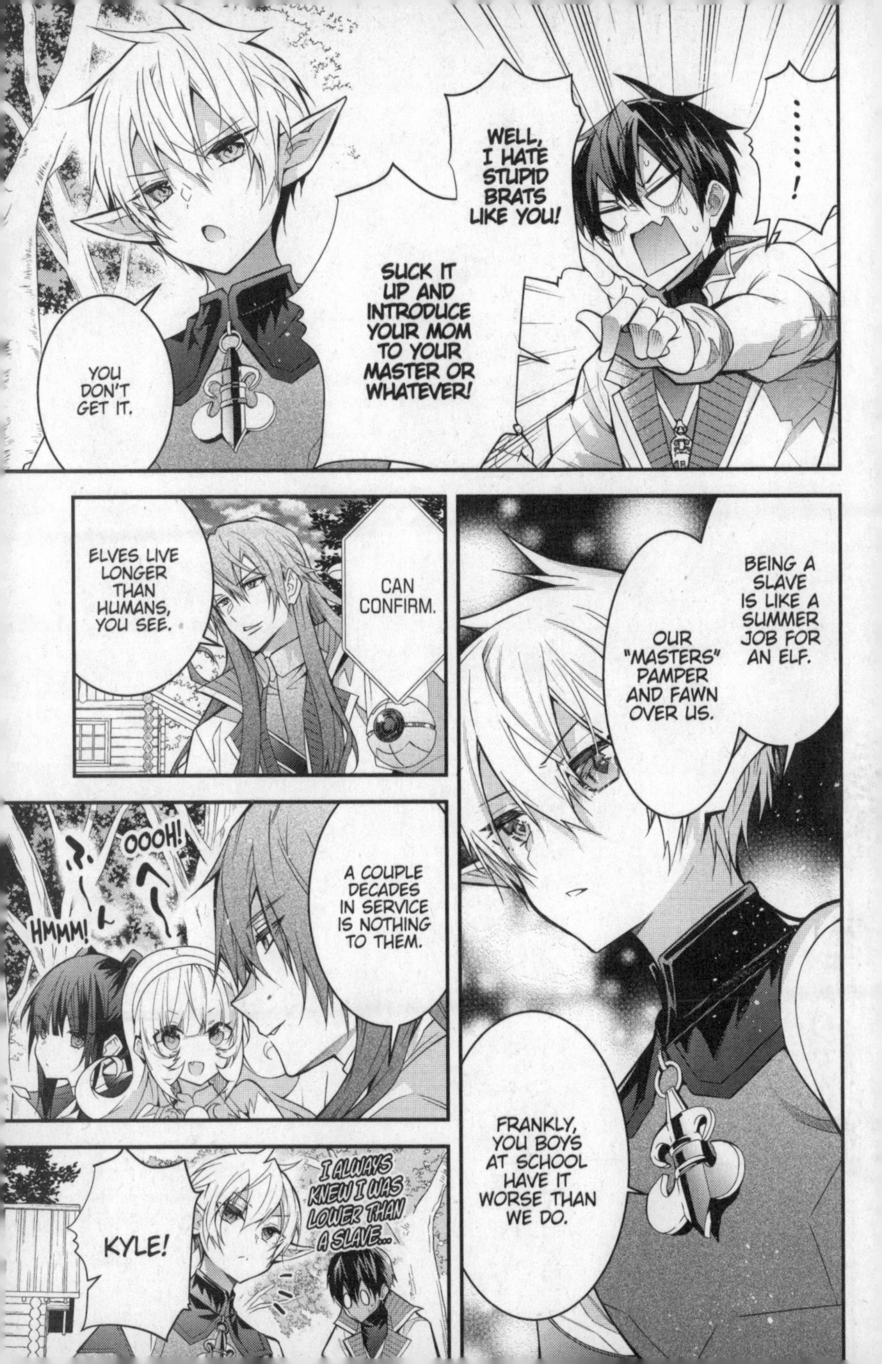
......!
WELL, I HATE STUPID BRATS LIKE YOU!
SUCK IT UP AND INTRODUCE YOUR MOM TO YOUR MASTER OR WHATEVER!
YOU DON'T GET IT.
BEING A SLAVE IS LIKE A SUMMER JOB FOR AN ELF.
OUR "MASTERS" PAMPER AND FAWN OVER US.
FRANKLY, YOU BOYS AT SCHOOL HAVE IT WORSE THAN WE DO.
ELVES LIVE LONGER THAN HUMANS, YOU SEE.
CAN CONFIRM.
A COUPLE DECADES IN SERVICE IS NOTHING TO THEM.
OOOH!
HMMM!
I ALWAYS KNEW I WAS LOWER THAN A SLAVE...
KYLE!

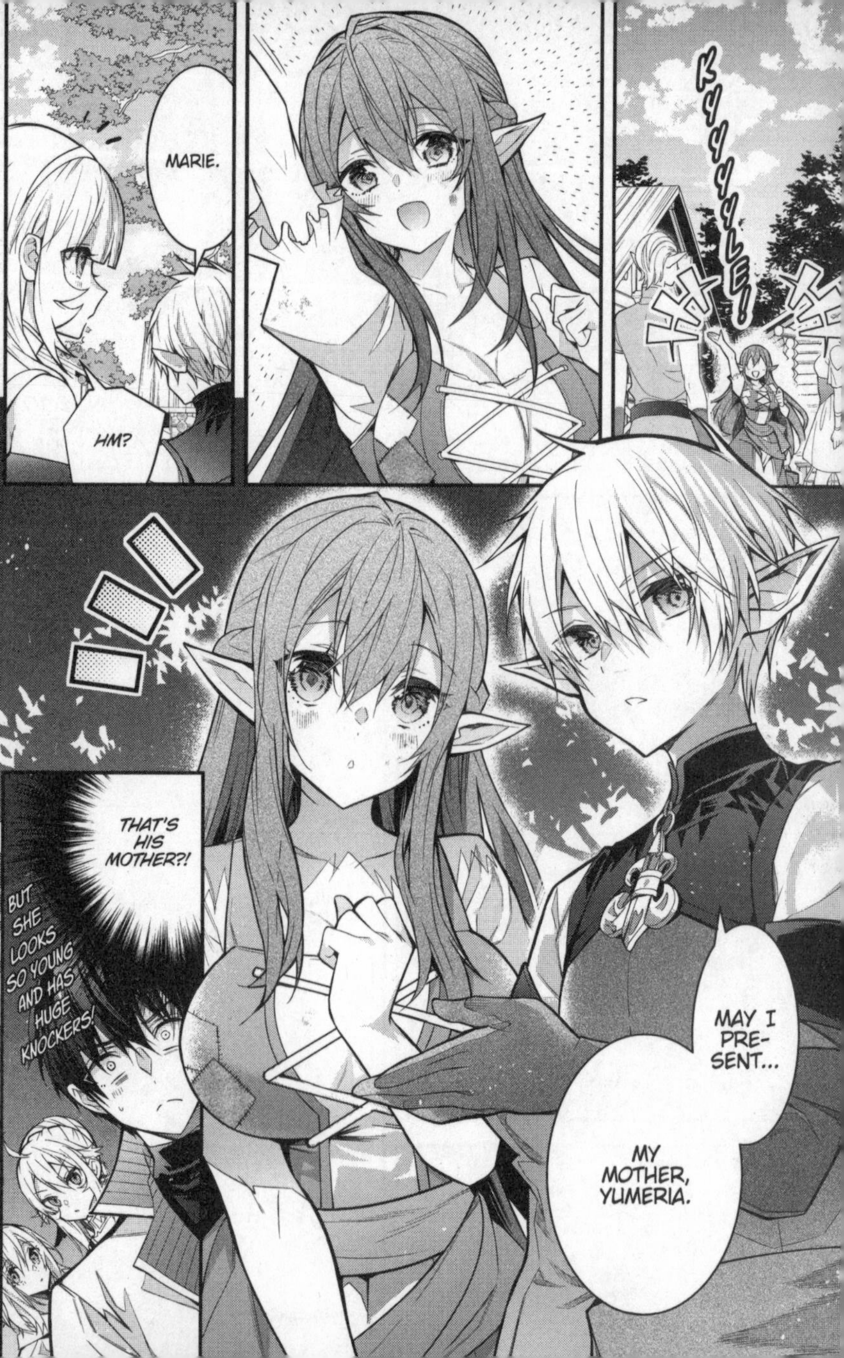

KYYYYLE!
MARIE.
HM?
MAY I PRESENT...
MY MOTHER, YUMERIA.
THAT'S HIS MOTHER?!
BUT SHE LOOKS SO YOUNG AND HAS HUGE KNOCKERS!

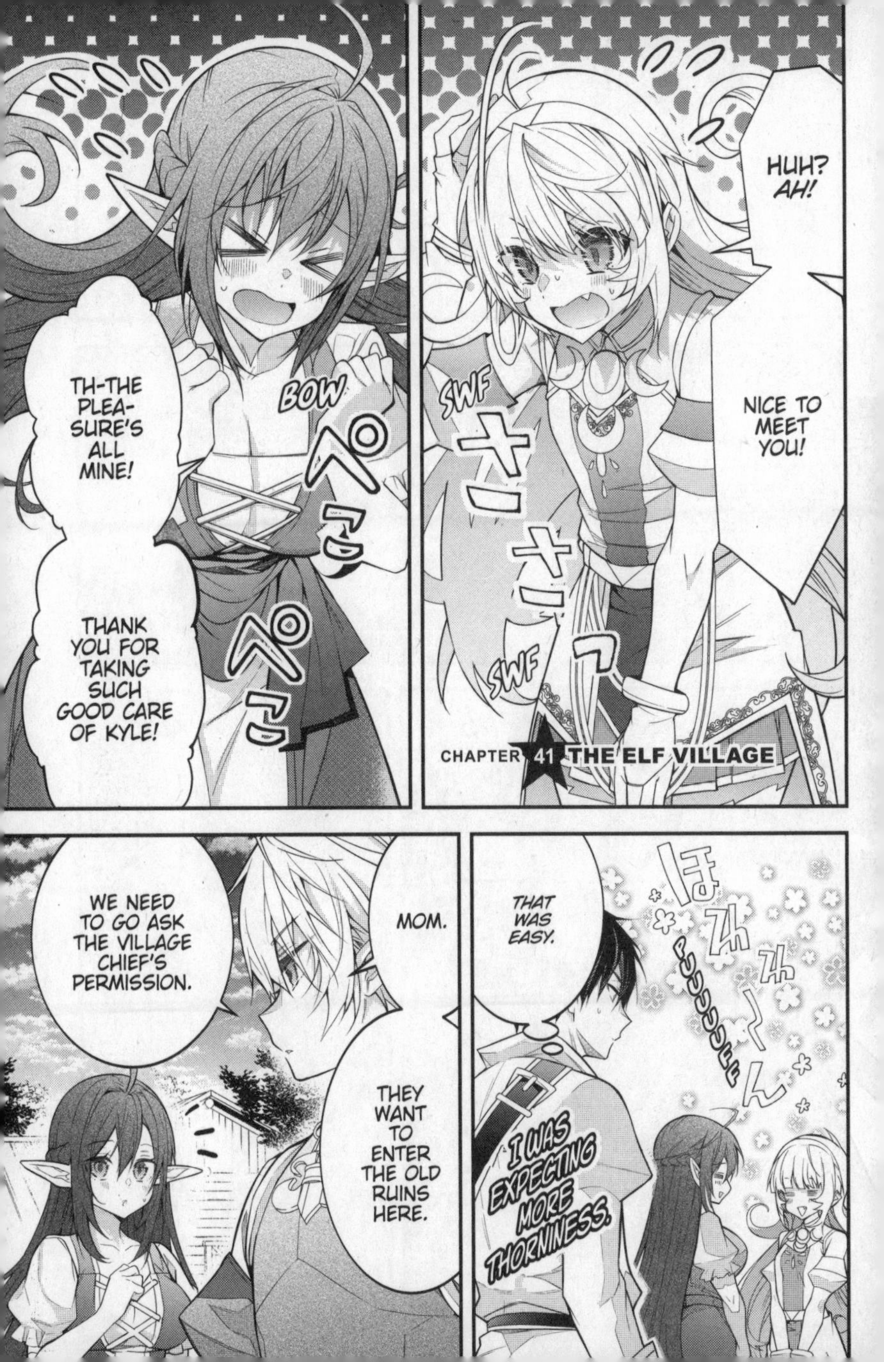
HUH? AH!
NICE TO MEET YOU!
SWF
SWF
CHAPTER 41 THE ELF VILLAGE
TH-THE PLEASURE'S ALL MINE!
BOW
THANK YOU FOR TAKING SUCH GOOD CARE OF KYLE!
THAT WAS EASY.
PUUUUUFF
I WAS EXPECTING MORE THORNINESS.
MOM.
THEY WANT TO ENTER THE OLD RUINS HERE.
WE NEED TO GO ASK THE VILLAGE CHIEF'S PERMISSION.

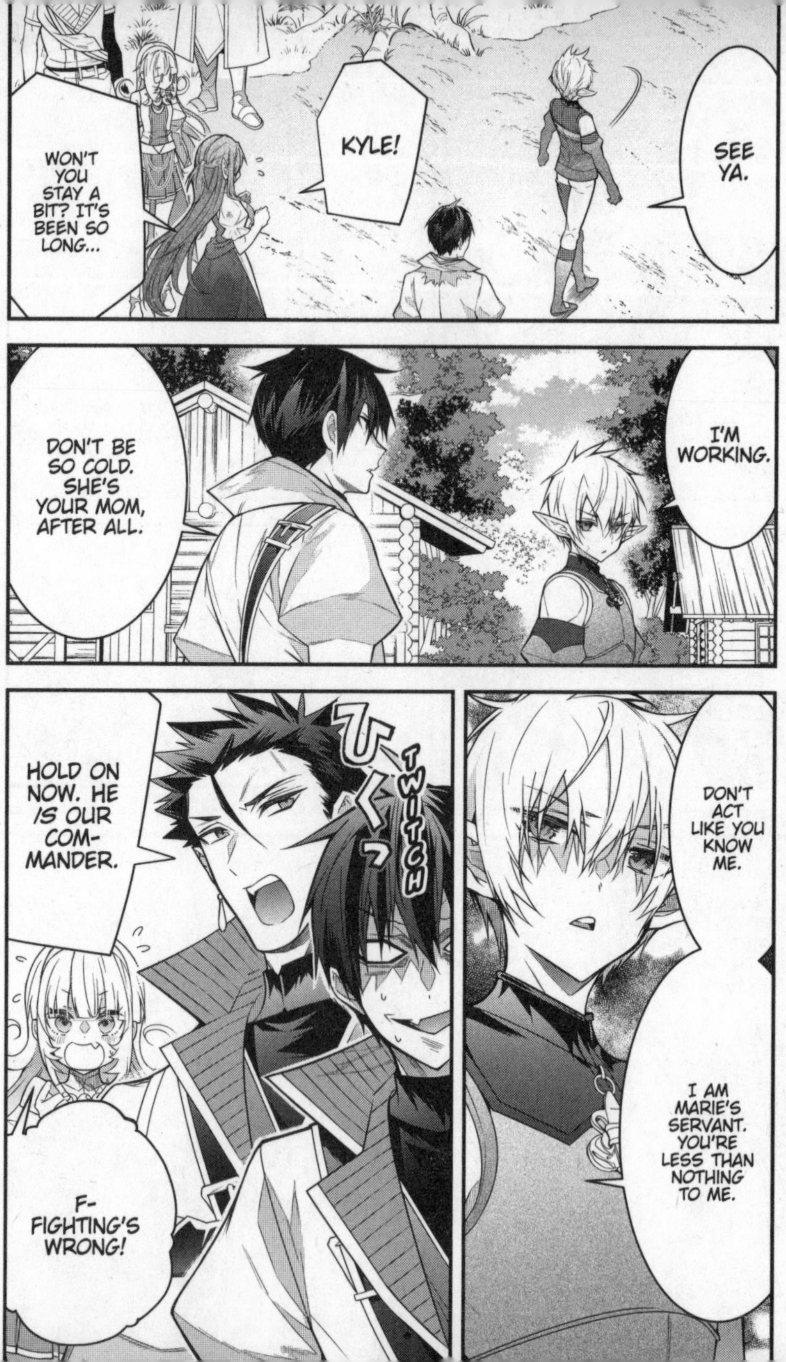
SEE YA.
KYLE!
WON'T YOU STAY A BIT? IT'S BEEN SO LONG...
I'M WORKING.
DON'T BE SO COLD. SHE'S YOUR MOM, AFTER ALL.
DON'T ACT LIKE YOU KNOW ME.
I AM MARIE'S SERVANT. YOU'RE LESS THAN NOTHING TO ME.
HOLD ON NOW. HE IS OUR COM-MANDER.
ひくっ
TWITCH
F-FIGHTING'S WRONG!

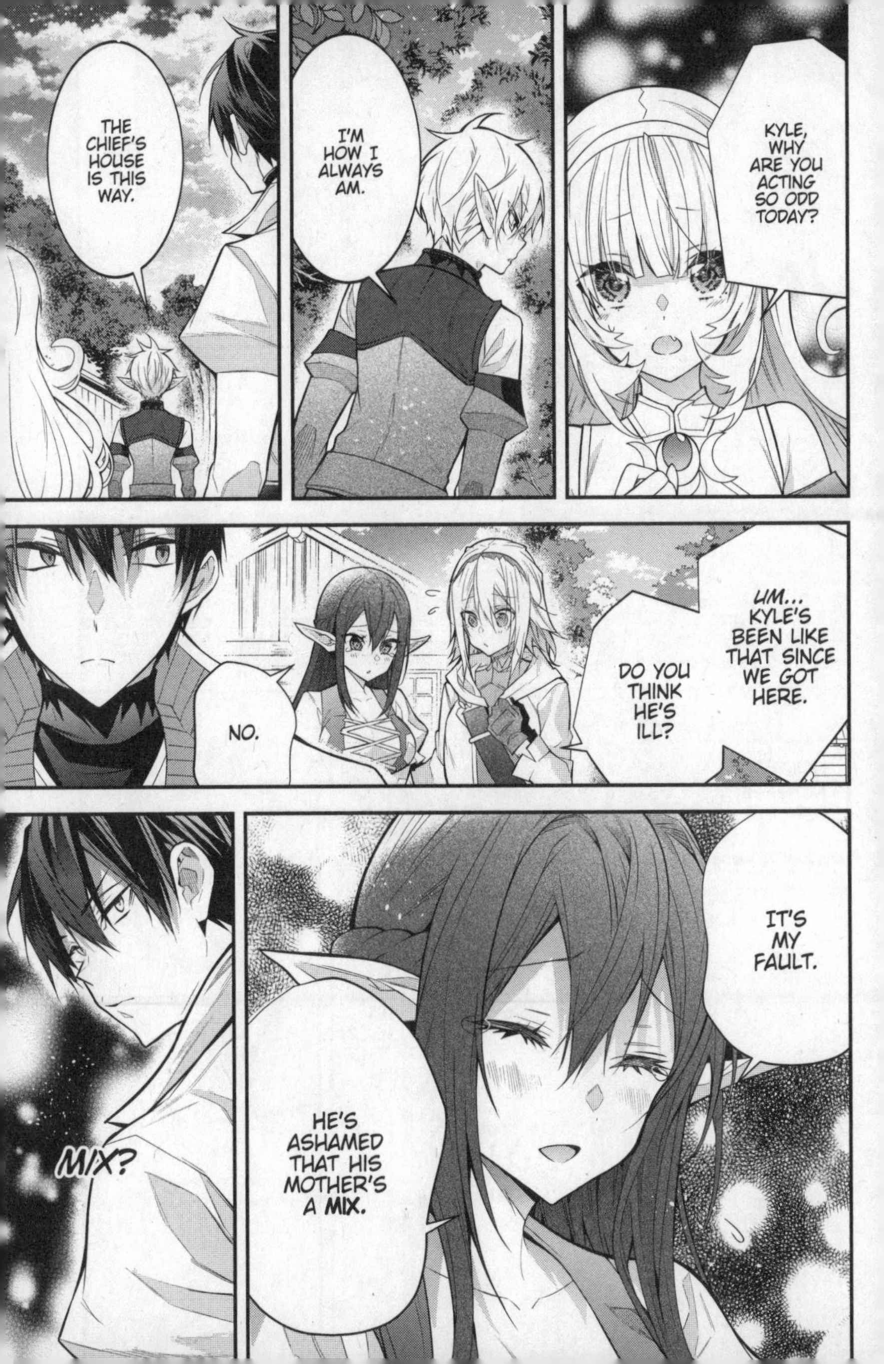
KYLE, WHY ARE YOU ACTING SO ODD TODAY?
I'M HOW I ALWAYS AM.
THE CHIEF'S HOUSE IS THIS WAY.
UM... KYLE'S BEEN LIKE THAT SINCE WE GOT HERE.
DO YOU THINK HE'S ILL?
NO.
IT'S MY FAULT.
HE'S ASHAMED THAT HIS MOTHER'S A **MIX**.
MIX?

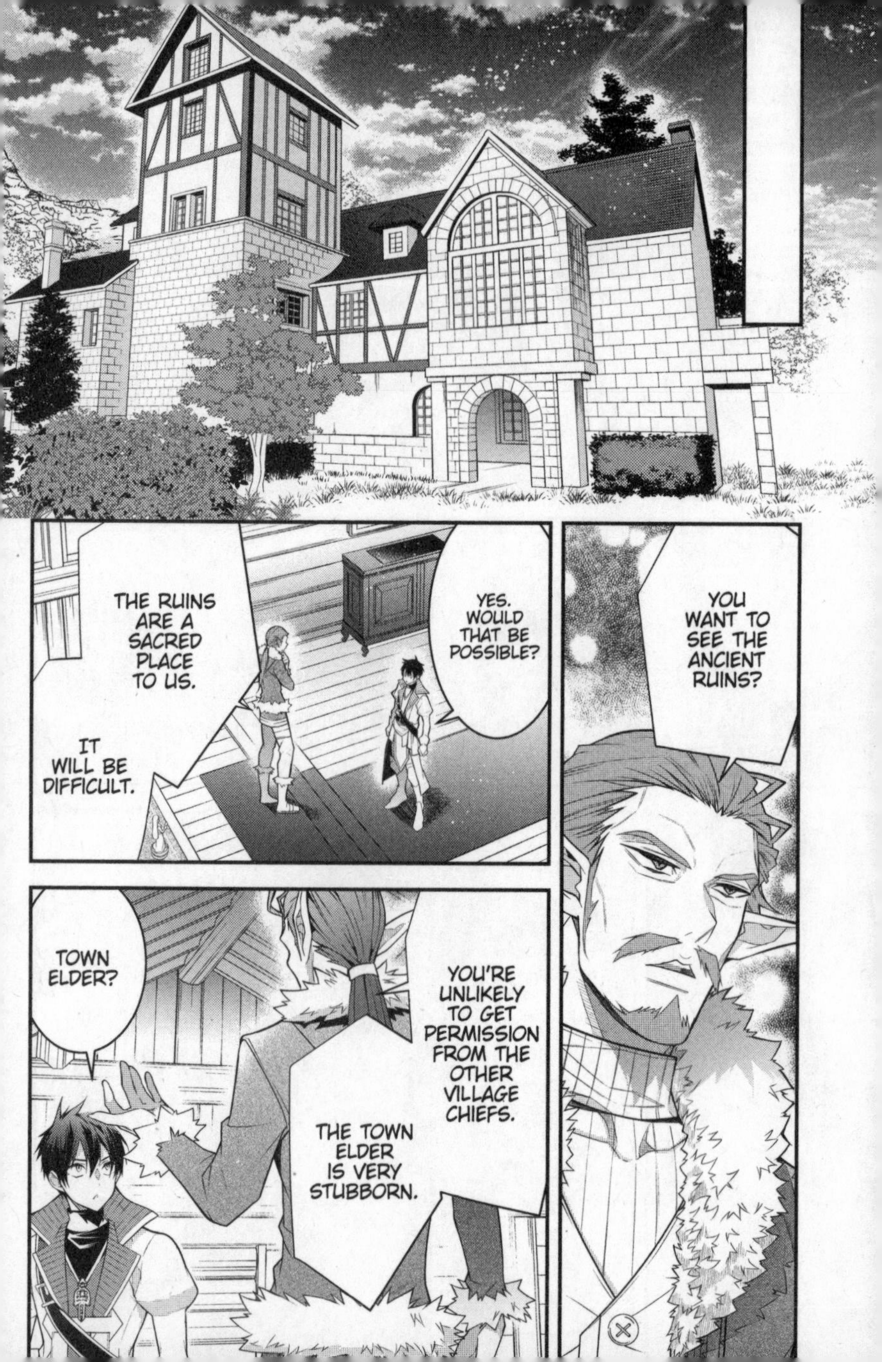
YOU WANT TO SEE THE ANCIENT RUINS?
YES. WOULD THAT BE POSSIBLE?
THE RUINS ARE A SACRED PLACE TO US.
IT WILL BE DIFFICULT.
YOU'RE UNLIKELY TO GET PERMISSION FROM THE OTHER VILLAGE CHIEFS.
THE TOWN ELDER IS VERY STUBBORN.
TOWN ELDER?

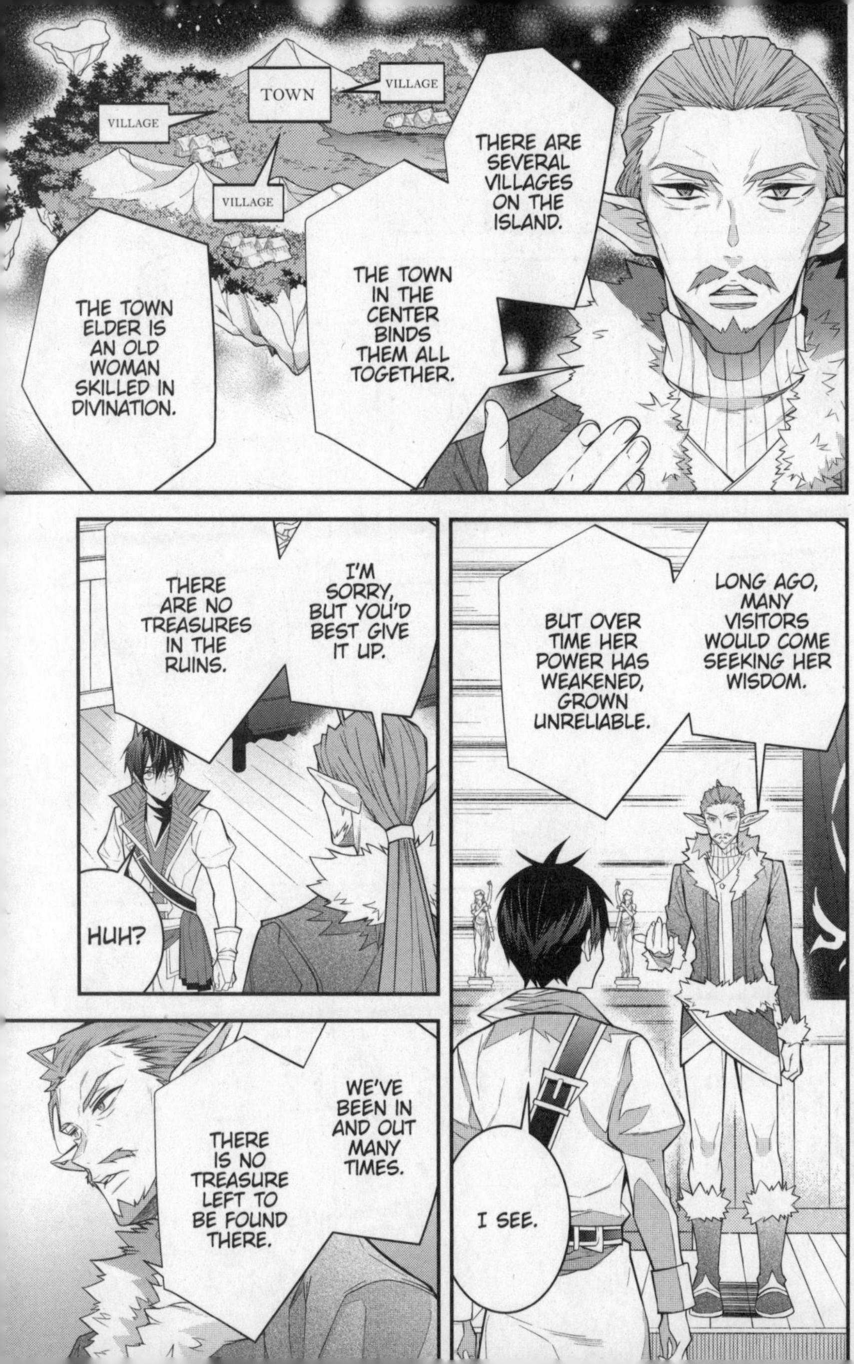
VILLAGE
TOWN
VILLAGE
VILLAGE
THERE ARE SEVERAL VILLAGES ON THE ISLAND.
THE TOWN IN THE CENTER BINDS THEM ALL TOGETHER.
THE TOWN ELDER IS AN OLD WOMAN SKILLED IN DIVINATION.
LONG AGO, MANY VISITORS WOULD COME SEEKING HER WISDOM.
BUT OVER TIME HER POWER HAS WEAKENED, GROWN UNRELIABLE.
I SEE.
I'M SORRY, BUT YOU'D BEST GIVE IT UP.
THERE ARE NO TREASURES IN THE RUINS.
HUH?
WE'VE BEEN IN AND OUT MANY TIMES.
THERE IS NO TREASURE LEFT TO BE FOUND THERE.

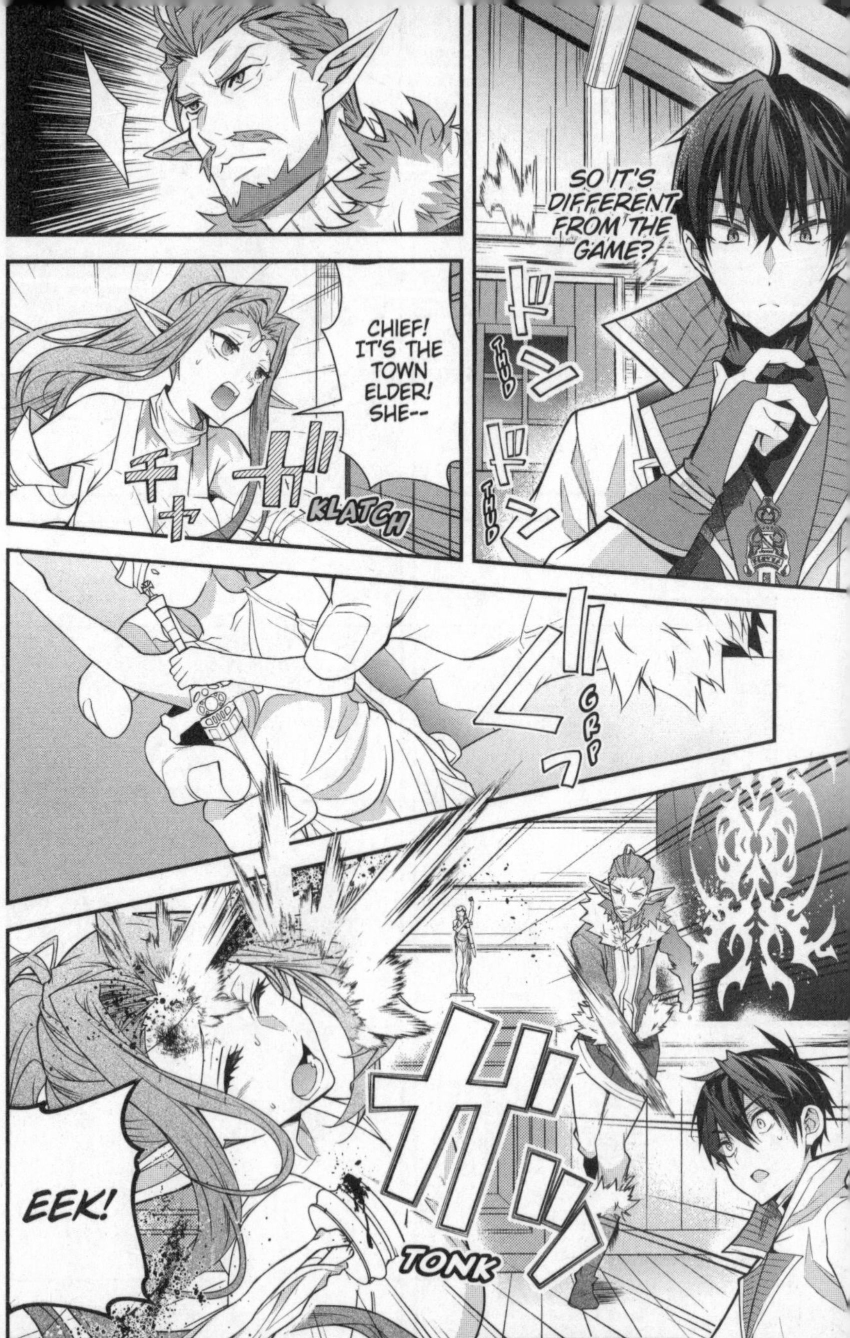

SO IT'S DIFFERENT FROM THE GAME?
THUD
THUD
CHIEF! IT'S THE TOWN ELDER! SHE--
KLATCH
GRP
TONK
EEK!

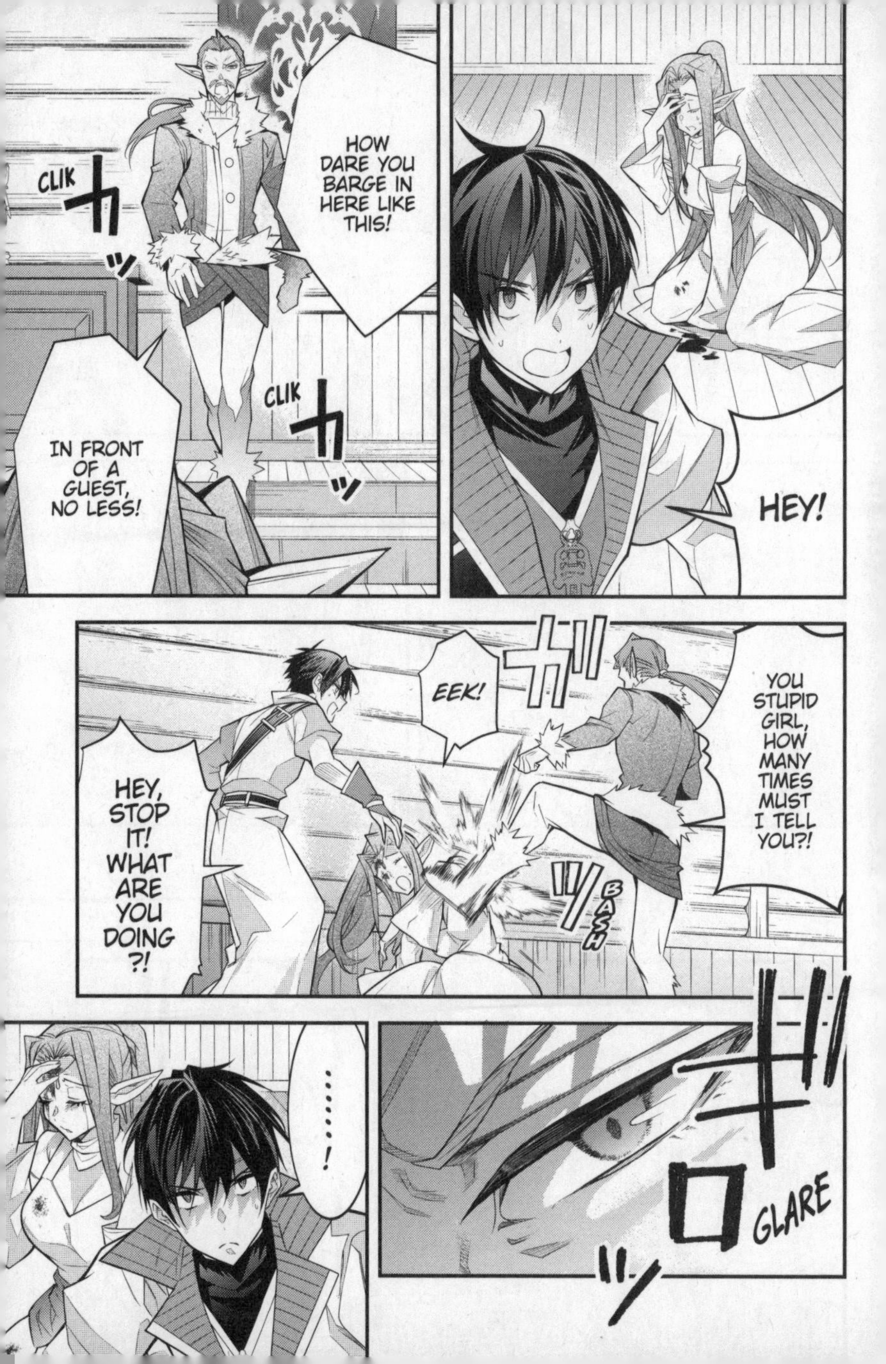
HEY!
HOW DARE YOU BARGE IN HERE LIKE THIS!
CLIK
IN FRONT OF A GUEST, NO LESS!
CLIK
YOU STUPID GIRL, HOW MANY TIMES MUST I TELL YOU?!
BASH
EEK!
HEY, STOP IT! WHAT ARE YOU DOING?!
GLARE
......!

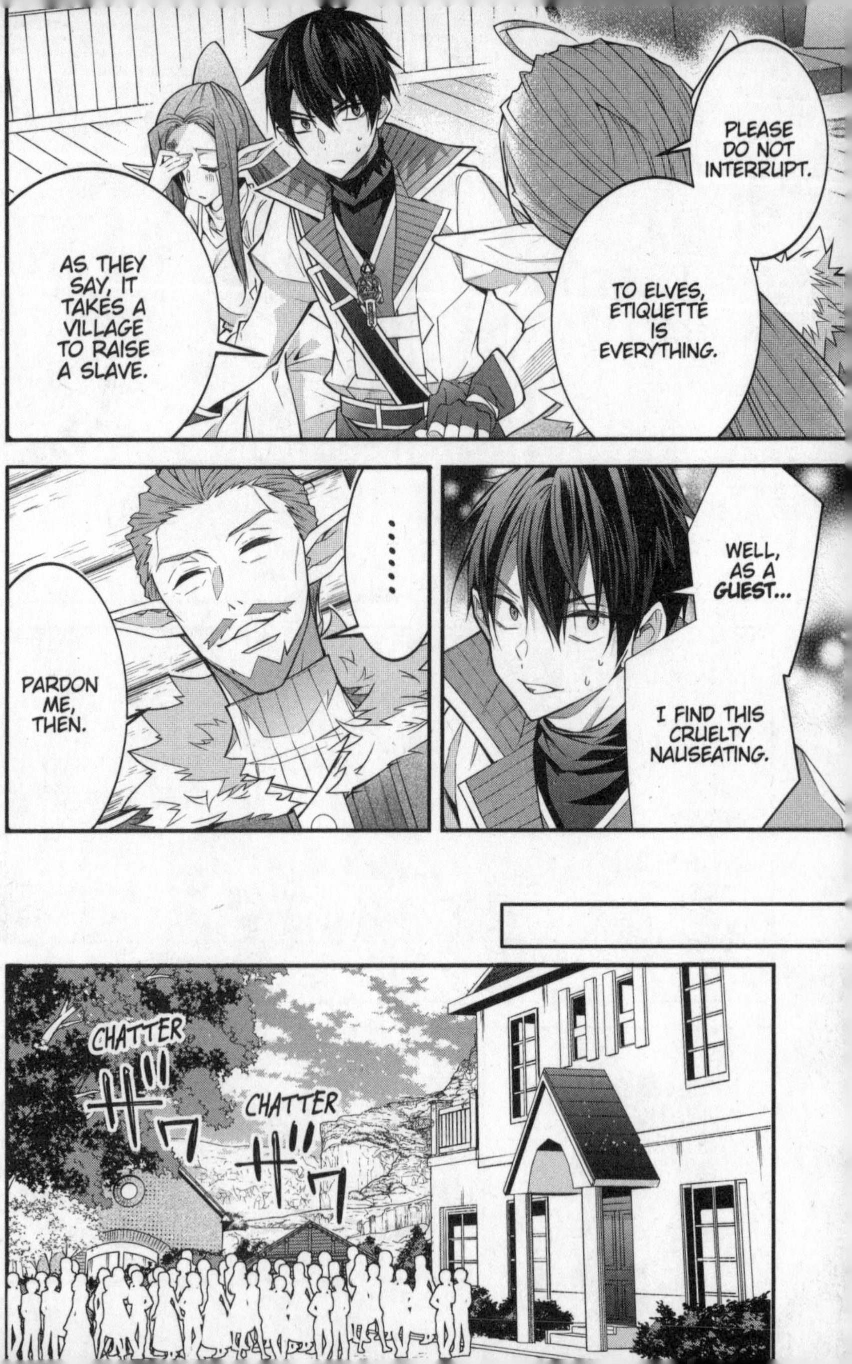
PLEASE DO NOT INTERRUPT.
TO ELVES, ETIQUETTE IS EVERYTHING.
AS THEY SAY, IT TAKES A VILLAGE TO RAISE A SLAVE.
WELL, AS A GUEST...
I FIND THIS CRUELTY NAUSEATING.
......
PARDON ME, THEN.
CHATTER
ザワ
CHATTER
ザワ

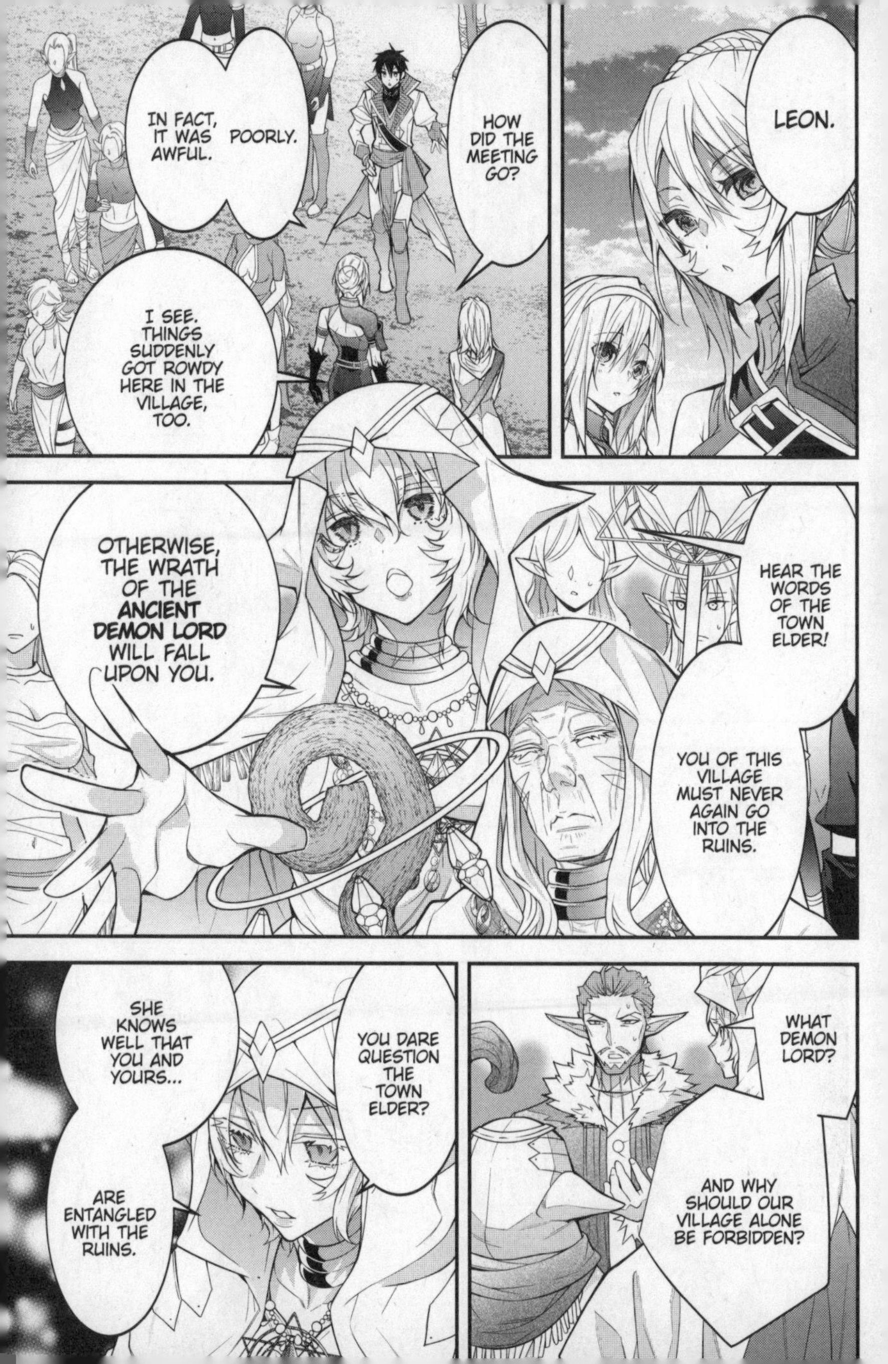
LEON.
HOW DID THE MEETING GO?
POORLY.
IN FACT, IT WAS AWFUL.
I SEE. THINGS SUDDENLY GOT ROWDY HERE IN THE VILLAGE, TOO.
HEAR THE WORDS OF THE TOWN ELDER!
YOU OF THIS VILLAGE MUST NEVER AGAIN GO INTO THE RUINS.
OTHERWISE, THE WRATH OF THE **ANCIENT DEMON LORD** WILL FALL UPON YOU.
WHAT DEMON LORD?
AND WHY SHOULD OUR VILLAGE ALONE BE FORBIDDEN?
YOU DARE QUESTION THE TOWN ELDER?
SHE KNOWS WELL THAT YOU AND YOURS...
ARE ENTANGLED WITH THE RUINS.

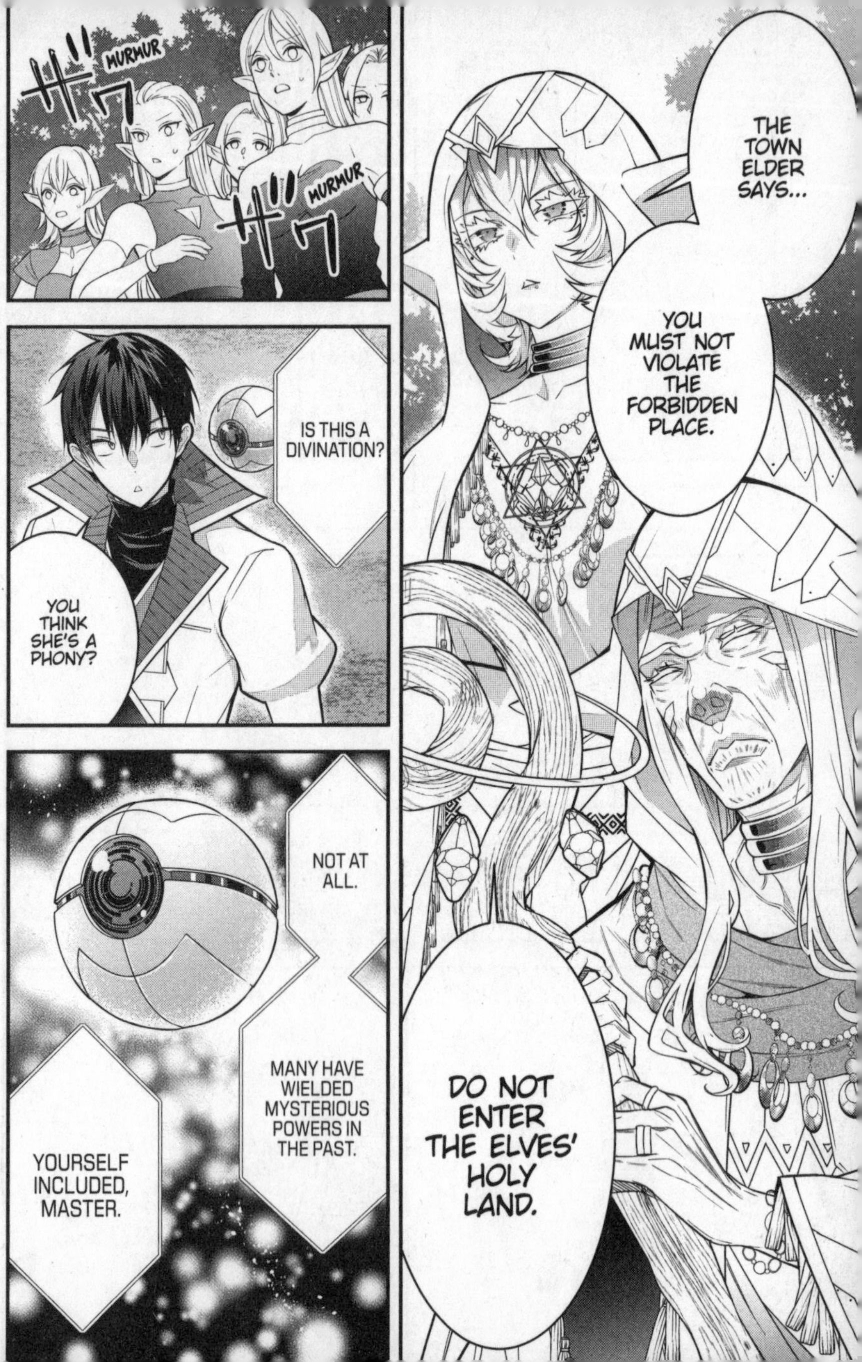
THE TOWN ELDER SAYS...
YOU MUST NOT VIOLATE THE FORBIDDEN PLACE.
DO NOT ENTER THE ELVES' HOLY LAND.
ザワ
MURMUR
ザワ
MURMUR
IS THIS A DIVINATION?
YOU THINK SHE'S A PHONY?
NOT AT ALL.
MANY HAVE WIELDED MYSTERIOUS POWERS IN THE PAST.
YOURSELF INCLUDED, MASTER.

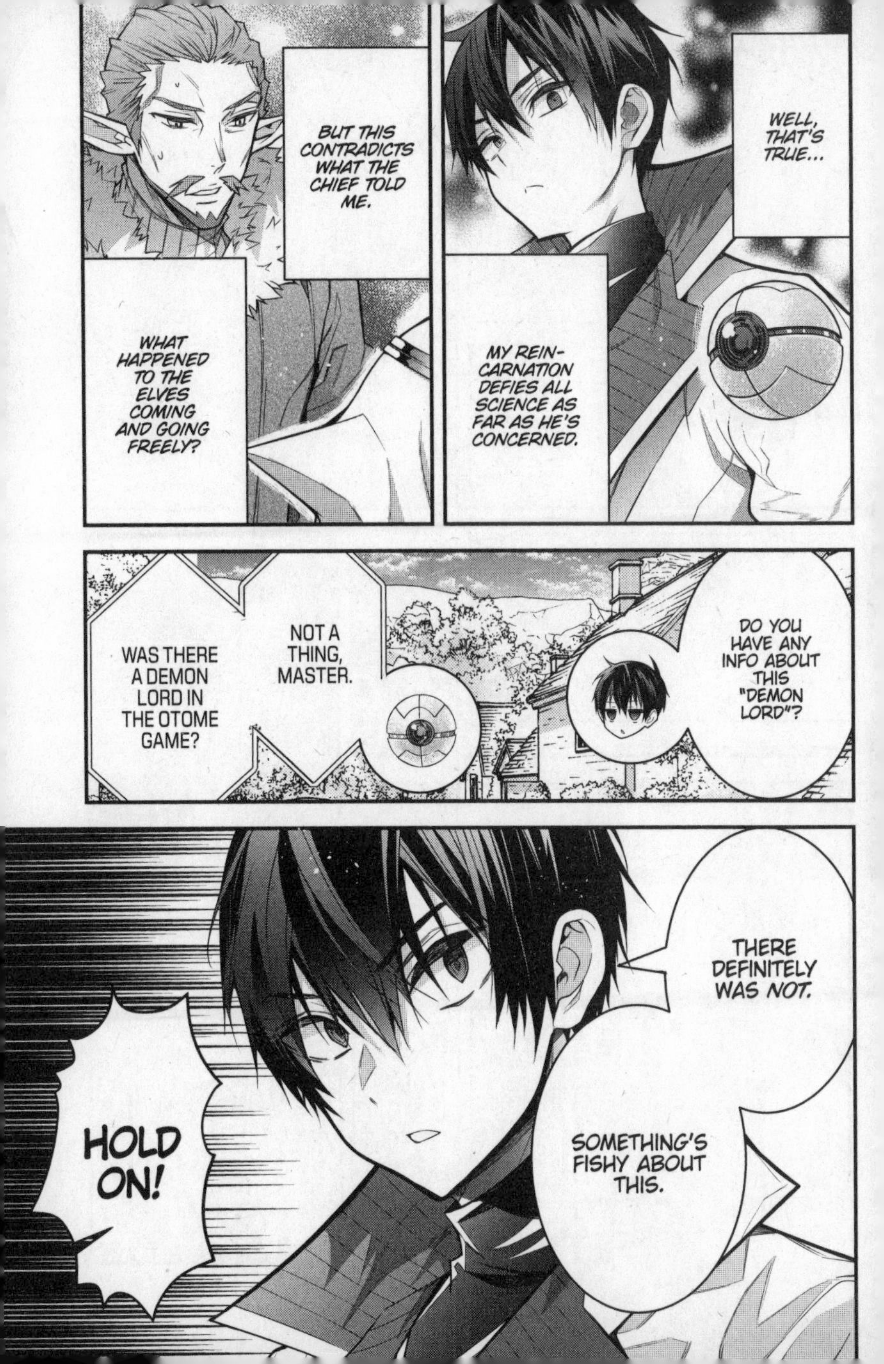
WELL, THAT'S TRUE...
MY REIN-CARNATION DEFIES ALL SCIENCE AS FAR AS HE'S CONCERNED.
BUT THIS CONTRADICTS WHAT THE CHIEF TOLD ME.
WHAT HAPPENED TO THE ELVES COMING AND GOING FREELY?
DO YOU HAVE ANY INFO ABOUT THIS "DEMON LORD"?
NOT A THING, MASTER.
WAS THERE A DEMON LORD IN THE OTOME GAME?
THERE DEFINITELY WAS *NOT*.
SOMETHING'S FISHY ABOUT THIS.
HOLD ON!

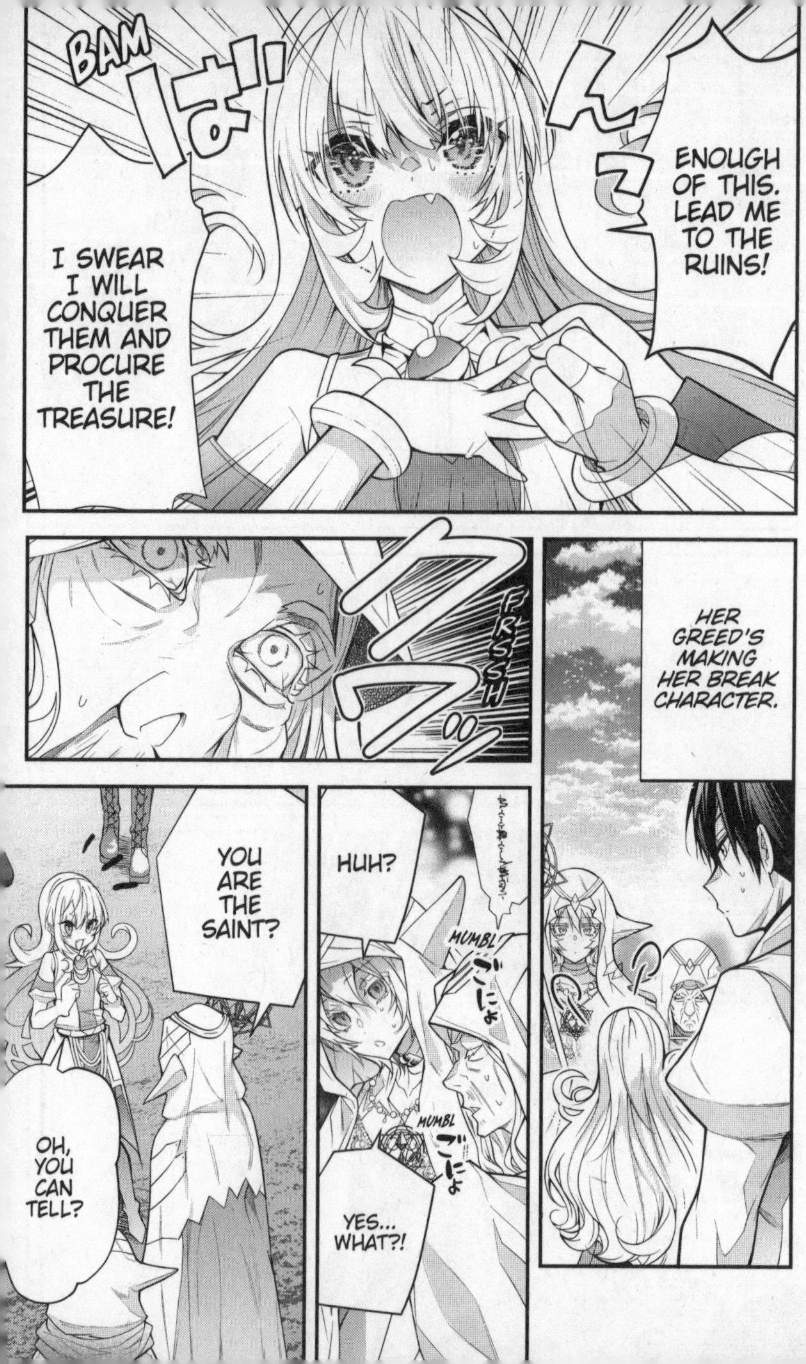
ENOUGH OF THIS. LEAD ME TO THE RUINS!
んっ
BAM
ばーん
I SWEAR I WILL CONQUER THEM AND PROCURE THE TREASURE!
HER GREED'S MAKING HER BREAK CHARACTER.
FRSSH
HUH?
MUMBL
ごにょ
MUMBL
ごにょ
YES... WHAT?!
YOU ARE THE SAINT?
OH, YOU CAN TELL?

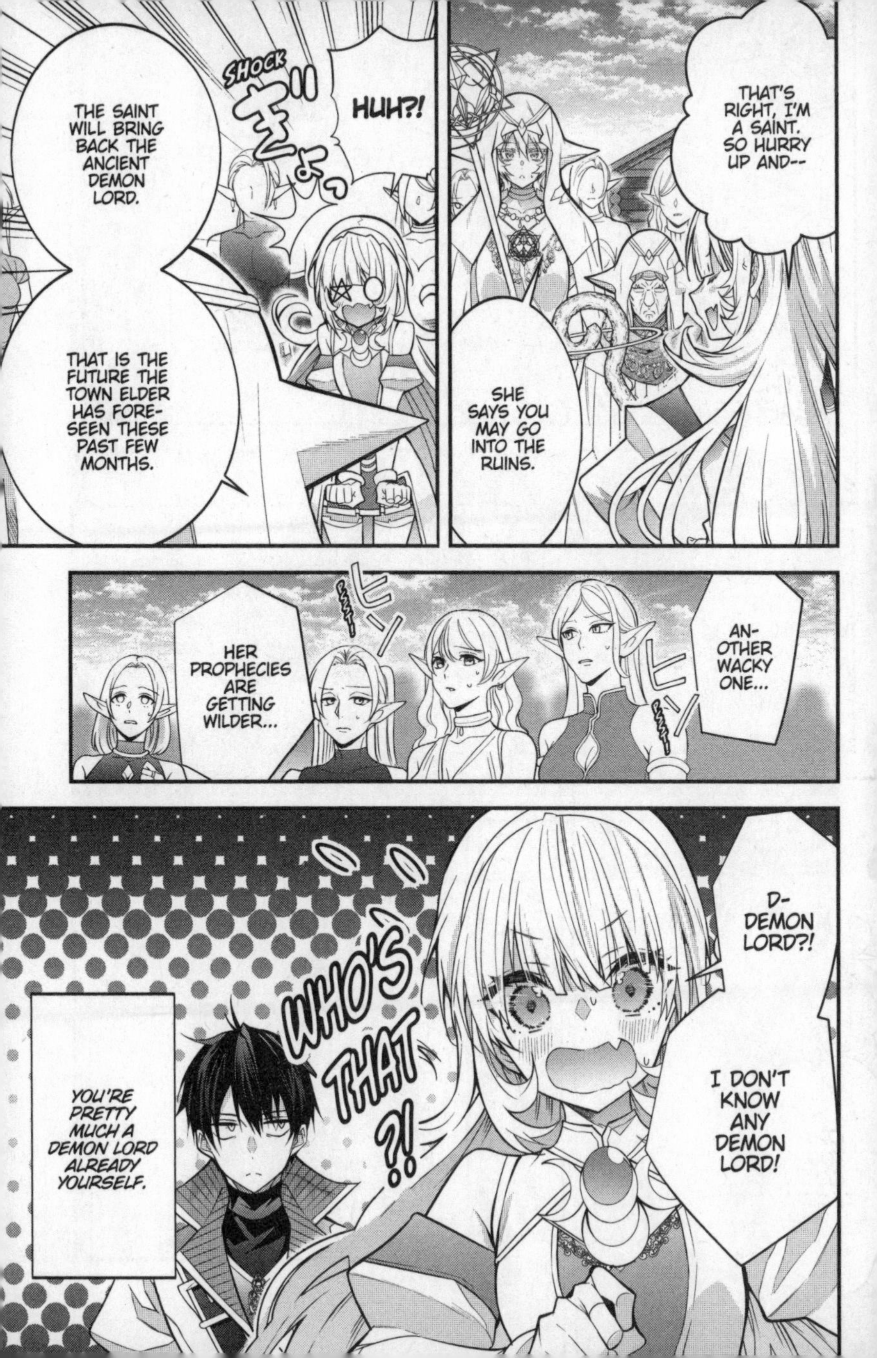
THAT'S RIGHT, I'M A SAINT. SO HURRY UP AND--
SHE SAYS YOU MAY GO INTO THE RUINS.
HUH?!
SHOCK
ぎょっ
THE SAINT WILL BRING BACK THE ANCIENT DEMON LORD.
THAT IS THE FUTURE THE TOWN ELDER HAS FORESEEN THESE PAST FEW MONTHS.
ANOTHER WACKY ONE...
HER PROPHECIES ARE GETTING WILDER...
D-DEMON LORD?!
I DON'T KNOW ANY DEMON LORD!
WHO'S THAT?!
YOU'RE PRETTY MUCH A DEMON LORD ALREADY YOURSELF.

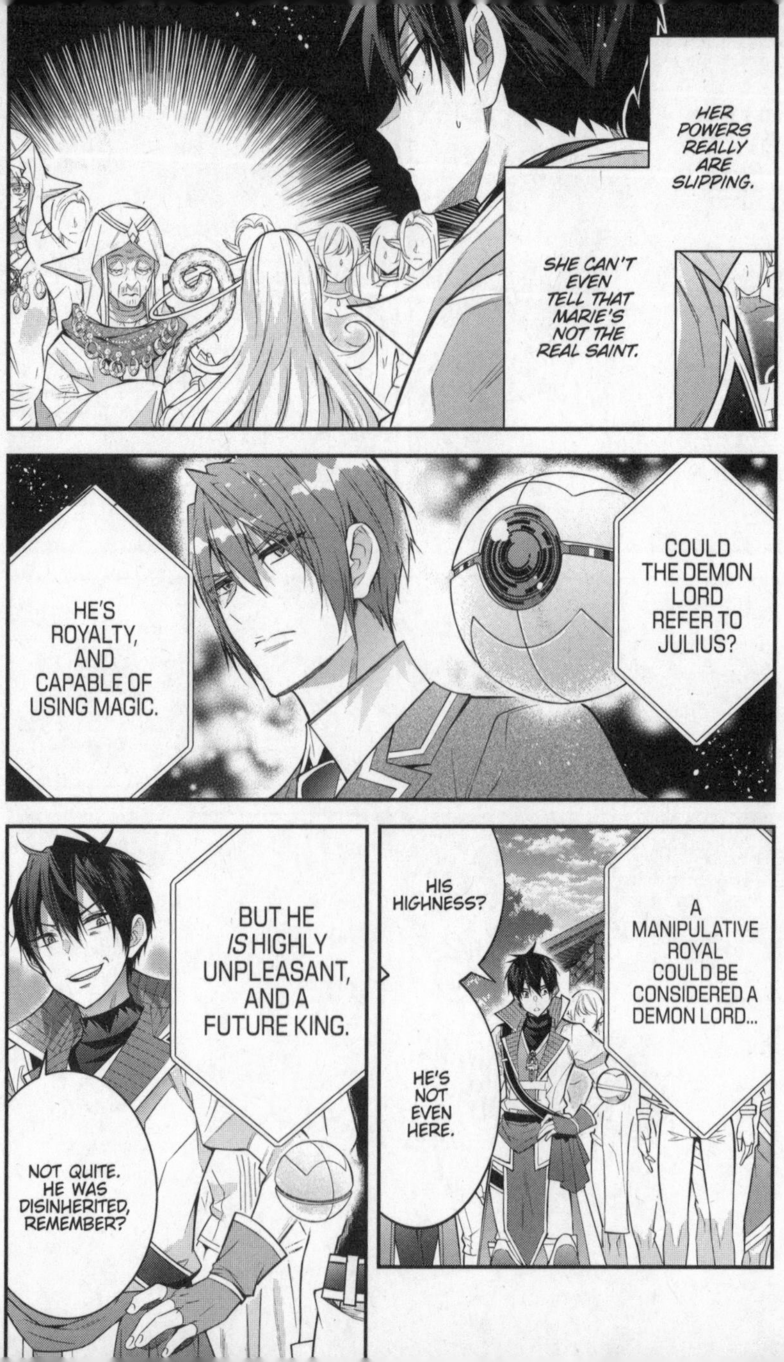
HER POWERS REALLY ARE SLIPPING.
SHE CAN'T EVEN TELL THAT MARIE'S NOT THE REAL SAINT.
COULD THE DEMON LORD REFER TO JULIUS?
HE'S ROYALTY, AND CAPABLE OF USING MAGIC.
A MANIPULATIVE ROYAL COULD BE CONSIDERED A DEMON LORD...
HIS HIGHNESS? HE'S NOT EVEN HERE.
BUT HE *IS* HIGHLY UNPLEASANT, AND A FUTURE KING.
NOT QUITE. HE WAS DISINHERITED, REMEMBER?

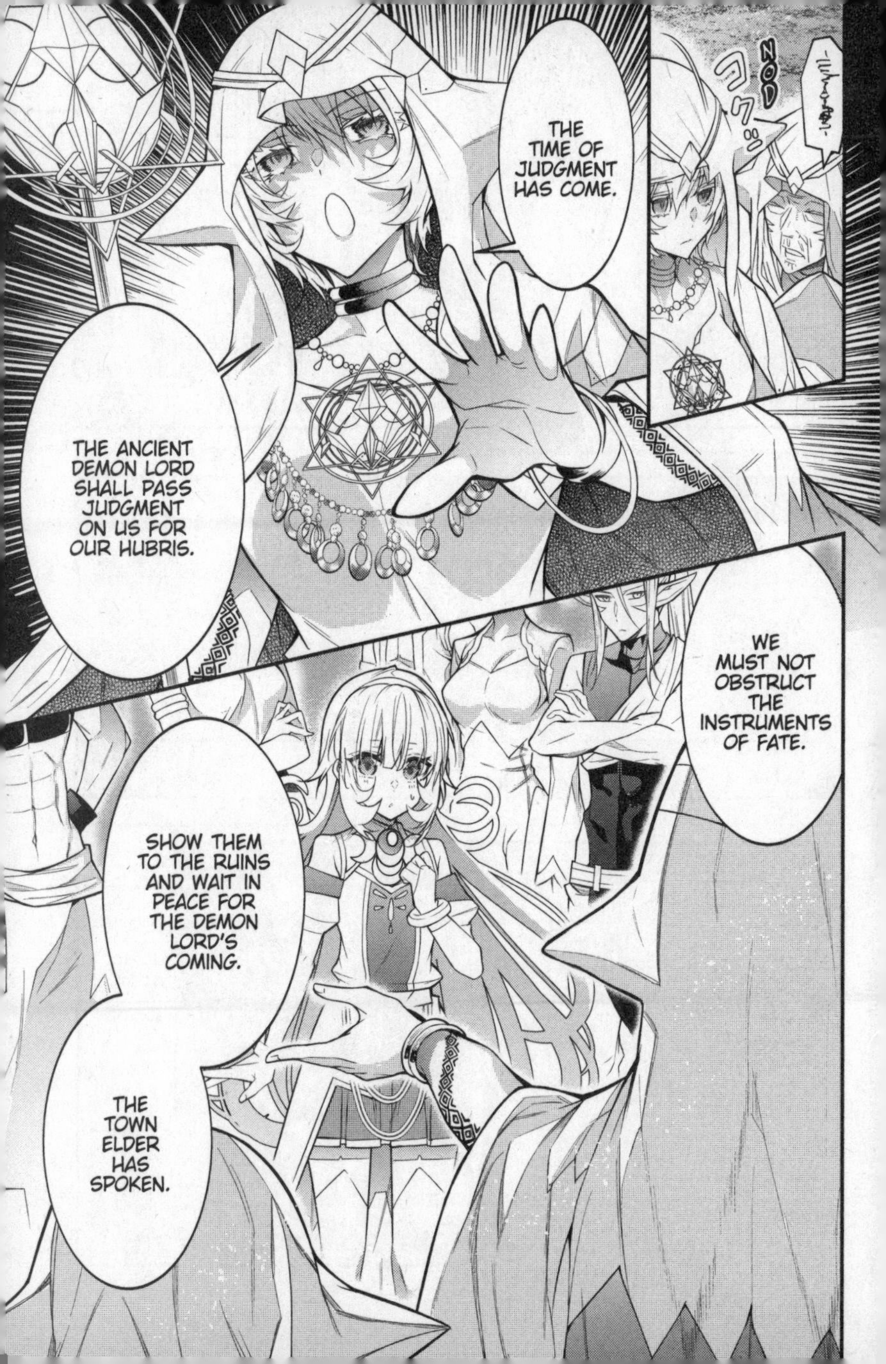
NOD
THE TIME OF JUDGMENT HAS COME.
THE ANCIENT DEMON LORD SHALL PASS JUDGMENT ON US FOR OUR HUBRIS.
WE MUST NOT OBSTRUCT THE INSTRUMENTS OF FATE.
SHOW THEM TO THE RUINS AND WAIT IN PEACE FOR THE DEMON LORD'S COMING.
THE TOWN ELDER HAS SPOKEN.

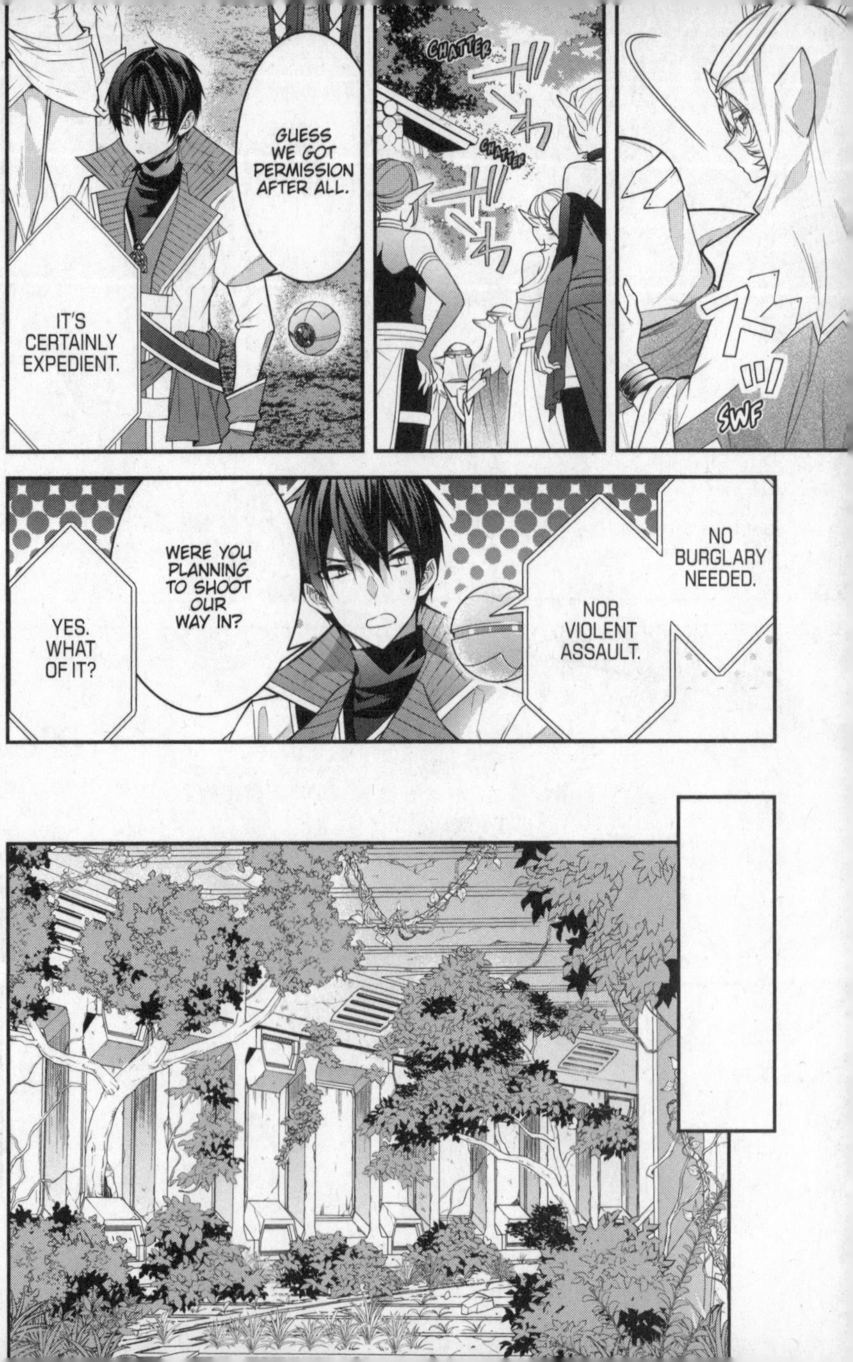
SWF
CHATTER
CHATTER
GUESS WE GOT PERMISSION AFTER ALL.
IT'S CERTAINLY EXPEDIENT.
NO BURGLARY NEEDED.
NOR VIOLENT ASSAULT.
WERE YOU PLANNING TO SHOOT OUR WAY IN?
YES. WHAT OF IT?

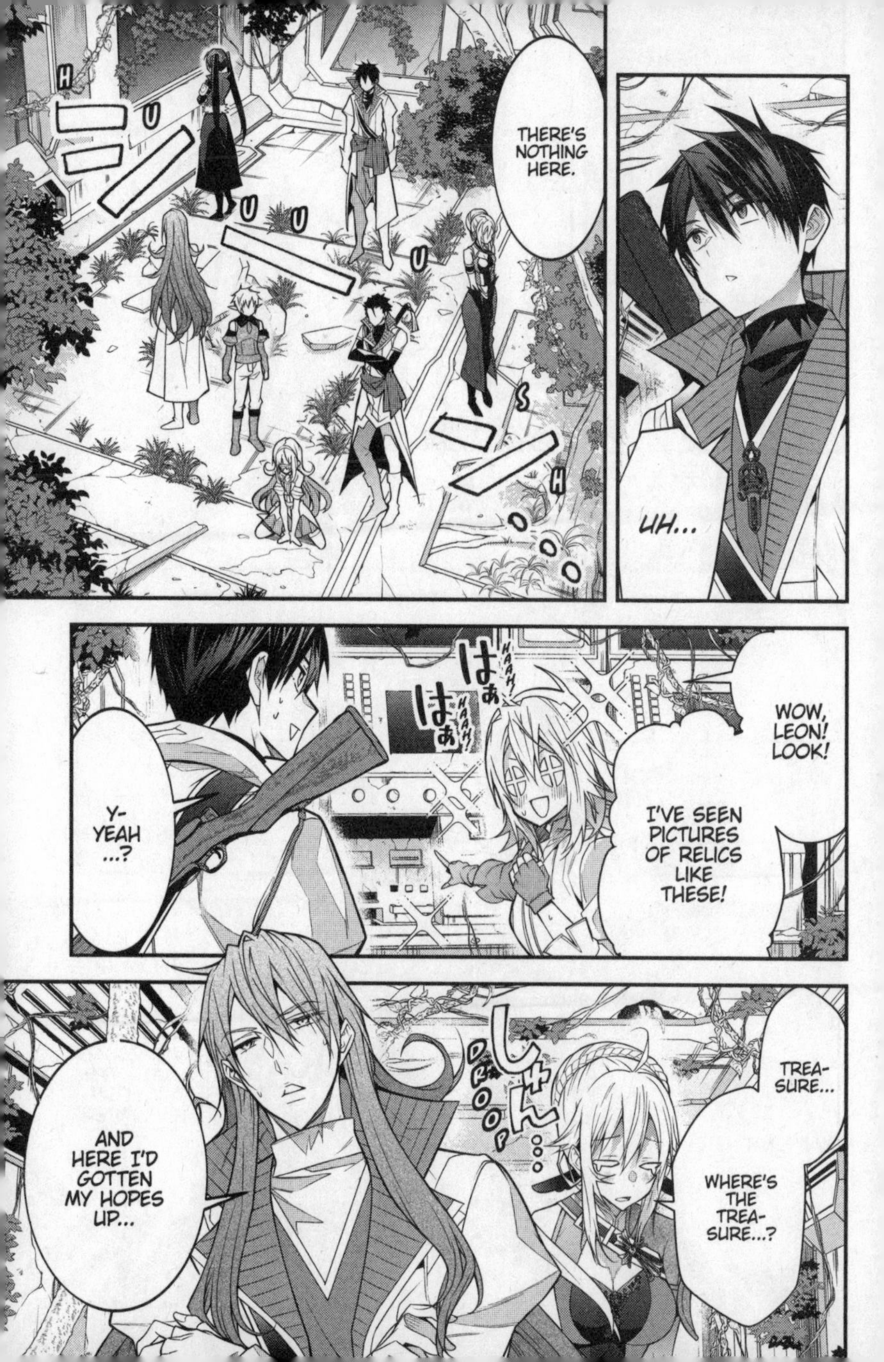
UH...
THERE'S NOTHING HERE.
HUUUU
SHOOO
WOW, LEON! LOOK!
I'VE SEEN PICTURES OF RELICS LIKE THESE!
はぁ HAAH!
はぁ HAAH!
Y-YEAH ...?
TREA-SURE...
WHERE'S THE TREA-SURE...?
しゅん... DROOOP
AND HERE I'D GOTTEN MY HOPES UP...

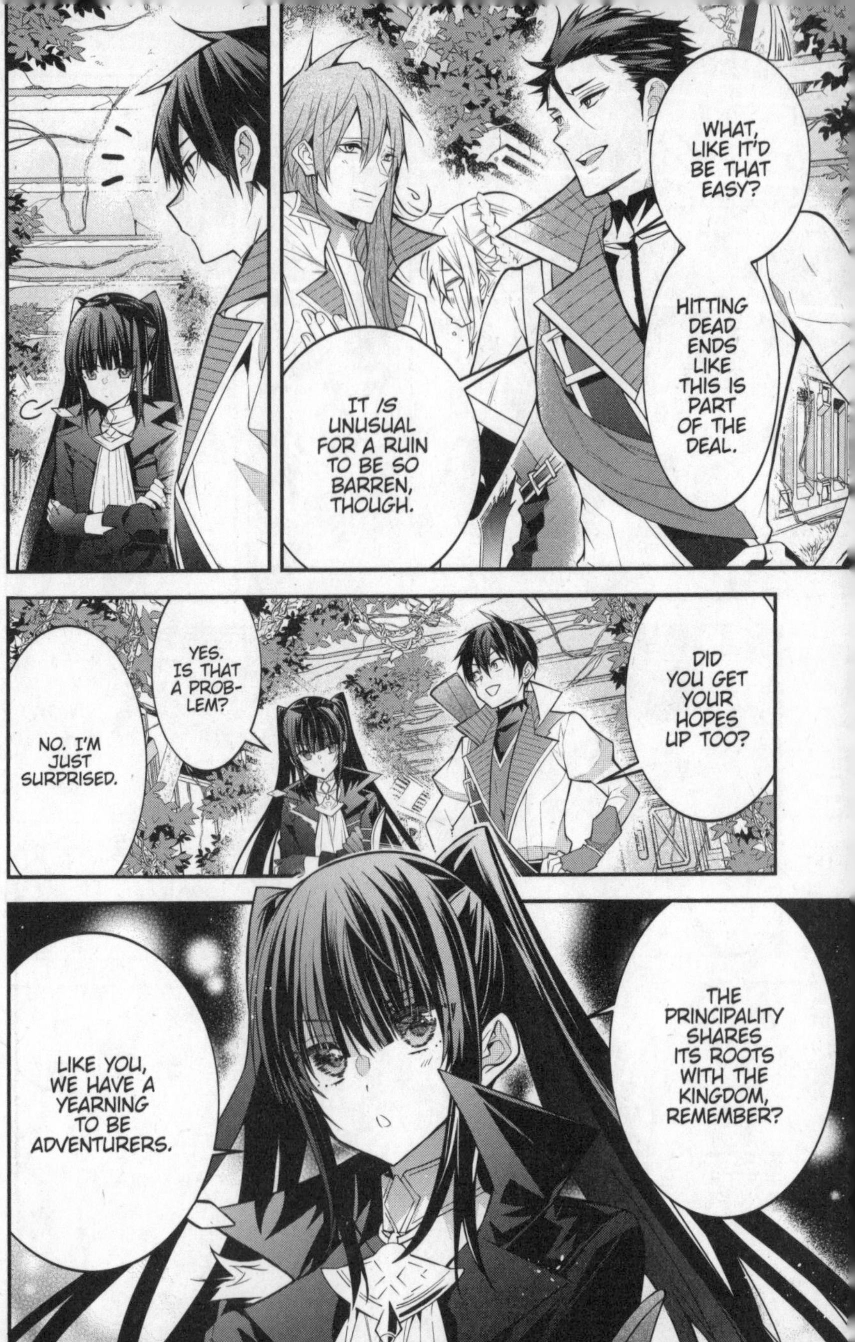
WHAT, LIKE IT'D BE THAT EASY?
HITTING DEAD ENDS LIKE THIS IS PART OF THE DEAL.
IT *IS* UNUSUAL FOR A RUIN TO BE SO BARREN, THOUGH.
DID YOU GET YOUR HOPES UP TOO?
YES. IS THAT A PROB-LEM?
NO. I'M JUST SURPRISED.
THE PRINCIPALITY SHARES ITS ROOTS WITH THE KINGDOM, REMEMBER?
LIKE YOU, WE HAVE A YEARNING TO BE ADVENTURERS.

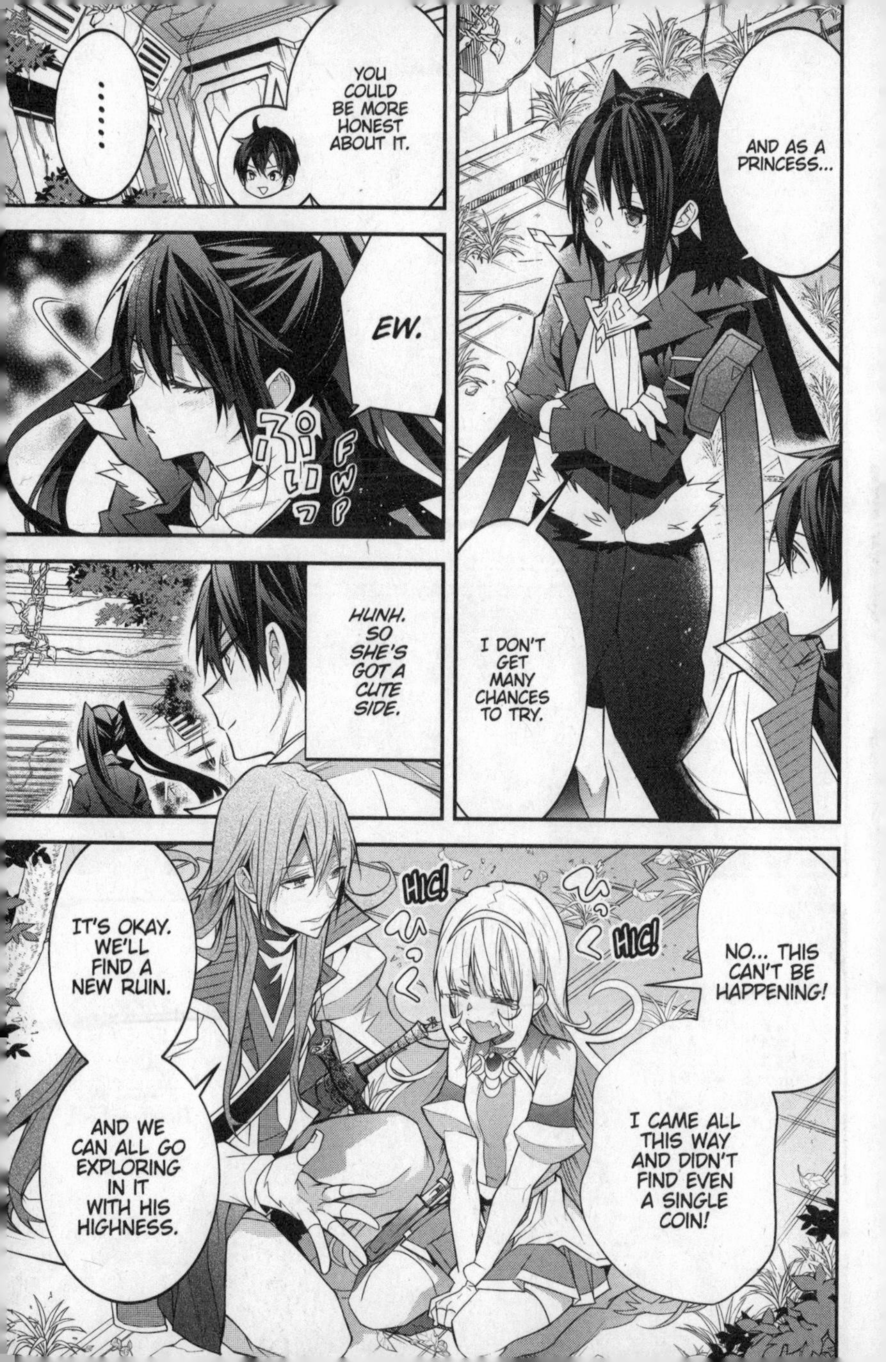
AND AS A PRINCESS...
I DON'T GET MANY CHANCES TO TRY.
YOU COULD BE MORE HONEST ABOUT IT.
......
EW.
ぷいっ
FWP
HUNH. SO SHE'S GOT A CUTE SIDE.
NO... THIS CAN'T BE HAPPENING!
I CAME ALL THIS WAY AND DIDN'T FIND EVEN A SINGLE COIN!
ひっく
HIC!
ひっく
HIC!
IT'S OKAY. WE'LL FIND A NEW RUIN.
AND WE CAN ALL GO EXPLORING IN IT WITH HIS HIGHNESS.

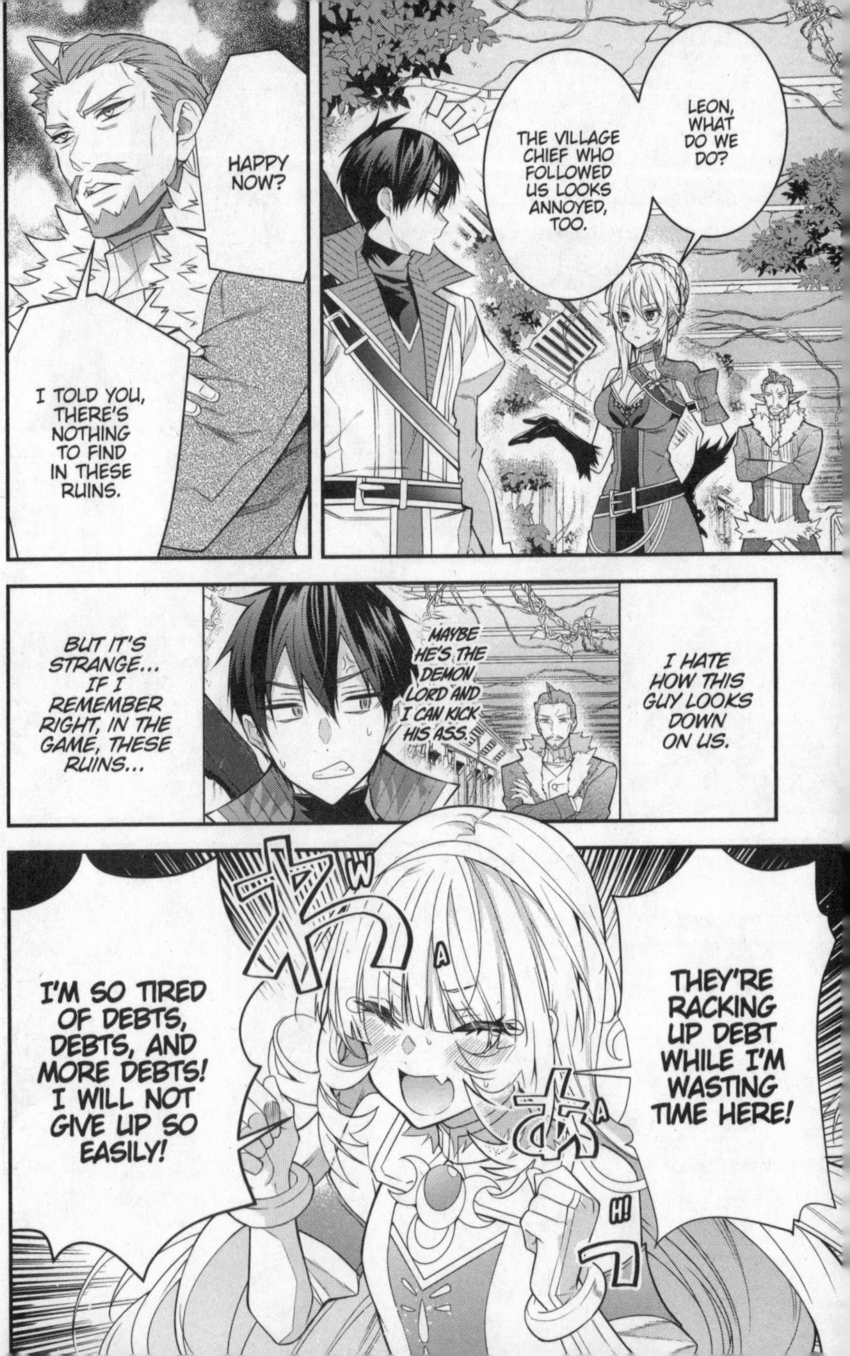
LEON, WHAT DO WE DO?
THE VILLAGE CHIEF WHO FOLLOWED US LOOKS ANNOYED, TOO.
HAPPY NOW?
I TOLD YOU, THERE'S NOTHING TO FIND IN THESE RUINS.
I HATE HOW THIS GUY LOOKS DOWN ON US.
MAYBE HE'S THE DEMON LORD AND I CAN KICK HIS ASS.
BUT IT'S STRANGE... IF I REMEMBER RIGHT, IN THE GAME, THESE RUINS...
W
A
THEY'RE RACKING UP DEBT WHILE I'M WASTING TIME HERE!
I'M SO TIRED OF DEBTS, DEBTS, AND MORE DEBTS! I WILL NOT GIVE UP SO EASILY!
A
H!

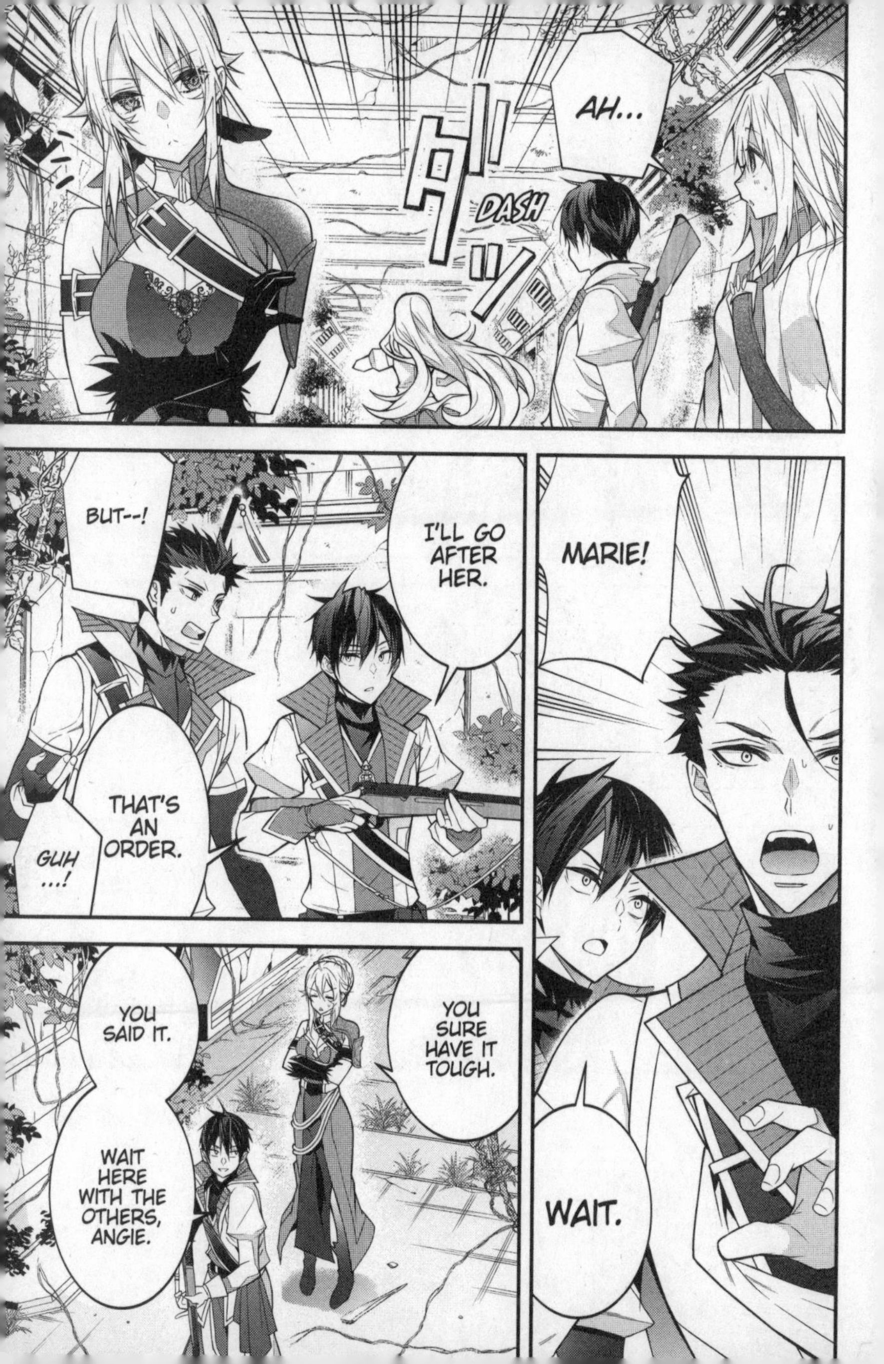
AH...
DASH
MARIE!
WAIT.
I'LL GO AFTER HER.
BUT--!
THAT'S AN ORDER.
GUH ...!
YOU SURE HAVE IT TOUGH.
YOU SAID IT.
WAIT HERE WITH THE OTHERS, ANGIE.

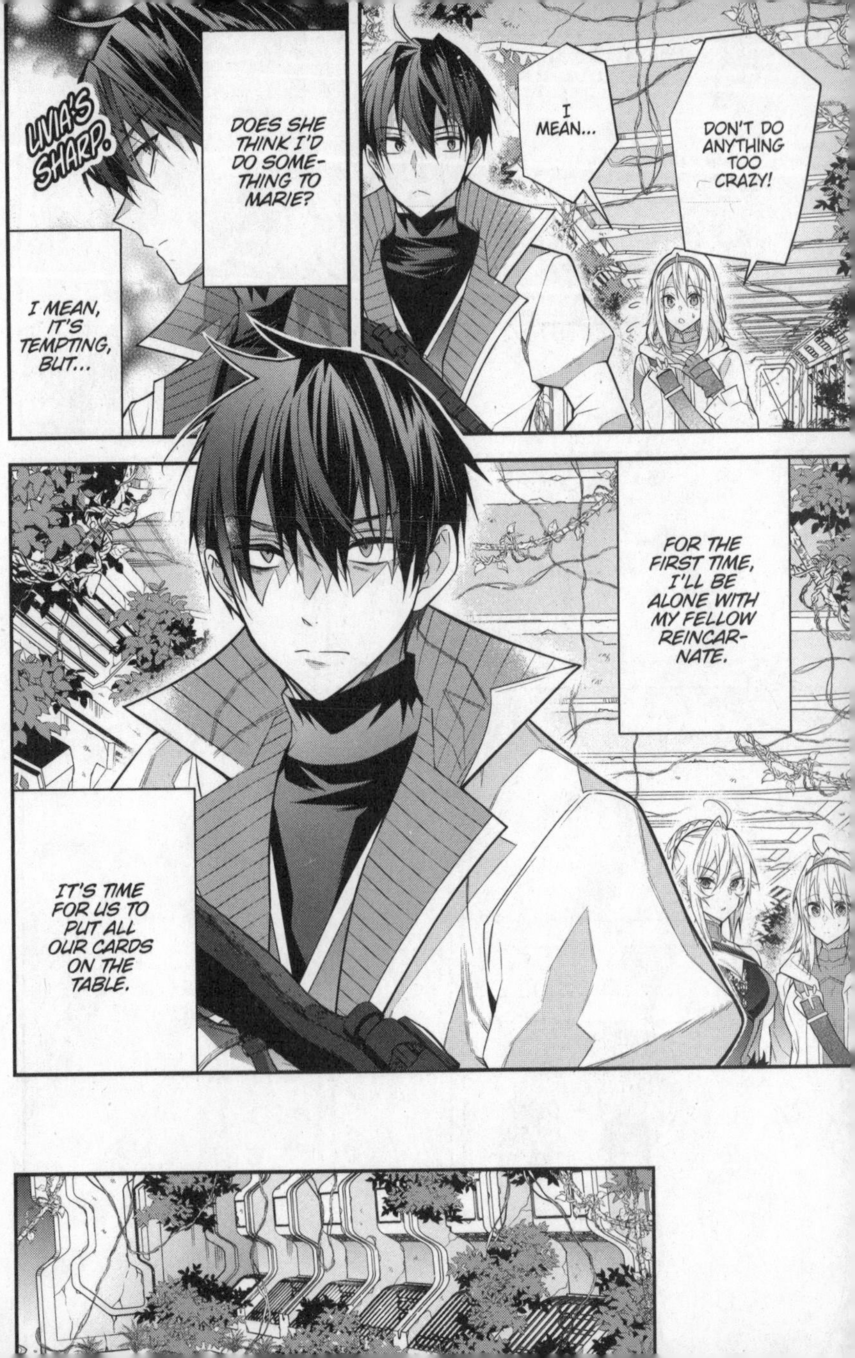
DON'T DO ANYTHING TOO CRAZY!
I MEAN...
DOES SHE THINK I'D DO SOME-THING TO MARIE?
LIVIA'S SHARP.
I MEAN, IT'S TEMPTING, BUT...
FOR THE FIRST TIME, I'LL BE ALONE WITH MY FELLOW REINCAR-NATE.
IT'S TIME FOR US TO PUT ALL OUR CARDS ON THE TABLE.

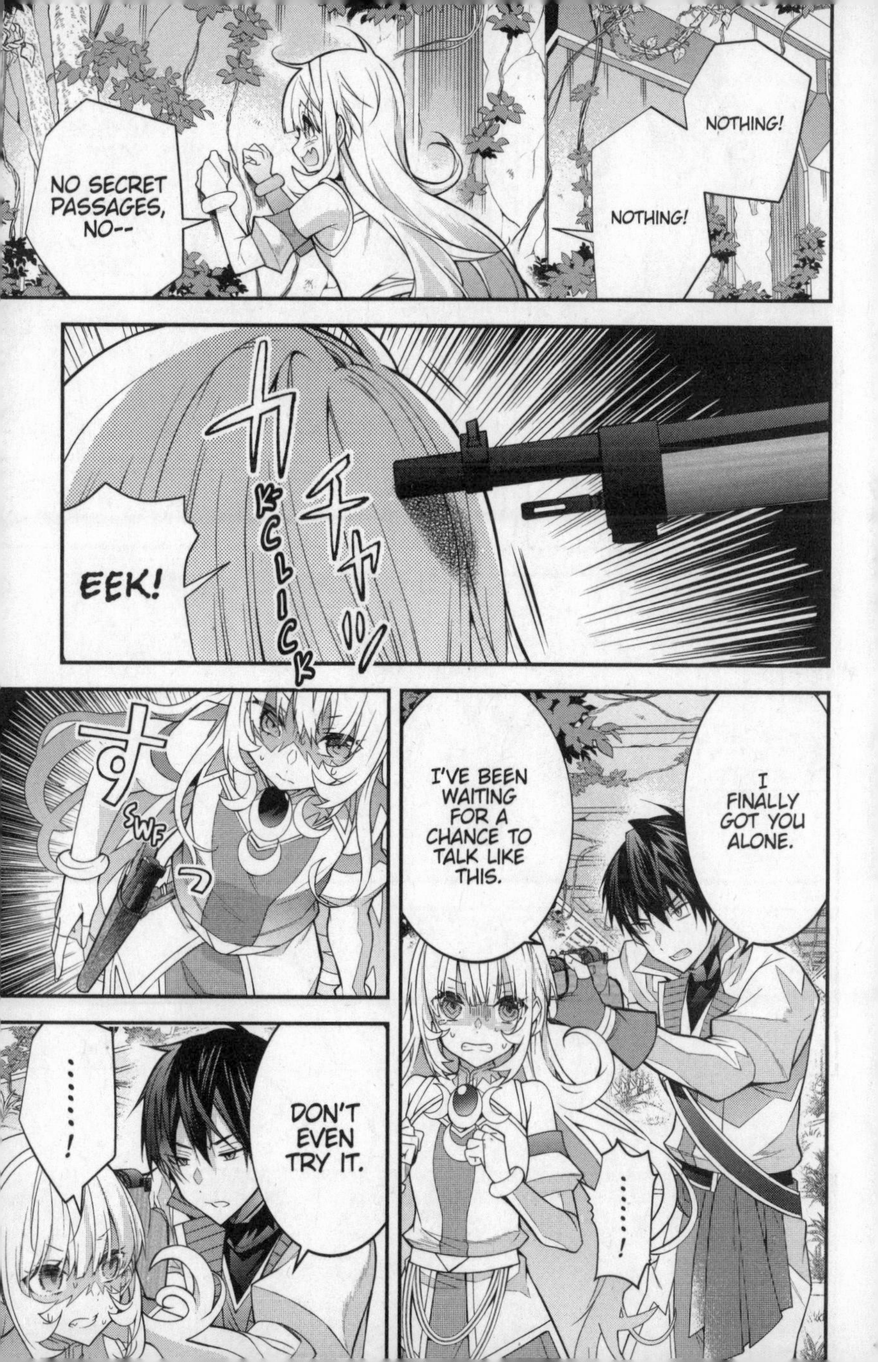
NOTHING!
NOTHING!
NO SECRET PASSAGES, NO--
カチャッ
KCLICK
EEK!
I FINALLY GOT YOU ALONE.
I'VE BEEN WAITING FOR A CHANCE TO TALK LIKE THIS.
......!
す
SWF
DON'T EVEN TRY IT.
......!

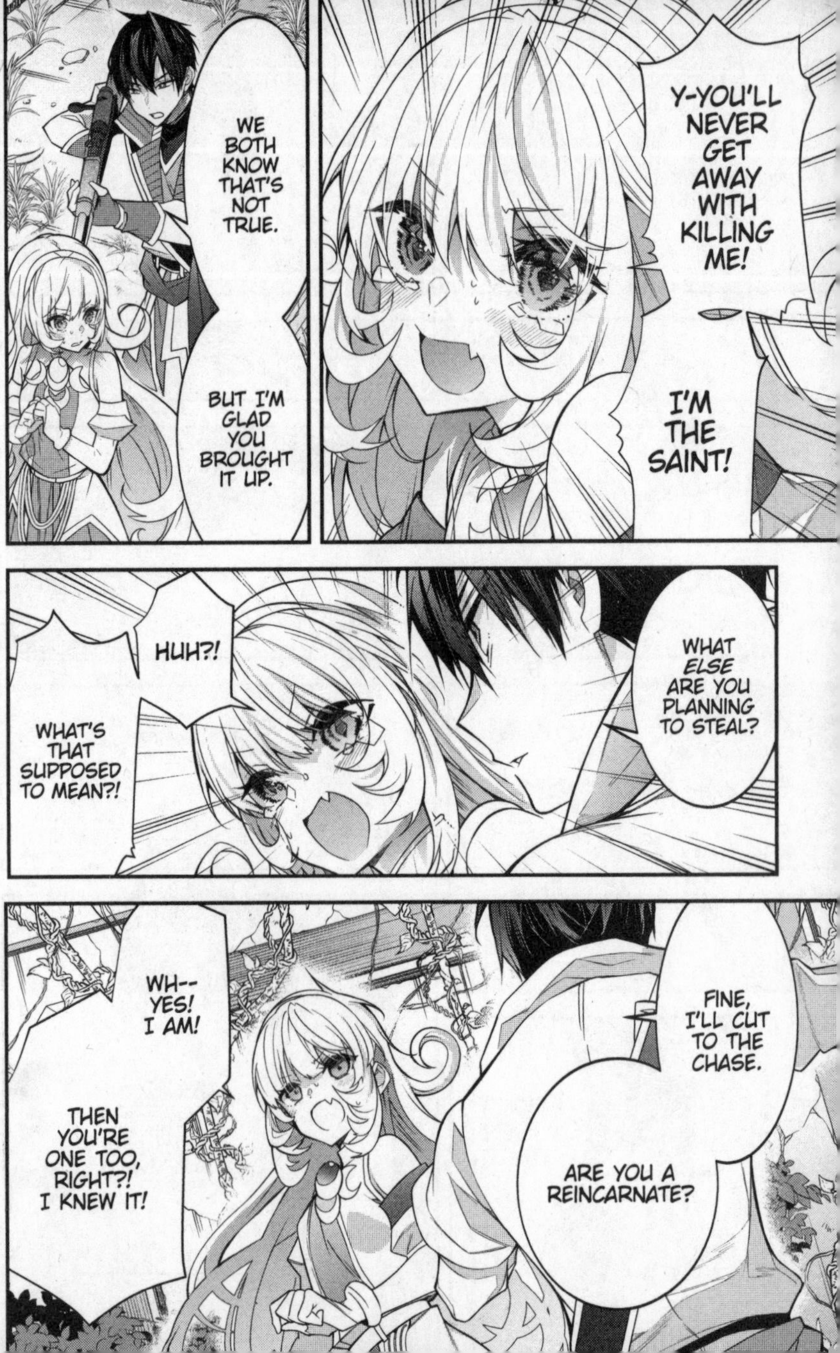

Y-YOU'LL NEVER GET AWAY WITH KILLING ME!
I'M THE SAINT!
WE BOTH KNOW THAT'S NOT TRUE.
BUT I'M GLAD YOU BROUGHT IT UP.
WHAT *ELSE* ARE YOU PLANNING TO STEAL?
HUH?!
WHAT'S THAT SUPPOSED TO MEAN?!
FINE, I'LL CUT TO THE CHASE.
ARE YOU A REINCARNATE?
WH-- YES! I AM!
THEN YOU'RE ONE TOO, RIGHT?! I KNEW IT!

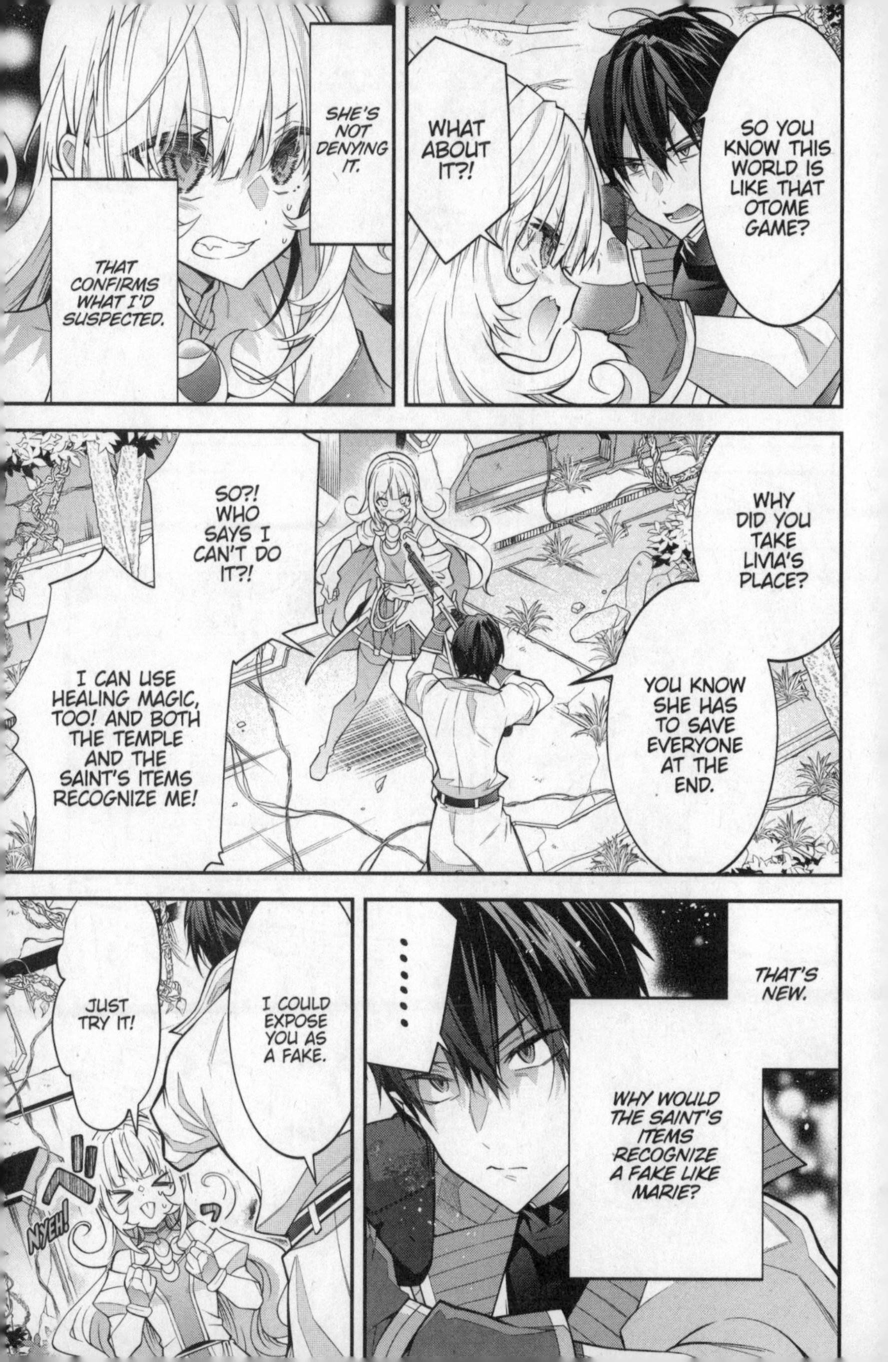
SO YOU KNOW THIS WORLD IS LIKE THAT OTOME GAME?
WHAT ABOUT IT?!
SHE'S NOT DENYING IT.
THAT CONFIRMS WHAT I'D SUSPECTED.
WHY DID YOU TAKE LIVIA'S PLACE?
YOU KNOW SHE HAS TO SAVE EVERYONE AT THE END.
SO?! WHO SAYS I CAN'T DO IT?!
I CAN USE HEALING MAGIC, TOO! AND BOTH THE TEMPLE AND THE SAINT'S ITEMS RECOGNIZE ME!
THAT'S NEW.
......
WHY WOULD THE SAINT'S ITEMS RECOGNIZE A FAKE LIKE MARIE?
I COULD EXPOSE YOU AS A FAKE.
JUST TRY IT!
NYEH!

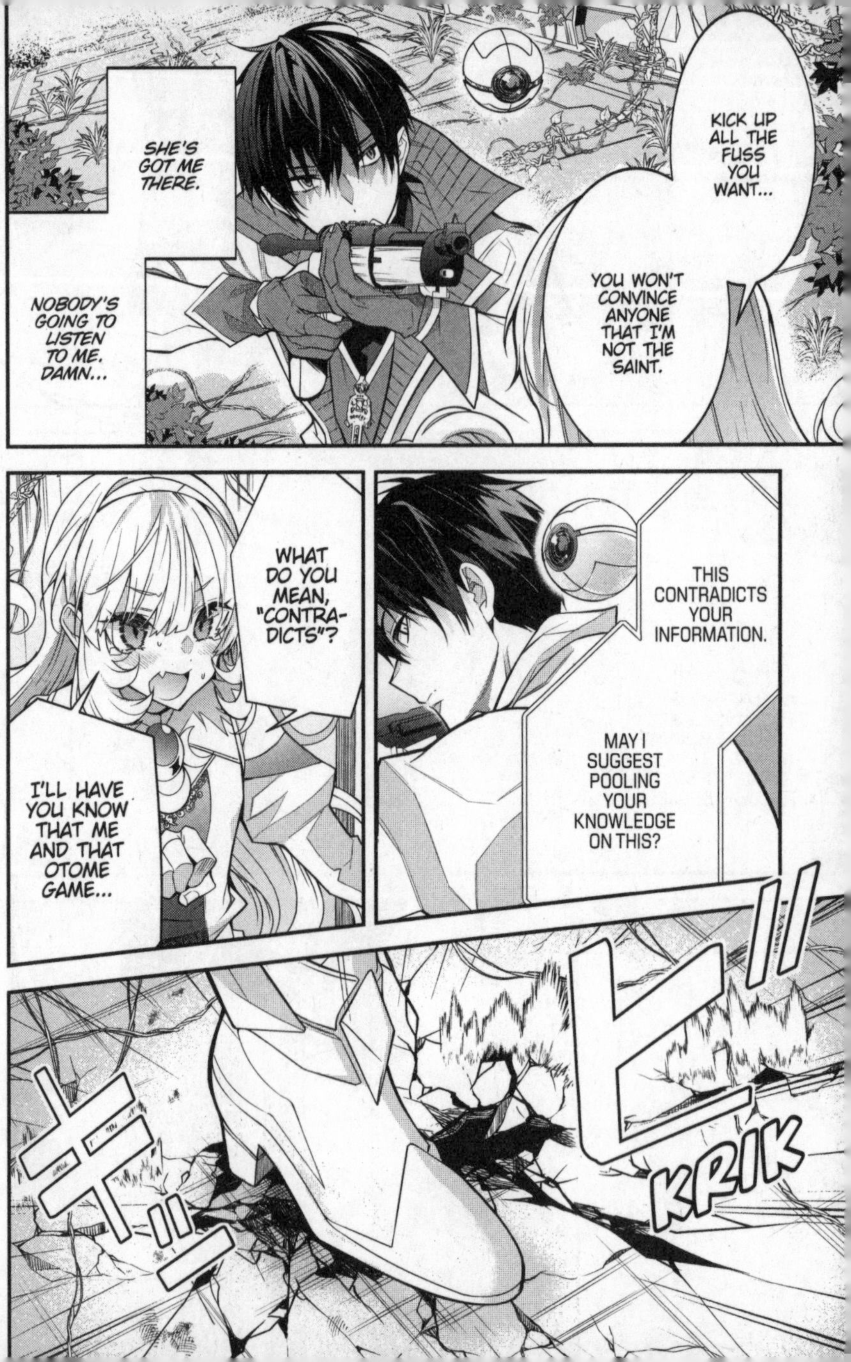
KICK UP ALL THE FUSS YOU WANT...
YOU WON'T CONVINCE ANYONE THAT I'M NOT THE SAINT.
SHE'S GOT ME THERE.
NOBODY'S GOING TO LISTEN TO ME. DAMN...
THIS CONTRADICTS YOUR INFORMATION.
MAY I SUGGEST POOLING YOUR KNOWLEDGE ON THIS?
WHAT DO YOU MEAN, "CONTRADICTS"?
I'LL HAVE YOU KNOW THAT ME AND THAT OTOME GAME...
KRIK

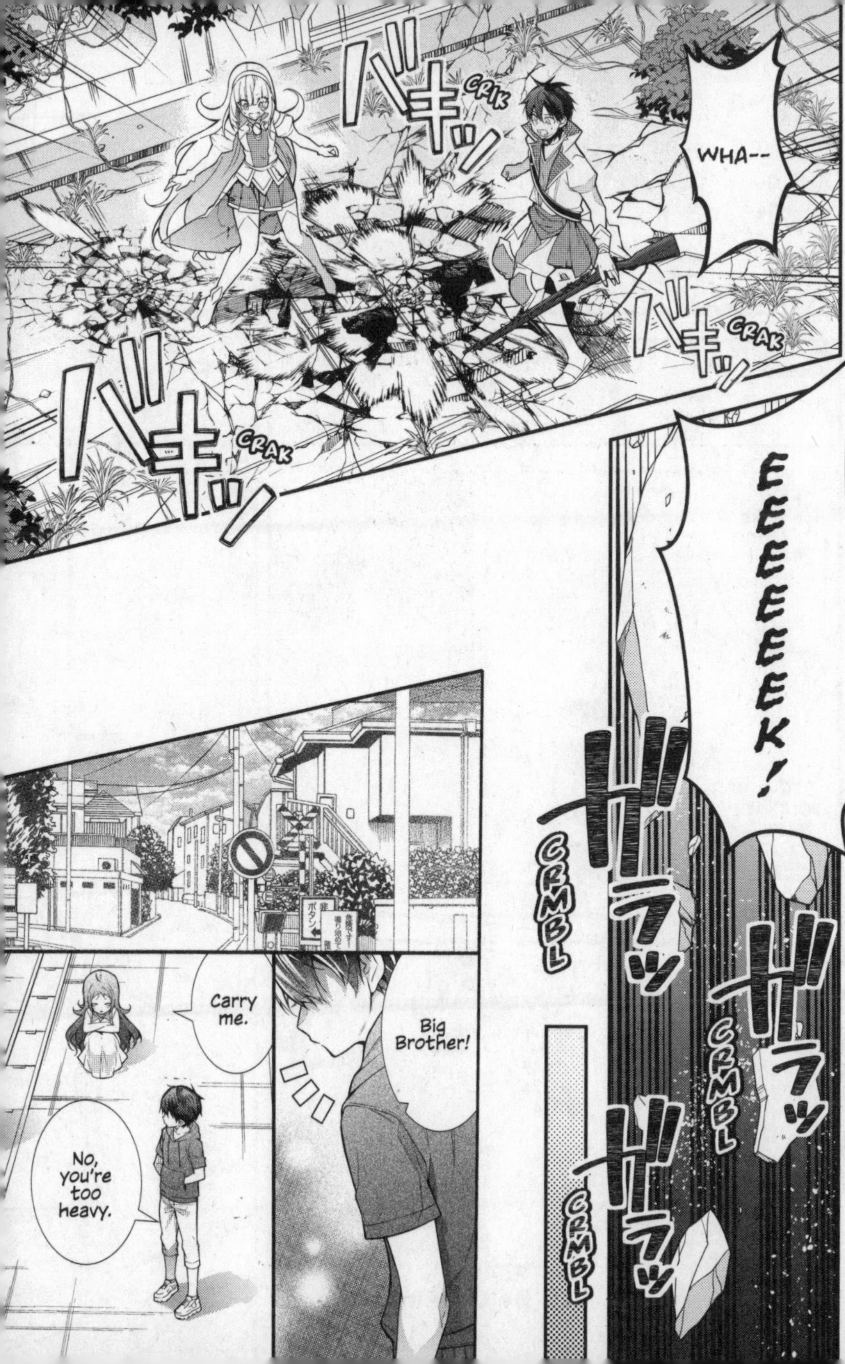
WHA--
バキッ
CRIK
バキッ
CRAK
バキッ
CRAK
EEEEEEEK!
ザラッ
CRMBL
ザラッ
CRMBL
ザラッ
CRMBL
Big Brother!
...
Carry me.
No, you're too heavy.

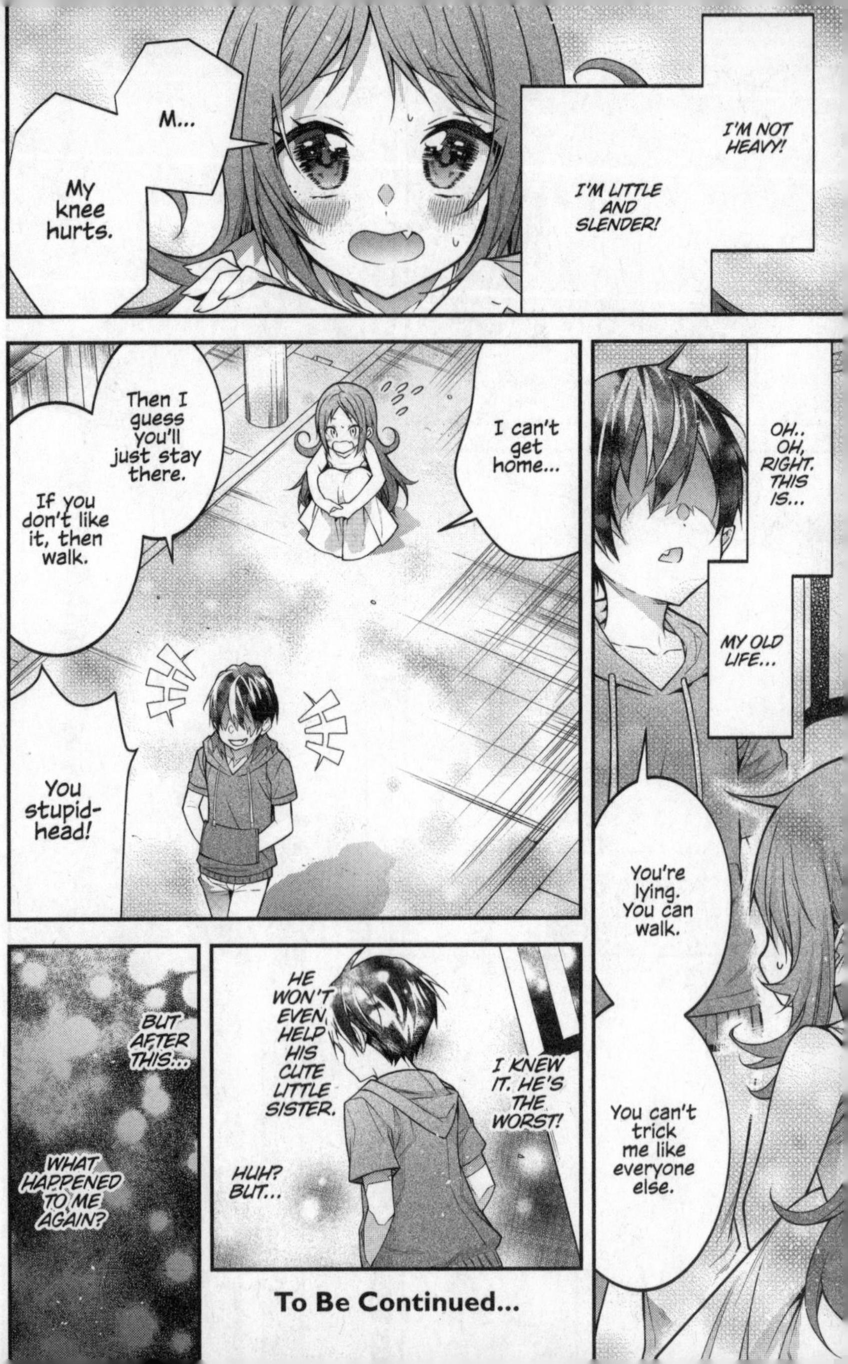
I'M NOT HEAVY!
I'M LITTLE AND SLENDER!
M...
My knee hurts.
OH.. OH, RIGHT. THIS IS...
MY OLD LIFE...
You're lying. You can walk.
You can't trick me like everyone else.
I can't get home...
Then I guess you'll just stay there.
If you don't like it, then walk.
You stupid-head!
I KNEW IT. HE'S THE WORST!
HE WON'T EVEN HELP HIS CUTE LITTLE SISTER.
HUH? BUT...
BUT AFTER THIS...
WHAT HAPPENED TO ME AGAIN?

To Be Continued...

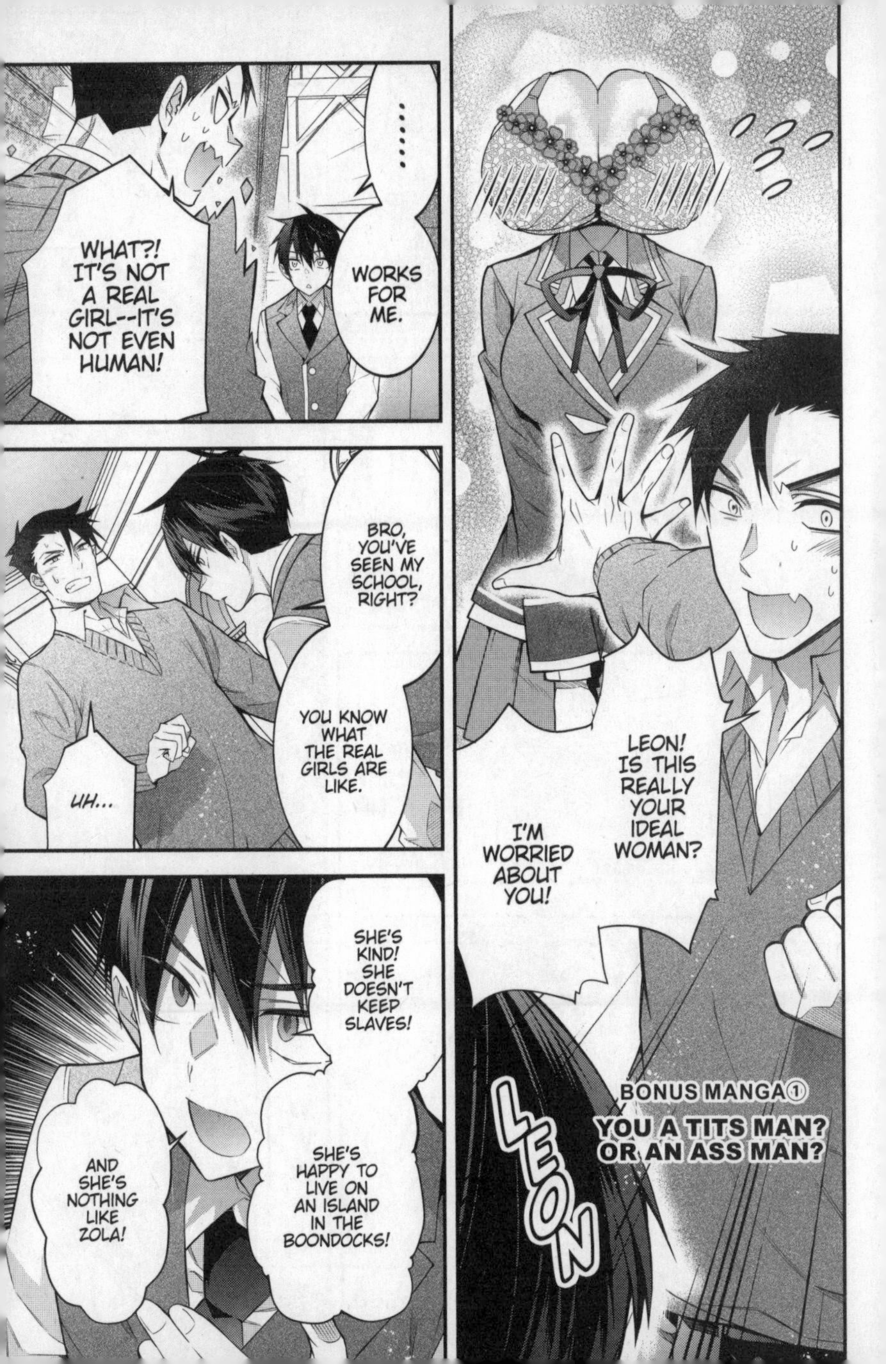
LEON! IS THIS REALLY YOUR IDEAL WOMAN?
I'M WORRIED ABOUT YOU!
BONUS MANGA ①
YOU A TITS MAN? OR AN ASS MAN?
LEON
......
WORKS FOR ME.
WHAT?! IT'S NOT A REAL GIRL--IT'S NOT EVEN HUMAN!
BRO, YOU'VE SEEN MY SCHOOL, RIGHT?
YOU KNOW WHAT THE REAL GIRLS ARE LIKE.
UH...
SHE'S KIND! SHE DOESN'T KEEP SLAVES!
SHE'S HAPPY TO LIVE ON AN ISLAND IN THE BOONDOCKS!
AND SHE'S NOTHING LIKE ZOLA!

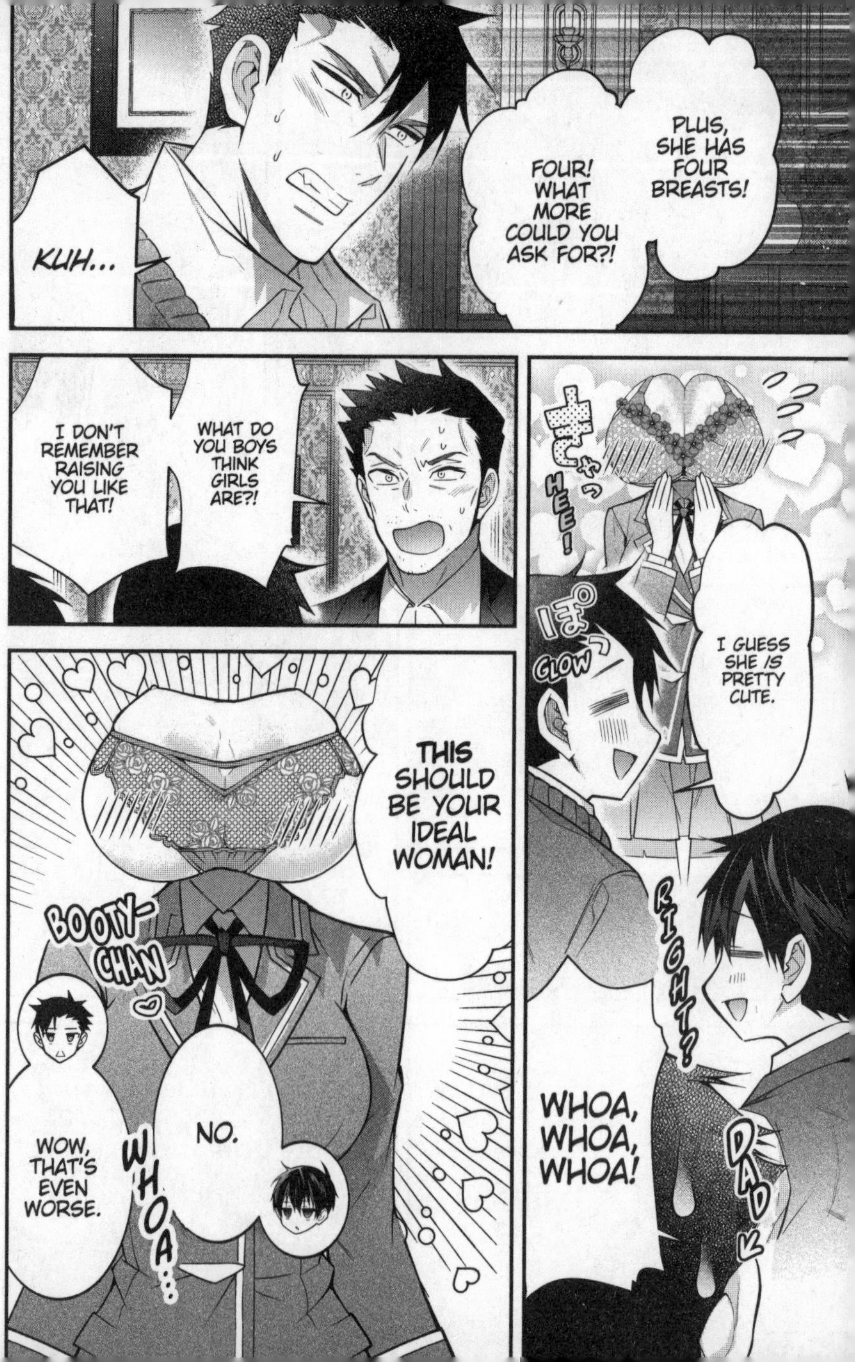
PLUS, SHE HAS FOUR BREASTS!
FOUR! WHAT MORE COULD YOU ASK FOR?!
KUH...
きゃっ
HEE!
ぽっ
GLOW
I GUESS SHE IS PRETTY CUTE.
RIGHT?
WHOA, WHOA, WHOA!
DAD
WHAT DO YOU BOYS THINK GIRLS ARE?!
I DON'T REMEMBER RAISING YOU LIKE THAT!
THIS SHOULD BE YOUR IDEAL WOMAN!
BOOTY-CHAN ♡
NO.
WOW, THAT'S EVEN WORSE.
WHOA...

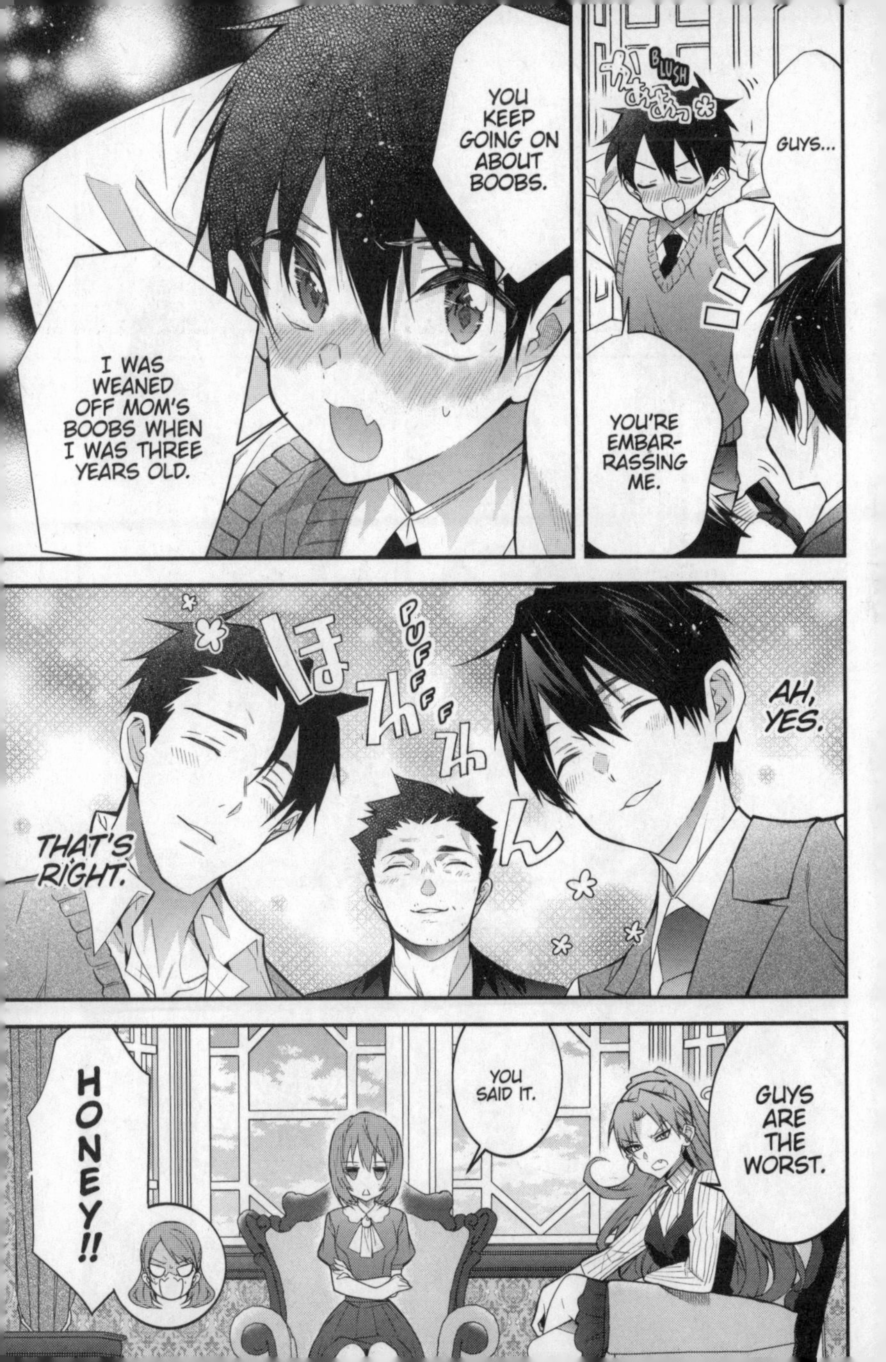
BLUSH
GUYS...
YOU'RE EMBARRASSING ME.
YOU KEEP GOING ON ABOUT BOOBS.
I WAS WEANED OFF MOM'S BOOBS WHEN I WAS THREE YEARS OLD.
AH, YES.
PUFFFF
THAT'S RIGHT.
GUYS ARE THE WORST.
YOU SAID IT.
HONEY!!

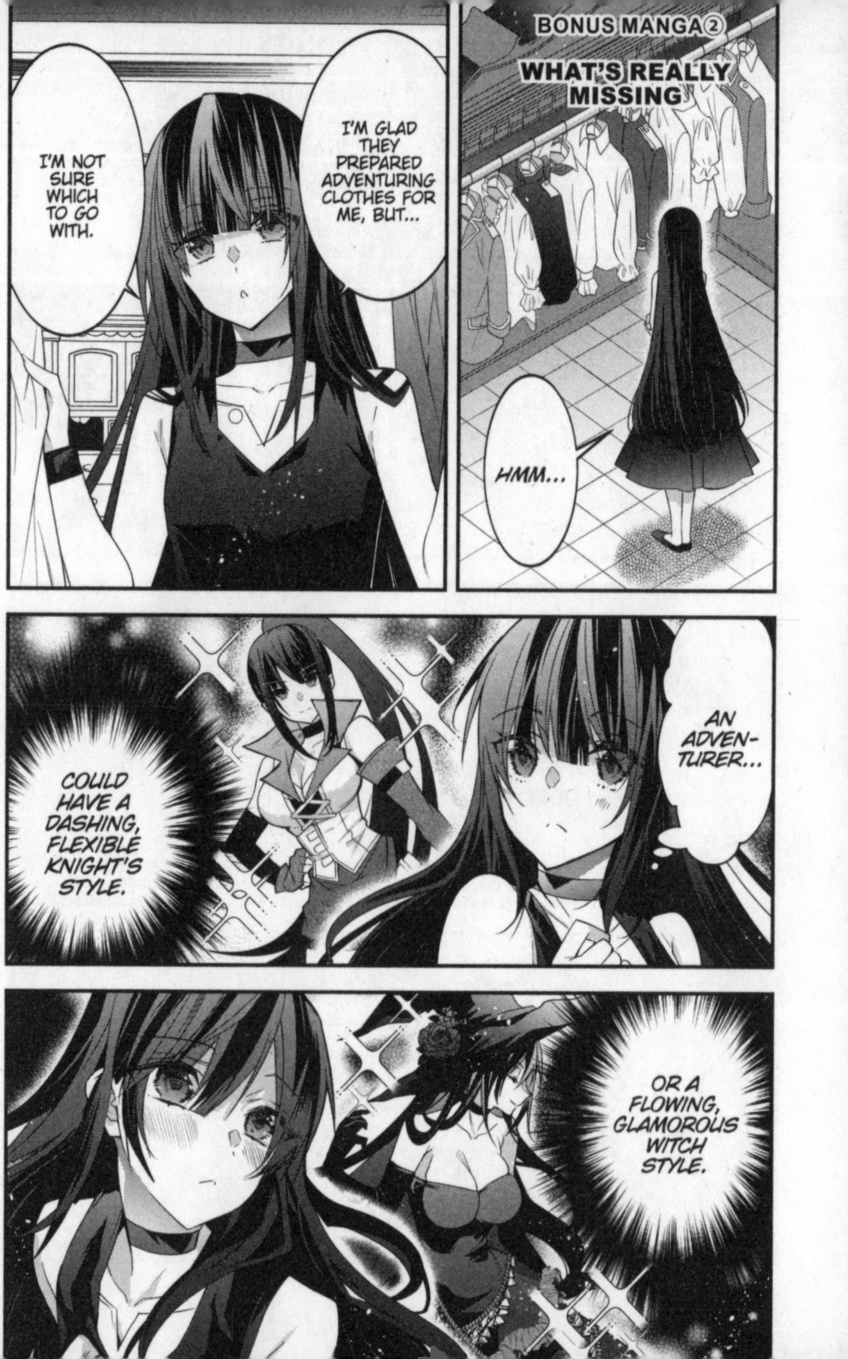
BONUS MANGA②
WHAT'S REALLY MISSING
HMM...
I'M GLAD THEY PREPARED ADVENTURING CLOTHES FOR ME, BUT...
I'M NOT SURE WHICH TO GO WITH.
AN ADVEN-TURER...
COULD HAVE A DASHING, FLEXIBLE KNIGHT'S STYLE.
OR A FLOWING, GLAMOROUS WITCH STYLE.

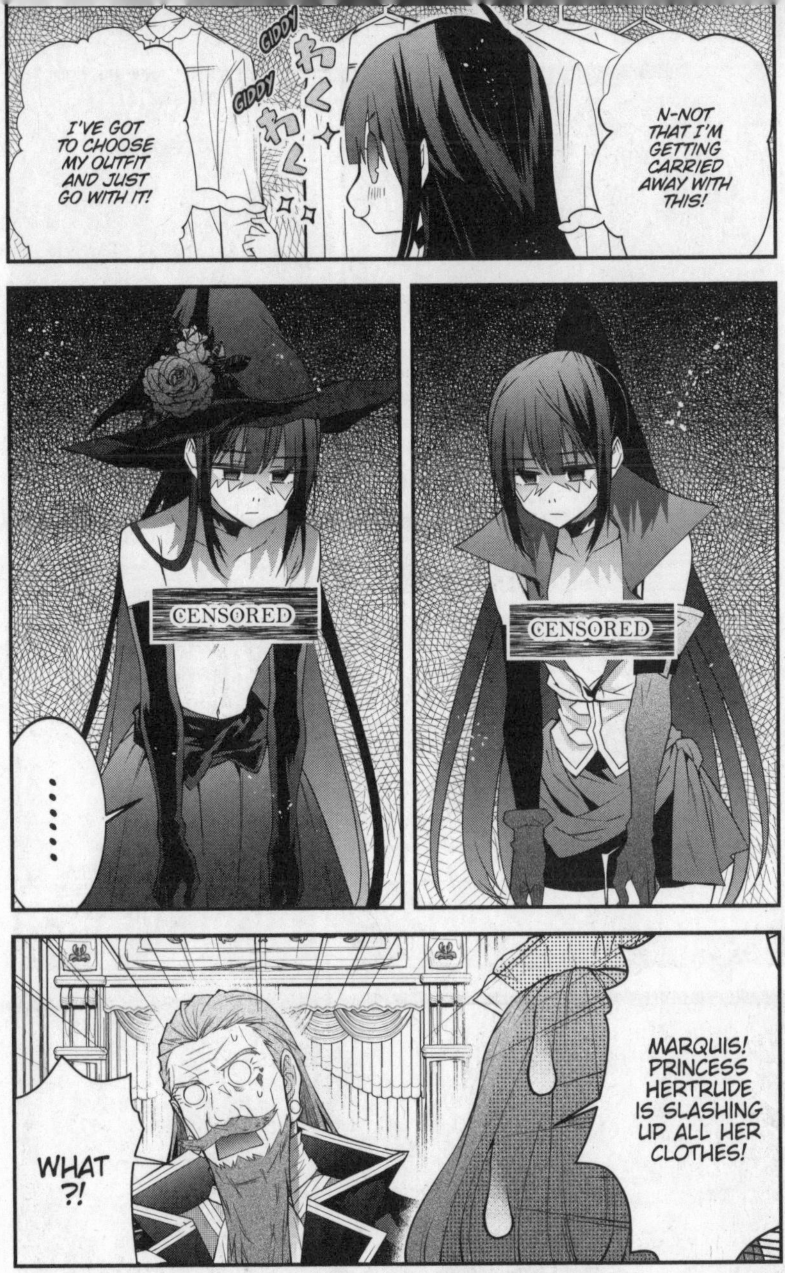
N-NOT THAT I'M GETTING CARRIED AWAY WITH THIS!
わくわく
GIDDY
GIDDY
I'VE GOT TO CHOOSE MY OUTFIT AND JUST GO WITH IT!
CENSORED
CENSORED
......
MARQUIS! PRINCESS HERTRUDE IS SLASHING UP ALL HER CLOTHES!
WHAT ?!

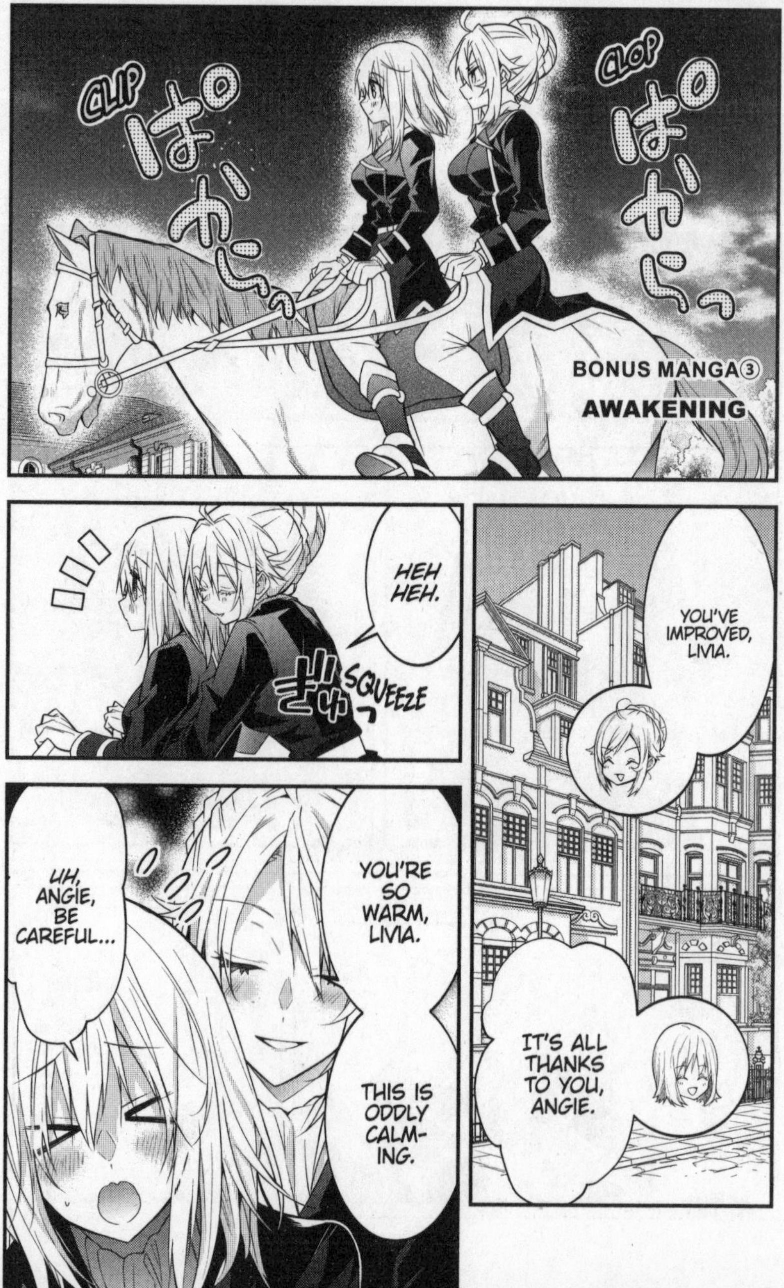
CLOP
CLIP
BONUS MANGA ③
AWAKENING
YOU'VE IMPROVED, LIVIA.
IT'S ALL THANKS TO YOU, ANGIE.
HEH HEH.
ぎゅっ SQUEEZE
YOU'RE SO WARM, LIVIA.
THIS IS ODDLY CALMING.
UH, ANGIE, BE CAREFUL...

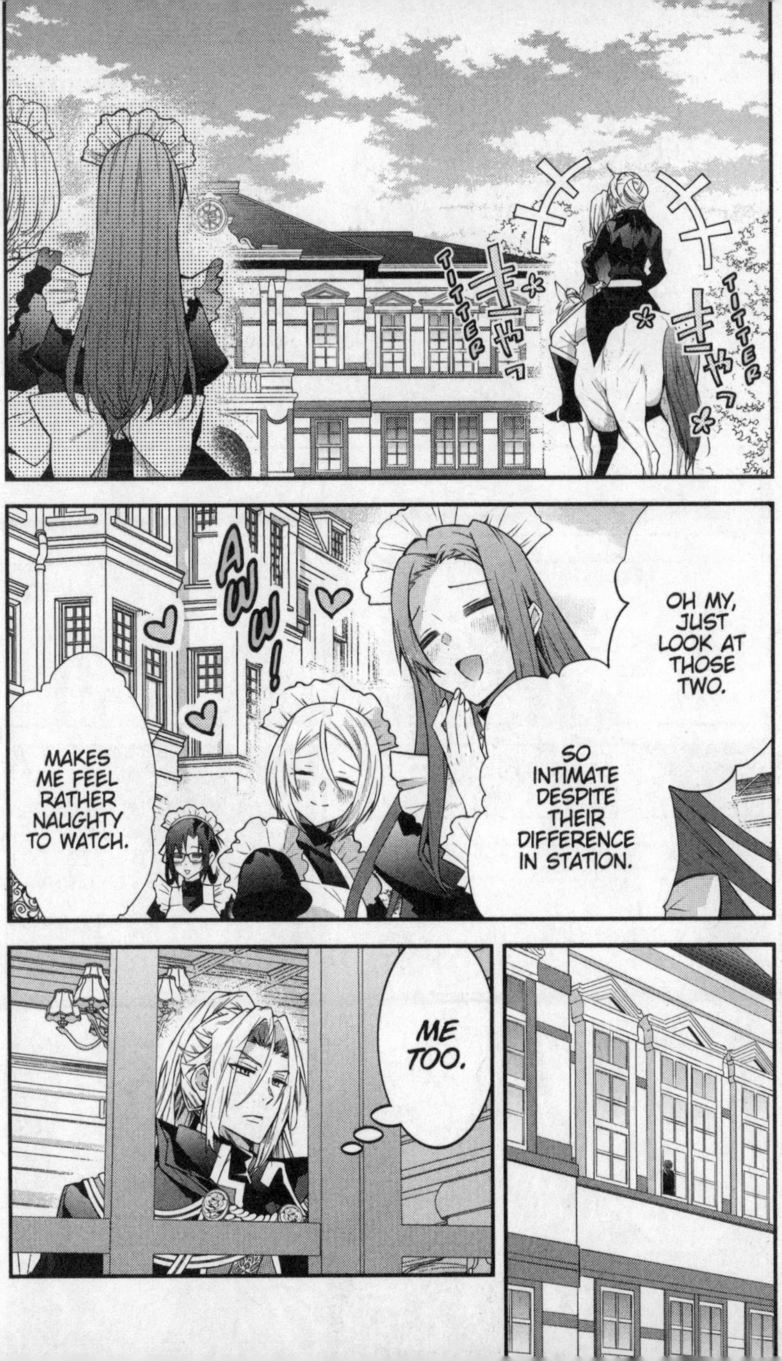
TITTER
TITTER
OH MY, JUST LOOK AT THOSE TWO.
SO INTIMATE DESPITE THEIR DIFFERENCE IN STATION.
AWW!
MAKES ME FEEL RATHER NAUGHTY TO WATCH.
ME TOO.

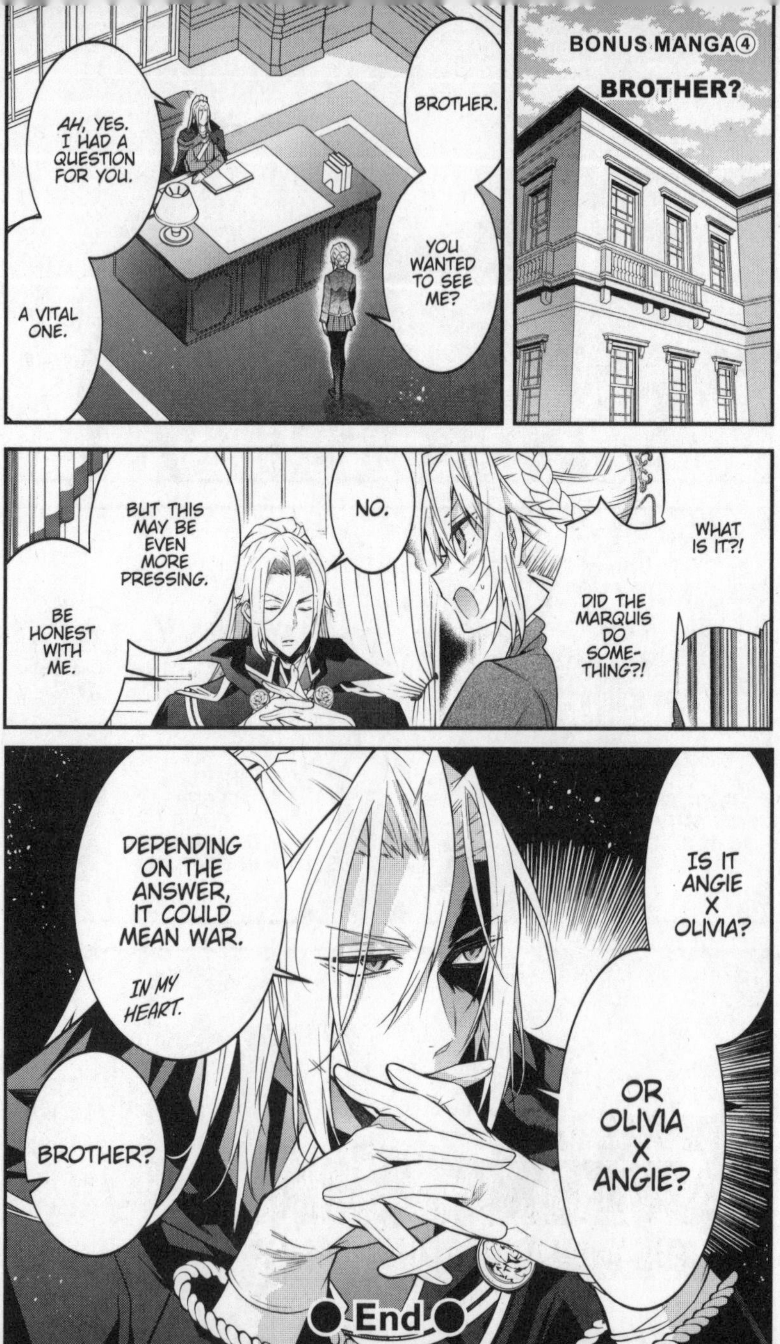
BONUS MANGA④
BROTHER?
BROTHER.
YOU WANTED TO SEE ME?
AH, YES. I HAD A QUESTION FOR YOU.
A VITAL ONE.
WHAT IS IT?!
DID THE MARQUIS DO SOMETHING?!
NO.
BUT THIS MAY BE EVEN MORE PRESSING.
BE HONEST WITH ME.
IS IT ANGIE X OLIVIA?
DEPENDING ON THE ANSWER, IT COULD MEAN WAR.
IN MY HEART.
OR OLIVIA X ANGIE?
BROTHER?
End

TRAPPED IN A
DATING SIM
THE WORLD OF OTOME GAMES
IS TOUGH FOR MOBS.

A short story to commemorate
the manga adaptation:

"Hertrude's Adventure"
Written by Yomu Mishima
Illustrated by Jun Shiosato

"Why's this place so stupid big?!" Hertrude, who had come to study in the Kingdom of Holfort, was wandering the interior of the airship *Partner* all by herself. Her long hair was held back in two pigtails as she paced the hallway with wider strides than usual. Turning her gaze to the left, she saw light come shining through the outer window. Hertrude narrowed her eyes.

"This really is a most irksome lost item." It wasn't the blinding light that had caused her to squint, but her apprehension at the sheer technological power of the airship. If it had merely been a matter of its ridiculously huge seven hundred-meter length, she'd be untroubled. But its flying speed wasn't proportionate to its immense size.

It was too fast.

And then there was the treatment applied to the windows.

Even though direct sunlight was shining in, it wasn't as bright as she'd have expected. No doubt it was constructed using technology that would be impossible to recreate in this day and age. The fact that such a vessel belonged to an enemy, Leon Fou Bartfort, was a problem that gave Hertrude a headache.

"And here I thought that going adventuring with the

saint could gain me some information," she said. By joining Marie in her treasure hunt, she could obtain firsthand intelligence on the ship that drove the principality's army to destruction. That had been one of Hertrude's goals; the reason she paid off her ward (who also doubled as her guide) and why she was currently in the process of investigating the ship alone in the free time she had bought.

Still, the place was too darn big.

"What's the point of it being so massive? Wouldn't a smaller size be better? What were they thinking, making such a huge airship?" The ship was ridiculously spacious, but oddly enough, it did not require a crew to operate it. Hence why Hertrude hadn't run into anybody on her solo expedition.

This would usually be a favorable condition for investigating, but for Hertrude, who was very familiar with airships, it was just too unnatural. On most airships, the only place you could be alone was your room. It's a given that you'd eventually run into someone somewhere. And yet, ever since boarding *Partner*, she'd been alone for the most part.

Far from military secrets, most of what Hertrude had gleaned so far was limited to: *Why is it so spooky? I wouldn't be surprised if someone told me this was a ghost airship.*

She was terribly lonely. Usually, she was prim and proper, but she was a princess being forced to study abroad by herself in an enemy country, and now was all alone. She tried not to let people around her catch on, but she was all nerves.

Thinking that she should go back, she stopped and turned around.

"*Eek!*"

When she did, she found a round, metal clump-like thing floating behind her. It had hand-shaped append-ages attached to it, and Hertrude recalled Leon referring to its kind as "operational robots." At the time, she hadn't felt fear, but now she was alone with one of the strange creatures. The operational robot, with its round ball of a form, didn't look like it was made for combat. It looked downright friendly, in fact. But in the silent, empty hall-way it took on an eerie appearance, and Hertrude was terrified. As she crept backward, the robot reached out its hands for her.

"Beep beep beep!"

It emitted an unfamiliar noise.

"Stay away!"

With tears in her eyes, Hertrude fled, tearing down the hall without looking back. She found a staircase and dashed upward, hoping to find a place where people were around. When she reached the deck, she spotted Leon and the others a ways off, and felt a wave of relief. Turning around, she saw the operational robot that followed her turn its back and retreat into the belly of the ship, disappearing from sight. Hertrude got her breathing under control and tucked her clothes back into place as she started walking toward Leon and his companions.

Apparently, the floating island that was their destination was in sight.

"Th-that was so scary."

She was trembling slightly, but by the time she appeared before Leon and the others, she was calm and composed.

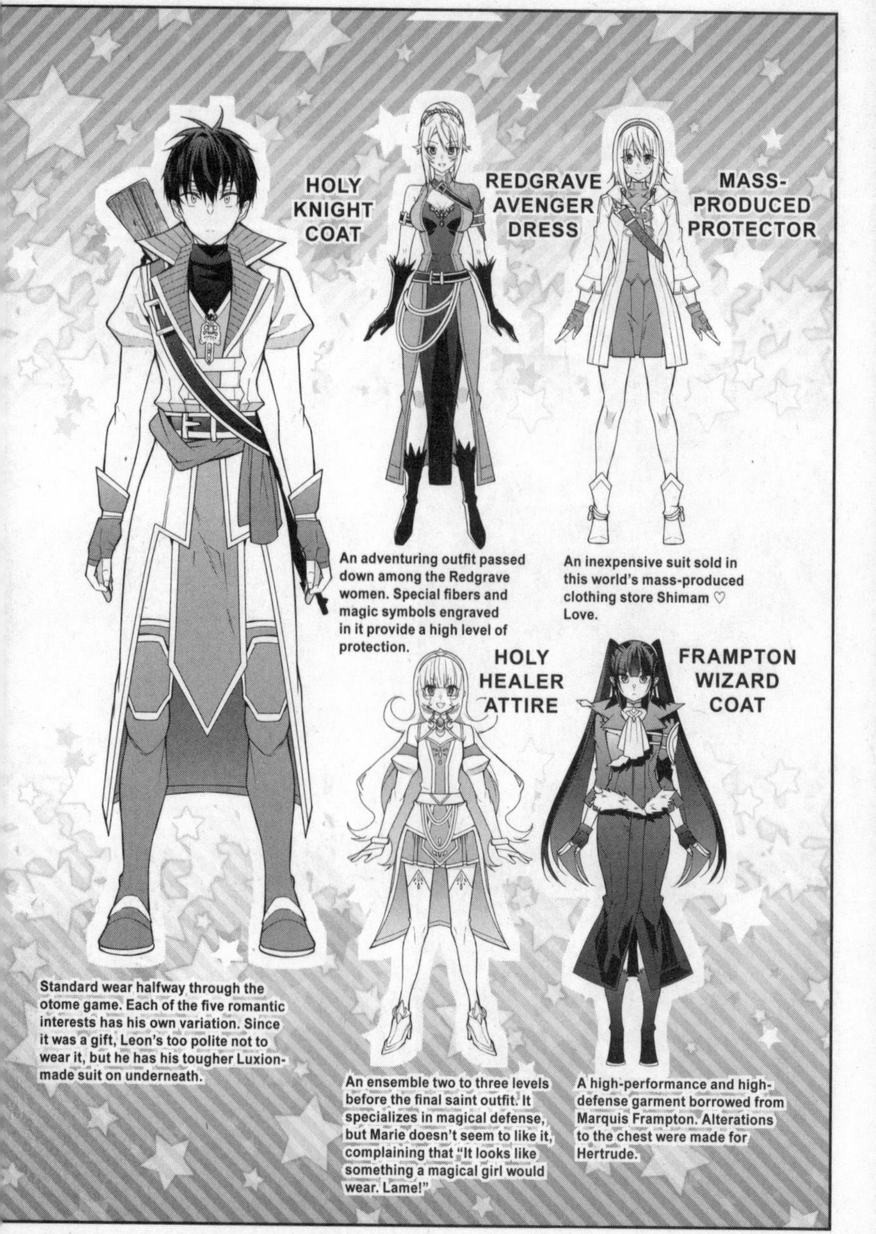
HOLY KNIGHT COAT
Standard wear halfway through the otome game. Each of the five romantic interests has his own variation. Since it was a gift, Leon's too polite not to wear it, but he has his tougher Luxion-made suit on underneath.
REDGRAVE AVENGER DRESS
An adventuring outfit passed down among the Redgrave women. Special fibers and magic symbols engraved in it provide a high level of protection.
MASS-PRODUCED PROTECTOR
An inexpensive suit sold in this world's mass-produced clothing store Shimam ♡ Love.
HOLY HEALER ATTIRE
An ensemble two to three levels before the final saint outfit. It specializes in magical defense, but Marie doesn't seem to like it, complaining that "It looks like something a magical girl would wear. Lame!"
FRAMPTON WIZARD COAT
A high-performance and high-defense garment borrowed from Marquis Frampton. Alterations to the chest were made for Hertrude.

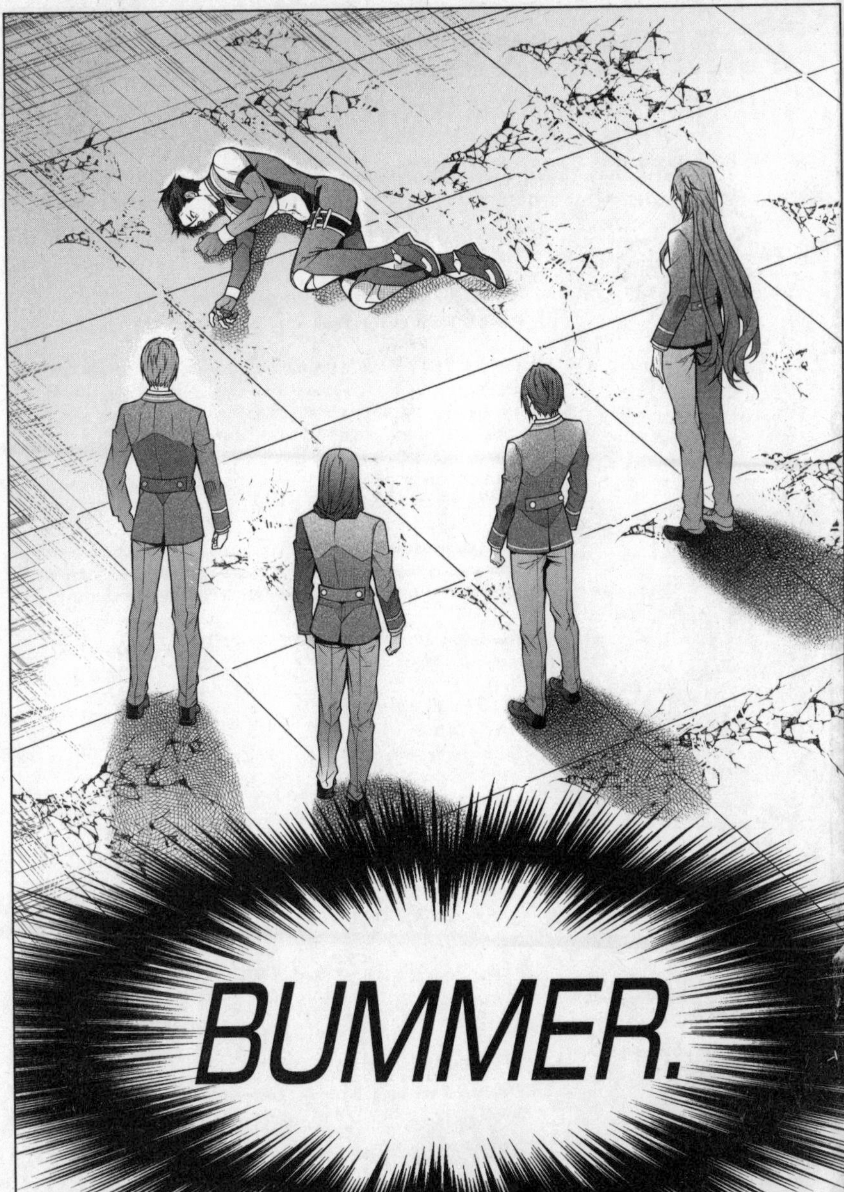
BUMMER.

SEVEN SEAS ENTERTAINMENT PRESENTS

TRAPPED IN A DATING SIM
THE WORLD OF OTOME GAMES IS TOUGH FOR MOBS. Vol. 8

art: **JUN SHIOSATO**   story: **YOMU MISHIMA**   character design: **MONDA**

TRANSLATION
Christine Dashiell

ADAPTATION
Brett Hallahan

LETTERING
James Dashiell

COVER DESIGN
H. Qi

LOGO DESIGN
George Panella

PROOFREADER
Krista Grandy

COPY EDITOR
B. Lillian Martin

EDITOR
Nick Mamatas

PRODUCTION DESIGNER
George Panella

PRODUCTION MANAGER
John Ramirez

PREPRESS TECHNICIAN
Melanie Ujimori
Jules Valera

EDITOR-IN-CHIEF
Julie Davis

ASSOCIATE PUBLISHER
Adam Arnold

PUBLISHER
Jason DeAngelis

OTOMEGE SEKAI WA MOB NI KIBISHII SEKAI DESU Vol.8
©Jun Shiosato 2022
©Yomu Mishima, Monda 2022
First published in Japan in 2022 by KADOKAWA CORPORATION, Tokyo.
English translation rights arranged with KADOKAWA CORPORATION, Tokyo.

Seven Seas press and purchase enquiries can be sent to Marketing Manager Lianne Sentar at press@gomanga.com. Information regarding the distribution and purchase of digital editions is available from Digital Manager CK Russell at digital@gomanga.com.

ISBN: 978-1-68579-921-2
Printed in Canada
First Printing: September 2023
10 9 8 7 6 5 4 3 2 1

READING DIRECTIONS

This book reads from *right to left*, Japanese style. If this is your first time reading manga, you start reading from the top right panel on each page and take it from there. If you get lost, just follow the numbered diagram here. It may seem backwards at first, but you'll get the hang of it! Have fun!!

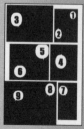

Follow us online: www.SevenSeasEntertainment.com